MORE PRAISE FOR
BRINGING CITIZENS
VOICES TO THE TABLE

"In her book, Lukensmeyer sends a message that our leaders in government and the private sector cannot ignore. It is her conviction (and I believe she is correct) that the very survival of our democracy depends on the ability of leadership to achieve a goal that has been horribly neglected. This is the goal of engaging the public as genuine partners in deliberating the nation's policies.

At present, the American public has been sidelined from policy shaping. Public opinion polls reveal a public that is discouraged, disillusioned, frustrated, and largely unaware of the consequences of the policies that our divided experts are pushing.

Lukensmeyer is one of a tiny handful of professionals who understand the seriousness of this failure to help the public reach sound and thoughtful public judgment, and who have the moral passion to do something about it."
—**Daniel Yankelovich**, Chairman and cofounder, Viewpoint Learning and Public Agenda

"As the old Chinese proverb states; 'Go to the people, learn from them, love them, start with what they know, build on what they say. . . . when their work is done the people will remark, we have done it ourselves.' The genius of America*Speaks* is built around these principles. This belief has brought millions of Americans to the 'gathering place' and offered hope and opportunity to build community's destiny and chart a course for justice and fairness. This is a must-read primer that is sorely needed today to bring back civility and community empowerment in the democratic way."
—**Norm Rice**, President, The Seattle Foundation; former Mayor, City of Seattle

"For the past three decades, few Americans have been as dedicated as Carolyn Lukensmeyer to ensuring that ours is a country of, by, and for the people. This book features numerous insights of use to citizens, civil servants, and civic leaders alike, and is a fitting capstone to an ennobling career spent in the service of American democracy."
—**David Gergen**, senior political analyst for CNN, public service professor of public leadership Harvard Kennedy School, and former adviser to four U.S. presidents

"Carolyn is one of the nation's leading experts on citizen engagement activities. This book makes a strong case for why it is important and how to help make sure that such efforts are successful."
—**David Walker**, former U.S. Comptroller General; founder and CEO, Comeback America Initiative

"Is it possible to create an authentic democracy, with government of, by, and for the people? Lukensmeyer's book not only makes the case that it is, she shows us what it could look like and how to create it. Drawing from her groundbreaking careers in government and the nonprofit sector, Lukensmeyer brings to life civic innovations from municipal, state, and federal levels. In the process, she charts a course for our country that could save us from our current dysfunction. Everyone who cares about the future of democratic governance—elected officials, government workers, and citizens of all views—should read this visionary and practical book."
—**Martha McCoy**, Executive Director, Everyday Democracy

"This important book is an owner's manual for democracy in the 21st century. We, the citizens, must reclaim our ownership; elected officials and public managers must bring us to the table. Carolyn Lukensmeyer helps us see how."
—**Stephen Heintz**, President, Rockefeller Brothers Fund

"This is the single most important book for managers and civil servants who want to engage the public in governance. Carolyn Lukensmeyer explains why and how to engage citizens, offering principles, evidence, practical strategies, and compelling case studies."
—**Peter Levine**, Director of the Center for Information & Research on Civic Learning and Engagement (CIRCLE) at Tufts University; author, *The Future of Democracy: Developing the Next Generation of American Citizens*

"Carolyn Lukensmeyer has been a key leader and innovator in the rapidly growing field of deliberative public engagement since its inception. In this book, she reveals the most critical lessons learned in this work, from new insights on the role of government in a democracy to practical tips for productively involving large, diverse numbers of people. Lukensmeyer provides an essential roadmap for public officials, practitioners, and other leaders interested in restoring trust and partnership between the people and their public institutions."
—**Matt Leighninger**, Executive Director, Deliberative Democracy Consortium (DDC); coauthor, *The Next Form of Democracy: How Expert Rule Is Giving Way to Shared Governance—and Why Politics Will Never Be the Same*

"Citizen engagement is at the heart of a healthy democracy. It is high time to revitalize our democracy and benefit from the wisdom of our citizens. Read this book for some informed opportunities to approach this challenge! As a person who has seen again and again just how wise citizens can be it thrills me to read concrete plans for how we can more effectively engage diverse communities."
—**Joan Blades**, cocreator, Living Room Conversations; cofounder MoveOn.org and MomsRising.org.

"Public employees need contact with the public to validate their passion for public service, and the public needs contact with public servants to understand and influence what they do. Our current method of communication through polls, press releases, and interest groups fails to create the human engagement necessary to create trust and a passion for action. *Bringing Citizen Voices to the Table* is an inspiring roadmap for responding to our polarized government by creating an engaged public that rekindles our democracy."
—**Bob Tobias**, Director, Key Executive Leadership Programs, American University; member, Internal Revenue Service Oversight Board

"Are you worried about the epic loss of confidence in government? Are you concerned about people's inability to influence the policies that affect everyday life? Is your institution looking for a better way to engage citizens and regain their confidence? Then this book is for you. Carolyn Lukensmeyer brings together a career of dealing with these questions and her experiences with the very successful America*Speaks* program to offer practical suggestions for bridging the divide that now separates the public from the government; our government, she insists."
—**David Mathews**, President, Kettering Foundation; author, *Politics for People: Finding a Responsible Public Voice.*

"Carolyn Lukensmeyer has been in the forefront of democratic innovation for several decades and brings a depth of experience in public management to meet the critical challenge that she sets for us in this important and timely book: how can we not only enrich citizen voice, so essential to our very identity, but also deepen democratic trust between citizens and government. Lukensmeyer brings unsurpassed practical wisdom and visionary leadership to the movement to revitalize our democracy on grounds that are inspired, yet institutionally realistic and workable."
—**Carmen Sirianni**, author, *Investing in Democracy: Engaging Citizens in Collaborative Governance;* Morris Hillquit Professor in Sociology and Public Policy, Brandeis University

"From the Tea Party to Occupy, it is clear that Americans are fed up. As the call rings out for localization of resources and services, we must rethink our governance. Dr. Lukensmeyer walks us from where we are to where we could be with specific strategies on how we get there."
—**David Smith**, Executive Director, National Conference on Citizenship

"Lukensmeyer is a passionate advocate for Jeffersonian democracy. Her book will really practitioners with new skills, tools and insights, and the inspiration to take more risks to bring citizens to the table."
—**Sterling Speirn**, President, W.K. Kellogg Foundation

"For years, Carolyn Lukensmeyer has been a pioneer in the work of restoring American democracy. Both in her outstanding contribution to public administration and then as the founding president of America-*Speaks*, she has been strengthening democratic practice throughout her career. Now she has brought that remarkable wealth of experience into sharp focus in a book that is guaranteed to provide a lasting contribution to democratic renewal in this country."
—**Daniel Kemmis**, author, *Community and the Politics of Place,* former Mayor of Missoula, Montana and Speaker of the Montana House of Representatives

"Carolyn Lukensmeyer is the Johnny Appleseed of democratic practices. This book is a must-read for any public servant who believes in harnessing the power and wisdom of we the people to help solve the problems of the nation."
—**Wendy Willis**, Executive Director, Policy Consensus Initiative

"Not since *Reinventing Government* has there been a book with such potential to shape the way we think about governance. The growing disconnect between the governed and the governing in our society is the greatest threat to the future we want for our children and our grandchildren. Authentically including citizen voices in public decision making will enable us to achieve our highest ideals as a self-governing people and to make decisions that produce better outcomes. In *Bringing Citizen Voices to the Table*, Carolyn Lukensmeyer describes a set of key strategies she has developed in her work at America*Speaks* and she shows us how to use those strategies to bridge the gap between citizens and their government."

—**Mark Funkhouser**, Director, The Governing Institute; former Mayor, Kansas City, Missouri

"Al Smith once said that the solution to the problems of democracy is more democracy. In this book Carolyn Lukensmeyer offers an imaginative and refreshing prescription for introducing that additional democracy at a time when we desperately need it."

—**David Abbott**, Executive Director, George Gund Foundation

"Carolyn pulls no punches in this book, but also provides a sorely needed road map for how public managers and citizens can create a new paradigm in today's world. In this book she is asking for nothing less than a concerted effort to revitalize 'American Democracy' and how it can be done. Her ideas are not a theory. They are based on almost a lifetime of practical experience. We would all be wise to heed her words."

—**Dan Basta**, Director, National Marine Sanctuary Program, NOAA, US department of Commerce

"Carolyn Lukensmeyer is at the forefront of building a new relationship between our government and the citizens it serves, and this work comes at a critical time for our country. The American people's expectations are not being met by our government and the consequence is a devastating loss of confidence, which in turn leads to greater public sector dysfunction. Dr. Lukensmeyer offers a strategy for addressing this disturbing downward spiral, and the public should be paying attention."

—**Max Stier**, President and Chief Executive, Partnership for Public Service

"This book has the power to not only inspire a current generation of public managers, and elected officials—but also a whole new generation who would join them. If you have ever considered a path of professional public service—or simply want to be the best citizen you can be—this book will convince you how much you are needed, reveal how much good work there is to be done, and share exciting ideas and resources to effectively engage your talents."
—**Jared Duval**, author, *Next Generation Democracy*; Demos Fellow and co-founder, Emerging Voices Initiative

"Citizen Engagement is the portal through which the wisdom of many can be harnessed for the greater good in the single institution that ensures a free society. For the public manager, citizen engagement as described here is analogous to the global IT revolution which has made services once reserved for the wealthy available to the masses. As servants of the people, we are obliged by our oath of office to embrace and leverage these new ways of tapping citizen voice—not just because it is now possible, but far more importantly, for the sake of our democracy."
—**Ron Redmon**, faculty at the Federal Executive Institute; former Chief Operating Officer of the Federal Quality Institute

"Carolyn Lukensmeyer's book, *Bringing Citizen Voices to the Table*, is a must-read for every organization involved in citizen engagement. Under Carolyn's leadership and through a national dialogue organized by America*Speaks*, our community found its voice."
—**JoAnn Turnquist**, President and CEO, Central Carolina Community Foundation

BRINGING CITIZEN VOICES TO THE TABLE

A Guide for Public Managers

Carolyn J. Lukensmeyer,

with

Wendy Jacobson

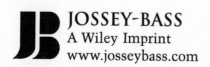
JOSSEY-BASS
A Wiley Imprint
www.josseybass.com

Published by Jossey-Bass
A Wiley Imprint
One Montgomery Street, Suite 1200, San Francisco, CA 94104-4594—www.josseybass.com

Jossey-Bass books and products are available through most bookstores. To contact Jossey-Bass directly call our Customer Care Department within the U.S. at 800-956-7739, outside the U.S. at 317-572-3986, or fax 317-572-4002.

Wiley publishes in a variety of print and electronic formats and by print-on-demand. Some material included with standard print versions of this book may not be included in e-books or in print-on-demand. If this book refers to media such as a CD or DVD that is not included in the version you purchased, you may download this material at http://booksupport.wiley.com. For more information about Wiley products, visit www.wiley.com.

Library of Congress Cataloging-in-Publication Data

Lukensmeyer, Carolyn J.
　Bringing citizen voices to the table : a guide for public managers / Carolyn J. Lukensmeyer.
　　　p.　cm.
　Includes bibliographical references and index.
　ISBN 978-1-118-23087-9 (cloth),　ISBN 978-1-118-28528-2 (ebk.),　ISBN 978-1-118-28251-9 (ebk.), ISBN 978-1-118-28343-1 (ebk.)
　1. Public administration–United States–Citizen participation.　2. Political participation–United States.　3. Public administration–United States–Decision making.　I. Title.
　　JK421.L855 2013
　　352.3'3–dc23

　　　　　　　　　　　　　　　　　　　　　　　　　　　　　　　2012026955

Printed in the United States of America
FIRST EDITION
HB Printing　10　9　8　7　6　5　4　3　2　1

*To my parents and grandparents
who first taught me the importance of voice
and standing up for what you believe.*

*For everyone who knows that America
only fulfills the promise of democracy
when all her voices are heard.*

The source of human suffering is that everyone chooses one side and refuses to see the other side, so reality becomes an alternating sequence of opposites with one leading invariably to the other.

CHUANG-TZU*

Never doubt that a small group of thoughtful, committed citizens can change the world. Indeed, it is the only thing that ever has.

MARGARET MEAD**

*Kia-Hway, Liou (trans.). *Œuvres complètes*. Paris: Editions Gallimard, 1969, unpaged.
**Kassarjian, Sevanne. Personal communication with Carolyn J. Lukensmeyer, May 10, 2012.

CONTENTS

FIGURES AND TABLES

FIGURES

TABLES

FOREWORD

Our representative democracy, of which Americans are justly proud, is in trouble. Partisan politics have paralyzed Washington. Instead of engaging in constructive dialogue aimed at working out pragmatic solutions to policy problems, political leaders are blaming and demonizing each other, focusing on the other side's perceived vulnerabilities, and avoiding serious discussions of what can actually be done to address challenges that face the country. These challenges are daunting—creating more jobs, stabilizing the rising debt, reducing reliance on fossil fuels, resolving the stresses of illegal immigration—but not unmanageable. Yet politicians snipe and bicker rather than working together to manage them. The problems worsen while gridlock reigns.

Partisan politics are nothing new, but polarization of the parties has intensified in recent years. There are many more party-line votes in Congress, fewer moderates in both parties, and diminished opportunities for cooperation or even socializing across the aisle. The tone of public discourse is more strident and accusatory.

Our Constitution, with its separation of powers and multiple checks and balances, has always made decision making slow and difficult. Getting things done in our system requires negotiation and compromise. With the parties so polarized on important issues and so unwilling to negotiate, the business of policymaking has nearly come to a dead stop.

Polls show that the public is disgusted with the political bickering and inaction. Congress's approval ratings have fallen to an all-time low, and trust in government has eroded from already-low levels. Remarkably, just as dictatorships are being overthrown by fledgling democratic movements in many parts of the world, the world's oldest and mostly stable democracy is losing faith in the ability of its elected officials to solve problems and, indeed, to govern.

But, wait—there is hope! It turns out that average citizens are far more able to engage in civil, constructive dialogue on public policy issues than politicians are, and they are more willing to hammer out pragmatic compromises. For a couple of decades, the public engagement movement has been bringing together groups of Americans from all walks of life in facilitated dialogues about difficult public issues, often at the local and state levels.

Typically in these dialogues, a representative group of volunteers, chosen with regard to diversity of gender, ethnicity, income, age, and other characteristics, works together for a few intense hours of interaction to try to resolve an issue on which they may have widely different views at the outset. These folks are not experts or policy wonks. Some have strong views on the issue in question; others may not have given it much thought. However, working from an agreed set of facts supplied by an unbiased source and following rules of civil discourse, time after time these groups of citizens prove equal to the task. They discuss the issue politely, although often passionately, and come to a solution that all or most can live with. The solution is not likely to be anyone's ideal choice, but it will be one that most find acceptable—far more acceptable than no decision at all.

In this book, Carolyn Lukensmeyer, one of the stars of the public engagement movement, draws on her years as founder and leader of America*Speaks* to describe how public engagement like this works and how it can contribute to breaking our nation's policy deadlock. She reviews what she and others have learned from the rich experience of hundreds of efforts to engage the public in serious dialogue with the explicit purpose of resolving a problem. She describes specific examples of public engagement in diverse settings and draws lessons and principles from them. Those who care about restoring trust in government and making better public decisions at all levels will find this an extremely informative and heartening book.

I have participated in public engagement events, some led by America*Speaks* and some led by other organizations, on issues as diverse as rebuilding lower Manhattan after the tragedy of September 11, 2001; neighborhood development in the District of Columbia; transforming the national health care system; and reducing the federal debt. I have always gone into these sessions with skepticism and emerged enormously encouraged by the common sense of ordinary citizens, their willingness to tackle hard issues, and their ability to listen respectfully to each other and seek common ground without betraying their principles. I often speculate about how public decisions would improve if we could take public engagement to a higher level with the active participation of elected political leaders. Carolyn Lukensmeyer takes this speculation seriously. She shares her hopes for involving far larger numbers of citizens in the decisions that affect their lives and changing the tone of public discourse from one of tearing down the other side to one of sharing ideas and coming to agreement on constructive solutions.

October 2012   Alice M. Rivlin

Alice M. Rivlin is an economist and public policy analyst. She is currently a Senior Fellow at the Brookings Institution and a visiting professor at the Georgetown Public Policy Institute. She served as Director of the Office of Management and Budget in the first Clinton Administration and as Vice Chair of the Federal Reserve board. She was the first Director of the Congressional Budget Office and chaired the District of Columbia Control Board. She was a member of the Simpson-Bowles Commission and cochaired the Bipartisan Policy Center's Debt Reduction Task Force.

PREFACE:
PUBLIC SERVICE AND
THE REVITALIZATION OF
AMERICAN DEMOCRACY

The great privilege of the Americans does not consist in being more enlightened than other nations, but in being able to repair the faults they may commit.

Alexis de Tocqueville, 1841*

In October 2011 I was invited to give the keynote speech at a ceremony for the recipients of the American University Robert W. Jones Award for Executive Leadership. The award recognizes federal public servants who produce outstanding results in their work. I give a lot of speeches. More often than not, I speak extemporaneously about the state of our nation's democracy and my work of over nearly two decades to do something about the challenges we face. At this particular moment, however, I was immersed in the process of writing this book about America*Speaks*'s citizen engagement practice. Knowing I would have more than one hundred public managers and other civil servants in the audience, it seemed a perfect opportunity to present some of the book's content: the importance of citizen engagement; the seven

---

*de Tocqueville, A., and Spencer, J. C. *Democracy in America* (H. Reeve, trans.). Vol. 1. New York: J. & H. G. Langley, 1841, 250.

strategies that underlie effective engagement efforts; case examples that demonstrate the application of these strategies; and some of the powerful results that have been achieved.

As often happens, however, while standing at the podium and taking the measure of my audience, I spontaneously pursued a different, unanticipated course. Instead of reviewing what would be in this book, I instinctively went directly to the fundamental issue of trust—how Americans have lost trust in the institutions managed and led by the very people sitting in front of me, and what I thought they could do about it.

I am glad that I followed my intuition, because after the speech, one of the honorees, John Montgomery, a forty-three-year employee of the U.S. Naval Research Laboratory, exclaimed that the talk had inspired him "to work another forty years." A woman in the audience approached me to say that she had been long contemplating her retirement but I had made her feel excited about going to work again the next day. So what did I say that touched such a responsive chord in these long-time, dedicated public servants?

I started with what everybody already knows: that the vast majority of Americans think our country is on the wrong track—eight out of ten of us are dissatisfied with where we are, and seven out of ten say they have little or no trust in government. Since Gallup began taking these polls at the end of World War II, the disconnect between the people of the United States and the institutions of our democracy has never been so serious (Saad 2011).

I said this state of affairs should not come as a surprise given forty-plus years of anti-government, anti-Washington demagoguery that has served as a core message in political campaigning. Both parties have been culpable. It began with Jimmy Carter's anti-Washington rhetoric in the 1970s; Ronald Reagan took it to a new level in the 1980s, making an anti-government mantra central to his campaign. Seeing how rhetorically effective it was, no matter how substantively inaccurate or misleading, candidates of both parties have been jumping on board ever since. As a result, "government as the problem" has become our official national narrative, repeated again and again by political candidates running for the highest offices in the land, and reiterated continually by the media. The cumulative impact is that mistrust and disdain are the first reactions of millions of Americans when they hear the word "government."

The tragedy of this is that it perpetuates a profound distortion of reality, and in so doing exacerbates what has become a massive gulf between what Americans have come to believe about their government and what government actually does for all of us. Of course there are many things about our government that should be reformed and improved, but we have lost sight of the fact that government's daily accomplishments are deeply and concretely connected to every aspect of our lives, from the quality of the food we eat, to the medicines we take, to the safety of our transportation systems, and on and on. As Abraham Lincoln so eloquently stated it in 1854: "The legitimate object of government is to do for people what needs to be done but which they cannot by individual effort do at all or do so well for themselves" (Lincoln 1907, 178).

And yet, Americans are repeatedly told they can do just as well without government. A pointed example: not too long before my speech at American University, on the floor of the U.S. House of Representatives a member of Congress said: "Why do we need the National Weather Service? It's a huge employee group at NOAA [the National Oceanic and Atmospheric Administration], and getting rid of it could save us millions of dollars. After all, we can get all that same information from the weatherman on the local news." The congressman's failure, or perhaps unwillingness, to acknowledge the facts in this situation is quite astounding. Have we truly come to a place where our national leaders feel free to disregard the obvious fact that investment in government infrastructure is often what makes it possible for the private sector to deliver its products? In this instance, that local weather reports are completely dependent on the work of the very federal agency he named. It is a stark illustration of why so many Americans have come to disrespect, and therefore to distrust, the very government that works for their benefit.

To reverse this trend, someone must take responsibility for increasing Americans' understanding and appreciation of what government actually does. Someone must also take responsibility for creating more effective mechanisms through which Americans can actively and positively influence government's decisions and connect to its work. I proposed to this audience of civil servants

that among others, that "someone" is them. In addition to everything else they are doing, they have a new task ahead: to take
responsibility for, and play their part in, rebuilding the public's
trust in our democracy. They must bring the voices of citizens to
the table.

KEY PATHWAYS TO
REBUILDING TRUST

There are three principal ways they could do this, I offered—key
pathways for turning around what has become a disturbing state
of affairs for the health of our democracy.

First, there must be a massive effort by government to communicate in new ways what it does—not so much the tasks themselves,
but the impact and benefits of carrying out those tasks. Public
managers have to look closely at all of their interfaces with the
public and deliberately use these to broadcast what government
provides for the public every day. Back to the congressman's statement, why not simply have a crawl running across the bottom of
our TV screens during every local weather report that says: "Data
supplied by the National Weather Service"?

The second pathway to rebuilding trust is for individuals and
organizations across our society that do understand the value of
government work to help dislodge the misleading picture of government that is so prominent. Public managers themselves will be
particularly effective in this task. As citizens of the United States,
they should be among those who bring together small groups of
people, in their homes, offices, meeting rooms, and throughout
their individual communities, to have discussions about the appropriate role of government in our lives. These gatherings should
not seek to teach or to lecture, but should allow the conversations
themselves to slowly build people's understanding of and connection to their own government.

A third pathway to rebuilding trust is for public managers to
commit to reinvigorating the ways in which government agencies
engage with the public—embracing new methods and strategies
that will fully and authentically bring citizen voice into decision
making. This pathway is the subject and purpose of this book.
New methods of engagement can and should be applied to key
governance processes, such as policy development and implemen-

tation, rule-making, and budgeting, among others. In any of these arenas, the informed, collective views of citizens must be part of decision making.

Communicate, develop real understanding, and engage. Richard Stem, a veteran of the U.S. Forest Service, described well the importance of these pathways to rebuilding trust:

> There are 450 District Rangers across the United States. They are usually located in small towns adjacent to a National Forest where they manage a staff of as few as 10 or as many as 80 people. There is an old expectation that these Rangers should establish relationships with local folks immediately so they understand who you are, what you stand for, and how you operate. If you don't establish those relationships from day one, when things get tough down the road, you have no respectful relationships to build upon. Right now, public agencies are forgetting that proactive wisdom. It is much more difficult to solve problems when you have to build respectful, trust-oriented relationships at the same time. We need to start public engagement before the next emergency [Stem 2012].

THE DESIRE IS THERE

It would be logical to question how a speech, even dramatically delivered, could move a soon-to-retire civil servant to sign up for another forty years of work. The answer lies not so much in the content of the speech as in the unrecognized nature of the audience. I have had this experience with public managers many times in my career—wherein a talk or a simple visioning exercise can quickly put them back in touch with the passion and drive that motivated them to go into public service in the first place. Most civil servants in our country have a profound respect for the common good. They care passionately about the issues they work on, and they believe they can make a difference. It is a very patriotic, core, democratic yearning that motivates so many Americans to pursue a career in public service.

Unfortunately, after many years of working in a large, impersonal bureaucracy in which there are few signals or responsibilities that take them back to their original inspiration to serve and actualize democratic principles, these feelings can get lost. But if you just scratch the surface, you hit a well of commitment to making a better world—to the belief that the best public policy must reflect the will of the people and protect our common good. In a February 2012 op-ed piece in the *Washington Post*, career Foreign Service Officer Jason Ullner captured this spirit:

> There was a time, not long ago, when government service was seen as a higher calling. That's the reason I decided to join the State Department in 2005—not because I wanted job security or good health benefits but because I wanted to devote my life to making this country stronger, to making the world a better, safer place . . . I still get excited to come to work every morning. I still get a thrill when I enter the State Department and see the flags of every nation with which we have diplomatic relations. And I certainly get chills each and every time I see the U.S. flag on one of our embassies . . . We don't do our jobs for glory, or money or power. We do them—and do them well—because we take pride in our work and pride in representing the United States of America [Ullner 2012, A15].

Words like these leave little doubt that dedicated and inspired public servants are an essential ingredient in revitalizing our nation's democracy.

As a passionate advocate both for strengthening democracy in our country and for the critical value of public service, I am challenged by, and excited about, making the connections between the two. It is the purpose of this book. Ensuring that America's democracy continues to strive to achieve the ideals of the founders will require nothing short of completely rethinking public engagement in governance. And at the core of this essential paradigm shift is the important role of government as convener—and the role of public managers as the designers and builders of the capacity and infrastructure needed to create authentic citizen engagement.

MY BACKGROUND

How did I come to these convictions? The trajectory of my life and work has led me directly here.

I was born and raised in a small town in rural Iowa, in a deeply religious family committed to hard work, helping others during difficult times, and building a better life for the next generation. My family church was, in fact, my first experience of self-governance. Similar to the Quakers, we were a lay congregation without an appointed minister or hierarchy. Leadership emerged as people felt moved by the spirit to suggest a hymn, offer a prayer, or give a sermon. Decisions were made by consensus of the elders in the community.

I came of age and experienced my political awakening amid the tumult of the Vietnam War. I was an undergraduate at the University of Iowa, where, it is not often remembered, the first draft card was burned. The university had a significant number of activist graduate students who were opposed to the war and a moderate, Midwestern undergraduate population that was generally supportive of the war. When campus governance structures began to break down in the face of these divisions, the university selected a small group of administrators, faculty, and student leaders to participate in a summer program on human relations and university governance. On returning from this program in the fall, I stepped into a principal role in designing meetings between students, faculty, and administrators to explore ways to reestablish governance guidelines. This work was recognized by a number of universities around the country, and after graduating I was recruited by the dean of students at the University of Rochester to create a similar program there.

These experiences piqued my interest in social change and organization and systems behavior, and I pursued a PhD at Case Western Reserve University in that field. With a desire to further understand the complex interplay among structures, processes, and human behavior, while working on my PhD I also pursued postgraduate studies at the Gestalt Institute of Cleveland. After receiving my degree, I launched an organization development consulting business, which I led for the next fourteen years. My consulting work focused on strategy, structure, and human resources: how to integrate these elements to successfully achieve an organization's mission and vision. In particular, I pursued understanding the differences in organization and management between the private and public sectors: as a function of the scale or size of the organization and as a result of gender differences in leadership positions.

In 1982, newly elected Ohio governor Dick Celeste was looking for a consultant to run cabinet and staff retreats and assist with a statewide strategic planning process. My name was given to him by several of my clients, including both multinational corporations headquartered in Cleveland at the time, Republic Steel, Jones and Laughlin, and TRW, as well as a number of the city's leading feminist coalitions and organizations. "Go find her," Governor Celeste told his staff, "she must at least be an interesting person!" During Celeste's first term I filled this consulting role, and in his second term he invited me to be his Chief of Staff—the state's first woman in that position as well as the first Chief of Staff in the country with a background in organization and management.

As Chief of Staff, I was in a position to be part of groundbreaking work that required new institutional relationships between sectors, inside the government, and with the public at large. Among other work, we built industry-university collaborations; completely reconfigured the mental health services system into a national practice model; clustered cabinet members across disciplines to increase their impact on such cross-cutting issues as economic development, education reform, and international trade; and created one-stop delivery for workforce development services. As a visionary leader and a highly skilled politician, Governor Celeste understood that to create significant large-scale system changes there had to be a public constituency committed to those goals. Because of his vision we were able to experiment with new methods of communication and engagement that brought collective citizen voice into governance.

I learned two significant lessons doing this work. First, the kinds of intractable issues that faced the state of Ohio—and that continue to face the country as a whole today—cannot be solved without true cross-sector collaboration. Businesses, nonprofits, and community organizations, as well as government, have to bring their best resources, both human and financial, to the table. The second lesson, equally important and the focus of this book, is that these intractable issues cannot be solved without the full engagement of the public. Based on the work we had done, I left my position in Ohio state government more optimistic than I would ever have imagined about how possible it is to change large government bureaucracies.

At the same time, I was more pessimistic and concerned than I ever imagined I would be about the health of democracy in the United States. During my four years as Chief of Staff, I saw the significant influence of money and special interests on decision making, how politically motivated redistricting efforts were disenfranchising a large number of citizens, and a host of other dysfunctional practices that continue to plague our democracy today.

And yet, even more motivated to express my vision and apply my skills at the national level, I moved to Washington, DC, in 1993 to join the new Clinton Administration, serving as the Deputy Director for Management of the National Performance Review, better known as the Reinventing Government Task Force. At the conclusion of my work on the National Performance Review I was invited to work as consultant to the White House Chief of Staff. From my office in the West Wing, I began to observe closely how our federal government's decision-making system actually works—and why it doesn't work. Within a few months I was saying: "I thought what I saw in Ohio was bad . . . " There I sat, at the nexus of our nation's major institutions, where the executive branch, Congress, the media, corporate special interests, and the Washington think tanks determine our policy frameworks, and I could see clearly that not one of them had the slightest interest in bringing in the public's views except through opinion polling. Further, it was clear that we were failing to make progress on the major challenges our country was facing in part because the public's voice was not at the table—because people couldn't demonstrate their will about these challenges to our governing institutions.

Although I was becoming increasingly disillusioned by the inner workings of our electoral and government institutions, I still held an unshakable belief in the democratic process itself. I chose to leave government in search of a new way to organize and elevate the public's voice on a large scale. I traveled across the country in pursuit of answers to a central question: How can we create an authentic connection between decision makers and the public so that citizens can have a tangible impact on the decisions that most affect their lives? I hoped to learn from people who had succeeded in organizing themselves, made an impact on policy, and created processes to sustain the engagement of citizens and leaders over time.

Based on my previous experience and what I saw and learned across the country, I created a conceptual model for large-scale citizen engagement forums and developed a vision for how these forums could be used in national dialogues on key public policy issues. I then returned to Washington and convened a group of elected officials, leaders of national associations, experts in dialogue and deliberation from the public and private sectors, foundation leaders, community organizers, and members of the media. I presented the model for feedback, and the response was uniformly enthusiastic. The ideas resonated strongly with this diverse group.

I founded America*Speaks* shortly thereafter to bring these ideas to life. Over the next two decades, America*Speaks* has used this model—which we call the "21st Century Town Meeting"—to give more than two hundred thousand people in the United States and around the world a voice in decision making on the critical issues that have an impact on their lives.

This book is filled with the stories of those efforts, each one reflecting the underlying strategies that made the work successful. It is my hope and dream that the key strategies we learned for effectively bringing citizens' voices into public decision making will take hold—that our nation will both embrace them and embed them in the everyday processes of how government works. I believe that if we do, we can realize the vision and the aspirations of our founding fathers and be a government that truly is "of the people, by the people, for the people."

INTENT OF THIS BOOK

This book seeks to inspire and support those who are willing to rise to the challenges of righting our democratic ship. It digs deeply into how public managers, civic leaders, elected officials, any interested parties for that matter, can successfully create strategic and effective processes of citizen and stakeholder engagement linked to decision making. My hope is that the lessons and foundational strategies of the deliberative democracy practice America*Speaks* has developed and pursued for nearly twenty years will inspire public managers to embrace the possibilities and then take the risks necessary to be leaders in revitalizing governance in America. To further that end, the book highlights the voices of highly experienced federal managers who have successfully used public engagement to realize their agency's goals. Their rich experiences and hard-earned wisdom demonstrate that robust, effective citizen engagement is both possible and mission-consistent, and is often even indispensable.

This book is a call to action. We are living in a time when the trust between citizens and government is profoundly broken. The survival of our nation demands that we not delay in taking steps to rebuild that trust. A wise public servant once said to me that when you lose or violate trust it evaporates by the ton, yet when you are trying to rebuild that trust it has to be done one thimbleful at a time. This graphic image of a daunting challenge aptly describes the road ahead of us. Nonetheless, we must rise to this challenge, make a place for citizens in public decision making, and restore trust in government: the future of our democracy depends on it.

Introduction: The Case for Citizen Engagement

What if millions of Americans regularly came together to deliberate about critical national issues such as health care, immigration, and the economy? What if the recommendations they made guided the actions of our national policymakers? What if the common ground they found was reflected in the tone of national politics? What if all the elements necessary to make it happen—the spaces to hold the discussion, the technology needed to bring millions of voices together, the human resources to facilitate it—were in place? If all this were true, we would be a nation that does more than just *aspire* to listen to its citizens and ensure our policies reflect the public will. We would be a nation that actually does so on a regular basis. We would be a credible democracy.

This need not be a thought experiment. For a long time, America has been a hotbed of innovation in developing a wide range of citizen engagement methods that would achieve these goals. We know how to do it with consistently good results. In fact, every element of the supportive infrastructure we need for robust citizen engagement already exists in some form in some places across the country. Not only do we have all of the knowledge and elements necessary to create robust citizen participation, but the American people really want to do it. In a nationwide survey, the National Conference on Citizenship (NCOC) found that more than 80 percent of respondents were supportive of regular, organized national discussions on critical issues, and that the support crossed political lines: 60 percent of Republicans and 70 percent of Democrats described themselves as "strongly" in favor (NCOC 2008, 12).

And yet our nation is a long way from having in place the supportive infrastructure we need to connect citizen voices to governance in this way. As a result, Americans today feel seriously *disconnected* from their government; they are deeply worried and frustrated that the critical problems facing the country are not being solved (Saad 2011). And their worries are not unfounded. Writing for *Time* magazine in 2010, political author and journalist Peter Beinart offered what has become a commonly held view of governance and democracy in America today: "What really defines our political era," he said, "is not the polarization of Americans but the polarization of American government. In the country at large, the disputes are real but manageable. But in Washington, crossing party lines to resolve them has become excruciatingly rare . . . 62% of Americans say most members of Congress do not deserve re-election, up 10 points from 2006. Public skepticism about the Federal Government and its ability to solve problems . . . is greater today than it has been in at least a decade and a half" (Beinart 2010).

This polarization not only affects Americans' confidence in government but also stymies dedicated public servants. After serving for seventeen years in the U.S. Senate, Republican Olympia Snowe of Maine announced in March 2012 that she would retire at the end of her term because of the way extreme partisanship had diminished government's productivity. Of her decision, Snowe said: "I have spoken on the floor of the Senate for years about the dysfunction and political polarization in the institution. Simply put . . . the greatest deliberative body in history is not living up to its billing. The Senate of today routinely jettisons regular order, as evidenced by the body's failure to pass a budget for more than 1,000 days; serially legislates by political brinkmanship, as demonstrated by the debt-ceiling debacle of August that should have been addressed the previous January; and habitually eschews full debate and an open amendment process in favor of competing, up-or-down, take-it-or-leave-it proposals" (Snowe 2012).

The Pew Research Center for the People & the Press confirms that most of us share Senator Snowe's assessment: just 22 percent of Americans say they can trust the government in Washington almost always or most of the time, among the lowest measures in half a century. Favorable ratings for both major parties, as well as for Congress, have reached record lows, and the public's impressions of elected officials as "corrupt, wasteful, self-centered, unwilling to compromise, and indifferent to the concerns of regular Americans" are widespread (Pew Research Center for the People & the Press 2010, 13).

This toxic environment has effectively stalled our nation. We face a host of urgent challenges crying out for resolution, from ensuring our fiscal sustainability and addressing our long-term energy needs, to resolving our immigration policies and fixing our schools. Yet as each issue takes its turn in the national spotlight, all we see is the continuous inability to make progress. Ours has become a system in which elected officials, to stay aligned with their ideology, refuse to make compromises in the interest of the common good; they are more concerned with gaining an advantage in the next election than they are with solving problems and governing the country.

Our two recent forays into national-level health care reform, arguably one of the most critical economic and social concerns we face, tell a compelling story of how corrosive politics stalls governance. In 1993–1994 substantive debates on health care reform were overtaken by highly politicized accusations of secretive processes and socialist agendas, and the issue was simply dropped. In 2009–2010 more progress was made: legislation was passed to extend health coverage to an estimated thirty-four million Americans, reform aspects of the insurance market, and slow the growth of costs. However, the deeper systemic reforms that were needed to actually bend the curve on health care costs were left untouched, and even without that level of structural change the new health care law quickly became the subject of twenty state lawsuits ("Georgia Joins Health-Care Reform Lawsuit" 2010) and a U.S. Supreme Court challenge. As a nation, we are developing a dangerous habit of leaving problems of grave consequence for the next generation to solve.

BRINGING CITIZEN VOICES TO THE TABLE

A healthy democracy depends on sound practices for elections and for governing. Many of the roots of the dysfunction just described are in electoral politics: partisan redistricting practices, the enormous amount of money influencing the outcomes of elections, and attempts at voter suppression, to name just a few. A full treatment of such concerns is outside the scope of this book. This book focuses instead on what happens *after* an election is over—when our officials turn their attention to governing. At this juncture we see another root problem: a failure to secure a place for citizens' authentic participation. Yes, we can vote and respond to polls or surveys; some of us get to participate in an occasional referendum; and we can comment on federal rule-making. But beyond that, meaningful opportunities for citizens to participate regularly in government decision making are few and far between.

If citizens are not given authentic opportunities to participate, then leaders cannot know their true values and their collective will. The absence of this collective citizen voice makes it impossible for our elected leaders and decision makers to come to compromises and make the tough choices that are necessary to meet the serious challenges facing our nation. We see their paralysis of action every day when we read or hear the news.

But this is a problem that can be solved. After nearly twenty years of experience in the field of deliberative democracy, I have witnessed over and over again that when citizens are given an authentic opportunity to engage in decision making—when public will is connected to political will—the power of special interests can be substantially reduced, decisions have greater staying power, and the public's trust in our governing institutions increases. Every elected official who has been part of one of America*Speaks*'s deliberative processes has immediately grasped the significant value of citizen engagement for governance. But how do we do it on a regular basis, all across our country?

To engage our citizenry and reinvigorate our democracy, three constituencies will have to reimagine their roles and begin to establish a new "business as usual."

The people will have to demand that they be given authentic opportunities to participate in governance on a regular basis. They must be willing to become more active citizens. The current level of public frustration about the problems facing our nation may finally be motivating citizens to demand a greater role. The Tea Party and Occupy Wall Street movements are potential signs of their readiness.

Elected officials will have to declare their allegiance to the idea of routine citizen engagement in decision making and take concrete action to implement it. They will have to ensure that citizens have the opportunities they are seeking to play a role in governance.

Public managers who lead our government agencies and programs will have to not only embrace this course but also creatively embed it in their daily work. Among these three key constituencies for action, public managers are the focus of this book. Their pivotal role in governance provides both ample opportunities for engaging citizens as well as the real promise of success. Because citizen engagement directly addresses some of the core challenges public managers face in their daily work, adopting it can be a high-payoff strategy.

ORGANIZATION OF THIS BOOK

A thorough consideration of the public manager's role in citizen engagement must begin with an understanding of the larger context: What is it and how has it been practiced in our nation? How does the America*Speaks* model fit into this field? What are its theoretical underpinnings? Has it proved successful? Answers to these questions make up the content of Chapters One and Two. Moving out of the realm of theory, Chapter Three offers a compelling case study of citizen engagement on the ground. It describes how in the aftermath of Hurricane Katrina and the devastating floods more than four thousand New Orleanians came together to make decisions about the future of their city.

With this case study as a backdrop, Chapter Four explores the work of citizen engagement from the public manager's perspective: What do public managers stand to gain? What challenges do they face? How might the Obama Administration's Open Government Directive, with its focus on transparency, participation, and collaboration, have an impact on their efforts?

The next seven chapters detail the core strategies that make up the citizen engagement methodology examined in this book. These chapters explore the importance of each strategy in the context of current democratic practice as well as our social, political, and cultural realities. They lay out specific steps for undertaking the work; provide case studies that illustrate how they operate on the ground; and explore the public manager's role in implementing them. Each chapter is accompanied by a case study from the perspective of a public manager who has done this work.[1] Taken together, these chapters provide a comprehensive blueprint for citizen engagement efforts. Following the seven strategies, Chapter Twelve provides an overview of how online methodologies hold promise for expanding citizen engagement.

Finally, Chapter Thirteen returns the reader to a broader perspective, exploring the larger context in which citizen engagement work takes place. It offers a vision of the infrastructure our nation needs to support a thriving democracy, including a legislative framework for participation, sufficient organizational and technological infrastructures, and robust civic education, among other components. To be sure, such topics, and the challenges they suggest, are far-reaching. But they are also critically important: creating day-to-day citizen engagement strategies will not alone bring about the needed sea change in our democracy. We must simultaneously build the underlying structures and systems that will support the ongoing participation we envision.

Under no circumstances can we fail in this task. Far removed from the voices of the citizenry, every day hyperpartisan politics undermine our government's ability to act on such critical issues as ensuring our fiscal sustainability, facing the realities of climate change, and addressing the crisis in immigration. Inaction harms all of us. Is this the democracy our founders envisioned? Is this the America in which we want to live? Are "of the people, by the people, for the people" merely antiquated words on the walls of our classrooms? They will be, unless we pursue a different course. As scholar David Orr so eloquently stated: "We can be reactionary and do . . . a series of disjointed, one-off, overly expensive *ad hoc* responses to external crises. Or, we can envision and create an integrated, well-thought-out system in which the parts reinforce the resilience and prosperity of the whole" (Orr 2012).

Bringing Citizen Voices to the Table

CHAPTER ONE

CITIZEN ENGAGEMENT IN THE UNITED STATES

The people are the only legitimate fountain of power, and it is from them that the constitutional charter, under which the several branches of government hold their power, is derived.

JAMES MADISON, 1788*

Our founding fathers had a deep and abiding belief in self-governance: the idea that power ultimately resides in the voices and wisdom of the people. They embedded this belief in our system of representative government. Our nation's founding documents— the Declaration of Independence and the U.S. Constitution— were a radical departure from any previous expression of the relationship between a people and their government. Today, our founders' vision is still an aspiration, not a reality. This chapter explores the extent to which U.S. citizens are currently engaged in governance and how we compare to other nations around the world in this respect.

---

*Madison, J. "The Federalist No. 49: Method of Guarding Against the Encroachments of Any One Department of Government by Appealing to the People Through a Convention." *Independent Journal,* Feb. 1788. [http://constitution.org/fed/federa49.htm]. Accessed 2012.

Use of the Word "Citizen"

The term "citizen" is used throughout this book to mean, simply, a resident of the United States of America. Many readers, particularly public managers, may choose not to use the word "citizen" in this broad way because it has become a highly politicized term that is full of complexity related to immigration status. Although this choice is understandable, I am deeply concerned that bowing to political correctness in this instance also means giving up core concepts and roles that are central to democracy. At a very fundamental level, a "citizen" is a person who feels, and is willing to act on, a sense of responsibility for the common good and the advancement of a nation.

To test this premise, several years ago America*Speaks* conducted focus groups with immigrants to ask their feelings about use of the word "citizen" in the context of deliberative democracy practice. The overwhelming response was that because their desire and intention was to become legal citizens of this country, they neither were offended nor felt excluded by the use of this term.

The work described in this book is based on a deep belief in the importance of citizenship, understood in its broadest sense. The use of "citizen" reflects that belief and is not meant to imply any other meanings of the word.

What Is Citizen Engagement, and Why Is It Important to Democracy?

The concept of "citizen engagement"—or "citizen participation"—has a wide range of meanings, associated ideas, and applications. For example, it might be used to refer to participation in mass social movements or to the development of class action lawsuits; it might be used to describe ballot referenda, or efforts by workers to gain control of their workplace. Depending on the circumstances, each could be a valid example of citizen engagement.

In this book, "citizen engagement" has a very specific meaning. It refers to a deliberative process through which groups of citizens representative of their communities learn, express their points of view, and discover common ground to influence government decision making. This kind of citizen engagement can be employed at many different stages in the governance process. As articulated by the Organisation for Economic Co-operation and Development (OECD), these stages include when policy agendas are first being set; when problems and strategies are being analyzed; when specific interventions are being designed; when the interventions are being implemented; and when they are being evaluated (OECD 2003).

At any of these stages, citizen engagement work can achieve several important goals. It can educate and energize the public. It can create opportunities for citizens to shape, and in some cases determine, government actions. It can improve the quality of government decisions by yielding better information about the issues at hand and ensuring that the voices of those affected by policy have been heard and considered, and their concerns addressed.

If these goals are achieved, citizen engagement can have a direct impact on the health of our democracy. Specifically:

- It reduces the inordinate power of special interests on decision-making processes.
- It produces policies that hold over time.
- It builds constituencies committed to specific outcomes.
- It increases trust in government programs, personnel, practices, and institutions.

Beyond these specific results, high-quality citizen engagement breathes life into our founders' deep belief in self-governance. Linking public will to political will is essential to solving the major issues facing our nation (see Figure 1.1).

The fundamental value of these results to a democracy is clear, and the case studies of citizen engagement offered throughout this book will return to these impacts again and again. Academics

Figure 1.1 Linking Public Will to Political Will

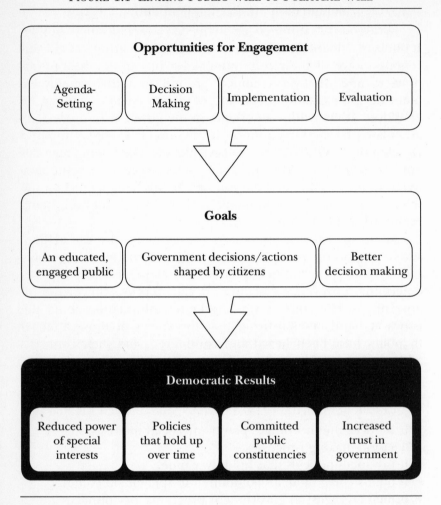

and practitioners in the field of democratic practice agree that the engagement of citizens on issues of public policy is a highly productive and worthwhile endeavor. The Kettering Foundation, a long-standing national nonprofit organization that has been conducting work and research in the democracy field since the 1990s, describes deliberation as "a time-honored way to make sound decisions." The foundation further states that "to make sound judgments, people have to weigh possible actions against what they consider valuable. This careful weighing is at the core of deliberation" (Kettering Foundation 2012).

In 2008 the National Academies Press published a book exploring the value of deliberation in government decision making. "Substantial evidence shows," the editors concluded, "that effective public participation can help agencies do a better job in achieving public purposes for the environment by ensuring better decisions and increasing the likelihood that they will be implemented effectively. Good public participation also helps build capacity in agencies and among participants" (Dietz and Stern 2008, 226).

Citizen Engagement in the United States: A Nongovernmental Enterprise

Despite the documented benefits of citizen engagement, across the country you can find only a small cadre of public managers and a handful of enlightened elected officials who embrace citizen engagement and practice it skillfully. The words and stories of a number of them are featured in this book. However, the U.S. government as an institution has taken a decidedly hands-off approach to citizen engagement.

Codified opportunities for citizens to *actively* lend their voices to the governance of the nation are quite limited and have not been adapted over time to the changing size and makeup of our country, or to the technologies now available to assist in this work. We do, of course, have the opportunity to vote (although 40 percent of us do not). In parts of the country where public referenda are constitutionally allowable and used, citizens can directly enact or reject specific ballot initiatives. In addition, since 1946 the Administrative Procedure Act has given us the legal right to weigh in on federal rules and policies while they are still being developed. A 1996 amendment to that act expanded this right, giving the public direct access to the committees in each agency that have the power to negotiate rules. The act further specifies mechanisms for including the views of affected people and requires that the president take steps to facilitate and encourage these efforts. Although these might sound like opportunities for participation, by and large they are taken up by a relatively small and narrowly drawn group: people who are paid to read the *Federal Register* every day—in other words, lobbyists representing special interests, not average citizens. As a result, what was conceptualized as a legislated vehicle for citizens to influence policy and governance has become, for the most part, a way for highly resourced special interests to wield their influence. Finally, there are very few budgets, authorizing mandates, or infrastructures for jump-starting and sustaining additional citizen engagement work within our government. President Obama's Open Government Directive (discussed in Chapter Four) is the beginning of a new direction.

In the meantime, the vacuum in codified citizen engagement in this country has been filled by nonprofit organizations, entrepreneurial practitioners, and academics. To be sure, these practitioners have succeeded in developing a wide range of engagement methodologies that can be used in a variety of settings and circumstances.[1] The National Coalition for Dialogue & Deliberation (NCDD), a nonprofit group that supports organizations working in the dialogue and deliberation field, has developed a useful framework for cataloguing the breadth of approaches in use. The framework, laid out in Table 1.1, identifies four streams of dialogue and deliberation and, for each, the explicit purpose as well as the methods that are best known and proven effective.

Organizations in the dialogue and deliberation field, and many others, are occasionally called on to assist the federal government with public engagement. However, these joint efforts tend to occur based on the personal interest, skills, and perseverance of a particular manager. Only a very small number of U.S. agencies have developed a comprehensive practice: the Environmental Protection Agency, the Department of the Interior, the Nuclear Regulatory Commission, the Fish and Wildlife Service, the Forest Service, the Army Corps of Engineers, and the Department of Transportation are notable in this regard. As a general proposition, however, it is fair to say that citizen engagement in the United States is understood and accepted to be the province of nonprofits pushing from the outside.

TABLE 1.1 CATALOGUE OF DIALOGUE AND DELIBERATION
METHODOLOGIES

Stream	Primary Purpose	Methods
Exploration	To encourage people/groups to learn more about themselves, their community, or an issue, and possibly discover innovative solutions.	• Conversation Café, • Intergroup Dialogue in the classroom • Wisdom Council • Wisdom Circles • Open Space • Appreciative Inquiry • Bohm Dialogue • Socrates Café
Conflict Transformation	To resolve conflicts, to foster personal healing and growth, and to improve relations among groups.	• Sustained Dialogue • Intergroup Dialogue in communities • Victim-Offender Mediation • Public Conversations Project Dialogue • Web Lab's Small Group Dialogue • Compassionate Listening
Decision Making	To influence policy decisions and improve public knowledge.	• National Issues Forums • Citizens Jury • Deliberative Polling • 21st Century Town Meeting • Citizen Choicework • Consensus Conference
Collaborative Action	To empower people and groups to solve complicated problems and take responsibility for the solution.	• Study Circles • Future Search • Appreciative Inquiry • Charrettes

Source: National Coalition for Dialogue & Deliberation, 2010.

Treating Polling as Participation

In the context of our nation's nongovernmental approach to citizen engagement, decision makers' increasing and misguided reliance on public opinion polling as a participation mechanism has become an ingrained habit.

Public opinion polling has long been viewed by policymakers, elected officials, candidates, and campaign consultants as an efficient and effective way to hear the voices of citizens and gather their "collective" views. Recent advances in technology (such as live and text response via phone, email, and a range of web-based platforms, as well as improvements in computerized modeling and sampling) have increased polling's appeal because the options now are even more plentiful and efficient. As a result, we conduct an enormous amount of polling in this country. In 2010 the 199 largest research firms spent $9.2 billion on polling; the full total, which is not measurable, is estimated to be nearly $15 billion (Honomichl 2011).

Well-designed, sophisticated polling that is used to gather moment-in-time preferences and reactions is a very important asset for developing corporate strategies, campaign plans, and even overarching policy frameworks in the public sector. But opinions on a spreadsheet do not equal participation and cannot create a public constituency that will stand behind the results. Long-standing democracy practitioners Daniel Yankelovich and Jim Fishkin have been among the strongest voices in the field arguing this point (Yankelovich 1991; Fishkin 1993). Standard polling, they say, only gives us a snapshot of the aggregate of individual opinions at one particular moment. Because these opinions can be, and are, dramatically influenced by specific events or strategies, such as a blitz of negative advertising in a political campaign, they do not provide the level of insight into the public's views that they often claim.

Further, standard public opinion polls do nothing to help individuals grasp and then wrestle with an issue's complexity. They don't help people understand their fellow Americans' views or provide them with an opportunity to develop creative, common-ground solutions to significant problems. Finally, polls fail to energize the public to stand by their opinions or to do their part in making the tough trade-offs embedded in policy decisions. Yet all of this effort is fundamental to developing what Yankelovich calls a stable opinion on a question of public policy (Yankelovich 1991). " 'You can't run a democracy if it is going to be based on raw opinion,' he concluded" (Melville and Kingston 2011, 53).

A public that engages only superficially with issues—that is, one that is unable to form a stable opinion—will always be a target for manipulation and influence. And a manipulated public is not a reliable basis for action by decision makers. Case in point, again, is health care reform. In1993–1994 in response to the Clinton Administration's health care reform proposal, the Health Insurance Association of America spent $14 million (equivalent to $20.4 million today) on the highly effective "Harry and Louise" television ads (Singer 2009), which were designed to evoke public fear and opposition. In the health care tumult of 2009–2010, 3,300 lobbyists worked the issue—equal to six lobbyists for every member of Congress—and were paid a total of $263.4 million for their efforts during the first six months of 2009 alone (Salant and O'Leary 2009). Both then and now, buffeted by highly spun information from lobbyists and special interest groups, the public could not reach a stable judgment about health care reform. As a result, decision makers did not have confidence that their actions would be supported, they failed to act boldly, and progress stalled (Teixeira 2009; Rivlin and Rivlin 2009). In short, tough policy decisions require a strong and stable public constituency. By relying primarily on shifting polling data to understand where the public stands, today's decision makers lack a viable foundation from which to act decisively—and so they generally do not.

Keith Melville, one of the founders of the National Issues Forums, and Robert Kingston of the Kettering Foundation, summarized well the important distinctions between opinion polling and the development of more stable views. "There is a fundamental difference between public opinion and the kinds of public judgments people reach in the course of deliberation," they said. "What public deliberation gives us is not a more detailed version of what opinion polls provide . . . [T]he goal of deliberative forums . . . is to illuminate why people support certain courses of action and what their reservations and main concerns are . . . The main contribution of public judgment is that it leads to the discovery of what we have in common. It reveals the concerns and priorities that public policy should reflect, and it sheds light on why they are important" (Melville and Kingston 2011, 71).

Even George Gallup, founder of the Gallup poll, recognized polling to be a "participation" mechanism that does not live up to its billing. In its November 2011 obituary for Gallup, the *New York Times* said he "lamented late in his life that politicians follow polls rather than their conscience" (Zernike 2011). In this Gallup acknowledged an important corollary truth: that almost every mechanism, if used for purposes beyond those for which it was designed, can become a problem rather than a solution.

RESULTS OF OUR NONGOVERNMENTAL APPROACH TO CITIZEN ENGAGEMENT

Our nation's externally driven citizen engagement practice, reinforced by the trends just described, has several unfortunate results, two of which are explored here. First, it has created inconsistency and unpredictability in the practice of citizen engagement, which in turn has undermined citizen engagement's potential to achieve momentum and, eventually, scale. Second, it has justified our unwillingness to prioritize developing a national deliberative infrastructure. Without this infrastructure, the task of bringing together the public to discover their collective voice is often seen by decision makers as too difficult and too costly.

LACK OF CONSISTENCY AND MOMENTUM

As noted earlier, localities, states, regions, and even the federal government sporadically use a variety of participatory methodologies. A few examples follow. In 2009 then-mayor of Harrisonburg, Virginia, Kai Degner used the Open Space methodology for a two-hundred-person summit on the environment and renewable resources (Jones 2009). Also in 2009, MacNeil/Lehrer Productions, working in partnership with the Center for Deliberative Democracy (CDD) at Stanford University, used the deliberative polling methodology to engage more than three hundred Michigan residents in discussions about the state's economy and budget choices (Center for Deliberative Democracy 2010). In 2010 leaders across sectors in Indiana brought four hundred citizens together in discussions aimed at establishing a long-term vision for a ten-county region (NE Indiana Regional Partnership 2010). Many more excellent examples can be found in Matt Leighninger's book *The Next Form of Democracy: How Expert Rule Is Giving Way to Shared Governance—and Why Politics Will Never Be the Same* (Leighninger 2006).

Although each instance of citizen engagement may be productive, taken together they constitute a patchwork approach that makes it nearly impossible to achieve real scale and sustainability. With only scattershot efforts at citizen engagement, the vast majority of Americans—not to mention the vast majority of public officials—have little inkling of the possibility of ongoing, substantive citizen participation and the ways in which it can positively affect government decision making on issues they care about. Fewer still have ever experienced such involvement themselves. This creates a reinforcing cycle that sustains the status quo: piecemeal citizen engagement efforts fail to create a widespread expectation of participation among the American public or among our decision makers. And without such an expectation there is no public demand for moving beyond our inconsistent approach.

LACK OF INFRASTRUCTURE TO SUPPORT DELIBERATION

A primary contributing factor to our approach to citizen engagement is that we do not have in place the infrastructure or the systems necessary to support meaningful, ongoing, routine participation. Rather, these systems have to be created each time a jurisdiction wants or needs to bring the public into a decision-making process. For example, in America*Speaks*'s work, every time we are brought in to facilitate citizen engagement, we find that the physical spaces needed to accommodate large numbers of people coming together to deliberate have to be set up; the technology needed to capture, distill, and disseminate citizens' views has to be brought in; and local organizations have to be paid to temporarily shift their work to citizen outreach to ensure representativeness in the process. Repeatedly recreating such an infrastructure is highly inefficient, yet it is what deliberative democracy practitioners in this country must continually do, searching each time for the necessary resources—from philanthropy, government, or both—to support the work and achieve the desired outcomes.

A case in point: to bring thousands of Washington, DC, residents together to deliberate about the municipal budget, and to advise the mayor of their priorities, the city had to pay the convention center exactly the same fee Microsoft had paid the week before for its annual exposition. As much as the convention center director might have wanted to support Mayor Williams's Citizen Summit by offering free space, given the facility's business model it was not an option. Similarly, in 2002 nearly $350,000 in philanthropic dollars was spent to house Listening to the City in the Jacob Javits Center, where 4,500 New Yorkers came together to weigh in on the conceptual land-use and architectural plans for rebuilding the World Trade Center site.

These kinds of expenditures on public participation have not always been required. In the 1960s and 1970s convention center space was routinely made accessible to mayors and other officials for important municipal gatherings. For example, during the rioting that followed Martin Luther King Jr.'s assassination, Carl Stokes, the first African American mayor of a major Northern city, sought to promote healing and rebuilding in Cleveland, Ohio, through a series of task forces that brought blacks and whites together on key issues. Many of the large organizing meetings of these groups were held in the Cleveland Convention Center at the mayor's request and at no cost to the city.

Today, without an established infrastructure for democratic deliberation, elected officials and decision makers must spend significant amounts of money and undertake complicated logistical work to engage with, listen to, and learn from citizens. A supporting infrastructure not only would bring citizens closer to their elected officials but also would go a long way toward building greater community identity and capacity for participation. Chapter Thirteen lays out the specific components of such a supporting infrastructure.

A Global Comparison

Our nation's scattershot and nongovernmental approach to citizen engagement stands in stark contrast to the approaches of other governments, which, facing many of the same challenges we face in the United States, have made a strong commitment to including citizen voices in their policymaking.

Denmark provides a particularly compelling example. For more than twenty-five years the government has subsidized the Danish Board of Technology, an independent institution established by law that engages citizens and experts in learning and debate about the impact of technology on Danish society. The board, which provides regular advice to the parliament on five to ten issues each year, describes its mission this way: "Knowledge and debate about technology is necessary at all levels to promote its development in a democratic manner. Therefore, the Board of Technology sees it as its duty to involve and help build bridges between citizens, politicians and experts in the assessment of technology. As an independent institution, the Board is duty bound to involve all parties concerned—businesses, research, interest organisations, a wide range of public and political decision-makers—in the assessment and debate on technology" (Leisner 2005, 4). In 2012, in a context of national economic concerns, whether or not to continue the Board of Technology became an issue of debate within the Danish government. Although a modified structure for the board seems likely for the future, it is important to note that during the debate there was extensive support for its work from members of the parliament, stakeholders, and citizens. The board reported that "most of the 111 responses on the settlement act find The Danish Board of Technology relevant, necessary, [and] a role model [that makes] economic sense for the society" (Danish Board of Technology 2012).

A different approach to citizen engagement that has been used broadly around the world is participatory budgeting. In the late 1980s the Brazilian city of Porto Alegre began experimenting with a new way of engaging citizens: inviting them to have a direct impact on overall budgetary spending as well as on the specific allocation of funds. The work was enormously successful and, according to the Participatory Budgeting Project, a nonprofit that supports this work across North America, in Porto Alegre participatory budgeting currently is an annual process "of deliberation and decision-making, in which as many as 50,000 city residents per year decide how to spend as much as 20% of the municipal budget. In a series of neighborhood, regional, and citywide assemblies, residents and elected budget delegates identify spending priorities and vote on which priorities to implement" (Participatory Budgeting Project 2012). Given its successes, participatory budgeting has spread across Latin America and has been increasingly used in Europe, Africa, Asia, and Canada. It has been identified by the United Nations as a "best practice of democratic governance" (Participatory Budgeting Project 2012).

It should be noted that participatory budgeting also has been used in the United States, first in a single ward in Chicago in 2009. Recently, in April 2012, the method was used in New York City, where four City Council members launched participatory budgeting processes in their districts to determine how to spend about $1 million in discretionary funding. More than 250 people directly participated in this process. The *New York Times* described one of the meetings as "the sound of revolutionary civics in action" (Sangha Mar. 2012).

Following are a few more brief examples of how other countries have consistently embedded citizen engagement in policymaking. In Canada, consulting with citizens is an expectation of all federal agencies as part of the country's management accountability framework, which stipulates that "policies and programs are developed 'from the outside in' and partnerships are encouraged and effectively managed" (Treasury Board of Canada Secretariat 2011). In Sweden, as many as two million people participate in study circles dialogues each year (Larsson and Nordvall 2010). Finally, over the last decade the European Union has funded more than thirty-five e-participation research projects with a total budget of over €120 million (Panopoulou, Tambouris, and Tarabanis 2009).

In 2009 the Ash Center for Democratic Governance and Innovation at Harvard University and the Center for the Study of Democratic Institutions at the University of British Columbia established an open knowledge platform called Participedia that is accumulating a global database of significant initiatives in participatory governance. At the beginning of 2012 Participedia had posted more than two hundred case studies from around the world of government-sponsored participatory efforts. Archon Fung, Ford Foundation Professor of Democracy and Citizenship at Harvard University and one of the site's developers, describes its utility this way: "Participedia builds knowledge about participatory governance and citizen engagement in a way that is totally open and itself participatory. Inspired by Wikipedia, anyone can contribute information about a case, an organization or a method. Over time, we hope to host the most complete repository of knowledge about participatory practices. The aim of this repository is to support the efforts of scholars, policy-makers, practitioners, and engaged citizens to understand and develop ever more effective democratic reforms and innovations" (Fung 2012).

WHY CAN'T WE DO THAT?

In 2005 America*Speaks*'s international brand, Global Voices, partnered with a U.K. firm, Opinion Leader Research, to organize and facilitate a national British citizens' forum for a thousand people. The topic was an issue that, as discussed earlier, has proven exceptionally difficult to navigate in the United States: health care reform. The U.K. initiative, called Your Health, Your Care, Your Say, was sponsored by the National Health Service (NHS), and was an extensive, multimodal citizen engagement and input process aimed at improving the country's national health care system. The U.K. Department of Health called it "one of the largest and most ambitious public engagement exercises ever mounted in the UK" (Warburton 2006, 3).

To develop a policy framework, Your Health, Your Care, Your Say sought guidance from the public on how health services could be better aligned with the realities of people's everyday lives. The deliberations produced a clear road map for change and a commitment from Prime Minister Tony Blair to ensure that the NHS worked with doctors to increase office hours, improved local access to treatment options, provided for additional in-home care, gave physicians greater control of the NHS's budget, and established a new emphasis on prevention, among many other commitments.

An independent evaluation commissioned by the U.K. Department of Health and conducted by Diane Warburton of the Brighton, England–based firm Shared Practice described the three objectives of Your Health, Your Care, Your Say this way: "1) for the public, providers of care, and government to work in partnership to determine policy priorities and design new approaches to future care; 2) to increase levels of public engagement in the policy decision-making process; and 3) to produce a public debate visible at local and national levels around the future of personalized and community centered care." A briefing for the evaluation suggested an additional, implicit objective: to "make some contribution to enhancing trust in Government, by reinvigorating public debate, and lead to better public service provision, by addressing the needs and concerns of service users and providers." The evaluation concluded that the initiative met all four of these objectives (Warburton 2006, 12–13).

Given that this initiative was sponsored and paid for by the British government, questions about cost and value naturally arose. To assess the strength of this concern, participants were asked, "At a time when the National Health Service's resources are in the news, and this consultation exercise obviously cost quite a lot, do you think this was money well spent, or not?" Nearly 60 percent of respondents felt it was money well spent; only 10 percent disagreed (Warburton 2006, 59).

For Americans caught in the quagmire of dysfunctional politics on this very issue of health care reform, the Britons' success story leaves a bitter aftertaste. The Obama Administration undertook major work on health care reform in 2009–2010. During this period deliberative democracy advocates and practitioners repeatedly suggested to the Administration that to arrive at policy recommendations that would withstand the toxic political environment in which the debate was taking place, authentic public engagement would be essential. But the Administration chose not to engage the public in a national discussion on the issue of health care reform. As a result, no meaningful connection was made between the public's will and political will, and from the moment it was enacted the health care law was the subject of multiple state lawsuits and continued partisan attacks. As noted earlier, in spring 2012 the constitutionality of the health care law was brought before the Supreme Court. Although it was upheld several months later, members of Congress and then-presidential candidate Mitt Romney continued to declare that they would work to overturn it.

These ongoing challenges can, in some measure, be attributed to the failure of the Obama Administration to truly engage the American people in developing health care reform policy. A two-hundred-person, California-based discussion America*Speaks* conducted about the new law after its passage (described briefly in Chapter Two) demonstrated that such an effort does, in fact, deepen and shift participants' views. Researchers found that "after receiving information on the problems and challenges facing the healthcare system that provided the impetus for the [Affordable Care Act, or] ACA, the primary goals of the ACA, and a fact sheet on how the law affects Californians (including specific cost information by income levels), participants were asked about how their views changed as a result of the information presented. For 66% of the people, their view of the law became more favorable; 19% did not change their views, and 10% of participants changed to have a more unfavorable view of the law" (Campbell, Sostrin, and Masters 2011, 9).

The Obama team's reluctance to hold discussions like these across the country reflected, in part, an unwillingness to risk the public coming to a collective view that the Administration did not support. But it was also a matter of habit. As described here, despite compelling models from around the globe, the United States has long held fast to its largely piecemeal and nongovernmental approach to citizen engagement.

Should we switch our national approach? Should government become the institution that provides our nation's primary support for citizen engagement? Should public managers, by virtue of their position in government, be the stewards of this work? The federal managers who have offered their stories for this book believe that engaging the public is not just feasible but actually vital to accomplishing their work. So, whose job is it to engage the citizenry?

The answer is that it is everyone's job. Citizens must be more proactive in claiming their seat at the table and demanding to be part of the decisions that govern their lives. Elected officials must provide leadership in order to achieve the aspirational democracy that our founding fathers so clearly articulated in the Declaration of Independence and the U.S. Constitution: we the people are capable of governing ourselves, and our collective voice is the final word. There is also a unique and special role for public servants to play at every level of government—local, state, regional, and national. Their myriad interfaces with the public create a multitude of opportunities to make the aspiration a reality.

CHAPTER TWO

AMERICA*SPEAKS* AND THE 21ST CENTURY TOWN MEETING

We came to the vast hangar at the Javits Center expecting the worst. Put 5,000 New Yorkers in a room, charge them with planning a hunk of the New York Future, and the result would be a lunatic asylum . . . None of that happened . . . From 10 a.m. to 4 p.m. they were presented with basic issues about the rebuilding of those 16 gutted acres in lower Manhattan. At each table they debated in a sober, thoughtful, civil way. They voted, offered comments, and moved on to the next item on the agenda . . . And because the process was an exercise in democracy, not demagoguery, no bellowing idiots grabbed microphones to perform for the TV cameras . . . In this room, "I" had given way to "we." It was absolutely thrilling. We have a word for what they were doing. The word is democracy.

PETE HAMILL, 2002*

Over the last thirty years, the field of deliberative democracy has evolved into a vibrant and eclectic set of practices across the United States and around the world. In 1983, Jane Mansbridge's *Beyond Adversary Democracy* marked the beginning of a deep exploration by both scholars and practitioners of the unitary model of democracy, as contrasted with the then-dominant adversarial

---

*Hamill, P. "Thrilling Show of People Power." *New York Daily News: Sports Edition Final.* Jul. 22, 2002, 8.

model. In the unitary model, the public engages in respectful deliberation, considers policy options in the context of trade-offs, and comes to a collective decision reflecting public will.[1]

Today, organizations and individuals use a wide range of citizen engagement methodologies to achieve the goals Mansfield outlined. Their practice is grounded in a series of shared principles, which include, for example: information for a deliberation must be objective and accessible; engagement should take place as early as possible in the policymaking process; the objectives of the engagement must be well defined at the outset, with clear roles and responsibilities for citizens and decision makers; and the results must be transparent and increase the public's ability to hold decision makers accountable, among others (Organisation for Economic Co-operation and Development 2012a).

In *Democracy in Motion: Evaluating the Practice and Impact of Deliberative Public Engagement,* Nabatchi, Gastil, Leighninger, and Weiksner (2012) build on these principles and identify three streams of current practice in deliberative civic engagement. The first stream of practice encompasses organizations and practitioners principally driven to take on day-to-day challenges, such as declining public resources; the second stream of practice includes those with an overriding interest in resolving conflicts, mediating disputes, and achieving cooperation among people of different views; and the third stream reflects those whose primary goal is to transform our larger democratic structures. America*Speaks* falls solidly in this third stream of practice. When I founded the organization nearly twenty years ago, it was to transform our democratic institutions so that they come closer to the founders' vision of self-governance. America*Speaks*'s 21st Century Town Meeting model of citizen engagement is a means to achieving that end.[2]

AMERICA*SPEAKS*'S 21ST CENTURY TOWN MEETING MODEL

Recognizing the power and efficacy of the traditional New England town meeting, America*Speaks*'s twenty-first-century version takes that process to scale. Through the use of technology, it enables thousands of people to deliberate simultaneously about critical issues, with their collective views strategically linked to live decision-making processes. The model revitalizes and actualizes this country's deeply held belief that naturally occurring conversations about important public issues have significant value and can lead to relevant decisions.

The 21st Century Town Meeting was purposefully developed to deepen the relationship between decision makers and the public by establishing a means for them to connect authentically with each other in a timely way on issues of immediate significance. In creating this connection, the model accommodates two conflicting realities. It acknowledges that decision makers who want to understand and act on the collective wisdom of their constituents are well served by the aggregate power of large numbers of representative citizen voices. At the same time, it recognizes that to develop collective, actionable views on an issue, citizens must be informed about it and participate in meaningful, in-depth discussions, which are most likely to thrive in small

FIGURE 2.1 A LARGE-SCALE 21ST CENTURY TOWN MEETING: NEW YORK CITY POST-9/11

groups. The 21st Century Town Meeting harnesses technology to move back and forth between small-group discussions and large-group decision making. It produces citizen deliberation that is well informed, synthesized, and directly connected to real opportunities for action.

Over nearly two decades America*Speaks* has put the 21st Century Town Meeting model into practice across this country and around the world. It has been used in nearly one hundred projects involving more than two hundred thousand people across five continents, effectively engaging diverse groups of as few as fifty citizens to as many as twelve thousand or more at the same time.[3]

The 21st Century Town Meeting has been adapted over and over again to a myriad of different needs and circumstances. It has been used to link citizens' voices and priorities to the rebuilding of lower Manhattan after 9/11; to planning for New Orleans in the wake of Hurricane Katrina; and to regional development, city budgeting, and national policymaking in critical areas. Through all of these, the methodology has proved unique in several respects. It works at the federal, regional, state, local, and international levels with "live" policy issues—that is, in cases in which critical decisions are actually pending. Further, it derives its power from the scale of engagement it can produce, the immediacy of its impact, the representativeness of participation, and its deliberate link to decision makers and governance processes. Finally, the method explicitly seeks to build public will and link it to political will to enable leaders to make tough decisions that hold.

How Does It Work?

The 21st Century Town Meeting model integrates technology and face-to-face deliberation methods to enable citizens to come together and develop an action-ready slate of recommendations about complicated public issues within one day.[4] A range of technologies and methodologies enable participants to distill and share their ideas and concerns. The back-and-forth between small- and large-group work can occur as many times as needed for participants to make collective decisions. The methodology comprises these elements:

- *Small-group dialogue.* Demographically diverse groups of ten to twelve participants come together with the support of a trained process facilitator for in-depth discussions of values, key aspects of the issue under consideration, and possible solutions. The small size of the group and the use of ground rules for participation help create a safe space, thereby enabling participants to learn from one another, react to ideas, use fact-based materials to inform their opinions, and ultimately arrive at a collective view that represents the best integration of each individual's perspective.
- *Networked computers.* Computers serve as electronic flip charts, creating instant records of the ideas generated at tables and ensuring that all voices are heard and no ideas are lost. This information is transmitted through a wireless network to a central computer and a team of analysts, setting the stage for the distillation of themes and minority reports from every table, and for the voting that will build final recommendations (see Figure 2.2).
- *"Theming."* Members of a "theme team" read electronic comments from all the tables in real time and distill them into key themes or messages. The themes are then presented back to the entire room so participants can respond to them and vote their preferences. The theme team can also highlight minority reports when appropriate.
- *Electronic keypads.* Each participant in a 21st Century Town Meeting has a wireless keypad for voting on issues and measuring his or her position with respect to the positions of other participants. Keypads also are used to establish the demographics of the participants, making it completely transparent who makes up the assembled whole. Keypad voting yields volumes of demographically sortable data that can be of great value to decision makers as well as to the media as they develop the story. For example, after the deliberation, decision makers and their staff can cross-tabulate and analyze the data to gain insight into and understanding of the differences in priorities and opinions across demographic subgroups. Equally important, keypad voting enables participants to see that their voices are being heard and that they are collectively making decisions.

- *Large video screens.* The use of large video screens for a large-scale deliberation creates the ability to develop plenary-wide understanding and agreements. The screens project data, ideas, themes, and information in real time to the entire gathering. When themes (and their corresponding levels of support in the room) are projected in this way, thousands of people can get instant feedback on how the results of their table discussions fit with what happened at other tables. Use of the large screens enables individuals to see the will of the whole as it gradually develops over the course of the day.
- *Virtual participation.* Through a wide range of linked platforms and online processes, citizens who are spread out across the country are able to participate in deliberative work before, during, and after a meeting. These platforms and processes include virtual summits, networked house parties, blogs, crowdsourcing, games, and policy simulations, among

FIGURE 2.2 PRODUCTION TEAM SUPPORTING
A 21ST CENTURY TOWN MEETING

others. Chapter Twelve explores how such online tools can support and extend citizen engagement.

What does a 21st Century Town Meeting actually look like from start to finish? The day begins with a welcome and brief opening comments from key political leaders to set the context for the issues under discussion and to establish that decision makers are listening. Participants begin by answering a series of demographic questions asking about age, gender, race, income, geography, and whatever other criteria are relevant to the issues being discussed. This is done using keypad polling, both to get oriented to the technology and to find out who is in the room. Before any deliberation takes place, a values discussion is held to help participants identify what is important to them, and to others, in regard to the issues at hand. This step is important because the values about which participants agree lay the foundation for the next four to five hours of discussion on key issues.

As described earlier, in each segment of the agenda discussions take place at individual tables; are "themed" in real time; and then presented back to the whole group for clarification and modification, and finally for voting. The last segment of time is used to evaluate participants' experiences; review next steps; and, most important, give time to decision makers to comment on what they have heard from participants and how it has influenced them.

Depending on the goals of the engagement, meeting sponsors can take intentional steps to capture contact information that can be shared and announce opportunities for continuing participation. Finally, the staff team quickly develops and reproduces a report summarizing the outcomes of the day to distribute to participants, the media, and decision makers as they leave (see sample in Figure 2.3). At the conclusion of the process, decision makers and citizens have heard the collective wisdom of a demographically representative cross-section of the public. Because decision makers have participated in the event and agreed to act on the recommendations, the collective voice that emerges from a 21st Century Town Meeting has a lasting impact.

FIGURE 2.3 A PRELIMINARY REPORT IS DISTRIBUTED TO ALL
PARTICIPANTS AT THE END OF THE DELIBERATION

Preliminary Report
July 20, 2002 • Jacob Javits Center

More than 4,000 people from New York and the tri-state area gathered on July 20 at the Jacob Javits Convention Center to play a role in rebuilding Lower Manhattan. Over the course of the daylong forum, participants in "Listening to the City" deliberated options for redeveloping the World Trade Center site and considered the critical issues that must be addressed to help people rebuild their lives in the aftermath of September 11 and memorialize those who were lost.

The public conversation was attended by many of the decision-makers and leaders who will ultimately decide the future of Lower Manhattan, including officials from the Lower Manhattan Development Corporation, the Port Authority of New York and New Jersey, the State of New York, and the New York City Mayor's Office and City Council. The results of the forum will be presented to these decision-makers to guide their work.

"Listening to the City" is a project of the Civic Alliance to Rebuild Downtown New York, a broad-based coalition of nearly 100 groups committed to devising strategies for the redevelopment of Lower Manhattan. The Civic Alliance was convened by the Regional Plan Association, in conjunction with New York University, New School University and the Pratt Institute. This 21st Century Town Meeting™ was designed and facilitated by America Speaks™.

The Civic Alliance sought to represent the rich diversity of the metropolitan region at "Listening to the City." This goal was achieved more closely in some areas than in others. For example, 53% of the participants were female and 47% were male, while the region is 52% female and 47% male. In addition, 27% of the participants were 20 to 34 years old, compared to 22% for the region. People 65 and older made up 10% of the forum, close to the regional figure of 12%. On the other hand, while 20% of the region is African-American, the room was only 7% African-American. Similarly, participation was higher among people in the top income brackets and among those who live in Manhattan. The Civic Alliance will continue to try to ensure that all voices are proportionally represented at future activities.

Forum participants related to the events of 9/11 and the rebuilding of Lower Manhattan in a variety of capacities:

8.9% had a family member who was a 9/11 victim
19.7% are survivors of the events of 9/11
23.6% lived in Lower Manhattan
41.4% worked in Lower Manhattan
33.5% were at or near Ground Zero on 9/11
21.5% became displaced/unemployed as a result of 9/11
6.2% were rescue or recovery workers
71.1% attended primarily as interested citizens

Demographics

Participants in the forum came from all walks of life and represented the rich geographic, racial and income diversity of the metropolitan region. These figures are compared below to the official demographics of the region.

Gender	July 20	Region
Female	53%	52%
Male	47%	48%
Age		
19 and under	4%	27%
20-34	27%	22%
35-54	45%	30%
55-64	14%	9%
65 and older	10%	12%
Household Income		
Less than $25,000	17%	26%
$25,000–49,999	21%	25%
$50,000–74,999	20%	18%
$75,000–99,999	14%	12%
$100,000–149,999	15%	11%
$150,000–199,999	13%	8%

Race	July 20	Region
African-American	7%	20%
Asian/Pacific Islander	13%	9%
Caucasian	66%	64%
Native American	0%	<1%
Mixed Race	5%	2%
Other Race	9%	n/a
Ethnicity		
Hispanic	10%	20%
Non-Hispanic	90%	80%
Geography		
Manhattan	46%	
Brooklyn	18%	
Bronx	3%	47%
Queens	10%	
Staten Island	1%	
Elsewhere in NYS	6%	23%
New Jersey	10%	30%
Elsewhere	6%	

WHEN DOES IT WORK BEST?

Although the potential applications for a 21st Century Town Meeting are numerous, America*Speaks*'s experience demonstrates that there are three types of public work (whether local, regional, national, or international in scope) that derive the greatest benefit from application of this methodology.[5] They are policy formulation, resource allocation, and planning.

POLICY FORMULATION

The 21st Century Town Meeting is particularly appropriate when critical public policy decisions are pending: when the issue is strongly and publicly contested, when a cross-section of the American public has a real stake in it, when polling data indicate that there is high public demand for a solution, or a combination of these factors. A 21st Century Town Meeting is ideal for working through contentious issues because the model creates a level playing field for all participants and follows a design that intentionally builds common ground by using values-based questions and then moving to tough trade-offs to arrive at concrete decisions. Such difficult issues as health care reform, whether or not to undertake unilateral military action, or immigration policy, for example, would be well served in this format. The first application of the method in a policy context was on the vexing issue of Social Security.

In 1998–1999 The Pew Charitable Trusts' Americans Discuss Social Security (ADSS) initiative used a combination of single- and multi-site 21st Century Town Meetings, smaller-scale local forums, and teleconferencing to bring almost fifty thousand citizens nearly fifty states into direct conversation with policymakers in Washington, DC, about addressing problems facing the Social Security system.

By the end of the project, ADSS demonstrated that Americans agreed on two top reform options: raising the cap on the level of earnings subject to payroll taxes and reducing benefits for people with higher retirement incomes. Notably,

FIGURE 2.4 DELIBERATION LOCATIONS IN THE AMERICANS DISCUSS
SOCIAL SECURITY INITIATIVE

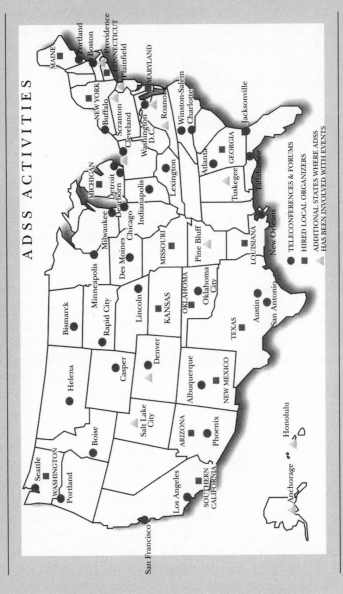

Source: AmericaSpeaks, 1998.

the deliberative experience had an impact on another option being considered at that time: permitting workers to direct a share of their Social Security contributions toward private investments. Although such private retirement investment accounts had received relatively strong support in surveys, when citizens came together in live forums and teleconferences to discuss the issue, their responses to this option turned out to be only mildly supportive to negative.

Ken Apfel, who was Commissioner of the U.S. Social Security Administration from 1997 to 2001, reflected on the work in this way:

> The Americans Discuss Social Security initiative was important because America faces a series of critical choices that will shape our social fabric in the 21st Century, and the voices of the people must be part of making these choices. One of the biggest relates to Social Security for future generations: given demographic changes underway, how do we define our individual and our societal responsibilities for economic security? While politicians will be the ones to develop changes in the laws affecting the Social Security system, it is the American people who need to help define the future path. Americans Discuss Social Security helped Americans understand the dimensions of the challenge and discuss their vision for economic security. We need more engagement like this [Apfel 2012].

RESOURCE ALLOCATION

Another context in which the 21st Century Town Meeting can be particularly useful emerges when elected officials must make tough decisions in establishing budget priorities. Public budgets have an enormous impact on our daily lives. They affect the quality of our schools, our roads, and our public services, among many other things. Further, because needs always outpace available resources, budget decision making tends to produce distinct winners and losers: Should we invest our limited resources in universal kindergarten, or do we put more police officers on the streets instead? Unfortunately, a win-lose environment is easily exploited by stakeholder and special interest groups that have the resources to exert influence over decision making.

The 21st Century Town Meeting model directly addresses this concern by creating a deliberative environment in which no organized groups can overinfluence the process. Everyone who comes participates in the same agenda, and all voices are equal. As a result, although the model works well when determining how to allocate surplus resources, it is even more effective when government has lost revenues and programs will have to be cut. Applying an equitable and highly transparent process to budget decision making increases the likelihood that resource allocation will reflect the common good rather than the priorities of the loudest voices or most organized special interests. It also creates a natural constituency for the budget as it moves through the political process.

Beginning in November 1999 America*Speaks* worked with the Washington, DC mayor's office to hold a series of 21st Century Town Meetings that would help set the city's strategic priorities for determining the allocation of local tax dollars. The largest of these meetings drew more than three thousand participants, and in 2000, The City Is Mine: Youth Summit brought together 1,400 young people ages fourteen to twenty-one. In the end, citizen input led to redirected spending priorities in a number of areas. Among others $70+ million was added to the education budget; $10 million in new funding was allocated to improving senior services; one thousand new slots for drug treatment were financed; new neighborhood-based supermarkets were approved; and funds were allocated to support continued neighborhood-based planning and citizen participation in governance.

PLANNING

City, state, and regional planning efforts are complex enterprises involving the weighing and prioritizing of a range of substantive issues—from economic development to the environment, from housing to education—while balancing trade-offs between short-term and long-term investments. The 21st Century Town Meeting model can support a large group of people working through the maze of issues in a planning process. The model's carefully developed participant guides and dialogue questions, combined with theme identification and instant voting technology, enable participants to rank order choices against a set of agreed-on criteria and values.

In January 2002 in Hamilton County, Ohio, America*Speaks* facilitated a 21st Century Town Meeting that enabled more than one thousand citizens to comment on elements of a comprehensive regional development plan (the first in thirty-five years), ratify a regional vision, set priorities, and offer strategies for action. Citizens gave specific suggestions for taking action in four priority areas: ensuring economic prosperity, building collaborative decision making, embracing diversity and equity, and balancing development and environmental protection. Elected officials from fifty-seven jurisdictions throughout the county unanimously approved the recommendations proposed by the public. Action teams were established to turn the citizens' suggestions into specific action steps.

Ron Miller, who was Executive Director of the Hamilton County Regional Planning Commission in 2002, shared these thoughts about the work: "I'm now retired from the Commission and have been teaching at the University of Cincinnati School of Planning for a couple of years. It's been a frequent occurrence during the past ten years that my 'civically-obsessed' colleagues come up to me and say 'I just want to tell you that the Community COMPASS meeting was the best public meeting I ever attended!' And others still ask, 'what do you have to do to make something like that happen?' and 'what do we have to do to get that many people to come to a meeting?'" (Miller 2012).

ADDITIONAL APPLICATIONS

In addition to policy formulation, resource allocation, and planning, a recent application of the 21st Century Town Meeting may be of particular interest to public managers. In early 2011 America*Speaks* (under the project name California*Speaks* 2) conducted seven community dialogue sessions across California, involving over 220 people, to assess the public's response to the core elements of the new national health care reform law. Each four-hour session included content presentations followed by facilitated dialogue and individual keypad polling. Participants were able to listen to presentations, review written and audiovisual materials, discuss focused topics in small groups, ask questions of experts, and share their opinions at key moments. The discussions not only explored the public's views but also identified what they could learn from different educational materials and discovered which parts of the law people wanted to know more about. The methodology could be similarly used to gather the public's views and input on an agency's implementation of new policies and practices.

Another instance in which the 21st Century Town Meeting methodology can be particularly effective is when decision making on a local issue can directly inform national policies, or, conversely, when local decision making calls for policymaking at the national level. For example, a number of local communities around the country that serve as gateways to national parks face similar concerns related to sprawl, congestion, and cost and revenue sharing and could benefit from coordinated policy development at the federal level. A 21st Century Town Meeting, using webcasts and other technologies, could efficiently facilitate simultaneous, multisite information sharing and deliberation on such a topic, improving the quality of local discussion and also quickly bringing key issues to national attention, potentially securing helpful action from federal decision makers.

AN IMPORTANT NOTE ABOUT SCALE

Many of the case studies and stories in this book are of citizen engagement on a truly large scale—they involve thousands of people at a time, include multiple jurisdictions, and seek to address highly complex public issues. For example: Listening to the City (in 2002) convened 4,500 people on rebuilding plans for lower Manhattan after 9/11; the New Orleans Community Congresses (in 2005) convened 4,000 people across twenty-one cities on developing a recovery plan in the aftermath of Hurricane Katrina; California*Speaks* (in 2007) convened 3,500 people on health care reform in California; and Our Budget, Our Economy (in 2010) convened 3,500 people on the nation's debt and deficit crisis.

America*Speaks*'s citizen engagement model was conceptualized as a vehicle for achieving national impact and was explicitly designed for work at this scale. The hope is that these large-scale examples will be inspiring and not intimidating to readers. This book does not assume that public managers will aspire to take on the large-scale, complex work that is at the heart of America*Speaks*'s practice. Rather, the goal of the book is to make transparent the underlying strategies and practices that have proven successful, and that can be applied *any time* a public manager wants to bring the voices of citizens into governance and decision making, at whatever scale and level of complexity are appropriate.

It is also important to note here that over the nearly twenty years of putting this method into practice, myriad uses for it on a small scale have been discovered. For example, the full methodology has often been used with as few as one hundred people, and the underlying individual components and strategies have regularly been applied to groups much smaller than that. The technology and infrastructure needs are less complicated on a smaller scale, but the dynamic processes operate in the same way regardless of size.

RESULTS

The 21st Century Town Meeting has shown that if you gather a group of demographically representative citizens in a safe, well-designed environment and give them a challenging policy issue to discuss, as well as the facts that go along with it, they will share their experiences and perspectives, increase their knowledge of the issue, think critically about trade-offs, and build workable solutions that can be directly linked to government decision making. It has also shown that what motivates the vast majority of people to participate is the nature of the opportunity and the sense of agency they experience. Finally, it has demonstrated that even reluctant decision makers can be effectively brought into these processes.

More specifically, independent evaluations of the work of America*Speaks* have found that it consistently produces results in three areas: (1) individuals across the political spectrum learn, change their opinions, and take action; (2) decision-making practices and cultures within institutions shift to make room for the views of citizens; and (3) in policymaking, the work breaks political impasses, shifts public funding, and changes the direction of municipal plans and public policy agendas. A few examples:

- In the aftermath of the 9/11 terrorist attacks in New York City, nearly six thousand people came together face-to-face and online to assess the conceptual plans for the redevelopment of the World Trade Center site. After consideration, the public rejected the original plans and identified the key elements of a framework for future plans.
- One thousand citizens of Mecklenburg County (Charlotte), North Carolina, crafted a priority agenda for the community's children that eventually led to a unified budgeting process.
- More than ten thousand people in the United States and abroad have participated in deliberations that shaped the development of health policy.
- Tens of thousands of Northeast Ohioans determined together how to make progress on the economic challenges facing their region.

Most recently, more than 3,500 ideologically and demographically diverse citizens came together across fifty-seven sites to wrestle with the extremely tough choices involved in resolving the country's long-term fiscal challenges. Something interesting happened at the deliberation sites for the Our Budget, Our Economy initiative: unlike what we witness almost nightly on the news, no fights broke out, there were no disruptive arguments, and people didn't scream at each other. Rather, members of local Tea Party groups sat together with activists from MoveOn.org and had civil conversations. The large majority of participants reported that they learned something and were influenced by what they heard from others. In the end, nearly 60 percent of the table groups achieved reducing the deficit by $1.1 trillion, or reached the target of a $1.2 trillion reduction by 2025; more than 75 percent were able to reduce the deficit by $800 billion or more. Alice Rivlin, founding Director of the Congressional Budget Office, former Director of the Office of Management and Budget, cochair of the Bipartisan Policy Center Debt Reduction Task Force, and member of President Obama's Fiscal Commission, said of the work, "All of you have restored my confidence in the ability of citizens to talk civilly about very hard issues. All of us need to challenge the politicians to do as well as we have done today" (America*Speaks* Aug. 2011).

The details behind this accomplishment are quite compelling: 85 percent of participants agreed to reduce defense spending by at least 5 percent; 68 percent agreed to at least a 5 percent reduction in spending on all nondefense programs; 62 percent of participants expressed support for at least a 5 percent reduction in health care spending; and 60 percent, across every age group, agreed to raising the cap on payroll taxes to 90 percent of earnings, among other results.

These percentages stand in stark contrast to how the media, and politicians of all stripes, have portrayed the public's views on these issues. They say Americans are divided beyond any hope of consensus. And yet this work clearly demonstrates that agreement on very difficult issues *is* achievable when citizens are given factual information and an opportunity to deliberate with each other in a safe and supportive environment.

Beyond the policy consensus they achieved, participants' assessments of the engagement process in Our Budget, Our Economy speak volumes. A participant from Portland, Oregon, described her experience this way: "The most important thing I learned from this process is that ordinary citizens could tackle a complex issue, filter it civilly through their own perspective, and come up with consensus. I literally did not think this was possible" (America*Speaks* 2011). A participant from Richmond, Virginia, concluded, "Regardless of our political perspectives, there is deep concern regarding the deficit, the ways in which our overspending will handicap the next generation and the fiscal stability of our way of life. Everyone at the table was willing to sacrifice to set things right. It was inspiring" (America*Speaks* 2011).

Because there was no existing legislation for the participants of Our Budget, Our Economy to respond to, from the beginning of this initiative the goal was to inform and influence the work of the president's National Commission on Fiscal Responsibility and Reform as well as the Senate and House Budget Committees. A week after the discussion, I testified at a public hearing of the commission and presented citizens' priorities to the budget committees. In addition, over the next few weeks, we briefed fifty-eight congressional offices and three caucuses (the New Democrat Coalition, the Blue Dog Democrats, and the Populist Caucus).

In November 2010, when Commission Cochairs Erskine Bowles and Alan Simpson released their recommendations, the work was met with surprise in that it openly tackled a number of "third rail" issues, such as cutting defense spending and undertaking tax reform. In formulating their recommendations, Bowles and Simpson used data from Our Budget, Our Economy that showed that there was more support for these issues among the public than in Congress. Our Budget, Our Economy provided the cochairs with a very valuable window into the current thinking of the American public on these issues. Simpson said: "Our Budget, Our Economy demonstrated that in this time of hyperpartisanship, while Congress puts politics above problem solving, the American people get it right" (Simpson 2012). Chapter Ten provides a closer look at how the Our Budget, Our Economy initiative discovered shared priorities among participants.

The next chapter offers a full story of what citizen engagement work can look like on the ground. It demonstrates a comprehensive application of the underlying strategies that public managers and others can tailor to their own purposes. Most important, it reveals the power that can be harnessed and the real results that can be achieved by bringing the voices of citizens into governance on a live issue of critical importance. The story of large-scale citizen engagement in New Orleans following Hurricane Katrina and the flooding is a moving and inspirational example of what citizens can accomplish together.

CHAPTER THREE

UNDERSTANDING THE POWER OF CITIZEN ENGAGEMENT

A Story of Post-Katrina New Orleans

We want our city. And we don't want it to come back like no Disneyland for adults. It was getting that way anyway. We don't want that. Just give us a chance to collect ourselves.

WYNTON MARSALIS*

We all got the same wake-up call. It was late summer 2005, and Hurricane Katrina and the devastating floods hitting New Orleans were all over the news. We watched, somewhat inured at first to the images of disaster victims making their way through rubble-strewn streets, carrying with them their children, their food, and the remnants of their lives. We've grown accustomed to pictures of natural disasters from faraway places.

But this time it was different. This time it was us. In horror, we realized that it was our fellow citizens, stranded and abandoned on their rooftops, who were calling out for help that was not coming. We can never forget the image of them, or their cry: "How can this be happening? We're Americans!" Glued to our

---

*Rutledge, D. (ed.). *Do You Know What It Means to Miss New Orleans? A Collection of Stories and Essays Set in the Big Easy.* Seattle: Chin Music Press, 2006.

television sets, and asking ourselves the same question, we watched our government fail before our eyes.

The deep destruction and tragedy in New Orleans after Hurricane Katrina and the subsequent flooding has been seared into our national consciousness. What is not widely known is that eighteen months later, and still in the midst of extreme chaos, four thousand New Orleanians came together in partnership with leaders and decision makers to establish a viable plan for rebuilding their city. It was a demonstration of authentic democratic practice that is rarely seen in this country—and one made all the more compelling by the extraordinarily challenging circumstances under which it happened. This chapter tells that story.[1] The work undertaken in New Orleans exemplifies all of the seven strategies for bringing citizen voice into governance laid out in Chapters Five through Eleven of this book.

GOVERNANCE GONE BAD

Many have argued that the failure of government in the face of Hurricane Katrina and the subsequent flooding was largely due to the fact that in the lead-up, in the moment of disaster, and in the following weeks and months, the wrong decisions were made at the wrong times. But what happened in New Orleans was worse than that. What Hurricane Katrina and the flooding brought into sharp relief was, in fact, a simmering crisis of democracy in that city and, by extension, in our nation.

For decades before Hurricane Katrina struck, New Orleans had been a place where citizen voice and public good were not respected. The systems to meet people's needs were largely inadequate or ignored. New Orleans writer and reporter Jason Berry described it this way: "You could not live in the city and avoid the dreary performance of democracy" (Berry 2006, 55). To cite just a few examples: requests for federal attention to the city's levees were repeatedly rejected by Congress; the city's public education system, among the worst in the nation, had long been left to fail; corruption in the public sphere—and years of citizen disenfranchisement—were accepted as simply characteristic of the city instead of recognized as a call to action.

Tragically, significant race and class inequities were ubiquitous. To give just two examples: in 2005 the difference in median household income between whites and blacks in New Orleans was 20 percent greater than the difference nationwide. The same year, the difference in New Orleans between the educational attainment levels of whites and blacks was nearly double the difference nationally (U.S. Census Bureau 2012).

Given this history, it is probably not surprising that in the months following Hurricane Katrina and the flooding, the Bush Administration said it would not release congressionally appropriated recovery and rebuilding funds to the city because of unclear and competing messages from the various jurisdictions in New Orleans and the state, including the City Council, the mayor, the Louisiana Recovery Authority, the state legislature, and the governor. "That's New Orleans for you," our national leaders said.

As a result, more than a year after Hurricane Katrina, federal dollars appropriated by Congress to help New Orleans remained largely in Washington, DC. With recovery activity proceeding painfully slowly, more than half of the city's population had still not returned. Those who remained fought to survive amid a decimated infrastructure. More than 70 percent of housing had been damaged, with entire neighborhoods virtually destroyed. Schools, hospitals, and police stations that had been shut down were struggling to reopen, and almost one hundred thousand jobs had been lost. Outdated water and sewer systems had been ravaged. The electrical grid was severely damaged. More than half the transit authority's buses and routes were destroyed, and two-thirds of its workforce had left (Rigamer 2006; New Orleans Community Support Foundation 2006). All of this destruction severely crippled movement around the city and inhibited efforts to recover.

Although the damage, destruction, and loss in every sector were unprecedented, the persistent failure of response, in the moment and in the ensuing months, was more than just an inability to surmount an unimaginably complex set of challenges. It was a profound and ongoing demonstration of what happens to people when governing systems go bad. And yet, eighteen months later, New Orleanians proved that by reengaging in these very governance processes—and by creating new ones—they could turn things around.

The successful recovery planning process that ultimately engaged thousands of New Orleanians was born out of a series of early missteps that were, in hindsight, largely predictable.

In their haste to get things going, New Orleans leaders seemed to ignore two important dynamics. First, citizens' already-low levels of trust in government had been lowered further by the failure of government at all levels to act quickly and effectively after the hurricane and flooding, and there were blatant disparities along racial and income lines in how New Orleanians fared. Second, the central issues in rebuilding were extremely charged, with many citizens feeling threatened by proposals to restrict rebuilding and turn whole neighborhoods into green space. The idea that displaced residents might not be able to return to their homes quickly became a seemingly insurmountable divide between black and white, rich and poor.

Turning a deaf ear to these issues, officials proceeded with a "business as usual" approach that bypassed the notion of broad public participation, ignored citizens' deep suspicions about government, and plunged into the rebuilding questions without attending to these divides and the need for sensitivity. One month after the hurricane, the Bring New Orleans Back (BNOB) initiative, sponsored by New Orleans mayor Ray Nagin and local developer Joseph Canizaro, convened an elite, mostly white commission to oversee a team of external planning experts. Without public consultation, the planners proposed not rebuilding many neighborhoods. When the BNOB plan was published in the *Times-Picayune,* thousands of people saw block after block of green space where their homes used to be. Needless to say, the plan faced enormous public opposition and wasn't viable. Next the City Council sponsored the Lambert Plan, named after the planning firm that produced it. Although praised for its neighborhood-level participation process, the plan did not include a comprehensive strategy for addressing the larger citywide recovery issues, and so it too failed.

In the wake of these planning debacles, the parameters of what it would take to launch and sustain effective planning efforts in New Orleans became clearer. Success would mean producing a coherent, collective view about both citywide and local neighborhood priorities in a very short time. To make the effort credible to both citizens and decision makers, representative participation of those still living in the city as well as residents in the diaspora around the country would have to be secured.[2] All of this would have to happen in a local culture unaccustomed to strong public participation and extremely skeptical of and fatigued by planning efforts. The long-standing and bitter legacy of racial mistrust and socioeconomic inequity that was laid bare for the world to see by Hurricane Katrina and its aftermath further complicated the task. Fully understanding and taking into account this complex context would be pivotal to effective planning.[3]

SEEKING A UNIFIED PLAN FOR NEW ORLEANS

In spring 2006 David Voelker, a prominent New Orleans businessman and trusted confidant of President George W. Bush, got things moving. Understanding the volatility and dysfunction of the situation as well as the necessity of having local and state leadership "on the same page," Voelker called a meeting of top leaders from all sectors. Fully aware of the consequences if they could not come to agreement, Voelker had already scheduled a press conference after the meeting, without knowing what the outcome of the meeting would be. This high-stakes gamble paid off. Officials came out of the meeting with a united purpose and got to work, and that summer, following months of intensive negotiations, the mayor, the City Council, the city planning commission, and the governor's appointed Louisiana Recovery Authority endorsed a new recovery planning process for New Orleans. The foundation-funded Unified New Orleans Plan (UNOP, also referred to in this chapter as "the Unified Plan" or "the Plan") would be run by the Greater New Orleans Foundation and overseen by the Community Support Organization (CSO), a newly created governance structure comprising citizen representatives from each of the five City Council districts, along with agency liaisons from the mayor's office, the City Council, the city planning commission, and the Rockefeller Foundation.

Without the risk-taking and leadership shown by Voelker, it might have been impossible to break through the entrenched positions of the various political players and gain the commitment of the Bush Administration to release funds in response to a comprehensive plan. When it comes to highly conflictual, intractable problems, it is almost always essential to find the leaders in a community who have the credibility to bring everyone to the table.

The Unified Plan process was to operate simultaneously at the neighborhood-, district-, and citywide levels. All together, eleven planning firms would work with thirteen planning districts to hold four rounds of meetings aimed at establishing recovery priorities for each of the city's seventy-three neighborhoods. Three citywide citizen meetings (to be called Community Congresses) would determine action steps on the overarching issues of flood protection, housing, schools, hospitals, public safety, utilities, and infrastructure. The final product would be an amalgam of the emerging recommendations, and would also incorporate the results of all previous planning efforts.

The urgent need to revive the city left a remarkably short time frame to accomplish all of this work: the citywide and thirteen district plans were to be completed—with full community participation—in under five months.

Despite the Community Support Organization's good intentions and reasoned approach to the task, the first effort, Community Congress I (CCI) held on October 28, 2006, actually repeated the mistakes of the past. There was limited outreach, and only about three hundred people attended. Worse than the small showing, the meeting did not *look* anything like pre-Katrina New Orleans. The low-income African American communities that had been so disproportionately destroyed by the storm were severely underrepresented, and affluent white people were far and away the largest group of participants. More than two-thirds of the pre-Katrina population were African American, whereas only 17 percent of CCI participants were African American. Only 25 percent of the pre-Katrina population had an annual household income greater than $75,000, compared to 41 percent of CCI participants. The headline in the *Times-Picayune* the day after CCI read: "Survey backs plan for smaller footprint, but demographics of voters questioned" (Krupa 2006, 1).

Every Voice Must Be in the Room

Learning from the failures in recovery planning up to that point, the Greater New Orleans Foundation recognized that to achieve credible and actionable results, large numbers of citizens, representative of the pre-Katrina population, would have to be involved.[4] The foundation invited America*Speaks* to work with planners to engage the New Orleans community and to use its 21st Century Town Meeting methodology to expand and deepen citizen participation in the process. A central problem would be how to find and authentically engage those New Orleanians who had been evacuated during and after the storm. Citizens and leaders alike had voiced a strong desire to include those who were in diaspora across the country. It was not only a plea for equity and justice but also an expression of people's need for healing, reconciliation, and hope as they faced a long and difficult road ahead.

In preparation for the next two Community Congresses, to be held in early December 2006 and late January 2007, America*Speaks* worked in close partnership with more than fifty organizations in New Orleans, Baton Rouge, Houston, Dallas, and Atlanta to conduct an outreach campaign aimed at finding and registering thousands of citizens to participate in those cities. In addition to simply generating large numbers, outreach efforts needed to capture demographics that matched the racial, ethnic, socioeconomic, and geographic makeup of pre-Katrina New Orleans.

Establishing partnerships with myriad neighborhood associations, professional groups, and social services agencies already well known and trusted in the various local communities was a critical first step. America*Speaks* also hired organizers to do outreach in neighborhoods whose existing organizational infrastructure was less robust.

Le'Kedra Robertson, Deputy Outreach Director for the Community Congresses, summed it up this way:

> The best gift any community can give is its trust. This kind of work is somewhat risky—if a project sours then the people helping with outreach can be burned in terms of their credibility.

In developing a successful post-Katrina outreach team, the messenger was as important as the message. We partnered with individuals and organizations well known and respected in their neighborhoods—people who neighbors felt comfortable with and who had tentacles into the local and diaspora grass-roots communities, in apartment complexes, survivor councils, churches and social networks.

The folks who stepped-up and put their trust in the process, and their credibility on the line, were a resilient group— passionate about re-connecting families and holding the government accountable [Robertson 2010].

So many individuals in the New Orleans community played vital roles. Glenda Harris, a former case manager and regional field coordinator for the Children's Defense Fund as well as a dedicated community advocate, had relocated to Texas after the storm, where she eventually became part of the Houston Community Congress outreach team. Harris was adamant about bringing families home to New Orleans and was an active participant in the Houston Survivor's Council. During her two years there, she built relationships with local churches and other community groups, and then used these resources to make sure her fellow displaced New Orleanians had the information and support they would need to rebuild their lives. In addition to using her professional connections, Harris tirelessly did whatever it took to find families who had evacuated from New Orleans. She went door-to-door, made an untold number of phone calls, and attended many, many events. Harris's personal efforts helped as many as two hundred dispersed New Orleanians connect to the critical planning work back home.[5]

In addition to individual efforts like this, a range of creative outreach strategies were used. In New Orleans's Treme neighborhood, organizers for the Episcopal Diocese held a traditional "second line" parade.[6] People walked through the streets, playing music and inviting others to join in behind the band leading the parade. Organizers marched along, distributing information and registering people as they went.

A young professionals group in New Orleans used its monthly "First Fridays" social gathering to recruit and register people. Members of this group were also able to pull in their aunts, their uncles, their grandparents, and others they knew who were not connected to the Internet or hooked into citywide activities. Through their efforts, the young professionals were responsible for bringing as many as one hundred people from a demographic that is especially tough to recruit to Community Congress II (CCII).

In Houston, Mayor Bill White had quickly opened Houston's school system to children arriving from New Orleans and made sure people had health care access and other critical resources. Parties were held for New Orleanians featuring food from back home and the New Orleans Saints on television, which drew big crowds and resulted in significant numbers of registrations. In Atlanta, the widespread geography and infrastructure of the city (the Atlanta metropolitan area has twenty counties and dozens of municipalities and organizations) had absorbed Hurricane Katrina evacuees, making it somewhat difficult to find them. However, a spirited young organizer named Anthony Payton helped jump-start the necessary networking process through a massive tailgate party organized around a Saints-Falcons football game. Free food and large-screen televisions drew about one hundred people. Participants not only had a good time but also became part of a critical healing and community-building network for New Orleanians living in Atlanta. People connected with neighbors, acquaintances, and even distant family members they had not known were in the same city. There were emotional reunions between people who had presumed each other dead.

Outreach staff used the event to provide information about what was going on back home with the recovery process, to register people for the next Community Congress, and to encourage them to take the information back to the networks of people they knew. Because many stayed involved, the event became a turning point in building momentum for participation. When outreach work got under way for Community Congress III (CCIII), the same group was able to help generate enthusiasm and registrations.

An obvious avenue for outreach in New Orleans itself was the public airwaves. Because authority figures at every level had lost credibility and let the citizens of the city down so many times, there was virtually no trust in information coming from public officials. This made it particularly urgent that highly reliable people be the ones to inform citizens about the Community Congresses and encourage them to participate. Respected New Orleans television news anchorman Norm Robinson was one of few people who could fill this role. Amid the chaos, his was a familiar voice people knew they could trust. Public service announcements by home-grown celebrities like Wynton Marsalis also helped build confidence and generate momentum. As outreach moved forward in New Orleans and across all of the diaspora cities, regular review of registrant demographics allowed outreach teams to shift their focus when the numbers for any population group were lagging. The promise of transportation to and from the Community Congresses; free meals; child care; and translation into sign language, Spanish, and Vietnamese enabled many who might otherwise have been left out to sign up and participate.

While participant registration was under way, so was recruitment for the hundreds of volunteer facilitators who would be needed to lead table discussions in New Orleans, Houston, Atlanta, Dallas, and Baton Rouge. In addition, facilitators would be needed in sixteen other cities across the country in which large numbers of New Orleanians were still in the diaspora. To accomplish this, America*Speaks* drew on its extensive national network of volunteer facilitators and interested organizations. People wanted to serve; more than five hundred facilitators signed up. Many of these people traveled at their own expense from around the United States, and from as far away as Canada and the United Kingdom, to volunteer their time and skills. Tulane University offered service learning credits for students who participated in the process, and about one hundred Tulane students became part of the Community Congress facilitation team.

Ameria*Speaks*'s leadership, working closely with local partners, did significant work for months to ensure that elected officials and other decision makers from every system and sector were committed to supporting the process. Not only was their participation critical to the credibility of the event but also it gave them co-ownership, along with citizens, of the outcomes. The mayor, the City Council, and the Community Support Organization provided contacts, lists, and other support to recruit participants.

CSO members traveled to diaspora cities to address outreach teams and community partners and help them understand how important it was to engage those who had been displaced. All of these officials were kept informed of citizens' feedback on the planning process so they could respond publicly to concerns and criticisms and follow up on the emerging recommendations.[7]

CITIZENS OF NEW ORLEANS ROLL UP THEIR SLEEVES

Community Congresses II and III brought together nearly 4,000 New Orleanians to deliberate with their fellow citizens about the future of their city and to make collective decisions about rebuilding priorities. These priorities would be reflected in the Unified New Orleans Plan, which, once approved, would drive how state and local governments used federal recovery funds. More than 2,500 people participated in Community Congress II, and 1,300 participated in Community Congress III.

At Community Congress II, New Orleanians—whether they had returned to the city or were still in diaspora—were asked to give input on specific planning issues, such as what steps to take to reduce the risk of future flooding, how to increase the availability of affordable housing, and how to allocate funds to rebuild the city's broken infrastructure. They had to make trade-offs, set priorities, review preestablished options, and create new ones of their own.

To make these tough decisions about allocating scarce resources in the face of staggering need, participants had to engage in difficult and honest conversations. They had to think together about the city as a whole. They had to quickly forge connections with each other and establish bonds of trust across their differences. The daylong deliberation began with a discussion aimed at helping to build that trust and connect people to their deepest feelings. The questions we posed were quite simple: "What do you love most about New Orleans?" and "What do you miss most about New Orleans?" Despite the simplicity of the questions, the transformation in rooms across the country, after people sat down together and shared what they loved and missed, was palpable. The atmosphere went from one of scattered energy, exhaustion, and anger to one marked by focus, keen interest, and a desire to get to the heart of the matter. People at every table had the opportunity to share what they believed to be the most important elements to preserve and to change as New Orleans was rebuilt.

With these ideas providing a solid foundation, the rest of the day focused on setting specific priorities, identifying and evaluating action steps in each priority area, and determining how to ensure resources would be available to move ideas into action. From among the thousands of ideas generated at Community Congress II, four strong priorities emerged: ensure safety from future flooding, by far the highest priority; rebuild safe and stable neighborhoods; provide affordable housing; and improve public services. The recommended action steps in these areas ranged from establishing different flood safety standards for different parts of the city, to providing incentives for public servants to return to New Orleans, to making schools 24/7 community centers, to finding alternate uses for blighted properties.

FIGURE 3.1 CITIZENS ESTABLISH THEIR PRIORITIES AT
COMMUNITY CONGRESS II

Following the work of CCII, city planners spent the next six weeks reviewing and integrating the public's recommendations into a final draft of the Unified New Orleans Plan. Given the public distrust and dissatisfaction that had characterized previous planning processes, it was essential that the final draft then be taken back to the public for an additional review. This was the purpose of Community Congress III: to give the people of New Orleans a last opportunity to provide input on the strategic recovery framework, rebuilding priorities, specific implementation activities, and financing strategy. The 1,300 New Orleanians who participated in CCIII assessed the revised plans to make sure citizens' priorities from CCII had been respected and incorporated. In the end, 91 percent of CCIII participants "agreed" or "strongly agreed" that the Unified Plan should go forward. This was a resounding statement of support for, and ownership of, the plan. The plan then proceeded through a multitiered approval process that began with the Community Support Organization and New Orleans Community Support Foundation; included the city planning commission, the City Council, and the mayor's office; and ended with the Louisiana Recovery Authority. It was approved at each step of the process.

In addition to establishing their rebuilding priorities, participants in CCIII were asked to review and identify options for ensuring meaningful ongoing citizen involvement. In a city in which over many decades people had had virtually no opportunities for participation, it is not surprising that one-third of those who took part in the Community Congresses advocated for quarterly citizen meetings and an annual Community Congress.

RECOGNIZING THE NEED FOR COMMUNITY HEALING

In the United States we place great value on our ability to move forward, take action, and not bog down in the past. As a result, we often fail to fully embrace experiences and rituals that enable community mourning and support closure. This can create problems in the aftermath of a significant trauma. Given the magnitude of the tragedy in New Orleans, there was an extraordinary need for grieving and healing. A series of large meetings that simply asked citizens to look at planning documents and make decisions would not have sufficed. The Community Congresses had to acknowledge and attend to these needs. They had to establish an emotional tone that would make it safe for participants to express whatever feelings arose as they worked through the day's agenda. This goal was consciously embedded into the design of Community Congress II.

Skilled facilitators created a climate of emotional safety at each table, helping people appropriately express their internal state of being, their needs, and their ideas for recovery. Grief counselors were present and constituency services tables staffed by city and state agency representatives helped participants with immediate needs, such as securing temporary housing, having enough food, finding an open school for their children, and so on. With these concerns sufficiently addressed for the moment, people could more fully participate in the meeting.

The Community Congresses did not, of course, bring closure to anyone's grief. However, they did allow a publicly shared and authentic honoring of those who had died, and they enabled everyone in the room to carry some of the emotions so that all could then join in the planning work that followed. Understanding the importance of healing as a basis for moving forward was essential for people to work productively and collectively. As one participant in Community Congress II said: "To see that energy—it was the closest I've felt to being in New Orleans since Katrina. Everybody was skeptical at the beginning, no one knew each other before, and at the end everyone was friends and hugging. . . . People saw the other sites. We all know they are out there, but we felt them. We've known they were there in our heads, but this time we felt them in our hearts. . . . Despite some differences . . . we were amazingly the same. . . . Healing? This is healing that's taking place right now, in this room" (America-Speaks 2007).

The creation of an environment that was conducive to the difficult work of the Community Congresses was absolutely vital to their success.[8]

Figure 3.2 New Orleans Musicians Play for
the Community Congress

Clear and Compelling Results

The citizen engagement work in New Orleans had a significant impact in many different ways. Among the clear and compelling results, the work drew demographically representative participation on a large scale. It helped restore hope in a thoroughly devastated city. It established clear priorities for the future. It engaged and influenced key decision makers. It tested citizens' commitment to the results of their deliberative efforts. It helped draw down critical financial resources. It changed aspects of local governance. And it reengaged public managers and other civil servants. Each of these results is explored in the subsections that follow.

Thousands of Citizens Came to the Table

Despite the fact that their lives were still in crisis, nearly four thousand current and dispersed residents of New Orleans participated in the Community Congresses. As planned, the participants

Table 3.1 Community Congress Participation by Demographic Category, Compared to the Population of Pre-Katrina New Orleans (by Percent)

	Pre-Katrina New Orleans	Community Congress II	Community Congress III
African American	67	64	55
White	28	27	34
Asian	2	4	4
Hispanic	3	2	2
Youth (ages 15–19)	7	2	6
Household income below $20,000	37	25	24
Household income above $75,000	19	20	22

Source: Lukensmeyer 2007, 7.

closely approximated the pre-Katrina demographics of New Orleans (see Table 3.1).

THEY CONNECTED WITH EACH OTHER AND HELPED RESTORE HOPE

By bringing citizens from across the diaspora together with those still living in New Orleans, showing them that they cared about the same things, and giving everyone a real voice in decision making, the Unified Plan process restored a sense of connection, community, and, ultimately, hope. What drew people to the events was the opportunity to speak and to be heard; and, unexpectedly, the work also reunited friends and families. A family coming into the meeting space in Dallas looked up at the large screens, and, as the images shifted to the Houston venue, they saw a family member they did not know had survived the flood. Dallas staff quickly called the Houston site, and the lost family members reunited and cried together over the phone, almost as if they were embracing one another in person. They had gone for a year and a half without knowing whether their relatives were alive or dead.

It was an incredibly powerful moment, and a searing reminder of the human side of what was being undertaken as well as the magnitude of systemic failure. In this era of instant data gathering and communication, it was simply shocking that life-and-death information was still not available eighteen months after the hurricane and flooding.

CITIZENS ESTABLISHED CLEAR PRIORITIES

The early and unsuccessful postdisaster planning processes had raised questions about the ability of citizens to contribute productively to the work that lay ahead. The slate of issues facing planners was unbelievably complex. A thoroughly devastated physical infrastructure, traumatized communities with divergent needs and interests, and a limited amount of financial resources to apply to the problems created an extraordinarily challenging situation. Under far tamer circumstances, decision makers have discounted the public's ability to grasp policy nuance and provide substantive input, to accept necessary trade-offs, and to put the common good above their individual needs.

The Unified Plan process concretely demonstrated that large numbers of citizens *can* engage with decision makers, even under the most challenging of circumstances, and contribute productively. Community Congress participants showed a remarkable degree of sophistication in their responses to planning options. For example, although they rejected the idea of government telling them where they could and could not live, they strongly endorsed the notion of incentives to help people make good choices about whether and where to rebuild. They were willing to take responsibility for reducing flood risk, even if it meant individual sacrifice. And they stood up for traditionally underrepresented members of their communities. Researchers who studied citizen participation in the development of the Unified Plan observed: "The participants were a good mix from various parts of the city and different income levels. . . . At most of the 16 tables that were observed, participants made decisions considering the needs of the whole city. While they may start a discussion grounded in their own neighborhoods, the discussions most often incorporated their understanding of the diversity of the city" (Wilson, Padgett, and Wallace 2007, 14).

The concerns that citizens raised accurately reflected where the plans were weak or where there were reasons to be wary about the planning process. Citizens were concerned about whether there would be adequate funds available; about how to transition from a temporary mode of existence to a permanent one; and about how local government could suddenly be successful in areas with which it had struggled before the storm, such as in reducing urban blight and effectively managing public housing and public schools.

In the end, the plan that emerged included dozens of policies, programs, and projects that directly corresponded to specific input citizens offered during the Community Congresses. One of the main concerns citizens identified was finding a way to help residents take responsibility for reducing flood risk. A strongly favored solution was to establish voluntary standards for rebuilding, and then provide incentives to help residents reach those standards. The final Unified New Orleans Plan made specific recommendations to achieve this, and the State of Louisiana's Road Home program provided financing for homeowners to elevate their houses.

The viability of the specific recommendations citizens produced resulted from two deliberate strategies: providing participants with accessible, factual information about the issues,[9] and meticulously designing the day so that they could produce collective views and shared priorities.[10]

DECISION MAKERS GOT ON BOARD

One of the more remarkable aspects of the Unified Plan process was the impact it had on local leaders, who, after early cautiousness, got deeply involved and agreed to be held accountable for follow-up actions they could not possibly know in advance.

Harvard University doctoral student Abigail Williamson interviewed twenty leaders before and after the process and found that eight of them were initially so skeptical that they had seriously considered not participating at all. As the process unfolded, however, it dramatically changed these leaders' perceptions and behavior—from skepticism to endorsement to active participation:

With most political leaders, it is difficult to understand whether a change in support indicates a genuine change of heart or a calculated decision. Whatever the reason, New Orleans political leaders are now publicly supportive of the Unified Plan. . . . After Community Congress II [planners] saw Councilmember Hedge-Morrell's support for the Unified Plan improve in terms of her articulation of [its] purpose and her responses to constituents at meetings. . . . Councilmember Arnie Fielkow, for instance, says that Community Congress II "gained credibility" and that "the full Council is in support of the [Unified Plan] process and sees it as a manifestation of the will of the people [Williamson 2007, 22].

Williamson went on to say, "Whereas before, Council members could get away with denigrating the Unified Plan with off-handed comments that suggested their lack of interest in the plan . . . after Community Congress II political leaders realized they could not 'get away with' that attitude any more" (Williamson 2007, 22).

One of the most notable of these "transformations" occurred in New Orleans Mayor Ray Nagin. The Mayor opened Community Congress II with a speech he had given many times since the hurricane, and to those in the room his delivery seemed flat and without much energy or real investment in what he was saying. The cumulative trauma of the hurricane, flooding, and planning experiences of the previous eighteen months had made it difficult for him to be in the present, open to his own emotions as well as those of others, and fully aware of the possibilities for moving forward. During the course of the day, however, Mayor Nagin experienced the energy and focus of people in the convention center and at other sites all across the country. Coming together with new life and new energy, he broke through his fog, and by the end of the day he was "back." He connected once again with his own passions and was able to join his community's energy and focus on planning for the future. In fact, Williamson reported that "soon after Community Congress II, the Mayor's newly appointed Executive Counsel began attending Community Support Organization meetings after a prolonged absence of any mayoral liaison. A top mayoral aide . . . allow[ed] that, 'At Community Congress II, the Mayor did realize the power of the people'" (Williamson 2007, 22).

The ability of the Unified Plan process to reengage decision makers was still in evidence several months after the Community Congresses. In response to a report issued in early March 2007 that was critical of the Unified Plan, New Orleans recovery director Ed Blakely said: "While the Unified Plan was not designed to provide an absolute blueprint for all of the actions necessary to complete our recovery, it does provide useful data based on a process driven by the people . . . We are developing a clear path for the recovery of the great city of New Orleans, and the Unified Plan is a critical part of this process" (Eggler 2007, 1).

Andy Kopplin, executive director of the Louisiana Recovery Authority at the time, may have best summed up the newly created link between citizens and decision makers: "It doesn't matter what the plan is if no one embraces it. . . . [T]he first time [in earlier planning] there was no connection between planners, politicians, and people. . . . [In the Unified Plan process] the ability for there to be a disconnect between the people and the planners was erased" (Williamson 2007, 13).

CITIZENS HELD THEIR GROUND

As effective as the Community Congresses were in the moment, it was essential that citizens stay involved in every stage of the work that followed. The multiple levels of local and state government review facing the Unified Plan, to say nothing of the long, arduous, and complex rebuilding process that lay ahead, would offer many opportunities for a return to politics and business as usual. In the face of this, the broad citizen participation and the decision making that had been accomplished would have to be sustained.

The first test came after only a few months. When the city planning commission announced public hearings on the Unified Plan, entrenched special interests in the city launched some harsh, politicized, and racially charged criticisms. In response, citizens themselves remobilized the network of participants, volunteers, and activists from the Community Congresses, and hundreds of people attended the hearings, a number of them providing direct testimony in support of the plan. Citizens were energized to make sure their accomplishments, their collective decisions, and their shared story were not lost in the cacophony of competing interests. This strong showing made it impossible for the city planning commission to delay moving forward on the plan. It was a turning point on the road to the plan's final adoption.

This example of sustained engagement is but one of many.[11] For more than four years following their participation in the Community Congresses, a group of inspired citizens actively fought housing policy that was keeping them trapped in Federal Emergency Management Agency (FEMA) trailers and preventing them from rebuilding their lives. By raising awareness about the direct and disastrous impact on families of prematurely ending support programs and withdrawing resources, the Rebuilding Lives Coalition successfully helped secure extensions for the Disaster Housing Assistance Program; for the FEMA Trailer Sales/Donation Program; for the Louisiana Swift Bus Service, which provided affordable transit among Baton Rouge, the River Parishes, and New Orleans; and on FEMA's deadline for closing the largest trailer park sites in Louisiana, Mississippi, and Alabama. The coalition was also instrumental in efforts to secure additional resources, including $5 million in state funds for emergency rental assistance for families transitioning from FEMA to Department of Housing and Urban Development (HUD) rental assistance, and $20 million in gap financing to homeowners as part of a rebuilding pilot program.

Unfortunately, despite these successes, the Rebuilding Lives Coalition was unable to gain sufficient traction on a comprehensive, coordinated case management model the organizations had painstakingly developed. As a result, many Hurricane Katrina survivors were—and still are today—left to manage largely on their own.

THE MONEY FOLLOWED

The Unified Plan made a strong and specific case concerning the desperate need for recovery funds. It identified a $14 billion gap between money that was already approved or on its way and what would still be needed. In June 2007, about five months after the last Community Congress, the New Orleans City Council and the Louisiana Recovery Authority approved the plan. Over the next six months the Louisiana Recovery Authority obligated $411 million in federal Community Development Block Grant funds that had been awaiting distribution to the city to help jump-start recovery projects. In addition, since 2007 billions of federal dollars have been committed by FEMA, the U.S. Department of Transportation, the U.S. Army Corps of Engineers, and other federal and state agencies, as well as by philanthropies and private investors, to fund projects identified in the plan and to work toward filling the $14 billion gap (L. Johnson 2010). In their 2010 work *Clear as Mud: Planning for the Rebuilding of New Orleans,* Robert Olshansky and Laurie Johnson provide a detailed look at continuing issues and concerns with federal resources like the Road Home program and the FEMA public assistance and hazard mitigation funds (Olshansky and Johnson 2010).

GOVERNANCE IN THE CITY CHANGED

The participation of thousands of citizens in the Community Congresses had an immediate impact on governance in New Orleans. The Unified Plan specifically delineated the various roles and responsibilities in the recovery process for the City Council, the mayor, and the Office of Recovery Management (ORM). The Unified Plan also educated the public about these roles, thereby solidifying urgently needed checks and balances and creating a clear path of accountability. The Mayor could not undermine the ORM, the ORM could not ignore the city's Development Authority, and so on. All of this provided the city with governance structures that had credibility with private sector leaders, with state and federal government officials, and with the citizens of New Orleans.

The Community Congresses, and the plan they helped produce, also achieved longer-term impacts on governance in New Orleans. One of the recommendations in the final plan was that the city planning commission revise the city's desperately antiquated zoning law and produce an updated master plan. The high-profile nature of the Community Congresses and the plan approval process had brought these issues into the public's awareness and fueled a demand to do something about them. In 2007 $2 million in recovery funds was designated for rewriting the zoning law and developing a new master plan. In August 2010, just after the five-year anniversary of Hurricane Katrina, the City Council unanimously approved a new citywide master plan that built on the Unified Plan. Although it had taken a number of years, a new culture of planning in the city was finally established. Engaging the public in solving significant problems laid bare by Hurricane Katrina and the flooding played a significant role in making this happen.

In winter 2012, six years after the Community Congresses, community leader Vera Triplett was asked if changes in the role of citizen voice in the governance of New Orleans remained. Her answer was emphatic. "Yes," she said, "to this day, every time there is a neighborhood association meeting a member of the City Council comes and listens or directly participates. That never happened before the Unified Plan work and the Community Congresses" (Triplett 2012).

Andy Koppelin, former Executive Director of the Louisiana Recovery Authority and currently Deputy Mayor and Chief Administrative Officer for the City of New Orleans, made the point strongly:

> There's no doubt that the Unified New Orleans Plan developed by citizens was the foundation for the city's final recovery plan and that it has had a significant, lasting impact on governance ever since. Just two days ago, during City Council budget hearings [in January 2012], Councilmember Cynthia Hedge-Morrell made reference to some things the city was supposed to do because they were part of the original UNOP plan. There has been no blinking by city managers on this—it is simply understood. We all know that the Plan was so big there would never be sufficient resources to implement it fully, but the city still very much keeps fidelity to the themes and priorities and moves forward on the action steps where possible [Koppelin 2012].

Public Managers and Employees Were Newly Engaged

For many years prior to Hurricane Katrina the civil service corps in New Orleans had been highly disenfranchised. The delivery of public services in the city was deemed troubled and substandard.

This negative reputation was acutely felt in the immediate after-math of the hurricane and flooding, when FEMA, without warning, changed the rules for emergency fund disbursement and required the New Orleans director of finance to recertify the city's needs four times before any funds were released. Standard procedure in these situations is that a certain amount of money flows imme-diately; the receiving jurisdiction then certifies conditions and needs; and if there are discrepancies, the jurisdiction returns the money. Federal agencies' distrust of the city's management capac-ity was exceptionally high. Many people in and out of New Orleans believed this distrust was motivated by partisan politics.

To break through the culture of distrust and dysfunction, about two months after the final Community Congress, America-*Speaks* facilitated the One New Orleans City Wide Planning Day, which brought together almost seven hundred New Orleans city employees for a first-ever summit aimed at engaging them in the citizen-driven priorities that had just been developed. Specifi-cally, the meeting was an opportunity for city employees to learn about the Unified New Orleans Plan, reflect on how they could help implement it, and discuss emergency preparedness for the future.

Participants focused on department-specific issues, took part in a neighborhood recovery exercise in which they had to make tough choices about recovery options given limited resources, and discussed what they would need to do as city employees working together inside and across departments and agencies to facilitate recovery.

City employees in New Orleans had been completely belea-guered. Not only were their personal lives profoundly disrupted but their ability to carry out their duties in city government had also been compromised. Participating in the One New Orleans City Wide Planning Day was like a breath of fresh air for them. For the first time, someone was investing time and resources to give them the opportunity to recognize their own struggles and heroism in the face of what had happened. At the same time, the planning day gave them a chance to understand the important insights and recommendations their fellow New Orleanians had developed in the Community Congresses. It was a cathartic and empowering experience for these employees. They left the day energized and focused on how to collaborate with each other, with the appropriate nonprofit and private organizations, and with the public itself to make the plan a reality. Yolanda Rodriguez, New Orleans Director of Planning, described the experience this way: "You have to understand that this was a very fragile time for city employees. Most of them were trying to get back to the city; there were lots of health and mental health issues . . . it was a very difficult time. The meeting gave us a chance to reach out and connect to each other—it had a very positive impact" (Rodriguez 2012).

KEEPING THINGS IN PERSPECTIVE

This chapter has explored the impact of the Community Congresses following the disastrous hurricane and flooding in New Orleans. At a point in time, America*Speaks* demonstrated that truly whole-community deliberation can influence governance. Obviously, however, severe race and class divisions, political corruption, and enormous systemic dysfunctions did not simply go away as a result of the community's coming together to make some big decisions. Considering the depth of these problems, it is not surprising that more than six years after the disaster, tens of thousands of New Orleanians are still displaced from their homes and remain disenfranchised from their rights as citizens of this country. Jordan Flaherty of the *San Francisco BayView* reported in September 2010: "Just as the storm revealed racial inequalities, the recovery has also been shaped by systemic racism. According to a recent survey of New Orleanians by the Kaiser Foundation, 42% of African Americans—versus just 16% of whites—said they still have not recovered from Katrina. Thirty-one percent of African-American residents—versus 8% of white respondents—said they had trouble paying for food or housing in the last year. Housing prices in New Orleans have gone up 63% just since 2009" (Flaherty 2010).

In one example of the systemic issues of race and class that have persisted, such rebuilding resources as the $11 billion federal Road Home program were made available exclusively to homeowners, leaving renters without access to a significant source of federal aid. Flaherty further reported: "Even among homeowners, the program treated different populations in different ways. U.S. District Judge Henry Kennedy recently found that the program was racially discriminatory in the formula it used to disperse funds. By partially basing payouts on home values instead of on damage to homes, the program favored properties in wealthier—often whiter—neighborhoods. However, the same judge found that nothing in the law obligated the state to correct this discrimination for the 98% of applicants whose cases have been closed" (Flaherty 2010).

Although the success of the Community Congresses in helping to release desperately needed federal recovery funds can be legitimately celebrated, we must all recognize that the road to full recovery for New Orleans and its citizens continues to stretch far into the future.

CRITICAL LESSONS

The practical lessons about meaningful citizen engagement that can be drawn from the Community Congresses in New Orleans are plentiful to be sure, and are explored throughout this book. Perhaps the most salient among them is that no obstacle provides a legitimate excuse for failing to engage citizens in the decision making that affects them. The work in New Orleans proved that you can secure substantial and representative participation under "hardest-case" circumstances. In this instance, most of the target population was living in postdisaster crisis mode, was openly skeptical of planning efforts, was angry with leaders and all public institutions, and was still living outside the city. Their commitment to participating in spite of all these issues demonstrates what citizens will do when they believe they will truly be heard and can make a difference.

In addition, the work demonstrated that through these processes you can, in fact, give full and equal voice to the most disenfranchised. Low-income citizens in New Orleans, African Americans in particular, who were disproportionately represented among the victims of Hurricane Katrina and who had been largely unheard in early recovery planning processes, were successfully included. So were New Orleanians dispersed to other cities who had not to that point been given any opportunity whatsoever to participate.

FIGURE 3.3 COMMUNITY CONGRESS PARTICIPANTS AT WORK

Finally, the effort proved that geography need no longer hinder face-to-face participation processes. The Community Congresses drew participation on a geographic scale few had ever attempted, using satellite broadcast to connect five sites in live conversation and enabling an additional sixteen sites to view the program through a webcast and submit their views in real time over the Internet.

BEYOND NEW ORLEANS

Although we may like to think of New Orleans as uniquely troubled, all around the country, in places like Detroit, Michigan, Camden, New Jersey, Compton, California, and so many others, slower and more invisible disasters caused by shifts in the industrial sector and the globalization of the economy have exacerbated the very same dysfunction in governance that Hurricane Katrina and the flooding brought into such sharp focus in the Louisiana Gulf.

In *all* of these and many other places, the voices and the will of the citizenry have long been lost. As happened in New Orleans, leaders from every sector—government, business, and nonprofit—and citizens themselves must create critical vehicles through which citizens regain their voice in governance.

FIGURE 3.4 LEADERS MUST CREATE OPPORTUNITIES FOR
CITIZEN VOICES TO BE HEARD

The moment is here, and the time is now. The experiences of America*Speaks,* other deliberative democracy practitioners, and those public managers who have been active in this work provide a solid foundation on which to begin. This foundation, taken together with the major breakthroughs in information technology, make it a perfect time to look at how citizens can more meaningfully be engaged in governance.

CHAPTER FOUR

CITIZEN ENGAGEMENT FROM THE PUBLIC MANAGER'S PERSPECTIVE

We will work together to ensure the public trust and establish a system of transparency, public participation, and collaboration. Openness will strengthen our democracy and promote efficiency and effectiveness in Government.

PRESIDENT BARACK OBAMA, JANUARY 21, 2009*

The citizen engagement work in post-Katrina New Orleans enabled thousands of people who had been through truly devastating circumstances to bring their voices to bear on the future of their city. The New Orleans story also demonstrates the many facets of citizen engagement work, as led by a nonprofit organization. In the context of a guide for public managers, this raises some important questions about undertaking such work in a government context. This chapter seeks to explore those questions.

DO PUBLIC MANAGERS WANT TO DO THIS WORK?

No matter how sound the rationale for citizen engagement or how effective the strategies for implementation, there is an important

---

*Obama, B. "Transparency and Open Government." [http://www.whitehouse
.gov/the_press_office/TransparencyandOpenGovernment]. Accessed 2012.

threshold question to be asked: Do public managers *want* to do this work? I believe that they do. To be sure, the many agency leaders featured in this book have demonstrated a commitment to citizen engagement. In most instances it emerged first as common sense ("There must be a better way to conduct our business"), then grew into true passion ("This really works; we need to reshape our agency culture around it"). But the desire goes beyond that of these select individuals.

In 1993, when I was a deputy director for Vice President Al Gore's reinventing government task force, I had a recurring experience that convinced me of federal managers' hunger for new approaches to "business as usual." For several months during that period I traveled around the country speaking to federal executive boards about the work associated with the Reinventing Government Directive. In those speeches, understanding how easy it is for all of us to get locked into a particular identity, I made it a practice to ask members of the audience to take off their "federal manager" hat and listen, instead, wearing their "citizen of the United States" hat. It is no exaggeration to say that in auditoriums of hundreds of managers, this mental shift routinely brought tears to the eyes of many. One simple exercise put them back in touch with why they went into public service in the first place, and reminded them that what they truly cared about was a government "of the people, by the people, for the people," and making a difference in the world.

I left this experience knowing that even though civil servants' career motivations often get publicly framed as a desire for the security that comes with a government job, the vast majority take these positions because they care passionately about the issues and want to make a difference on a large scale. It is illustrative of this point that when the Partnership for Public Service gives out its Service to America Medals every year, the recipients' speeches reflect a core desire to serve and make a difference. A recent example: on receiving an award in 2011, Diane Braunstein, Associate Commissioner for International Programs in the Social Security Administration, described her work as "the opportunity of a lifetime . . . In terms of making a positive change in people's lives, it was a chance to work on a national scale—to make a difference in scope that is simply unparalleled" (Partnership for Public Service 2012). Braunstein speaks for many public managers whose enthusiasm and commitment drive them to take on new strategies to achieve their goals.

Public managers no doubt have a passion for the mission of their agency, but do they want to do citizen engagement work? Again, I believe many of them do. To start, federal agencies often call on America*Speaks* to consult and provide technical assistance on citizen engagement practice. As further evidence, in 2006 we published a paper sponsored by the IBM Center for the Business of Government called *Public Deliberation: A Manager's Guide to Citizen Engagement* (Lukensmeyer and Torres 2006). In the first year this paper was the IBM Center's most-often-downloaded report; six years later, as this book was going to press, it was still being accessed by significant numbers each year. Clearly a great many public managers see that bringing citizens into the governance process adds value to their efforts to achieve their agency's mission. Further, they are excited to have resources that support this work.

WHAT PUBLIC MANAGERS HAVE TO GAIN

Citizen engagement is an important tool for public managers for two principal reasons: it can help them address core challenges in achieving their mission; and it is a fiscally and operationally prudent strategy, especially in tough budget times. Each of these reasons is discussed in the subsections that follow.

CITIZEN ENGAGEMENT CAN ADDRESS CORE CHALLENGES

There are a number of ways in which citizen engagement can help public managers address the core challenges they face. To start, public managers, to accomplish their program goals, must routinely navigate complex relationships among diverse constituencies that have competing agendas—work made even more complicated in today's highly toxic political environment. If a manager does not effectively navigate these relationships, and if policymaking is hijacked to serve the interests of a few, the integrity and credibility of the policy outcome as well as of the governing agency itself will be diminished.

Well-crafted citizen engagement processes help address such concerns. As discussed earlier, these processes can create a level playing field among general interest citizens, competing stakeholders, and special interest organizations, thereby enabling these various parties to reach common ground. As the U.S. Forest Service's Richard Stem observed following an extensive citizen engagement process by his agency: "We could only have achieved unified recommendations and implementable plans by bringing all the relevant stakeholders to the table" (Stem 2012).

Another core challenge facing public managers is that the politics that often accompany controversial policy questions can stymie not only decision making but also program implementation. In such high-stakes environments, citizen engagement can build an active public constituency that feels ownership of, and commitment to implementing, the outcomes of a deliberative process. Public managers who are able to demonstrate that the actions they plan to take are solidly supported by a diverse group of citizens and stakeholders are in a strong position to diffuse political gamesmanship. The Centers for Disease Control and Prevention's Roger Bernier put it this way: "Agencies face many difficult or stalemated policy decisions which have a component of competing values that are particularly challenging to work through. Public engagement can produce sounder, more population-relevant decisions" (Bernier 2012).

Finally, high-quality citizen engagement increases the respect the public has for government and public managers, and is therefore an effective avenue to building the public's trust in government programs, practices, and institutions. Tony Faast of the U.S. Fish and Wildlife Service put it quite succinctly: "When we discovered that we didn't have all the answers, we should have engaged rather than postured. It is so important to be authentic" (Faast 2012). Patricia Milligan of the U.S. Nuclear Regulatory Commission agreed: "Sometimes you have to be prepared to embrace your dirty laundry proactively," she said, "own up to it, put it out there, and address it directly. This builds trust through transparency" (Milligan 2012).

CITIZEN ENGAGEMENT IS FISCALLY AND OPERATIONALLY PRUDENT

Economic trends in this country clearly signal that already-diminishing resources available to government will most likely continue to decline for the foreseeable future. This reality could be expected to have a chilling effect on public managers' willingness and ability to take on new strategies and responsibilities. In tight budget times, any work not classified as urgent or mission-critical is likely to be dropped or scaled back. Further, because public engagement activities are only in the authorizing legislation of a small number of U.S. agencies, such as the Environmental Protection Agency, the Fish and Wildlife Service, and the Department of Transportation, the great majority of public managers in this country are currently working in an environment with no preexisting internal commitment to providing resources for these activities.

The limited availability of resources for citizen engagement work might seem to present a considerable challenge. And yet, paradoxically, a context of reduced revenues and budget cutting is actually one in which agencies should *strengthen* their connections to citizens. Under these circumstances, it is particularly vital to engage the public in the process of identifying their priorities as well as the specific budgetary or program trade-offs they would support. With this information in hand, agencies can make the necessary tough decisions, confident of public backing as opposed to simply waiting for the inevitable backlash against cuts that have been chosen unilaterally.

In addition, although citizen engagement done right is costly, the cost is likely comparable to, if not less than, what government agencies routinely spend on public opinion polls and public relations strategies ostensibly used for the same purpose. And, as described in Chapter One, these costly poll results ultimately have limited utility when it comes to backing up tough decision making. Describing the importance of such "backup," the Forest Service's Richard Stem noted: "The concept of trying to stop action or not working together toward common objectives was just not tolerated by the many that worked within the collaborative" (Stem 2012).

Building on this point, meaningful engagement of the public on controversial issues can mitigate the likelihood of expensive controversies and lawsuits over decisions the public or stakeholders felt they had no opportunity to influence. A long-term federal manager in a regulatory agency said: "Were it not for an open process, there may have been potentially damaging and costly litigation. Successful public engagement was likely a significant factor in reducing those risks."

Finally, rather than being viewed as an additional expense during tight budget times, citizen engagement processes can actually be an antidote to budgetary constraints. For example, these processes can help reduce expensive staffing redundancies that result from a failure to work effectively across programs; or costly work-arounds made necessary by an inability to implement key policy changes; or, as noted earlier, the labor-intensive work of managing complex relationships among diverse constituencies with competing agendas. In each of these areas, the strategic use of citizen engagement processes can both bring greater efficiencies and increased program effectiveness.

In short, public managers charged with shaping policies, implementing programs, and managing crises can be well served by championing citizen engagement. Long-term federal manager Rich Kuhlman put it quite simply: "For federal managers who have no experience with public engagement, I would say: 'try it, you'll like it.' Even though it can require enormous effort, when you experience success, you'll say: 'we should have been doing this all along'" (Kuhlman 2012).

CHALLENGES TO BROADER GOVERNMENT USE OF CITIZEN ENGAGEMENT

Although there are many reasons for public managers to do citizen engagement work, there are also a number of persistent challenges to overcome.[1] America*Speaks* has studied this phenomenon, looking closely at the intersections between the broader field of deliberative democracy and the citizen engagement work of public agencies. We have observed it in the course of our work; have twice published research on it (Lukensmeyer and Torres 2006; Lukensmeyer, Goldman, and Stern 2011); and have spearheaded multiple cross-government, cross-sector leadership roundtables on the topic.[2]

Through this work, we have been able to cluster the predominant challenges facing public managers into six categories. Taken together, these challenges describe an organizational culture and environment in which it can be difficult to undertake citizen engagement efforts, despite what may be a genuine desire on the part of a public manager to do so. It is important to note, however, that for each category there is also a track record of agencies successfully overcoming the associated challenges.

NEGATIVE PERCEPTIONS OF THE PUBLIC

Deliberative democracy practitioners have long observed that citizens are often perceived to be incapable of contributing to policymaking processes. Citizens are believed to be insufficiently informed about the issues and likely to put individual perspectives ahead of the common good. In some respects, this view is understandable. Wild swings in public polling data combined with the media's often inflammatory presentation of citizen opinions on the issues can certainly leave an impression that the public holds simplistic, self-referential views.

In addition, the way that most public meetings are structured and managed contributes to and reinforces this view. For example, the people who attend such meetings are generally the "usual suspects": preidentified or invited stakeholders who are directly connected to a particular cause or position. By definition, this group cannot reasonably be expected to focus on the larger public good; they will, instead, advocate for their respective positions. Unfortunately, when such stakeholders do not focus on the broader public good, public managers too often use this as data to support their perception that the same is true of the general public. Yet in practice, the field has demonstrated time and again that unaffiliated citizens are quite capable of making decisions in the interest of the broader public good.

For public managers deeply embedded in a data-driven, "expert" culture, it is often particularly difficult to imagine ordinary people being able to make substantive contributions on technically complex issues. And it is true: without the proper information and support, the public would struggle to participate effectively in discussions on such questions. However, it is also true, and has been repeatedly demonstrated by democracy practitioners, that when given accurate and fair information, the public can and indeed does rise to the occasion. Olivia Ferriter, Deputy Director of the Office of Policy Analysis in the U.S. Department of the Interior, recognized the pattern: "We still encounter some staff who say 'I'm the expert, why would I want to partner?'" she said. "It is important for our employees to understand the rules we have to follow, the authorities that govern what we do, and that frame what is possible. However, they also should know where flexibilities exist in order to be a better partner. When you tap the community's expertise, it can make them more willing to join you" (Ferriter 2012).

The U.S. Forest Service's Richard Stem agreed: "Once you turn over decision-making power to the public you have to trust that they will give you the best answers," he said. "We used to think that it would be a mob mindset with bad outcomes, but after you begin to treat them as partners in the process, you quickly see a different result" (Stem 2012). The case studies in this book, starting with the story of citizen engagement in the previous chapter, offer compelling examples of how citizens can and do make valuable contributions to important policy discussions.

LIMITED ENGAGEMENT REPERTOIRE

Citizen engagement practitioners recognize a spectrum of strategies that ranges from simply informing the public to truly empowering them. Table 4.1, originally developed by the International Association for Public Participation, delineates this continuum.

TABLE 4.1 PUBLIC INVOLVEMENT SPECTRUM

Inform	Consult	Engage	Collaborate	Empower
Provide the public with balanced and objective information to assist them in understanding the problem, alternatives, opportunities, and/or solutions.	Obtain public feedback on analysis, alternatives, and/or decisions.	Work directly with the public throughout the process to ensure that public concerns and aspirations are consistently understood and considered.	Partner with the public in each aspect of the decision including the development of alternatives and the identification of the preferred solution.	Place final decision-making authority in the hands of citizens.

Source: International Association for Public Participation, 2012.

Although these are all valid forms of public involvement, and each may be well suited to a particular situation, if the overall objective is meaningful citizen engagement, they are not all equal in value. Simply informing and consulting are, in fact, quite thin and frequently pro forma techniques of participation that often fail to meet the public's own expectations for involvement. Moving to the right on the spectrum shown in Table 4.1, the depth of involvement and the value to the public increase.

Unfortunately, the engagement methods habitually employed— often, in fact, mandated—by government, such as public hearings, citizen advisory councils, and public comment periods, are generally limited to the far left side of the continuum. Although they are important strategies for information exchange, they do not support members of the public in considering the issues or trading ideas with people of diverse opinions and experiences. Nor are they designed to surface areas of agreement and enable members of the public to develop shared views that can translate into collective recommendations. In short, they reflect a one-way, top-down orientation that is wholly unsatisfactory if the goal is to actually engage citizens substantively in the governance process.

Further, because public hearings, citizen advisory councils, and public comment periods constitute "engagement" in name only, they can actually undermine citizens' confidence in the value of the concept. In the absence of other meaningful engagement opportunities, overreliance on these strategies can be counterproductive, feeding citizen frustration and increasing mistrust of government. Roger Bernier, who first joined the Centers for Disease Control and Prevention in 1978 as an Epidemic Intelligence Service Officer, put it this way: "Federal managers need to realize that public engagement—done poorly—causes more harm than good. There can be a reduction in trust and social capital, and a commensurate increase in public cynicism. You are better off not asking for advice from the public if all you are prepared to do is use what's consistent with your own opinion" (Bernier 2012). Tony Faast of the U.S. Fish and Wildlife Service agreed: "In too many cases, federal managers are just jumping through the hoops—sending out notices, convening information sessions, responding to the usual objections from the usual interest groups with the same level of arrogance and stubbornness. Even in situations where meetings have lots of attendance and little controversy, you have to get out of the short-term thinking that says "let's just see if we can get the group to agree with us by the time we're done" (Faast 2012).

To rebuild public trust and truly involve people in governance, credible citizen engagement practice must offer opportunities beyond what has been traditionally available.

CULTURE OF RISK AVERSION AMONG CAREER CIVIL SERVANTS

Anyone who has worked in the federal government or in top levels of state, county, or city government has experienced the tension that can exist between political appointees and career civil servants. The former must develop policy in a political context, whereas the latter must implement that policy in a nonpolitical way. In the context of their different roles, political appointees often lack appreciation of and respect for civil servants' deep content knowledge and understanding of what it takes to implement policy on the ground. Civil servants often do not appreciate or respect all of the political dimensions of the policy environment that appointees must satisfy. All of this can lead to significant levels of mutual distrust and defensiveness, resulting in a culture of risk aversion. Political appointees may not invest enough trust in civil servants to work in a truly collaborative way, and civil servants may simply be seeking to "survive" the tenure of a given administration.

This is a highly dysfunctional way for any organization to operate. In such an environment, if an agency's mandates and operating structures do not already value and expect citizen engagement, and very few do, it would be quite risky and unusual for a public manager to step out and implement such engagement. Chapter Six explores the importance, in the context of citizen engagement, of bridging the divide between the political and career workforces, and it offers strategic approaches for accomplishing this goal.

FRAGMENTED POLICY AND PRACTICE ENVIRONMENT

Compounding a culture of risk aversion, government policy and practice around citizen engagement have a history of being fragmented, poorly coordinated, and characterized by limited inter- and intra-agency knowledge sharing. As described in more detail in Chapter One, existing legislation, such as the Administrative Procedure Act of 1946, has provided insufficient incentives to deepen citizen participation practices and offered no guidance about how to actually do the work more effectively. Further, systems to ensure internal coordination of such efforts are lacking. For example, public managers who have been doing high-caliber public engagement work for decades report that their efforts often remain completely unknown to the political appointees who are brought in to oversee "external affairs" or other interactions with the public.

Institutional Roadblocks

Public managers face a series of structural barriers to citizen engagement from within government. The Federal Advisory Committee Act (FACA) provides a useful example of this concern. Enacted in 1972, FACA was intended "to ensure that advice by advisory committees is objective and accessible to the public." To that end, it established a process for "operating, overseeing, and terminating these advisory bodies" (U.S. General Services Administration 2012). In assessing the impact of FACA, researchers Rebecca J. Long and Thomas C. Beierle said: "It has had a profound influence on who participates in government decision-making, when they participate, how they participate, and what influence participation has on policy" (Long and Beierle 1999, ii). More specifically, they argue that although the act was principally intended to make transparent the influence of special interest groups on advisory processes, the procedural requirements and limitations it imposed are so onerous that it has had an overall chilling effect on government efforts to undertake public engagement.

John Kamensky, Senior Fellow at the IBM Center for the Business of Government, agrees. He has identified two primary constraints on agencies resulting from FACA: a cap on the number of advisory committees, instituted by the Clinton Administration in 1993, and the requirement that the General Services Administration (GSA) both be "consulted" before an agency creates a new committee and receive a justification for the committee every two years thereafter. "As a result of these constraints," Kamensky said, "agencies are reluctant to set up new advisory committees and instead use loopholes in the law to create them, for example directing a contractor to set up an advisory committee to support the contractor's work, but taking advantage of the advice themselves. Currently, some in Congress are trying to remove the loopholes, which could have the effect of further restricting citizen engagement. The Administrative Conference of the United States, an independent federal agency that works on governance process improvements, recently recommended lifting the cap and shifting GSA's role in approving FACA committees to the agencies themselves" (Kamensky 2012).

Regrettably, FACA is not the only institutional barrier facing government managers who seek to engage the public. In 2012 staff at the U.S. Department of Health and Human Services were formulating plans to gather public input on their open government work. They hoped to use an electronic survey. The federal Paperwork Reduction Act (PRA), passed in 1980 in an effort to ease paperwork burdens for individuals and groups communicating with the federal government, presented a significant roadblock. In effect, the PRA prevented the use of a quick survey instrument and would in any event have required developing a new system of records for the incoming data. Pursuing a one-time exemption from the Office of Management and Budget to allow for the gathering of public input would have taken several months. It is certainly ironic, if not enormously frustrating, that federal regulations inhibited efforts to engage the public about how the federal government can be more inclusive of that same public.

Exhortations to get rid of such institutional barriers to engagement have been made repeatedly by advocates outside government as well as by managers inside. Although the Obama Administration tasked the Office of Management and Budget with resolving some of these concerns, many of them persist.

DYSFUNCTIONAL NATIONAL DEBATE

We are in the midst of the most heated political and media debate about the role of government that this country has seen since the Great Depression. Sadly, it has mostly been limited to discussions about the "size" of our government, as opposed to representing a serious look at government's goals, roles, and responsibilities. In this limited framework, Republicans have come to own the position that smaller is always better, whereas Democrats hold to the flag of a more expansive government role. As typifies our political discourse these days, such a narrow context has opened up deep ideological chasms, and the debate has devolved into demagoguery and accusations on both sides.

While campaigning in Iowa early in the 2012 presidential race, then-candidate and former Texas governor Rick Perry said about the federal Social Security program: "It is a Ponzi scheme for these young people. The idea that they're working and paying into Social Security today, that the current program is going to be there for them, is a lie . . . a monstrous lie" (Daly 2011). In December 2010 Representative John Boehner of Ohio explicitly extended the criticism to public servants themselves. The *New York Times* reported that "the top Republican in the House called it 'nonsense' that 'taxpayers are subsidizing the fattened salaries and pensions of federal bureaucrats'" (Parker 2011).

As evidence of the severity of the problem, the Partnership for Public Service, created ten years ago to attract young talent into government careers, has deliberately expanded its efforts to focus on improving attitudes and perceptions about civil servants among the public. Career Foreign Service Officer Jason Ullner published a moving plea in the *Washington Post*'s editorial section in February 2012: "All I hear these days are the once and future leaders of our country tripping over themselves to denigrate the work we do . . . I implore you: Stop using the government work-force as a political football . . . it is counterproductive to drive away the best and brightest from working for the betterment of this country" (Ullner 2012, A15).

By demeaning government workers, our national debate has created an environment that is not conducive to efforts by public managers to interact positively with the public, let alone seek to broadly engage them. The strategies for citizen engagement described in this book are an antidote to this problem. As public managers expand their existing citizen engagement practice and create new, authentic opportunities for citizens to influence critical decisions, the public's views about government will change.

FURTHER CONTEXT FOR PUBLIC MANAGERS: THE OPEN GOVERNMENT INITIATIVE

In a nation that has long delegated citizen engagement work to the nonprofit sector, the Obama Administration's Open Government Initiative represents a change in course. Although it has produced mixed results to date, it has nonetheless elevated the visibility of citizen engagement opportunities for public managers across the government.[3]

Developing the Open Government Directive

In January 2009, newly in office and facing a host of challenges, from war in the Middle East to a national economic crisis, President Obama determined to make good on what had been one of his most consistent campaign promises: to carve out a more authentic role for citizens in the governance of the country. Remarkably, the *first official act* of the new administration was the Executive Memorandum on Transparent and Open Government: a mandate for government to be not only transparent but also participatory and collaborative (Obama 2012).

The 2009 Executive Memorandum on Transparent and Open Government tasked the Office of Management and Budget with issuing an Open Government Directive (OGD) that would operationalize the objectives of transparency, participation, and collaboration across the federal government. The moment the executive memorandum was announced, many organizations in the United States began to collaborate on a unified message to the administration about how to implement it. Under America-*Speaks*'s leadership, a broad spectrum of senior federal agency leaders, managers, and staff were twice brought together in forums aimed at providing the White House with the distilled wisdom of those who had been doing the best public participation work in the federal government for decades. Many of the challenges discussed earlier were explored in these initial meetings, which were attended by White House representatives.

After nearly a year of stakeholder and public input, on December 8, 2009, the Obama Administration issued the Open Government Directive, which laid out in exacting detail the steps that executive departments and agencies would be required to take to publish government information online; create an enabling policy framework for open government; improve the quality of government information; and create and institutionalize a culture of open government. Each agency would also be required to describe at least one new "flagship" initiative in the area of transparency, participation, or collaboration (Orszag 2009). Four months later, on April 7, 2010, every federal department published its open government plan.

Successes of the Open Government Work

In the first two years of the Open Government Initiative the most significant actions taken by the White House and federal agencies were responsive to the stated goals for achieving transparency. In particular, these actions focused on releasing data that were previously inaccessible to the public or available only in difficult-to-digest formats. To achieve this, agencies hired chief technology officers and other staff, including professionals in a whole new job category related to the use of social media. Online platforms like Data.gov were created. By the beginning of 2011 agencies had released more than three hundred thousand data sets for public consumption through Data.gov.

In addition, the OGD required all federal agencies to create an open government website that would give the public direct opportunities to provide input on the agency's open government plans; enable publication of key data sets; and be a platform for advertising opportunities to participate in agency activities. Finally, the OGD established new policies guiding agency behavior related to issues of transparency, such as expediting responses to Freedom of Information Act requests.

Some important work was also completed in the areas of participation and collaboration. Agencies launched wikis, crowdsourcing platforms, and other online tools to solicit public feedback and generate innovative ideas from citizens, stakeholders, and employees (these and other online tools are discussed in detail in Chapter Twelve). The Obama Administration created new offices and initiatives to enable and encourage greater use of these tools, especially in the area of online contests and engaging the public to identify new solutions to problems faced by government. The Administration also focused heavily on improving online public input into agencies' rule-making processes.

WHERE THE OPEN GOVERNMENT WORK HAS FALLEN SHORT

Through all of the efforts just described, the OGD has improved how government interacts with the public. But for the practice of citizen engagement, it has not been a game changer: it has not called for or supported high-quality public deliberation linked to decision making on important policy issues.

The majority of the participation activities and accomplishments under the OGD sit on the far left side of the public involvement spectrum described earlier in Table 4.1. They have principally been efforts to use online platforms to provide the public with more data and engage them more frequently in two-way consultative processes. In other words, the efforts have gathered public input through contests and requests but have not done much to engage the public in the development of mutually determined plans or solutions. This emphasis on information-gathering and information-sharing strategies can be explained, in part, by the fact that these are the most familiar and easily executed strategies available to federal agencies. Further, because the OGD's incentives and awards focus on transparency and data access, that is the work that agencies prioritized.

By contrast, the OGD's instructions for engaging, collaborating, and empowering, referred to as "collaboration" and "participation," are less clear to many inside government. For example, the OGD divides its participatory work into four general categories: engaging the public online, engaging the public face-to-face, engaging the public through formal input mechanisms or procedures, and changing agency culture to support greater participation. Yet there is little guidance about what these activities entail—about how to define *good* public participation and then assess and evaluate the efforts. As a result, confronted with the requirements of the directive, a federal manager might legitimately wonder: What are the minimum standards for good participation? What constitutes adequate levels of participation by the public? What kinds of participation are most appropriate for different circumstances? What are the most useful measures for tracking and evaluating participation efforts?

From a public manager's perspective, it is not clear where the answers to these questions are supposed to come from. For all of these reasons, the "take-up" of authentic citizen engagement work under the OGD has been minimal. By not providing more specific guidance, expectations, and incentives, the OGD has left agencies and federal managers without the clear direction and tools they need to demonstrably increase citizen participation. If the Administration had placed as high a value on participation as it did on transparency, and if it had led with the same effort and experimentation that went into the transparency and data access objectives, public managers across the board would have increased their knowledge about dynamic ways of bringing the public into decision making. The impact could have been significant.

OPPORTUNITIES FOR PUBLIC MANAGERS

Although incomplete, the open government work does strengthen and enrich the relationship between government and citizens. Its influence on agencies, represented best by the twenty-three-member Open Government Working Group (the interagency task force leading OGD implementation), is driving increased availability of important, useful information for citizens. New channels, models, and spaces for interaction between policymakers and citizens are being opened and strengthened. The spirit of the OGD is fostering new tools and forums for joint work.

The OGD was described in some detail here because it is the most extensive federal effort at citizen engagement in this country to date. In this regard, it represents potential movement from our nation's historically nongovernmental approach to public participation to an approach that is initiated by, and embedded in, our government. It will also offer important object lessons about the practice of citizen engagement work for public managers, or for anyone wanting to extend and deepen his or her practice of citizen engagement. Because the open government work is under way in every agency in our federal government, public managers interested in building their citizen engagement practice will undoubtedly come in contact with and be able to build on these efforts.

It has taken decades to advance the practice of deliberation and meaningful citizen engagement at all levels of government. The same will be true for the principles, processes, and tools of the Open Government Initiative. As these trends mature, gain institutional footholds, and are incorporated into management and performance policies, the ability of citizens, elected officials, and public managers to govern together will be profoundly strengthened.

SEVEN STRATEGIES FOR BRINGING CITIZEN VOICE INTO GOVERNANCE

This book has argued that our democracy, founded on strong principles of self-governance, has lost its way on the journey to actualizing these principles. It has looked at the citizen engagement strategies our nation has tried, and offered a clear picture of a different path forward: a more robust way of engaging the public in decision making that not only will improve the effectiveness of our policies but also will help us reach the aspirations expressed in our founding documents.

The chapters that follow are the "how." They explore the many ways in which public managers, civic leaders, elected officials—or any interested parties—can design and implement strong citizen engagement opportunities that link the voices of the public to government decision making. A comprehensive engagement methodology is explored through seven specific strategies:

1. Know the context.
2. Link to decision makers.
3. Achieve diverse participation.
4. Create a safe public space.
5. Inform participants.
6. Discover shared priorities.
7. Sustain citizens' engagement.

These strategies are explored in detail: their importance in the context of current democratic practice, specific ways to undertake them, what they look like on the ground, and the public manager's role. Taken together, these chapters do not just lay out a practice methodology—they provide a strategic road map for rebuilding trust in government and strengthening our democracy.

CHAPTER FIVE

STRATEGY ONE: KNOW THE CONTEXT

Man is prisoner of his own way of thinking and of his own stereotypes of himself . . . This old world was characterized by the need to manage things . . . The new world is characterized by the need to manage complexity. Complexity is the very stuff of today's world.

STAFFORD BEER, 1975*

In authentic, high-impact citizen engagement processes, the voices of the people will directly affect important decisions. To have such an impact, the engagement work must be relevant, comprehensive, and targeted in its approach. This can be achieved only with a thorough and ongoing assessment of the context in which the citizen engagement will take place—that is, the significant demographics, history, economics, geography, leadership, institutional landscape, stakeholder interests, decision scenarios, and politics that are in play. An understanding of this full context must be deliberately applied when planning the citizen engagement initiative. This chapter explores the importance of knowing the context and presents case examples to illustrate how a full contextual analysis can be accomplished at the earliest stages of planning.

---

*Beer, S. "Thesis." *Platform for Change.* West Sussex, UK: John Wiley and Sons, 1975, 15.

WHY KNOWING THE CONTEXT IS IMPORTANT

In some respects, the importance of knowing the full context seems self-evident. Any leadership or management team worth its salt knows that you cannot develop viable plans or leverage desired resources unless you have an understanding of the context in which you are operating. But years of experience in the field of citizen engagement have repeatedly shown that in-depth contextual analyses are rare. Rather, the preparatory work for citizen engagement tends to be perfunctory or habit driven. It follows familiar paths and focuses on known constituent and stakeholder groups. It often shies away from an in-depth political analysis. To simplify logistics and implementation, it regularly prioritizes simplicity over complexity, sacrificing all the richness that would come from a detailed contextual analysis.

Because a quality contextual analysis provides the background for *every* aspect of an engagement process—from the makeup of the planning team to the sequence of the deliberation agenda— a cursory investigation can have quite a negative impact on the results. For example, if the work of citizens does not reflect the span of realities that constrain public officials' actions, that work can be easily brushed aside as uninformed or irrelevant. Further, decisions that have not taken account of and included all voices in the community will face immediate challenge as well as ongoing opposition or obstruction from those who were left out. This opposition can become particularly active in the realm of social media. As a result, policymakers can lose control of the discussion, and false information or misinformation can predominate. Finally, by not taking the full context into consideration, the effort may shortchange its own ability to deliver solutions. For every constituency that is not included in the process or every aspect of an issue that is not explored, potential solutions and their related opportunities are lost.

Olivia Ferriter of the U.S. Department of the Interior illustrated the point with this story: "I went to a workshop a few years ago in West Virginia where federal agencies, NGOs, partners from Columbia, South America, and the strip mining industry were discussing how to improve the habitat of cerulean warblers. It was a great workshop but, at the end of the day, we realized the land owners would be the ones to decide if they wanted a golf course, or trees planted on their property after strip mining . . . and they were not even in the room. You can't have a one-legged stool; you need support and participation from all the different sectors" (Ferriter 2012).

STRATEGIES FOR KNOWING THE CONTEXT

The context surrounding citizen engagement work exists simultaneously across several dimensions. Time is one very critical dimension. There can be little doubt that the life of a public policy issue is constantly shifting and evolving, and that these changes are informed by past and current events as well as ongoing expectations about the future. In the time it takes to go from conceptualization of a citizen engagement effort to its implementation, the landscape can change significantly: financial circumstances may shift due to predicted as well as unseen forces; elections and other political events may sweep out long-standing partners and bring in new ones; stakeholders adjust their priorities based on many considerations; and the intensity or urgency of an issue can rise or fall based on changing conditions and new technology or information. Because any shifts like these can have a direct impact on whether a citizen deliberation produces actionable results, a contextual assessment must, in addition to assessing the current state of affairs, take full account of the history of an issue and anticipate what events may create shifts as the work is in progress.

The assessment must take into account the significant demographics, geography, leadership, institutional landscape, traditional and nontraditional stakeholders, media outlets, decision scenarios, and politics. These last two in particular often encompass a formal aspect, such as the elected or appointed officials, as well as an informal aspect, such as the people who are locally known to have political or community influence though they hold no actual position.

A holistic assessment of the institutional landscape is also critical, including all of the organizations, large and small, public sector and private, that have a discernible relationship to the issue. Finally, because the media's role in information delivery is so central to the public's ability to participate in substantive discussions and make good decisions, the contextual analysis must include a thorough review of the relevant media outlets, including social media; their capacity; and how they have covered the issues under consideration.

The planning team for a citizen engagement initiative must pay close and ongoing attention to multiple data points along all of these dimensions to ensure that the work remains relevant and retains its potential for impact. A long-term federal manager in a regulatory agency made this point when he said: "If we do not have an idea of what all the stakeholders want when we write regulations, we are toast." Following are step-by-step strategies for identifying, gathering, and then using the contextual information.

IDENTIFYING THE INFORMATION

The full contextual analysis envisioned here hinges on a series of critical questions, such as the following: What is the history of the issue in the identified locality and in whatever political jurisdictions are affected—local, state, regional, national? Who are the leaders, key players, and affected constituencies, and what is their level of involvement, if any? What do the political, budgetary, and population landscapes look like? What are the geographic and institutional considerations? As noted earlier, it is not enough to simply answer these questions in the moment. To ensure that all bases are covered, each element of the context must be understood in terms of what has happened in the past, what the present conditions are, and what the range of future configurations might be. David Kuehn, Cochair of the Environmental Justice in Transportation Committee of the Transportation Research Board, summed it up this way: "In some cases, greater knowledge of communities and networks of relationships are the most important factors in designing and carrying out successful public engagement efforts. You may need to understand prior history with the community and the context in general because you cannot come in cold and expect to generate trust and high levels of engagement" (Kuehn 2012).

Naturally, the data that are gathered must be continuously monitored and updated throughout the planning, designing, and convening phases of the engagement work to ensure that they accurately reflect the current context. The matrix in Table 5.1 provides a way to conceptualize this task and organize the necessary information. Although this matrix no doubt goes beyond what an individual public manager might reasonably do in the course of planning for a public engagement initiative, it is presented in such detail here to give a "helicopter view" of the full

TABLE 5.1 MATRIX FOR CONTEXTUAL ANALYSIS

Contextual Component	Past	Present	Possible Future
The issue	• What is the history of the issue locally and more broadly? • What information has been made available about it in the past, and by whom?	• How is the issue described and understood? • Does it lend itself to a deliberative process? • What misinformation is circulating about this issue? • Which groups are providing current information?	• How might this issue be different in six months? One year? • What is the range of possible policy outcomes?
Key leaders and players	• Who were they? • What were their views? • What were their leverage points?	• Who are they? • What are their views? • What are their leverage points?	• Who might they be? • What will their views be? • What will be their possible leverage points?

(*Continued*)

Table 5.1 *(Continued)*

Contextual Component	Past	Present	Possible Future
Engaged sectors and constituencies	• Who were they? • What was the nature of their stake? • What leverage did they exert?	• Who are they? • What is the nature of their stake? • What leverage do they exert?	• Who might they be? • What will be the nature of their stake? • What leverage might they exert?
Not engaged (although affected) sectors and constituencies	• Who were they? • Why were they not engaged? • Did they have any leverage points?	• Who are they? • Why are they not engaged? • Do they have any leverage points?	• Who might they be? • Why might they not become engaged? • What possible leverage points might they have?
Political landscape	• Who held political power on this issue, and who was excluded from power? • From where was there pressure for change? • Who gained and lost as this issue's policy or budget framework evolved?	• Who has political power on this issue, and who does not? • From where is the pressure for change? • Who gains and loses as this issue's policy or budget framework evolves?	• Who might have political power on this issue, and who might not? • From where might the pressure for change come? • Who might gain and lose as this issue's policy or budget framework evolves? • From where might a future surprise emerge?

TABLE 5.1 *(Continued)*

Contextual Component	Past	Present	Possible Future
Budgetary landscape (both of the affected municipality and of the engagement initiative itself)	• What resources were vital to this issue? • What were the primary budgetary gaps and their consequences?	• What resources are vital to this issue, and who is providing them? • What is the state of the current budget as it pertains to this issue? • Who is financing the engagement work, and what is the significance of their involvement?	• What resources might this issue require? • Who will need to provide resources? • What will be the state of the budget as it pertains to this issue? • Can sustained engagement be financed in the future?
Population landscape	• What were the demographics of the full population?	• What are the demographics of the full population?	• What might be the demographic make-up of the population in future years?
Geographic considerations	• What were the geopolitical as well as the perceived boundaries?	• What are the geopolitical as well as the perceived boundaries?	• What might be the geopolitical as well as the perceived boundaries?
Institutional infrastructure	• What were the key institutions, and what roles did they play? • Which institutions were not involved, and why?	• What are the key institutions and their roles? • How and why has the institutional landscape changed?	• What will the landscape look like? • Why will it change (or not)?

(Continued)

TABLE 5.1 (*Continued*)

Contextual Component	Past	Present	Possible Future
Media landscape	• What was the composition of the media landscape (outlets, vehicles, predominant slants, individuals, resources)? • How was the issue reported across the media landscape?	• What is the current composition of the media landscape (outlets, vehicles, predominant slants, individuals, resources)? • What has changed from the past, and why? • Use and prevalence of traditional and new media; Internet access • How is the issue being reported across the media landscape?	• What might be the future composition of the media landscape (outlets, vehicles, predominant slants, individuals, resources)? • What is the anticipated use and prevalence of traditional and new media; Internet access? • How might the issue be reported across the media landscape in the future?

range of priority areas and questions. The matrix can easily be adapted to fit the specific circumstances.

Use of such a matrix ensures that all relevant information is gathered and that no important data are missed. Because every citizen engagement effort is unique, the most critical aspects of a contextual analysis will be different each time. As described in Chapter Three, for example, the dispersal of New Orleanians across the country post-Katrina meant that the historical population demographics were more vital to determining the citizen engagement initiative's participation targets than were the current demographics. In the California*Speaks* health care initiative, the political history of the issue, which included gubernatorial vetoes of single-payer health care legislation, had to be balanced with current polling that showed especially strong support for a single-payer system among specific subgroups of the population and in particular areas of the state.

In addition to highlighting the specific issues that are most salient for any given project, a comprehensive contextual analysis can provide a holistic view of the issue that is truly critical in today's complex and interconnected world. Even a cursory analysis of any of the major issues facing our society today—for example, our budget deficit, our climate, our health and education systems—quickly reveals that they cannot be resolved by any one sector alone, but will take a collaborative commitment from a wide range of players from all sectors.

Gathering the Information

Some of the information in the matrix is likely to be already known to individuals spearheading the citizen engagement work. Some of it, in particular the quantitative data, should be easily accessible through sources inside government or through external Internet resources. Beyond this, however, public managers seeking to "fill in" the matrix should anticipate the need to venture into the community in a series of group and individual discussions aimed at surfacing critical and nuanced information about the landscape.

For example, in preparation for the first Citizen Summit in Washington, DC, America*Speaks* held more than fifty of these exploratory meetings, working with organizations and citizens in every ward of the city to discover their views and priorities. Although this was an unusually large number of preliminary meetings, due to the completely broken state of governance in the District at the time, they served an important dual purpose: they not only brought in critical contextual information for planning but also advised the community about the upcoming citizen engagement initiative and helped citizens begin to get committed to participating. It is important to note that under appropriate circumstances, exploratory meetings like these can also be done on the phone or through electronic methods.

USING THE INFORMATION

What is done with contextual information once it has been gathered? The information is used to inform virtually every aspect of the citizen engagement work, from determining who is part of the planning team to deciding how the discussion content should be framed and what the best timing for the deliberation would be. The analysis helps determine the substance and presentation of the informational materials and agenda, and is the basis for the participant recruitment strategy, the media engagement work, the approach to key decision makers, and the selection of the venue, among other components. All of this work is discussed in detail in upcoming chapters.

In addition to shaping the engagement process, an extensive contextual analysis is an excellent vehicle for public education. As already described, public managers may tend to focus on their known world. However, they are not the only ones to fall prey to this habit. Everyday citizens do the same. It is simply human nature to want to stay within our comfort zones; to focus on what we know from our own particular vantage point. And yet, to participate effectively in high-stakes decision making, citizens must have a broad-based understanding of the issue and the affected groups. As noted earlier, the process by which contextual information is gathered is therefore also an opportunity for heightening awareness and understanding about the issues among potential participants. It encourages them to develop a more comprehensive view of the opportunities as well as the constraints. The case study that follows elaborates on this mutually reinforcing information-gathering strategy.

KNOWING THE CONTEXT: A CASE STUDY

The sixteen counties that make up the Northeast Ohio region have faced some daunting challenges. Home to more than four million people, in the early 2000s the area lagged far behind the country in job growth, wages, and many other facets of economic opportunity. The big cities—Cleveland, Akron, Canton, and Youngstown—had experienced significant losses in manufacturing jobs, which resulted in enormous budget shortfalls and steep population declines over two and a half decades. Between 1980 and 2005, for example, Cleveland alone lost more than one hundred thousand manufacturing jobs—42.5 percent of its manufacturing employment—and overall it was gaining jobs at a rate of less than one-quarter of the national rate; wage increases were about one-third of the national average (Atkins et al. 2011). Efforts to address these and other substantial concerns were plagued by leadership challenges in both the private and public sectors. An additional complication was the fact that the region's over five hundred political jurisdictions often acted parochially.

In June 2005 the Fund for Our Economic Future stepped into this situation, sponsoring Voices & Choices, which at the time was the most extensive citizen-based regional planning effort to be undertaken in the United States. A partnership among the fund (itself an unprecedented collaboration among over eighty philanthropic organizations from across Northeast Ohio), America*Speaks*, and the Universities Collaborative, Voices & Choices would, over the next eighteen months, directly engage more than twenty-one thousand people across sixteen counties in setting an action agenda to revitalize their region's ailing economy. Through this initiative, citizens would identify the region's strengths, pinpoint and prioritize its most persistent challenges, and brainstorm solutions.

Voices & Choices incorporated more than three thousand citizen interviews; 1,200 leaders participated in interactive workshops and summits; 13,500 citizens engaged in local community conversations; 1,700 expressed their views through engaging in an online survey called a Choicebook; 1,650 participated in regional town meetings; and hundreds of thousands were engaged in the conversation through a range of media strategies. Voices & Choices produced a clear agenda for regional development, uniting the people of Northeast Ohio behind a collective commitment that was responsive to hard economic realities. More specifically, the initiative developed shared views on the region's six most pressing challenges:

- Training workers for current and future jobs
- Improving racial inclusion and income equality
- Attracting and growing businesses

- Reducing government fragmentation and inefficiency
- Ensuring equitable school funding and accountability
- Reducing sprawl and improving regional connectivity

Across these six challenges, twenty specific goals and forty-nine solutions were developed based on citizen input and expert refinement. At a culminating town meeting, citizens assessed the slate of goals and solutions and established their priorities. Finally, in creating the regional action plan, the initiative built an extensive network of citizens and leaders who would remain engaged, and eventually established Advance Northeast Ohio, which continues to serve as the coordinator of the region's economic competitiveness agenda.

Rather than exploring these remarkable accomplishments, this chapter offers Voice & Choices as a case study because of some of the initiative's lesser-known work: the early activities aimed at generating an understanding of the full context in which the citizen engagement would subsequently take place. Reflecting on both successes and missteps, the case study clearly shows the importance of an in-depth analysis of key contextual elements and how a deliberate and broad-based information-gathering process can contribute to that analysis. A less robust contextual analysis would have meant missing unique opportunities that were critical to the eventual impact of citizens' voices on priorities and strategies for revitalizing the region.

Assessing the Leadership Context

Given the very large number of cities, towns, and villages in Northeast Ohio, one of the most important tasks in understanding the context for Voices & Choices was to develop an accurate picture of the leadership landscape. As it turned out, this landscape was rather unusual. Unlike many regional development efforts that are spurred by local government and business leaders or by a regional planning commission, Voices & Choices was completely initiated by the philanthropic sector. More than eighty philanthropies (acting together as the Fund for Our Economic Future) launched, led, and funded the citizen engagement work. The Fund also supported development of an economic dashboard, and made numerous grants to emerging businesses. To be sure, the region was enormously fortunate in the depth and commitment of its local philanthropic leadership. However, the philanthropic sector's role also signaled their recognition of a significant leadership vacuum in the political and business sectors.

And, in fact, analysis of the political and business sectors in Northeast Ohio revealed that strong leadership in the region had been lacking for decades. The two-term Republican governor, along with Republican majorities since 1994 in the state house and senate, had not treated the economic challenges of Northeast Ohio with the sense of urgency and creativity that was required given the structural changes in the economy that continued to erode the role of manufacturing there. Exacerbating this problem, as noted earlier, was the fact that the region's multiple political jurisdictions (cities, counties, towns, and villages) had grown accustomed to acting unilaterally, making it extremely challenging to pinpoint effective regional-level leadership. On the business side, leadership was equally sparse. Whereas in 1983 Cleveland had been "home to the headquarters of 12 Fortune 500 companies, including manufacturers of steel, paint, and appliances, Standard Oil of Ohio, and American Greetings" (Atkins et al. 2011, 7), by 2011 only five Fortune 500 corporate headquarters remained ("FORTUNE 500: Our Annual Ranking of America's Largest Corporations" 2012). Following the departure of key corporations, a new set of business leaders with a strong regional vision had not emerged in their place. This analysis of the regional leadership landscape became a driving force in shaping Voices & Choices. Early workshops that engaged more than one thousand cross-sector leaders (detailed later in this chapter) were specifically designed both to get a better understanding of—and begin to address—the identified leadership gaps and to create an opportunity for these leaders to develop their collective views on the six citizen-identified challenges facing the region.

But although the analysis and leadership workshops proved very effective in this regard, the Voices & Choices steering committee, principally Fund members, failed to conduct a similarly self-reflective analysis of the leadership of the initiative itself. After determining that the region lacked a solid base of strong, high-level political and business leaders, the Fund decided to go forward without identifying potential leaders from these sectors to join the steering committee. They chose to wait until a later time to expand the team, limiting it initially to member philanthropies, and the two organizations contracted to do the on-the-ground work and analysis. Even though this decision streamlined the immediate work, in the long run it had negative consequences. America*Speaks* sought to shift the steering committee's approach as the initiative reached its final months, unsuccessfully suggesting that the full set of leaders who *could* influence the economic development of the region, and who would without a doubt play an important role in the implementation of recommendations, be included. Yet it was not until months after Voices & Choices was completed that the business and political leaders who would be critical to implementation were eventually brought into the leadership of the initiative. The late addition meant that the transition from engagement to implementation was slowed by almost a year. A contextual analysis that had included a full and open assessment of the impact of the steering committee's composition could have prevented such unnecessary implementation delays.

Assessing the Geographic Context

In *Reflections on Regionalism*, the Brookings Institution's Bruce Katz notes that academics, corporate leaders, and political activists alike are increasingly identifying the critical role of regions in our society. He says "more and more of us travel across city, county, even state borders every morning on our way to work. Our television, radio, and print media rely on a regional marketplace. Our businesses, large and small, depend on suppliers, workers, and customers who rarely reside in a single jurisdiction. The parks, riverfronts, stadia, and museums we visit draw from, and provide an identity to, an area much larger than a single city. The fumes, gases, chemicals, and run-off that pollute our air and water have no regard for municipal boundaries" (Katz 2000, 1). Defining a region tends to require a mix of data-based decision making, intuition, and flexibility. This turned out to be quite true in Northeast Ohio.

In the early development of Voices & Choices, the planning body had defined the Northeast Ohio region as consisting of fourteen counties surrounding the major urban hubs of Cleveland, Akron, Canton, and Youngstown. These boundaries had been drawn based on an alignment of shared interests, employment patterns, the existing economic engines, and a sense that the general public as well as existing leaders in those areas defined themselves as connected.

However, as staff fanned out into the region to collect data about the context through leadership meetings, community-based gatherings, and individual interviews, it became clear that several adjacent counties identified with the region and had an equal and compelling interest in the work. Leaders from these counties began, in fact, to lobby for their inclusion in the effort. The steering committee quickly recognized that given these leaders' commitment and interest, and given that a significant portion of

FIGURE 5.1 VOICES & CHOICES CLOSELY ASSESSED THE GEOGRAPHY
OF THE REGION

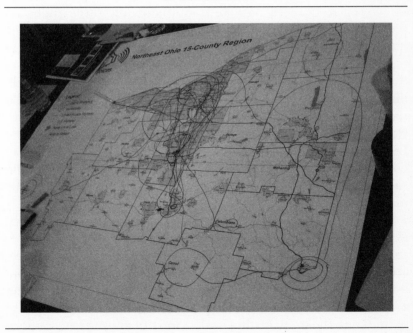

the population in these counties was employed in the already-designated region, it would strengthen the project to add them. This is an excellent example of how the contextual analysis reshaped a core element of the work: in this case, the geographic boundaries of the initiative.

Information-Gathering Strategies

In conceptualizing Voices & Choices, the Fund for Our Economic Future sought to find a few critical leverage points whereby investment could build on regional assets and stand a reasonable chance of having a positive impact on the economy. To ensure the integrity of the citizen engagement process, it would be important not to impose the priorities of the steering committee by predefining these potential investment opportunities, but rather to organize the deliberation around citizens' views on these questions. Three initial activities designed to gather these views were: cross-generational and cross-geographic one-on-one interviews; leadership workshops held in geographic clusters; and a large-scale public deliberation.

Voices & Choices recruited approximately three thousand people from across the sixteen counties to participate in the interviews. "Appreciative inquiry," an asset-based approach to organizational development and strategic planning,[1] was used as the interviewing technique. Although the interviews were self-directed, they were intended to solicit specific input on the region's assets, strengths, and core values as well as on citizens' vision for the future. Following the interviews, a team from the Levin College of Urban Affairs at Cleveland State University randomly selected 1,006 interviews, proportionally representing each county and its demographics, for analysis, and identified the major themes.

While these interviews were under way, eleven leadership workshops—each involving approximately one hundred participants—were held across the region. The workshops were geographically clustered and had cross-sector participation from the faith, nonprofit, business, education, and government communities. Because the workshops were organized around local boundaries, the participating leaders were operating in a comfortable setting: near home and with people they were likely to know. This safe and positive experience built relationships and laid important groundwork for the initiative's ultimate challenge to participants: devising regional goals and plans with people they might *not* know. The full America*Speaks* participatory technology, with a computer at every table and a keypad in every hand, enabled planners to distill important themes across the eleven leadership workshops.

It is important to note that although the interviews and leadership workshops were essential to the contextual analysis and contributed information to begin building the initiative's agenda, they simultaneously served two additional purposes. First, they began to build a network of leaders and citizens who would commit to ongoing participatory work. Second, they helped lay the foundation for a sense of regional identity and common community across the usual divides of geography, age, race, and economic status. All of this would make the planned deliberations among diverse citizens that much more effective.

USING THE INFORMATION

Planners used the data gathered from the interviews and leadership workshops as the basis for the initiative's first regional town meeting, in which 750 people prioritized the challenges and assets of the region. Those results informed the next phases of the engagement process, which focused on developing solutions. In one notable instance, the path from information gathering to prioritization yielded unexpected results.

Analysis of the sixteen-county region had revealed that, as in other regions throughout the United States, institutional structures and practices had left minorities in Northeast Ohio disproportionately affected by such negative trends as stagnant school funding, limits in access to quality health care, and overall racial segregation and discrimination. Although the steering committee for Voices & Choices had acknowledged the importance of these concerns early on, these leaders also believed that issues related to economic justice would have to be "forced" onto the larger citizen engagement agenda because the majority population in the region would not identify them as a priority. However, to the surprise and satisfaction of the steering committee, these issues *were* consistently raised during the interviews and leadership workshops, and achieving racial and economic justice emerged as citizens' second highest priority in the regional town meeting.

This is an excellent example of how the results that can be achieved through deliberative engagement are different from those that come from opinion polling. Had the initiative not included early mechanisms for getting a more complete and accurate reading of the context, leaders might have continued to believe they had to push this issue onto the agenda, not recognizing that the public already held it as a high priority. As a result, in the implementation phase of Voices & Choices, leaders discovered they had greater traction when it came to action steps on racial and economic justice because the public had prioritized the issue independently. It was a wonderful example of linking public will with the political will of the leadership team to create a strong constituency to confront systemic economic inequities.

Another example of how information gathering directly informed the content for the deliberation was in relation to the region's history of "brain drain." As was true across many distressed rust belt states, the best and brightest young people were leaving Northeast Ohio at a rapid rate, either to attend college elsewhere or to find a job once they graduated from a local college or university. To gain insight into this phenomenon, planners identified eighteen- to thirty-year-olds as a key group for information gathering and engaged people from this demographic group to conduct interviews with their peers. Analysis of the interview data indeed confirmed that "very few people named job opportunities as an asset the region possesses. Still fewer young people, the very group that the region hopes to attract and retain, feel that job opportunities in the area are strong" (Chupp 2005, 21). In the end, two of the most widely supported recommendations from Voices & Choices were linked to this information: making postsecondary education more affordable and accessible, and improving workforce training programs. Digging more deeply into an aspect of the context that had not been fully understood proved to be powerful. The information gathered had a lasting impact throughout the life of the project.

Knowing the context and intentionally gathering data throughout the life of the project were critical ingredients in the success of Voices & Choices. By understanding the public's basic views and positions before the deliberative work took place, the initiative was able to address key topic areas that might otherwise have been overlooked, such as the relationship between quality elementary education and a robust economy and the link between a clean environment and quality of life, among others. In addition, grounding the content in the views of citizens gave Voices & Choices a level of credibility it would not have had if the agenda had been driven exclusively by the steering committee. Finally, the contextual analysis reshaped the planned geographic parameters of the initiative. Without on-the-ground exploration of the identified region and, critically, an openness to modifying the original plans based on the outcomes of this exploration, the initiative would have excluded important leaders and population groups. This case study also illustrates how creative citizen engagement strategies—in this instance, appreciative inquiry interviews and leadership workshops that began to bring citizens into the larger process—can be a core part of the contextual analysis.

THE PUBLIC MANAGER'S ROLE IN KNOWING THE CONTEXT

The Voices & Choices initiative was citizen engagement on a truly large scale. To be sure, this level of effort may be beyond what a public manager is likely to undertake and accomplish in the context of his or her work. Recognizing this, the case study presented was intended not to suggest replication, but rather to offer inspiration and encourage adaptations that incorporate the underlying strategies and best practices that have been shown to increase the quality of citizen engagement. In many contexts, starting small is wise. But regardless of the scope of the effort, approaching the contextual analysis in an active and comprehensive way will help ensure that the planning process leads to the best possible outcomes.

As alluded to earlier in this chapter, the challenge for public managers in this regard is largely one of habit or discipline.

Although most managers are accustomed to undertaking "environmental scans" on an issue, too few routinely go beyond mapping out the familiar stakeholders and assessing current leaders' views on the issues. Further, because the great majority of public managers are career civil servants, undertaking explicitly political analyses, although certainly appropriate in nonelectoral contexts, is not common practice. Finally, most public managers rarely venture into the community to interview citizens and community groups as a way to gain a more robust understanding of the context surrounding an issue that is slated for public engagement. And yet all of this work is precisely what is needed.

Another habit, or subconscious practice, that leads to inadequate contextual analysis is taking too narrow a view of an issue. It is natural for people who are immersed in a problem for a long time to define the boundaries of the context in a way that is familiar to them and reduces complexity and "the unknown." Standard training in problem-solving methods reinforces this tendency, generally teaching that the most direct route to a solution is to simplify scenarios wherever possible. Again, this is the opposite of what is necessary in planning and executing robust citizen engagement processes and for solving intractable issues. Further, the more complex the issue, the more important it is to resist the temptation to simplify. Because simplifying takes away the richness and variability of a situation, it increases the probability that things will go wrong, or that there will be unwanted surprises. In *Managing the Unexpected: Resilient Performance in an Age of Uncertainty*, Karl E. Weick and Kathleen M. Sutcliffe (2007) present a detailed rationale for learning to live with and embrace complexity rather than simplifying problems. The reluctance to simplify, they find, is a characteristic of organizations that are both highly reliable and resilient.

Therese McMillan of the Federal Transit Administration recounted her own experience with managing complexity while doing public engagement work:

> It's important not to run from complexity, but rather to interpret and manage it. This lesson was brought home to me in a public engagement session in Detroit, as I watched our opening presentation and realized that participants' confused expressions and distracted body language meant we were not connecting with them. At the end of the session, I stood up and said,

"we blew it today," and I asked people to share their experiences. One person said: "You lost me four slides in; I just couldn't follow what you were saying." After that honest exchange, we re-tooled our presentation. In addition to clarifying information, we took a close look at all of the technical details. We took out those that were not critical, but we were very careful not to take out so many that issues would be misrepresented in any way. We struck a better balance [McMillan 2012].

A brief reference to systems theory also helps illustrate this point. In any federal agency there are a series of program offices and, within each, a number of work units. Each of these units is simultaneously a subsystem of a larger unit and a suprasystem of a smaller unit. If the issue for resolution is how four work units can solve conflicts and collaborate more effectively, instead of simply focusing on those four, an alternative strategy would be to move up a level and examine the entire program in which the work units exist. Are there dynamics or rules or practices that might have an impact on the problem from that perspective? What are leverage points that would have influence? Equally valuable would be to move down a level and look at the individuals within the teams to determine who is most capable of solving the problem and what authority and resources they would need to do it. Instead of focusing purely on the four units in question, embracing a more systemic analysis can surface surprising and creative solutions.

Asking a broader range of strategic questions along the lines of those offered in the matrix presented earlier in this chapter, and being willing to physically venture into affected communities to listen to people, are the high-impact strategies public managers need to embrace. To be sure, pushing practice outside the usual boundaries in this way will require both intentionality and discipline. Yet public managers who are energized to demonstrably increase the impact and value of their citizen engagement practice will have to step up to these challenges. Individual efforts can generate a multiplier effect. By fully accounting for the context, citizen engagement work will achieve more compelling results that, in turn, will increase interest in replication across the country. Replication will help institutionalize a new role for citizens in our governance.

Public Manager Perspectives

The Light Brown Apple Moth and the Importance of Knowing the Context

Jane Berkow, lead strategic planner, Animal and Plant Health Inspection Service, U.S. Department of Agriculture

The Context

The Animal and Plant Health Inspection Service (APHIS) at the U.S. Department of Agriculture seeks to protect and promote U.S. agricultural health. In particular, as a regulating agency, APHIS seeks to keep out—or contain and, if possible, eliminate—exotic pests that can have a significant, negative economic impact on local agriculture and domestic and international trade. APHIS works in partnership with state departments of agriculture to accomplish its mission by providing scientific expertise and federal funding to the state. APHIS's work can be particularly challenging in urban areas, where the methods to eradicate an exotic pest can face substantial public opposition.

In spring 2007 APHIS confirmed the detection of the light brown apple moth (LBAM), a pest not native to this country, in Alameda County, California. Given the extensive host range of this pest, APHIS was concerned that it would have a significant impact on U.S. agriculture and the environment if the pest's population were allowed to grow unchecked. The California Department of Food and Agriculture (CDFA), working closely with APHIS, intensively surveyed the area to determine the extent of the infestation. Surveys indicated that the pest was primarily in residential and urban areas throughout a six-county area stretching from Monterey County in the south to Alameda County in the northeast, just a short distance from the rich and fertile agricultural production areas of the Salinas Valley and the San Joaquin Valley.

Operating on scientific knowledge of the insect's biology and considering the fact that any treatment would have to be applied in and around areas where people lived and worked, CDFA and APHIS determined that the aerial release of a mating disruption pheromone would be the most effective method to eliminate the insect from this area. The pheromone was designed to disrupt the moth's mating cycle and to cause a swift population decline, as the moths would be unable to reproduce. The U.S. Environmental Protection Agency had determined that the LBAM pheromone is safe, with no adverse impact on public health or the environment, and therefore it could be applied aerially over residential areas. Prior to initiating activities to distribute the pheromone, CDFA conducted a considerable number of meetings (with local and elected officials and the public) and distributed informational materials throughout the affected areas to notify local officials and citizens of the threat the moth posed to California agriculture and the environment, and the steps that would be taken to eliminate it.

To APHIS's surprise, the public's reaction to the plan to aerially disperse a benign pheromone was intensely negative. A small group of concerned citizens quickly made use of social media—a newly emerging technology—to create the appearance of a groundswell of opposition. In a very short period of time, this small group of citizens effectively used the Internet to form a sophisticated opposition network. Not anticipating such a response, CDFA and APHIS were unable to stop the rapid spread of misinformation about the pheromone and allegations that the moth posed little or no threat to

California's agricultural and natural resources. Agricultural producers, normally APHIS's primary stakeholders, partners, and vocal supporters in these situations, went silent in the face of this opposition. Although they were supportive of APHIS's plans to contain the moth and keep domestic and foreign commodity markets open, they, too, were unsure how to respond, especially because they wanted to maintain good relations with this group of energized citizens who were also their neighbors.

Lessons Learned and Changes to Agency Practices

The events surrounding the detection of the light brown apple moth in the California Bay Area created a watershed moment for APHIS. In the past, the science behind the strategy to deal with a pest outbreak had been enough to reassure the public that something needed to be done. No longer was that true. In this situation, the science didn't matter, and we quickly realized that we had to give greater consideration to the public's willingness to accept a particular solution—regardless of the scientific, economic, and environmental feasibility of that solution. And despite the large number of public meetings we had with local officials and the public, we realized that we had spent most of our time talking to people about what we planned to do rather than engaging them in a dialogue on this issue. Taking these lessons on board, the agency has since shifted its practice in some important ways:

- *Giving greater consideration to the types of pest management solutions from the perspective of the people on whom our actions will have an impact.* From a scientific perspective, the decision to aerially disperse the pheromone made sense, and the agency assumed the public would find the scientific basis for the strategy to be reasonable. What we learned after the fact, or perhaps what we knew but didn't stop to consider at the time, is that aerial spraying of any substance over densely populated areas—especially areas with a high degree of environmental consciousness—would raise serious concerns about public health effects and harm to the environment. It might be an effective way to quickly disperse treatments over extensive tracts of agricultural and forested land, but it wasn't politically acceptable in a residential or urban context. APHIS now works to more actively solicit, identify, and consider the perspectives and perceptions of the individuals in an affected area—including the types of solutions they are willing to accept—prior to determining a tactical response to the problem.

- *Moving the conversation to where the people are.* Managers and staff in APHIS are working to become adept users of social media—both in consistently tracking what is out there relative to our mission and in proactively using these media to showcase our work, raise issues, answer questions, and build new relationships. In addition, APHIS has set up user-friendly websites, such as HungryPests.com, that provide a more engaging and interactive approach to education about pests and pest management efforts. Beyond providing useful information, these sites include action steps individual citizens and groups can take. The new sites are getting much more traffic than APHIS's main website.

- *Scanning the context more broadly.* As a result of the LBAM experience, we know that when we propose a response to a pest we must comb the stakeholder environment much more extensively than we ever did before to make sure we reach both traditional and nontraditional stakeholders. No stone can be left unturned in terms of who might possibly be affected and what our responses should be.

- *Developing new partners.* Because increasing numbers of pest detections have an impact on suburban and urban residents, in addition to those who live or work in agricultural areas, APHIS now considers a wide array of potential partners—from traditional stakeholders, such as agricultural producers and other regulatory agencies, to more unconventional organizations that may not appear at first glance to be aligned with our mission, goals, or objectives. For example, we have established new working relationships with the Nature Conservancy and local community leadership groups, among others.
- *Changing management expectations.* Executive management in the agency now routinely sets the expectation for program managers to conduct the broadest contextual analyses possible and to consider stakeholder input when developing pest management strategies.
- *Remembering that government is "of the people, by the people, for the people."* For years APHIS has successfully led efforts to eliminate pests that threaten agriculture and the environment. But in the last decade, the rapidly changing political and social landscape, coupled with the emergence of the Internet and social media, have given the American public a stronger voice in directing the role of government. In response, before determining action, APHIS now actively seeks to gauge the public's interest in an issue and strives to understand their willingness to seek federal assistance in resolving a situation.

CHAPTER SIX

STRATEGY TWO: LINK TO DECISION MAKERS

You can't see people when they answer polls; but you could see people at CaliforniaSpeaks. Governor Schwarzenegger was standing there when the live video of other sites came in on satellite feed from across the state. It was real. He could look at people face-to-face and ask them for their help in trying to achieve something on health care reform.

HERB SHULTZ, SENIOR HEALTH POLICY ADVISER, OFFICE OF THE GOVERNOR OF CALIFORNIA, 2011*

Citizen deliberations can change the terms and outcomes of decision making, the shape and content of a policy or plan, and the way dollars are allocated in a budget. Whatever the subject matter, people will seriously engage in the process only if they believe they can have a real impact. Their sense of agency is critical. To achieve such an impact, the work must have the buy-in of key decision makers and be directly connected to "live" governance processes (that is, where a decision is actually pending). If not, citizens' time and effort are at risk of being misused, even wasted, and the compounding loss of faith in the process will further erode public trust. This chapter explores the importance of linking citizen engagement work to decision makers, including, but not limited to, elected leaders. It presents case examples to

---

*America*Speak*s. "California*Speaks*: Working Together for Better Health Care." [http://americaspeaks.org/resources/videos/], 2007.

illustrate how this can be accomplished, and reviews the particular challenges and opportunities for public managers who will be designing the connections among citizens, stakeholders, and decision makers.

WHY LINKING TO DECISION MAKERS IS IMPORTANT

My personal experiences have led me to understand why linking citizen engagement to decision makers is so important. As I noted in the Preface to this book, in 1994, after more than ten years of working at high levels of state and national government, I was no longer able to quell my concerns about the complete disconnect I routinely observed between citizens and their elected officials. This disconnect not only resulted in missed opportunities for collaborative, high-quality decision making but also reflected a huge gap between the core ideals of our democracy and the actual practice of government.

To more deeply understand this problem, I left my position at the White House and traveled the country for several months, talking with scores of people about their views on, and experiences with, public engagement. Among the various reasons people cited for their lack of interest in civic participation, by far the most dominant was that they were certain their efforts would not make a difference—that nobody was listening.

Scanning the field of deliberative democracy at the time, it was apparent that most of the methods in use were focused on quality public deliberation, but they did not place a high priority on ensuring decision makers were listening, and that participants could therefore have an impact on the issues in real time. In fact, the opposite theory was commonplace: that engagement work should be conducted independent of decision makers to avoid any undue influence by them on the discussion.

To be sure, conducting participatory work that is independent of decision makers could prevent real or perceived undue influence. And there is certainly inherent value in people getting together and talking, regardless of whether or not the discussion is connected to a live decision-making process. People learn through these experiences; they come to understand difficult issues in a broader context, appreciate differences in perspective, and open themselves up to community problem solving. But I knew from my experience as chief of staff to Ohio governor Dick Celeste that without a direct connection to decision-making processes, citizens' deliberations have little or no impact on policy or on budget choices.

In my role, I received a steady stream of information about citizens' views from a wide range of nongovernmental organizations. In most cases, these organizations were advocacy groups sharing polling data to bolster their respective positions. Although the issues identified were often quite important to the state, the information had to be treated as reflecting special interest positions. In those cases in which the information did not come from an advocacy group, very often the background information and questions given to the public for deliberation did not fully encompass key aspects of the issue that had to be resolved in the political process. In the end, if the work of citizens did not reflect the real context in which public officials would be taking action, the views were easily brushed aside as uninformed or irrelevant.

These combined experiences helped me understand that for the collective voice of the people to make a real difference in public policy it must be explicitly linked to live governance processes—early and consistently. Decision makers and their staff must be engaged in the framing of the issue, the development of the materials and agenda for the deliberation, as well as the event itself. This is *not* so that they can dominate or control the process, but rather to secure a commitment to action that they can then uphold because the recommendations are viable in real-world contexts and fully integrated with existing legal and operational frameworks. To be sure, decision makers will never commit to everything that is on the table, nor should they. But real agency for citizens requires decision makers' commitment that the process—and its results—will have some demonstrable impact on how the issue moves forward. Tony Faast of the U.S. Fish and Wildlife Service explained it this way: "It is imperative to link citizen engagement to the highest levels of decision making in the agency so that the processes are supported. Agency leaders are in a unique position to think about and take action on the big picture" (Faast 2012).

Strategies for Linking to Decision Makers

Every decision maker—and decision-making context—is unique. However, the following principles and strategies can help ensure an effective link, in just about any circumstance, between the citizens engaging on significant issues and the decision makers who are responsible for addressing those concerns.

- *Elected leaders and top decision makers must make a public commitment to action.* The governor, mayor, member of Congress, senator, agency secretary, or director responsible for the issue must be fully and visibly committed to taking action on the outcomes of the deliberation. If the public knows their collective decisions will be acted on, they are more than willing to put in the necessary time and effort. Equally important, a leader's visible commitment to citizen participation on the toughest issues facing the jurisdiction will refute the assertion by the media and prospective participants that the deliberative event is merely window dressing or a photo opportunity. One strategy for demonstrating such commitment is for top-level decision makers to make themselves available to the public for questions and answers both before and after a deliberation through live, in-person appearances, Internet chat, or the use of other media. California governor Arnold Schwarzenegger held a press conference to announce his commitment to incorporating the results of an upcoming health care reform deliberation into legislation.
- *High-level officials must participate in the planning process.* All of the people or departments with expertise in, accountability for, and influence over the selected issues must be present or represented at critical junctures throughout the planning process. Their participation is crucial to informing and framing the presentation of the substantive issues and to developing an acceptable range of options for public decision making. Their role is to inform and advise so that the process remains aligned with political and contextual realities. They do not exert control over the outcomes, but rather clarify the

legal and "real-world" parameters in which the engagement must take place.

- *Planners as well as participants in the initiative must have access to official data and information.* To arrive at recommendations that are viable, participants must have access to the same data and information that decision makers will use in their own assessments. The relevant government entities must not only make that information available but also actively participate on the team that develops the materials citizens will use to inform their deliberations. This idea is explored more fully in Chapter Nine. Technological advances coupled with new government efforts to make data and information more widely available and accessible to the public can facilitate achieving this goal.

- *Top decision makers must be visible in the participant recruitment process.* Successful participant recruitment hinges on the top decision maker(s) lending an official "stamp of approval" to the deliberation. Equally important is the endorsement of appropriate business and nonprofit leaders and other key community stakeholders. Such visibility may include having the person's name and endorsement appear prominently on fliers, advertisements, and email blasts; their endorsement can also be included in public statements and appearances. Washington, DC, mayor Anthony Williams used drive-time radio interviews to call for public participation in an upcoming deliberation on the city's strategic plan; New Orleans mayor Ray Nagin lent his voice to "robo calls" that invited citizens in diaspora cities to participate in post-Katrina recovery deliberations. In each instance, a leader's public declaration of the desire to hear from people about their views—as well as a commitment to acting on them—helped build the necessary credibility with citizens and the media.

- *Top decision makers must be present at the deliberation.* The top decision maker, or his or her credible representative, must be in the room as citizens are deliberating. This does not, and should not, require speeches or other intensive leadership. Being present is simply the powerful symbol that states: "I am here and listening." In this way, the public's efforts to respectfully explore their differences will not be just a story told after the fact, but rather a visceral experience that energizes the decision maker and gives him or her a new understanding of the public's commitment and capabilities. During a 3,500-person, multisite deliberation on health care reform in California, Governor Arnold Schwarzenegger, pictured in Figure 6.1 in Los Angeles, spent the day listening to participants deliberate and changed his proposal on health care reform as a result.

FIGURE 6.1 CALIFORNIA GOVERNOR ARNOLD SCHWARZENEGGER PARTICIPATES IN A TABLE DISCUSSION DURING CALIFORNIA*SPEAKS*

During an initial, New York City–based deliberation in the wake of the 9/11 terrorist attacks, Stephen Heintz, President of the Rockefeller Brothers Fund, had an experience that also demonstrates the importance of ensuring leaders are in the room. Heintz had been randomly assigned to the same table as a man who had worked as a janitor in the World Trade Center. After listening to the man's story and hearing his views on rebuilding priorities and strategies, Heintz said:

"What became so clear to me was the fact that the lives of ordinary people are not adequately understood or talked about by those of us in decision-making circles. We tend to lose touch with these experiences. It made me see very clearly that these circles must be substantially broader—that they have to comprise the full community. All voices have to have an opportunity to influence the outcomes" (Heintz 2012). When decision makers and leaders participate in these events and hear citizens speak, unfiltered by media or staff analysis, the learning for them can be transformative. As is true for all of us, it is actual—not secondhand—experiences that enable us to change our mind-set and dramatically shift our perception of reality.

- *Follow-up work must be transparent and timely.* Transparent communication, both during and after the deliberation, is critical to maintaining credibility with the public and holding decision makers accountable for the commitments they have made. Accomplishing this communication entails determining at the outset who will do the following: (1) analyze the data that come from the public, (2) objectively synthesize the information for key themes, and (3) pass this information through the necessary internal points of review and prepare it for top-level consideration. After the deliberation, communicating the results to all participants, stakeholders, and the media in real time is crucial. And, most important, decision makers must communicate their responses and action plans as soon as these have been determined.

Attending to these steps and conditions in the development of a citizen engagement initiative will firmly connect decision makers to the process and the outcomes. As a result, the work can yield policy priorities, resource decisions, and planning options that are actionable. The public will know that their voices have made a difference.

LINKING TO DECISION MAKERS: A CASE STUDY

The Washington, DC Citizen Summits held between 1999 and 2005 constituted the longest-running series of large-scale town meetings in the United States. Over a six-year period more than thirteen thousand people reflecting the city's demographic diversity participated in a series of deliberations with their fellow residents. Their efforts significantly influenced the District's priorities, legislative actions, and annual spending in regard to education, housing, economic growth and development, public safety, and other key concerns. One of the critical success factors in the Citizen Summits was the way in which the city's complex web of leadership was fully engaged in the process.

By the mid-1990s Washington, DC, had become a city that was completely broken. The municipality was $700 million in debt, and decades of corruption and mismanagement had led to an epic failure of governance as well as pervasive distrust of the city's leadership by its citizens. In 1995 a congressionally mandated financial control board and an appointed chief financial officer (CFO) took over governance of the city's finances. Under this system the elected mayor reported to the CFO, and the control board had the power to override decisions made by the DC City Council. It also had the authority to oversee the District's budget, veto legislation, and appoint senior officials. It was the equivalent of putting the elected government of the District of Columbia under conservatorship because democracy was bankrupt.

In 1998 the control board's CFO, Anthony Williams, decided to run for mayor on a platform of government accountability and improved service. As a career public servant rather than a politician, Williams rejected many traditional campaign strategies, and instead spent a great deal of time in each of the District's neighborhoods holding listening sessions with citizens. Through this process, Williams discovered commonalities across what were largely believed to be intractable socioeconomic and geographic divides in the city. Once elected, Mayor Williams determined to continue what he had started and build hope in the District's future by actively engaging the community in governance. He knew that if the public could experience what he had experienced while campaigning, they would discover that the great majority of the city's people cared about the same things. He set out to give them that opportunity, and to prove that government would listen to and act on what residents had to say.

Given citizens' high levels of distrust of their government, and given a legacy of disengagement and disenfranchisement, it was critical that the planned citizen engagement effort demonstrate a strong connection to both decision-making processes and the actual decision makers. If the District's citizens were going to take the time to join Mayor Williams's first Citizen Summit in the convention center, they would need to believe that real action would come from their efforts. Reporting on the November 20, 1999, Citizen Summit the day after, the *Washington Post* pursued this angle: "The proof of whether the Summit is worthwhile will be in what action follows, if any," the article read (Cottman 1999, C01).

In the end, the first Citizen Summit produced something quite significant. The public's priorities for investment of discretionary dollars were embraced by the mayor and his administration and became the blueprint for the city's 2000–2001 budget. This outcome was possible because decision makers were involved in and committed to the process.

PLANNING AND DEVELOPMENT

Despite a raft of logistical and scheduling challenges, for six months leading up to the first Citizen Summit America*Speaks* met regularly with different groups in the administration—including the CFO and policy and budget staff reporting to Mayor Williams. Equally important were four sessions held with the entire mayoral cabinet, during which as many as forty-five high-level individuals worked together to create a citywide strategic plan that would be taken to the public for review and revision.

As is typical in public budgeting, a particular challenge in this planning process was the fact that in the city's $5 billion 1999 budget, only $1.2 billion represented discretionary funds. Because discretionary programs in the District had been underfunded for decades, individual agencies had a significant stake in securing these undesignated resources. However, the teamwork-based process challenged cabinet members and agency heads to think beyond their own respective agencies and adopt a broader, city-wide view. Further, by surfacing and resolving contentious issues during the planning and development phase, such issues were less likely to "pop up" during the citizen deliberation and sidetrack the work. Incidents of individual agency heads "side-dealing" with the City Council, which can often subvert an administration's agenda, were substantially diminished by the fact that the agency heads felt ownership of the strategic plan because they helped create it.

Participant Recruitment

Mayor Williams and city leadership were actively involved in recruitment for the Citizen Summits. In all of their public appearances leading up to the first summit, they spoke from strategically worded talking points and messages about the importance of the effort to the city. They issued personal invitations to the people of Washington, DC to attend. As described earlier in this chapter, one particularly effective recruitment technique was having the mayor interviewed live by all the high-profile drive-time radio hosts in the city. His personal invitation to citizens to attend the summit was enhanced by the fact that it was delivered on the programs of such trusted sources of community information.

Participation in the Event

The unique circumstances of governance in Washington, DC, and the extreme levels of public distrust that had built up over time, called for an equally extreme demonstration of the city's commitment to taking citizens' views seriously. To achieve that, all forty-five members of the mayor's cabinet and policy team were present at and actively participated in the first Citizen Summit. When participants arrived that day, they were greeted by name and given informational materials to take to their assigned table. Then, as they entered the hall, they walked through a two-sided receiving line that included every cabinet member, each of whom personally welcomed them to the event and thanked them for their participation. Later, when reflecting on the day, both cabinet members and participants identified this as one of their favorite features of the experience.

In addition, throughout the day cabinet members moved around the hall and sat at tables for twenty to thirty minutes at a time, listening to the citizens' discussions; learning on a personal level what citizens thought; and seeing how they could reach collective decisions, even across their differences. While they circulated in the hall, cabinet members and their top deputies were also able to answer questions or provide clarifications on substantive issues raised in the discussions. At the end of the day, cabinet members and their staff made themselves available to respond to individual concerns, such as a dead tree or an abandoned car that needed to be removed.

A different story can be told about the Washington, DC City Council's involvement in that first summit. In a city struggling to function within a challenging new governance structure, there was little love lost between the Williams Administration and the City Council. Over the years, mayors and City Councils often sparred in the District, but the overarching authority of the control board had exacerbated this tendency. So although members of the City Council had been invited to attend the Citizen Summit, they had not been involved in the intensive planning work that led up to the event. As a result, on the morning of the Summit, few City Council members were present—most had simply sent staff in their place. However, when word got out that there were three thousand citizens deliberating in the convention center, many more Council members came quickly. As they arrived, each was introduced from the stage, and they were then able to observe and participate in the work of the day.

The next day, the *Washington Post* reported that City Council member Jim Graham "had come to the summit with some skepticism, but after a morning sitting at a table working on priorities with eight residents, he said he was won over" (Cottman 1999, C01). The compelling scale of the event helped bridge an ongoing leadership divide, and made it clear to City Council members that it was important for them to be part of future Summits.

FOLLOW-UP

At the end of the first Citizen Summit, participants were informed that the government would need a number of weeks to integrate what had been heard. A follow-up event would be held to publicly review the decisions the administration had reached. This follow-up event would also be hosted by Mayor Williams and his full

FIGURE 6.2 LOCAL ARTIST PRESENTS HIS PAINTING OF THE DC
CITIZEN SUMMIT TO MAYOR ANTHONY WILLIAMS

cabinet. Due to an unexpected snowstorm, this event had to be
cancelled and quickly rescheduled. Despite this last-minute adjust-
ment, an overflow crowd of 1,500 people showed up to make sure
their voices and priorities would truly hold sway.

Although unbeknownst to most of the public, in the lead-up
to this second event, decision makers' commitment to valuing the
priorities of citizens was put to a significant test. At the first Citizen
Summit, one of the public's highest priorities for investment of
discretionary dollars had been education. This directive presented
a challenge, however, in that the mayor did not control the education budget—those funds were under the control of an independently elected school board and the City Council. Yet to honor
citizens' priorities, the mayor committed to giving $70 million of
his discretionary funds to the superintendent of schools to invest
in an initiative to improve the quality of school principals. In so
doing, the mayor was, in effect, taking these funds away from the
numerous city agencies over which he did have direct authority.

The heads of those agencies, who had been intimately involved in planning for the Summit and who, it is important to note, had been in the convention center and watched the participants vote in support of increased funding for education, supported this redirection of funds, despite the fact that it was against their own program interests. The power of citizen engagement to move decision makers was clear. In a very dramatic moment, Mayor Williams stood up and said that if the school board agreed to spend the money in a dedicated and accountable way, he would respond to the voices of the people and transfer the money—even though he would lose oversight of these funds. He did, and it worked.

RESULTS

Over a period of six years, the Citizen Summits instituted a new governance process in the District of Columbia that had significant impacts. The work transformed the relationship between citizens and the development of the municipal budget; established new governance structures through which neighborhoods and individual residents would play a strategic and sustained role in governance (described in Chapter Eleven); and led to the creation of a youth advisory council with a statutorily based role in budget development, only the third in the nation.

In addition to the new governance structures, for every budget cycle during Mayor Williams's two terms in office, the Citizen Summits led to the allocation or reallocation of hundreds of millions of dollars based on citizens' collective decisions. Some highlights from those priority choices include the following:

- $70 million for education added to the city's 2001 budget; an additional $10 million allocated for senior services; and one thousand new drug treatment slots funded
- $25 million added to the city's 2003 budget for a housing trust fund and $2 million added to support further neighborhood-level citizen involvement in governance
- $200 million made available for education in 2005 and an additional $20 million included for police and juvenile-related initiatives

- In the 2007 budget, an additional $123 million added for school system modernization efforts; $21 million allocated for workforce development, targeting youth and the hard-to-employ in particular; and $16 million added for public library construction and renovation, among other improvements

Looking back on the work and its accomplishments, Mayor Williams had this to say: "Public trust in DC was so broken when I became mayor. I knew that I personally had to convince the public that the Citizen Summits would make a difference—that if they came together and worked to create city-wide priorities, my administration would act on them. The pay-off was beyond my expectations because we created a meaningful connection between myself, my administration and the public. It could not have been accomplished any other way" (Williams 2012).

FIGURE 6.3 CITIZENS OF WASHINGTON, DC
ESTABLISH PRIORITIES FOR THEIR CITY

The Public Manager's Role in Linking to Decision Makers

This chapter has established the importance of directly and substantively linking citizen engagement efforts to live governance processes and decision makers. Because public managers are well positioned to steward citizen engagement work in government agencies, they are likely to be the ones to engage appropriate decision makers in the various ways described. This task may be complicated by the fact that some decision makers will be resistant, not initially seeing the value, importance, or potential benefit of citizen engagement. They may also be concerned about the risks, or they may want to politicize the engagement process. Therefore, in addition to bringing in decision makers, public managers may have to guard the fact-based neutrality that is so critical to a credible engagement effort.

Another challenge is that public managers consulting on or directly designing an engagement process may not have direct access to the critical decision makers. Roger Bernier, retired from the Centers for Disease Control and Prevention, recognized this difficulty. "Federal managers are part of a decision making chain, but often not the final stop," he said. "In the end, you may have to conduct a project without one-on-one conversations with the decision maker. For example, if you are a level seven manager in a bureaucratic hierarchy, and a decision maker is at level ten, you would likely only speak to that decision-maker on rare occasions. This might make it difficult to get clarity of purpose on an initiative, so to succeed, you'll have to find a different way to get that clarity" (Bernier 2012).

Further, managers who have experience with citizen engagement work have often deliberately conducted this work under the radar to avoid political and bureaucratic entanglements. Openly educating and engaging the managers and political appointees above them may feel like a potentially risky shift in their operating strategy. The value of taking this risk is that it is likely to increase the impact of the citizen engagement work.

Another potential trouble spot may be ensuring the neutrality of the agenda and materials for a citizen deliberation. This work can require navigating the challenging terrain between an agency's political objectives and its routine program operations. In the final analysis, enabling political appointees to help frame development of the agenda and materials while not allowing them to dominate the process can be difficult work.

As suggested earlier, creating the space for citizens to make collective recommendations, without knowing in advance what these will be, can be perceived by decision makers as too risky. But citizen engagement work has demonstrated over and over that the results justify the risk. Public managers seeking to engage top decision makers can address this issue head-on. One strong argument is that failing to fully engage the public often leads to costly and time-consuming lawsuits over those decisions the public and certain stakeholders do not accept. Describing an extensive engagement process, the U.S. Forest Service's Richard Stem noted: "There were very few disagreements . . . [and] no litigation or serious appeals that held up progress." (Stem 2012).

To successfully take on these challenges and new roles, public managers will also need to wrestle with the impermanence of top management in a federal agency. Long-standing civil servants may naturally be reluctant to work for culture change in their respective programs because they have often seen such work lose support when administrations change. A strategic approach for a public manager committed to building a more robust culture around citizen engagement is to capitalize, where possible, on the best the political appointees have to offer in this regard, such as an appreciation for public listening sessions or a belief in the need for data from the public. They can build capacity and embed it in the parts of their agency that will not change as upper management moves on, for example by bringing in career staff with outreach experience so that public meetings will involve a more diverse set of participants, or by ensuring that the agency's public documents are written in accessible language. Career development in such areas as outreach, process design, facilitation, and cultural competence, among others, will serve public managers well in stewarding citizen engagement work in their respective agencies. As more and more individual managers develop these capacities it will, over time, enhance an agency's overall comfort with, and ability to conduct, high-quality citizen engagement work. As more agencies establish this capacity, the public's voice in governance will become stronger and stronger.

Public Manager Perspectives

The Public Engagement Project on Pandemic Influenza

Roger Bernier, former Senior Adviser for Scientific Strategy and Innovation, Center for Immunization and Respiratory Diseases, U.S. Centers for Disease Control and Prevention

---

The Context

After the call in 1999 to reduce or eliminate thimerosol, a mercury-containing preservative, from vaccines, disagreement over the potential link between vaccines and autism diminished trust between a segment of the concerned public and the Centers for Disease Control and Prevention (CDC). Staff who worked in this area knew the research was solid, but some members of the public were not accepting this version of the facts. Because of the serious gap in trust, new research was effectively "dead on arrival" with the public, and simply layering on more research would not solve the problem. Vaccine policy in this area needed to move forward—the problem had to be addressed.

As a CDC scientist on special assignment, I began to explore possible solutions. From my work experience, I knew that collaborating with others is a way of building trust. Thus, after a couple of years of research and planning with colleagues in the field to determine what kinds of work could realistically be done with the public, we developed a new model of public engagement related to difficult policy decisions.

An opportunity presented itself to test the new model when one such difficult decision arose in the course of planning for pandemic influenza, namely: who first to vaccinate in the early days of a pandemic when vaccine supplies are expected to be very limited. The Public Engagement Project on Pandemic Influenza (PEPPI) would engage the public and stakeholders to learn what the federal government should recommend to state and local health departments on this difficult issue.

Public Engagement Strategies

To engage ordinary citizens and stakeholder organizations on vaccination strategies for an influenza pandemic, the PEPPI used a new model called a Consequential Public Engagement Table (CPET). The model was termed "consequential" because it contained specific design elements to help ensure that the advice given by the public was relevant to a real pending decision and would be seriously considered—that is, that it was "needed and heeded." The key design elements included

- Focusing on undecided policy choices involving technical and values considerations
- Joint refining of the question for discussion
- Opportunities for participants to learn from balanced and credible sources
- Neutral facilitation

- Structured opportunities for frank dialogue, mutual learning, genuine deliberation, and reaching agreement on the question of interest—not consensus or unanimity but understanding and expression of opinion
- Integration of citizen and stakeholder perspectives into one collective public viewpoint
- Linkage to government decision-making processes and decision makers
- Feedback to the participants about the decision made and the reasons for it

The PEPPI began in July 2005 with plans to forward a final report to the secretary of the U.S. Department of Health and Human Services (HHS, the agency governing the CDC) and other decision makers in advance of the release of national guidance on the issue in late 2005. In those four to five months, 100 unaffiliated citizens in the southern part of the United States and 35 stakeholders in Washington, DC, met separately to discuss and consider competing goals for a pandemic influenza vaccination program. The stakeholders integrated the results of the deliberations into a single collective statement and presented this for discussion to another 150 citizens in the western, eastern, and central United States. The project was evaluated independently by the University of Nebraska Public Policy Center. Commenting on the deliberations, one observer noted: "What I liked about it was there were no shrinking violets. People were quick to say 'I don't get this; can you explain it to me better?' Or 'I totally disagree.' I know that in the working group I was in, everyone spoke loud and long."

Through the deliberative process, both the citizens-at-large and stakeholder organizations decided with a very high level of agreement that ensuring the functioning of society should be the first immunization goal in a moderately severe pandemic, followed in importance by reducing individual deaths and hospitalizations. There was little support for other suggested goals—to vaccinate young people first; to use a lottery system; or to take a first come, first served approach.

Linking to Decision Makers

When the PEPPI was developed, the plan was for the citizen and stakeholder work to inform the decision making of the two expert committees that routinely advise HHS on vaccine issues: the Advisory Committee on Immunization Practices and the National Vaccine Advisory Committee. Unfortunately, however, delays in funding and organizing meant that these expert committees had already met jointly *before* the public engagement work got off the ground.

To make things more complicated, the experts and the public reached quite different conclusions about who should be vaccinated first: the experts prioritized decreasing health impacts by vaccinating people at high risk of death and hospitalization, whereas the public prioritized minimizing societal impacts by vaccinating people tasked with key social functions (for example, firefighters, police officers, emergency medical technicians).

In issuing its first set of national guidance in November 2005, HHS accepted the advice of its expert committees. However, in an unusual caveat, HHS also stated in its guidance document that "as other sectors are increasingly engaged in pandemic planning, additional considerations may arise" HHS leaders then directly referenced the public's view: "Though findings of the outreach are preliminary, a theme that has emerged is the importance of limiting the effects of a pandemic on society by preserving essential societal functions" (U.S. Department of Health and Human Services [HHS] 2005, D-10).

Although the results of the PEPPI did not directly shape the content of the *first* national guidance, they did compel HHS to question the finality of its expert-derived recommendations and to see the public's viewpoint as the basis for further discussion and exploration. Approximately one year after the initial guidance was issued, HHS decided to revisit it.

In fall 2006 a new interagency work group was established under the leadership of HHS and the Department of Homeland Security to set forth new guidance. The interagency group conducted a second public engagement project in 2007 using the CPET model, which came to conclusions similar to those of the first public engagement project. This time, however, leadership adopted many of the public's recommendations in preparing its national guidance (issued in July 2008).

Although the first public consultation was carried out as a pilot project without official sanction, it nevertheless had the participation of government managers as stakeholders. The second public consultation was actually carried out with the official approval of HHS and the Department of Homeland Security and with the participation of public managers throughout the process. Thus the results were well understood by government staff and could be presented directly to decision makers.

Final evidence of the critical link to decision makers was the strong statement by HHS secretary Mike Leavitt when the second set of national guidance was released: "This guidance is the result of a deliberative democratic process. All interested parties took part in the dialogue; we are confident that this document represents the best of shared responsibility and decision making" (HHS 2008).

CHAPTER SEVEN

STRATEGY THREE: ACHIEVE DIVERSE PARTICIPATION

I think this may be the first time that people of all races, creeds, and from various neighborhoods actually had an opportunity to sit down with each other and engage in discussion. A lot of times we create perceptions of each other based on what we see in the media, what we read in the newspaper, and never have had the opportunity to sit down and talk with people who could only be a couple blocks away from us. We broke down barriers that have existed for a long time in New Orleans.

TARENCE DAVIS, ATHLETIC DIRECTOR AT ALGIERS
CHARTER SCHOOLS, NEW ORLEANS, 2007*

Participation by people of diverse backgrounds is a cornerstone of effective and successful citizen engagement. It enables citizens with different experiences and unique perspectives to talk to and learn from each other. Diverse participation builds credibility for the results of the deliberative process, helps leaders make tough choices in the face of political risks, and lays important groundwork for sustaining broad-based citizen involvement over time. This chapter discusses the importance of achieving and sustaining diverse participation and presents case examples that demonstrate how to accomplish it.

---

*Williamson, A. "Citizen Participation in the Unified New Orleans Plan." Unpublished doctoral dissertation. Cambridge, MA: Kennedy School of Government, Harvard University, 2007, 21.

Why Achieving Diverse Participation Is Important

Public officials feel much more confident about taking action on an issue when they are doing so on behalf of a diverse and demographically representative group of citizens. They want to know that all voices, from across their various constituencies, have been at the table and been given an opportunity to contribute to the results. Broad support from people of different perspectives lends their decisions the validity and credibility necessary to withstand political opposition. Further, as described in Chapter One through the example of health care reform, decisions that are made without broad-based public involvement and ownership tend to have a relatively short life. Senator Kent Conrad of North Dakota said it this way: "The people who participated in Our Budget, Our Economy discussions in my state and around the country were from all walks of life and of all political persuasions. Such diversity of opinion helps produce meaningful dialogue. It is that informed discussion with a wide array of citizens that helps me to reach a fair and balanced conclusion on the important public policy issues that I must vote on. It is very important to hear fully from all sides of an issue" (Conrad 2012).

Despite the importance of having a representative cross-section of constituent voices standing behind decision makers, the more predominant forces in decision making today are wealth and connections to highly influential stakeholder groups. The substantial impact of increasing amounts of money in politics and governance has been so widely reported, and is so generally accepted as truth, that it needs little elaboration here. The 2010 "Citizens United" ruling by the Supreme Court (*Citizens United* v. *Federal Election Commission* 2010) allowing corporations to spend as much money as they want on political campaigns and reintroducing anonymous giving is a recent example of the extent to which we have given the wealth and well-connected more power.

Special interest and advocacy groups also have significant influence in our governance processes. Of varying sizes and different levels of financial backing, these stakeholder groups have multiplied and extended their reach over the last decade as advances in technology have facilitated direct connections with large numbers of citizens as well as with elected officials. In just one example, in January 2011, covering the reaction to legislation aimed at curbing Internet piracy, the *New York Times* reported that in a very short period of time 4.5 million people had been moved to sign a Google petition on the issue; more than 2 million had posted about it on Twitter (four times the usual traffic); a group called Engine Advocacy reported to be averaging about two thousand calls per second to members of Congress; and Wikipedia said four million people had searched for contact information for their local representative (Wortham 2012). The advocacy and interest groups concerned with the issue were able to mobilize an unprecedented number of citizens in a very short time frame. Their efforts paid off: lead sponsors of the bill withdrew it, indicating that they would have to go back to the drawing board.

The creation of such effective communication and information-sharing networks among dispersed individuals and communities is a positive outcome of the expanding reach of advocacy and stakeholder organizations. Yet there are reasons for concern. Although arguably their influence is less pernicious and patently unfair than that wielded by corporations and wealthy individuals with private business and financial interests, these groups can have disproportionate access to decision makers. Further, there is a direct correlation between such disproportionate access and the amount of money such groups are able to bring to the table. The Center for Responsive Politics reported that in 2010 "527 advocacy groups (tax-exempt organizations that raise money for political activities such as voter mobilization and issue advocacy) spent more than $590 million on these various activities" (Center for Responsive Politics 2012).

Of further concern is the fact that many people have come to accept advocacy and stakeholder groups as representative of, or synonymous with, "the public." Government programs seeking public input often focus largely if not exclusively on stakeholder groups to fulfill this mandate.

To be sure, stakeholder organizations play a vital role in our democracy, especially to the extent that they represent groups and causes that are less powerful. But often their increasing level of influence in decision making crowds out the views of unaffiliated citizens. Their growth is also crowding out many non-issue-specific, prodemocratic organizations, such as the League of Women Voters, the National Civic League, and the YWCA, among others, thus leaving citizens with fewer and fewer opportunities for civic participation that is not linked to a particular issue or position.

What is particularly worrisome about these trends is that stakeholder groups cannot substitute for citizens in government decision-making processes for a simple and important reason. Stakeholder groups generally represent a fixed position and will come to any governance process with the predetermined goal of securing that position. And yet the real value of citizen engagement as a basis for decision making lies in its ability to do the opposite—to develop and bridge participants' views; to enable people to genuinely consider the opinions of others and find compromises that support the common good. By definition, stakeholder groups are not in a position to serve this goal.

As long as wealth or membership in a stakeholder group are the dominant mechanisms through which citizens reach decision makers, "of the people, by the people, and for the people" does not hold its rightful place in our democracy.

Strategies for Achieving Diverse Participation

Democracy practitioners have long been concerned with securing representative participation in citizen deliberations. There are a range of strategies for accomplishing this goal including: understand the needs of potential participants, use enrollment targets to make tactical adjustments, partner with community leadership, craft the deliberation agenda thoughtfully, hold information sessions, discover the barriers to participation and address them, and conduct broad-based outreach, among others. Specific tactics in each of these areas are discussed in the following subsections.

Understand the Needs of Potential Participants

At first blush, deciding who needs to be present at a citizen deliberation may seem fairly simple: a spectrum of representatives from the groups or communities affected by a given issue or decision should be at the table. Yet simply opening the doors and inviting everyone to come will not achieve that goal. The dynamics of power and group membership generally result in open-door forums being dominated by groups with greater resources, higher levels of education, a stronger sense of entitlement, and more participatory experience. More promising from the standpoint of achieving real representativeness are forums that aim to bring together a demographic microcosm of the community. Achieving that microcosm requires in-depth assessments of the participant landscape. Several key dimensions for analysis include the following:

- *Logistics.* Do all of the different demographic groups have ready access to transportation, child care, and other things they will need to be able to participate?
- *Participant characteristics.* Various demographic groups will have distinct histories of, and levels of comfort with, engaging with political or government institutions. Their relative sense of entitlement or marginalization will shape whether and how they participate. Has this variable been explored for each group, and have accommodations been made to facilitate engagement opportunities for everyone?
- *Participant skills.* The ability of different groups to participate successfully in a deliberation will depend on their language skills and education levels. Have participants' needs been assessed, and are they reflected in the design and format of the session and related participant materials?
- *Issue-specific considerations.* Although some groups are persistently and recognizably marginalized, the topic of a public policy deliberation will often bring to light groups that might only be marginalized in a particular context. For example, when conducting a large-scale deliberation on health care reform in California, participants' insurance status (for example, employer based, open market, or government program) was an essential demographic variable to be considered that would have been irrelevant in other contexts.

It should also be noted that assessments of the participant landscape are critical not only at the outset of an initiative but also on an ongoing basis as enrollment numbers emerge.

USE ENROLLMENT TARGETS TO MAKE TACTICAL ADJUSTMENTS

Conveners of the citizen engagement initiative should make representational goals and targets transparent from the outset, periodically assess enrollment against these preestablished targets, and then adjust outreach accordingly. For example, while recruiting for America*Speaks*'s Listening to the City initiative it became apparent that young Hispanics were not enrolling proportionately to their numbers in the population. In addition to shifting more community organizers into particular neighborhoods, when the initiative simulated an actual discussion table on the NY1 television station, a twenty-six-year-old Hispanic woman from Brooklyn was deliberately included. Following the show, registrations among young Hispanics increased dramatically. It was a powerful illustration of Daniel Yankelovich's concept of "proxy dialogue," which "harnesses the power of identification" (Yankelovich 2001, 159, 168). When people see someone participating who is like them, or with whom they identify, it influences their own views and can inspire them to actually participate.

PARTNER WITH COMMUNITY LEADERSHIP

It is a basic principle of human behavior that when we are curious about or considering doing something we have never done before, what most often moves us beyond our ambivalence is to be encouraged or invited by someone we know and trust. Because citizen engagement is something of a rarity in many communities, outreach is best led by local organizations and people who either live in the community or are identified by community members as one of their own.

Therefore, forums are ideally developed in partnership with a community advisory group that can help with outreach as well as provide input and feedback on the meeting design and agenda.

In most cities in America, for example, African American churches are a mainstay of the community, often serving to link the issues that citizens care about to the politics that influence them.

FIGURE 7.1 Every Voice must Be Heard

Craft the Deliberation Agenda Thoughtfully

When designing the agenda for the deliberation, the concerns of disadvantaged groups must be included. It cannot be assumed that the voices of these groups will be powerful enough to make themselves heard on their own once the deliberation has begun. Young people, for example, are one of the most consistently underrepresented groups in public policy discussions. To bring them in, their voices must be part of the development of the agenda and the informational materials. In the Voices & Choices initiative discussed in Chapter Five, a deliberate effort was made to include the input of young people. That work paid off. Across the various components of this initiative, 26 percent of participants were ages fifteen to thirty-four.

HOLD INFORMATION SESSIONS

Planners should meet with community members in advance to explain the process, introduce the technology, address concerns, and garner support. As already mentioned, in preparation for the first large-scale Citizen Summit in Washington, DC, more than fifty such meetings were held. In the end, a diverse group of more than three thousand residents, statistically representative of the whole city, participated in that first Summit.

DISCOVER THE BARRIERS TO PARTICIPATION AND ADDRESS THEM

Although every locality and issue will present unique circumstances, the most common obstacles to participation by underrepresented groups include such things as language barriers, access to transportation, and a lack of child care. Planners must thoroughly address all known barriers. In the case of the Washington, DC Citizen Summits, the public transportation system did not provide equal access from all parts of the city to the downtown convention center where the Summits were held. To address this problem, the initiative worked with the local transit authority and local churches to make a convoy of buses available to transport participants either to the convention center or to a bus or metro that could then take them there. The local YMCA and YWCA, Boys & Girls Clubs, faith-based organizations, and child care facilities are often likely partners to provide activity-based child care that will enable parents and caregiving grandparents to attend.

Listening to the City staff used a creative approach to ensure that youth could fully participate in the deliberation on post-9/11 rebuilding strategies. They collaborated with a youth leadership group called Global Kids to develop a youth-oriented curriculum on the issues to be discussed, and to train youth who planned to participate in some of the skills they would need to do so. Adult participants who sat with these young people commented on their impressive command of the issues and their ability to articulate their perspectives.

The concrete results that are possible when barriers to participation are addressed were recently demonstrated in New York

City. As briefly described in Chapter One, using an engagement methodology called participatory budgeting, in 2012 four New York City Council members from four different districts engaged the public in direct decision making about the use of $4 million in discretionary funds. To engage members of the public living in those districts, materials were translated into a wide range of languages. The initiative did not require people to formally register to participate and did not impose citizenship status or criminal records as barriers to participation. Another important step was to make voting convenient by holding it over several days and in high-traffic locations. The *New York Times* reported some remarkable results from these efforts: in one of the four districts, although only 1 percent of voters had an annual household income of less than $25,000, 10 percent of the participatory budgeting voters were from this income group. In another district, although 39 percent of local voters were Latino, 47 percent of the participatory budgeting voters were Latino. In yet another district, the greatest number of votes came from residents of a public housing development (Sangha Apr. 2012). The additional efforts to reach these underserved communities had a tangible impact on the ability and willingness of people who are often marginalized to participate in a high-impact citizen engagement process.

CONDUCT BROAD-BASED OUTREACH

Looking back on his more than twenty years of experience in the U.S. Fish and Wildlife Service, public manager Tony Faast concluded that deliberation planners must "engage all of the interested parties with the same commitment, but with different approaches. Organized stakeholder groups and under-represented community members require very different kinds of outreach and engagement" (Faast 2012).

When it comes to marginalized population groups in particular, the work is challenging, but the goals are attainable. These citizens tend to demonstrate low levels of civic engagement because many of them have had life experiences in which their individual voices were not adequately heard, or in which they were unable to make a difference. As a result, they may not have an interest in participating unless they perceive that things will be different this time.

Recognizing the importance of having a fully representative sample of citizens in the room, America*Speaks* uses the following central pillars of a comprehensive outreach strategy:

- Strategic use of decision makers and community leaders
- Media partnerships focused on mass media outlets as well as retail media, such as neighborhood or population-specific newspapers
- Partnerships with a wide range of mediating organizations in a community
- Grassroots organizing efforts conducted by people and organizations that have local credibility
- Connecting to unique or iconic events in the community that resonate with a wide range of citizens and demographic groups
- Online and technology-based vehicles, such as text messaging and social networks. Using online tools, discussed in detail in Chapter Twelve, is less resource intensive than many on-the-ground strategies, and can be particularly helpful in reaching certain demographic groups

PAYING DELIBERATION PARTICIPANTS: DISAGREEMENTS AMONG PRACTITIONERS

As would be expected in a diverse field of practice, there are strategies for achieving representative participation that engender strong differences of opinion. For example, some practitioners believe that paying citizens to take part in forums is vital to ensuring representative participation of traditionally marginalized groups and to avoid overrepresentation of people who already have a strong civic impulse. Others believe that paying participants creates a mixed motivation for attending, which may have an impact on their commitment to deliberation and diminishes the likelihood that they will remain involved after they have received their payment. The 21st Century Town Meeting model is based on this latter view, and does not compensate people monetarily for their participation.

Another example of a tension point pertains to the use of random sampling to achieve representative participation. America*Speaks* uses random sampling when the politics of the issue are so contentious that external validation of representative participation is necessary. However, there are a number of demographic groups, for example young people or people without telephone landlines, that most often do not respond to random sampling efforts. Further, because it operates "under the radar," recruitment using random sampling can limit opportunities to create public excitement and community interest before an event. Combining random sampling with targeted recruitment is a strong approach. For the California*Speaks* health care reform initiative, a random sample was critical because of the intense political pressure surrounding the issue and the initiative. However, to end up with a fully representative group of people in the room, targeted outreach activities were also necessary, particularly with youth, Hispanics, and low-income people.

ACHIEVING DIVERSE PARTICIPATION: A CASE STUDY

A particularly powerful example of achieving diverse participation took place in a 2002 initiative to engage the public in the rebuilding efforts in lower Manhattan following the 9/11 terrorist attacks.[1] Listening to the City brought thousands of New Yorkers together to deliberate and make specific recommendations on the highly contested plans for redevelopment of the World Trade Center site. A first deliberative event brought more than 650 people from throughout the metropolitan area together with experts and regional leaders to discuss the vision and principles that should inform the rebuilding process. This information was used to develop a series of conceptual plans. When that work was finished five months later, more than 4,500 people gathered at the Jacob Javits Center to review and respond to these plans. The public discussed and came to collective decisions about transportation issues, commercial and residential use, cultural and civic options, and other topics. Those assembled always kept in mind the importance of remembering and rebuilding in a way that would honor and respect those who lost their lives on 9/11.

Figure 7.2 Citizens Discuss Vision and Principles to Inform the
Rebuilding Process

The engagement of the public was vital to moving the redevelopment of the World Trade Center site forward. Early planning had surfaced stark differences of opinion among survivors, business leaders, developers, and residents about the future of the site, and had been roundly criticized for not being responsive to the full range of people and communities that had been so directly and tragically affected by the events of 9/11. Writing for the *New Yorker* at the time, architecture critic Paul Goldberger described the magnitude of the task this way: "The future of the World Trade Center site . . . has inspired more public forums, hearings, debates, op-ed articles, and design proposals than any urban-planning question in the city's history. . . . Dealing with the site is the greatest logistical challenge the city has faced in modern times, and deciding how to handle this challenge is, in effect, a referendum about what the city's symbolic center should be . . . [it is] a struggle between the forces of participatory democracy and the notion of the big idea, the bold gesture" (Goldberger 2002, 1, 4).

Civic leaders and members of the general public feared that development and political interests would prevail unless public consensus emerged. In this environment, New York's leaders, both city and state, needed broad-based public backing to make decisions that would hold.

To meet the need for diverse and representative participation, highly effective outreach on a massive scale was necessary. America-*Speaks* conducted a detailed analysis of the demographics of the city and affected region. Based on this analysis, they pulled together an experienced team of more than a dozen full- and part-time field organizers who lived or had worked extensively in the communities from which they were recruiting participants. This outreach team developed strong relationships within each target community and secured assistance and commitments from organizations and leaders to support the event and help with recruitment. As the registrations grew, the outreach team regularly assessed which demographic populations were underrepresented and redoubled their efforts in those communities. They increased person-to-person outreach, ran more advertisements in newspapers and on television, brought credible leaders to the various target communities to demonstrate their commitment, and invited people from those communities who had already registered to become part of the outreach work.

One of the most significant challenges the planners of Listening to the City faced was finding a way to reach and engage undocumented immigrants. This community had lost large numbers of people in the Twin Towers; was significantly affected by the loss of jobs in the area; and was, by virtue of being undocumented, thoroughly disconnected from civic life in general, and participation in governance processes in particular.

As outreach for Listening to the City was getting under way, New York State was simultaneously working on a strategy for granting amnesty to the large number of World Trade Center employers who had hired undocumented immigrants to work in the buildings. The government had to have the names and contact information for these individuals so their families could be notified of their death. Gathering this sensitive information required help from service organizations working closely with immigrant communities. Because America*Speaks* was participating in these discussions, the organizations serving immigrants came to trust us and later agreed to promote participation in the deliberation, on the condition that personal data normally gathered during the registration process would not be required.

When Listening to the City was held on July 20, 2002, among the 4,300 people at the Jacob Javits Center were nearly 450 undocumented immigrants—an extraordinary level of participation for this profoundly affected but almost always unheard part of the American community.

Listening to the City had lasting results. Within a week the governor of New York reiterated the citizens' directive to go back to the drawing board on site design options, develop mixed-use plans, reduce the density of the site, and find new solutions to the issue of commercial space. Three months later, the voices of citizens were still being heeded as new decisions were made about the redevelopment of Ground Zero. When the Lower Manhattan Development Authority released a worldwide "Request for Qualifications" for new design proposals, the great majority of the public's recommendations were written directly into the document. Without the participation of the whole community, in all of its diversity, producing a unified voice, it is unlikely that the public's recommendations would have held such sway.

Ten years later, as the new site at Ground Zero was taking shape, architecture critic Goldberger said that the selected master plan by Daniel Libeskind "struck a careful balance between commemorating the lives lost and reestablishing the life of the site itself." This vital compromise was at the heart of the messages citizens delivered in Listening to the City. Goldberger went on to offer this moving description:

> You feel a sense of dignity and repose, and you see the shapes of the renewed city in the rising skyscrapers, as you should. Ground Zero can't be a place where your thoughts escape completely into history, as at Maya Lin's extraordinary Vietnam Veterans Memorial, or on the battlefield at Gettysburg. You are in the middle of the city, part of an urban life that was as much a target of the terrorists in 2001 as the lives of three thousand

people. The people will not come back, but the life of the city has to. When you stand in [architects Michael] Arad and [Peter] Walker's park and look toward the footprints ringed by names and the new towers behind them, you feel the profound connection between these two truths [Goldberger 2011].

THE PUBLIC MANAGER'S ROLE IN ACHIEVING DIVERSE PARTICIPATION

This chapter has made the argument that diverse participation is vital to effective citizen engagement; that it brings credibility to deliberative processes so they can provide decision makers with the public backing they will need to make tough choices. This chapter has also given concrete examples of how broad-based and strategic outreach is critical to achieving diverse participation.

For many public managers, undertaking such outreach would mean adopting a decidedly new approach to their work. First, it would require differentiating "stakeholders" from the general public. As noted earlier, members of a stakeholder group, when they take part as representatives of that group, are by definition unlikely to be open-minded enough to participate authentically in an open-ended engagement process. And yet, by habit and sometimes by mandate, government programs seeking public input often focus largely, if not exclusively, on these groups. America*Speaks*'s rule of thumb, by contrast, is that to ensure the integrity of a citizen engagement process, 60 percent of participants should be representatives of the general public.

This work would also be new for public managers in that they would have to conceptualize and implement their outreach strategies much more broadly. For example, simply posting notices for public comment will for the most part attract only the "usual suspects": stakeholder groups and lobbyists who routinely read the *Federal Register*. To go beyond these known groups, public managers will have to set enrollment targets that reflect the desired diversity, and then, to meet the targets, work collaboratively in communities. They will have to discover the existing and potential barriers to participation and take proactive steps to address them. They will have to conduct a substantially wider range of outreach activities and possibly hold information sessions in the lead-up to the citizen engagement initiative to build the public's commitment to participating.

To effectively execute this new approach, public managers will need to work in partnership with a range of local, regional, or even national organizations that have strong ties to the target communities; have the credibility to help bring in participants; and can assist with developing the agenda, the materials, and other critical aspects of the engagement process. As Olivia Ferriter of the U.S. Department of the Interior described it, the concept of partnering should become ingrained in the agency culture. "We have some remarkable success stories, but the biggest one is that our Department's leaders do not have to tell employees to partner. They want to do it because they understand the value. We can always do more. There are always new employees to orient, issues to discover, and citizens to engage, so the cake is always baking" (Ferriter 2012).

One challenge in developing these critical partnerships is that they should, to the greatest extent possible, be with issue-neutral or nonstakeholder organizations. If they are not, public managers are likely to simply recreate the scenario already described in which stakeholders come to dominate the engagement process; diversity of participation is lost; and the impact, and in some cases even the integrity of the outcomes, are compromised. Unfortunately, our nation suffers from an increasing lack of issue-neutral organizations that have sufficient capacity to bring unaffiliated citizens to the table. As a result, public managers may have to be creative in building the connections that will help them achieve diverse participation. For example, while I was working as chief of staff to the governor of Ohio, the state was able to give a number of grants to issue-neutral mediating organizations to build their capacity to link the public to the state's policymaking process.

Another example of a creative approach comes from America-*Speaks*'s work with a key partner organization in Columbia, South Carolina: the Central Carolina Community Foundation. America-*Speaks* was preparing for a large-scale citizen deliberation on the federal budget deficit, and although the Community Foundation was not focused on democracy or budgetary work per se, the board of directors and staff were able to make a significant contribution to the recruitment process by quickly tapping into more than thirty organizations whose combined networks touched every subpopulation of the community. Around the country, nearly seven hundred communities and regions are served by a community foundation that is likely to have a similar capacity to support citizen engagement and play a leadership role in convening the community.

At the national level, the Federal Mediation and Conciliation Service (FMCS) is an example of another possible source of support and partnership. Established in 1947 to help federal, state, and local government agencies resolve disputes, design conflict systems, and build capacity for constructive conflict management, FMCS has field offices in over fifty cities throughout the United States and could be brought into broader engagement efforts involving the public.

By strategically partnering with local, regional, or national groups that are in a position to help secure diverse citizen participation, public managers can significantly improve their capacity to bring a diverse cross-section of the public into agency decision making.

Public Manager Perspectives

Achieving Diverse Participation on Civil Rights Policy

Therese McMillan is a Deputy Administrator of the Federal Transit Administration (FTA), part of the U.S. Department of Transportation. McMillan recently led a review of the FTA's civil rights program, including an extensive public involvement process that could be a model for other federal agencies. In light of her leadership, I talked with McMillan to learn about what FTA had done. The following is a summary of our conversation.

The Context

When Deputy Administrator McMillan came to FTA in 2009, one of her first tasks was to lead a comprehensive assessment of the agency's civil rights responsibilities under Title VI of the 1964 Civil Rights Act and the 1994 Executive Order 12898 concerning environmental justice (EJ). This area of work was receiving increased scrutiny under the Obama Administration, and FTA had a decidedly mixed track record, due in no small part to regulatory guidance that had been unclear and incomplete.

The internal evaluation resulted in clear, high-priority recommendations that FTA's Title VI Circular be significantly revamped,[2] and that the agency's expectations around environmental justice be clarified and highlighted in a stand-alone EJ Circular. Recognizing that the implementation of civil rights regulations demands knowledge about, and engagement of, affected communities, FTA knew it had to get broad-based public input on the specific policy and program changes it was contemplating. In 2011, therefore, the agency designed and launched an unprecedented national public engagement effort.

Public Engagement Strategies

To capture the country's geographic and demographic differences, FTA planned information sessions and extended community outreach in five of its ten regions, with hubs in Boston, Atlanta, Detroit, the San Francisco Bay Area, and Kansas City. It was critical for the agency to be aware of the historical context and to understand how a region's diversity influenced local expectations for the agency's work as well as the actual impact it was having. The local meetings and outreach would provide a lens through which the agency could fully assess Title VI and EJ issues.

To establish the context for the meetings and design effective community outreach campaigns, the agency partnered with a cross-section of transit operators, metropolitan planning organizations (MPOs), state departments of transportation (state DOTs), advocacy groups, community-based organizations (CBOs), minority and low-income community members, and FTA regional staff who would implement the revised circulars. Each of the information sessions was officially sponsored by FTA and hosted by an MPO or local transit agency. Historically, these two groups did not always work well together. The outreach campaign was deliberately used as an opportunity to create a better dialogue between them because they were ultimately responsible for leveraging FTA's resources to increase local transit capacity through planning and service delivery.

To achieve the widespread, diverse participation and meaningful dialogue needed to accomplish its goals, the agency pursued several strategic and tactical steps:

- *Outreach.* Given that the agency needed first-person perspectives on specific transit system needs (as opposed to the views of representatives), extensive outreach to culturally and socioeconomically diverse communities—especially low-income people—was critical. The effort successfully used "nontraditional" strategies (that is, those used by communities themselves) to engage typically hard-to-reach individuals. FTA partnered with local advocacy, stakeholder, and citizen advisory groups, which then conducted direct recruitment. Outreach strategies included CBO-to-CBO efforts, an e-blast flyer campaign, and old-fashioned word of mouth. To include people without computer access, FTA used an "RSVP website" that allowed individuals to respond for others.
- *Meeting structure.* The structure of the public engagement meetings was carefully planned to encourage diverse participation. To begin the meeting, a leader from a local CBO welcomed everyone, shared ground rules, and set the context.

After an FTA presentation about the content of the proposed Title VI and EJ Circulars, participants broke into small-group conversations facilitated by known leaders from various federal, state, and local groups. Each small group reviewed the ground rules and worked from a set of guiding questions designed to spark discussion and ensure that diverging ideas would be shared and heard.

These efforts created a nonthreatening environment: participants did not feel pressure to come up to the microphone and quickly share their perspective. The small-group format also allowed more people to express their views and enabled professionals and community members to comfortably engage with each other. Throughout the meetings, McMillan and FTA's Chief Counsel Dorval Carter walked the floor, listening intently to participants' comments, answering questions, and demonstrating that the agency was indeed open to input.

- *Accessibility and accommodations.* FTA worked with an MPO and a transit agency to translate meeting materials into multiple languages, including Spanish, Korean, Chinese, Vietnamese, and Russian. Foreign language and sign language interpreters worked at some of the information sessions, and all locations were compliant with the Americans with Disabilities Act and transit-accessible. In addition, the agency wrote the updated circulars in "plain language" and developed PowerPoint presentations and related materials that would be understandable to people with a high school education. Meetings were held in the evening and lasted no more than two hours.
- *Online engagement.* Resource constraints limited the face-to-face information sessions to five cities. To achieve the wider public participation that was necessary, FTA kicked off its outreach effort by

hosting a series of Title VI and EJ webinars. These online sessions engaged transit operators, MPOs, and state DOTs in Alaska, Hawaii, Maine, and Florida, yielding important feedback that was then woven into the information sessions as well as the circulars themselves. The webinars did not, however, allow the agency to feature a community-based leader or enable participants to break into small groups. As a result, the online discussions were less cohesive than those that took place in person. For these reasons, FTA holds to the principle that blending face-to-face and online public engagement efforts is critical.

Results and Lessons Learned

FTA's engagement efforts brought more than 1,700 people into the policy development process. The agency received feedback about the proposed circulars from more than 200 commenters through the traditional *Federal Register* process.[3] More than 500 people participated in the Title VI and EJ information sessions, and more than 1,000 participated in the webinars. By providing a forum for local transit providers, citizen advocacy groups, and riders to come together with regional, state, and federal managers, the agency more clearly understood the gaps in policy recommendations and the barriers to implementation. As this book went to press, the agency was in the process of finalizing its new circulars.

One of the major lessons learned—an important breakthrough for FTA's public engagement work going forward—pertained to a seemingly simple point. Although the complicated work of federal agencies must be broken down in ways that those who are not federal bureaucrats can understand and use, it is also vitally important not to *oversimplify*. When too much complexity is removed, the issues under discussion run the risk of being misrepresented, and participants' input will lose its validity and utility.

Another significant lesson learned related to the timing of the work. It was logistically complex to squeeze all of the planning for and implementation of the information sessions and webinars into the *Federal Register* review and comment period. In the future, these efforts—in particular the outreach—should start much earlier.

FTA continues to receive positive feedback about its outreach process, in particular about the opportunities it provided for meaningful input on the Agency's policies and programs. An additional source of validation came when the San Francisco Bay Area chapter of the Women's Transportation Seminar named FTA as the 2012 recipient of the Rosa Parks Diversity Leadership Award. The award recognized FTA for holding information sessions across the United States (including in the San Francisco Bay Area), thereby promoting diversity, inclusiveness, and multicultural awareness.

CHAPTER EIGHT

STRATEGY FOUR: CREATE A SAFE PUBLIC SPACE

What does the open space of democracy look like?

In the open space of democracy there is room for dissent.

In the open space of democracy there is room for differences. . . .
Democracy can be messy and chaotic. It requires patience and
persistence . . .

When minds close, democracy begins to close. Fear creeps in;
silence overtakes speech. Rhetoric masquerades as thought.
Dogma is dressed up like an idea. ... The lie begins to carry
more power than the truth until the words of our own founding
fathers are forgotten and the images of television replace
history . . .

An open democracy inspires wisdom and the dignity of
choice . . .

Democracy is built upon the right to be insecure. We are vulnerable.
And we are vulnerable together.

Democracy is a beautiful experiment . . .

This is what the open space of democracy looks like.

Question. Stand. Speak. Act.

Make us uncomfortable.

Make us think.

Make us feel.

Keep us free.

TERRY TEMPEST WILLIAMS, 2004*

---

*Tempest Williams, T. "Commencement." *The Open Space of Democracy.* Great Barrington, MA: The Orion Society, 2004, 8.

Democratic and productive deliberation requires that every voice is heard, that no ideas are lost, and that diverse citizens can confidently and civilly air their differences. It gives participants the freedom to express their individual perspectives, no matter how unpopular, and to change their viewpoints as they choose. A safe deliberative space is a prerequisite for achieving these goals. This chapter explores the importance of creating such a space for citizen engagement and presents case examples that illustrate how to do it.

Why Creating a Safe Public Space Is Important

As human beings, we are dependent on the social and contextual cues in our immediate environment. We can all identify physical spaces that represent safety for us, whether they are places of worship, community locations we frequent, particular rooms at home or at work, or special places in nature. In these spaces, we are "at home." We feel a sense of safety, and we know we can be ourselves, voicing with confidence what we think and believe. In such spaces we can tackle unknowns, think creatively, and operate from our highest selves.

There might be no more stark contrast to these safe spaces than the following image: *an unfamiliar public space that is far from home and is filled with total strangers from diverse backgrounds, with different experiences and opinions with whom one is expected to dialogue on complex and sometimes personal issues.* It is difficult to imagine feeling instantly confident that one would be heard, understood, and respected in such a space. Yet this describes the space in which most public participation takes place.

Exacerbating this problem and intensifying the need to create safe spaces for deliberation are some unfortunate trends. Politics in our nation have become increasingly polarized, marked by ideology, anger, hyperbole, and blaming the other side. International democracy practitioner Lyn Carson described it well when she said: "We're working in a landscape where the job description of politicians is to destroy each other" (Deliberative Democracy Consortium 2008, 37). As our political discourse has deteriorated, our civil society has increasingly come to reflect these attributes.

The recent aggressive and antidemocratic distortion of the traditional American town hall meeting is a case in point.

In August 2009, as the country was engaged in a vigorous debate about health care reform, congressional recess town meetings intended to further this debate actually became vehicles for violating our Constitution's guarantee of free speech. In multiple instances, members of Congress who had come to a town hall to discuss their views on the issue were hanged in effigy, surrounded and followed by taunting crowds and threatened with injury and death. Anyone expressing a positive or even neutral view of the Obama Administration's health care reform efforts was shouted down. At events supposedly designed to allow citizens to air their views, aggression and sometimes even violence were used to achieve the opposite. Further, many attendees had been organized outside the congressional districts, trained in disruptive tactics, and then bused to the town halls. In a remarkable departure from the tradition of these local gatherings, members of Congress were facing angry mobs with no connection to their respective districts whatsoever. This kind of pure political theater also made more difficult the important work that public managers and others were doing on the key policy issues under discussion.

These "town hall meetings" had a chilling effect on the willingness of decision makers and other public servants and officials to engage face-to-face with voters. Two years after the 2009 health care town hall meetings, the *Washington Post*'s David Fahrenthold reported that congressional town hall meetings were down by almost 25 percent, and described "the broken state of the national town hall meeting, a staple of congressman-voter interaction, and of American democracy more generally . . . [in which] it now counts as a defeat if one's opponent is allowed to make a point in peace" (Fahrenthold 2011).

Further, these events had an equally negative impact on citizens' willingness to get civically involved. Betty Knighton, Director of the West Virginia Center for Civic Life, which creates opportunities in communities around the state for citizens to become involved in deliberative dialogues on common problems, summed it up well when she said: "Despite diligent efforts to communicate about the power of non-partisan, civil dialogue, most people have trouble getting beyond what they've either personally experienced or what they've seen in the media: long lines at the microphone at a school board meeting, or a loud and contentious public hearing. Most people don't want to put themselves in an environment like that" (Knighton 2010).

The health care town hall meetings were a dramatic departure from American tradition and values. But even when this level of disruptive intent is not operating, public meetings today are still too often dominated by repetitive ax-grinding, grandstanding, and demagoguery. Targeted invitation lists and limited outreach mean that they are largely a showcase for the "usual suspects," and that participants and decision makers simply hear and reaffirm their own views rather than opening themselves up to considering opposing perspectives and discovering common ground.

When our civic spaces for convening and deliberating are captured by decidedly nondemocratic processes, citizens take away two messages: first, that there is little meaning in these events; second, and worse, that there is an actual risk in participating. This is a precarious state of affairs. Our government will remain gridlocked unless and until we revitalize the link between the public and elected leaders. To achieve the robust, productive public dialogue that will help reestablish this link, deliberative spaces must be accessible and safe for every member of the community, including our elected officials.

Something amazing happens when people find themselves in a safe public space: there is a willingness to open up to new ways of thinking about long-held beliefs, and real relationships are built across differences. A participant in the Our Budget, Our Economy initiative (discussed in detail in the Chapter Ten) put it well when she said: "It was so refreshing to have civil discourse among people of different ages, persuasions, and backgrounds. Congress could learn a lot from our experience. The tone of our discussions was polite, respectful, and everyone contributed" (America*Speaks* 2011).

STRATEGIES FOR CREATING A SAFE PUBLIC SPACE

The task of creating a safe, accessible, deliberative space has multiple dimensions, two of which will be highlighted here: creating the literal physical space in which the public comes together to participate, and creating the psychological space in which the public will be doing the challenging, interactive work. Both of these dimensions work together to create an opportunity for effective engagement, and each is vitally important for success of the process.

The physical attributes of a safe deliberative space are specific and clearly achievable. They include ample room without crowding; comfortable furniture, lighting, and temperature; a nonconfining room layout and use of technologies that enable everyone to see and participate in the program with equal access; presentation materials that match participants' diverse abilities, for example in regard to language, literacy, and special needs; and ease of access to the venue, meaning proximity of public transit, availability of parking, and so on. Surprisingly, spaces that meet all of these criteria are very difficult to find in many American communities.

Ensuring a safe psychological space for citizen dialogue is a somewhat more involved undertaking. The goal is to establish a level playing field on which all members of the public feel safe enough to participate fully. Several strategies are required to create such a space:

- Make sure all of the planning work is grounded in an in-depth demographic analysis
- Attend to the symbolism of the location
- Create a welcoming and supportive atmosphere in the hall
- Plan table seating so that it ensures interaction across demographic and ideological groups
- Provide experienced process facilitators for every table, and moderators for online dialogue, to ensure everyone can participate and to keep the discussions focused and productive
- Present clear expectations for the work, its purpose, and desired outcomes

A discussion of these strategies follows.

MAKE SURE PLANNING IS GROUNDED IN AN IN-DEPTH DEMOGRAPHIC ANALYSIS

Despite the increasing diversification of our society, most public engagement modalities used in the United States today are still designed around the expectations and conversational style of educated white males. The planned progression of the work is often linear, logical, and based on data, even though the lingua franca of many participants may be more oriented toward the use of personal contexts, stories, and emotions. For *all* participants to be comfortable participating, for them to have the psychological space they need to speak their individual truths, such differences must be taken into account in the design of a deliberation, in the framing of the informational materials and questions, in the order of the agenda, and in the place and time of the event.

To accomplish this, the planning team for an engagement process must assess the range of possible differences among participants. They should start by imagining a room full of people representing every part of the community affected by the issue under discussion. Do all elements of the process enable all people to participate equally? Does the process work just as well for women as it does for men, for people of different ages, and for all minority and ethnic groups? The team should review these questions, and on discovering that there are groups for which they do not know the answers they must meet with the groups in their own environment and have a conversation about what group members will need to feel comfortable and confident about fully participating in the public process being designed.

In a democracy, members of all groups should have access to a public meeting. They should have equal opportunity to understand and influence the substance, and they should feel safe and confident enough to speak their mind and respectfully listen to others.

ATTEND TO THE SYMBOLISM OF THE LOCATION

An important part of the analysis just described is an assessment of the physical attributes as well as the symbolism of the proposed deliberation location. Use of federal office or auditorium space, although perhaps the most convenient and least expensive option for a host agency, can send a message that participants are guests in the deliberation and that their views will be listened to politely but are not necessarily considered equal to those of the host. Use of a community-based setting, such as a library, community college, recreation center, or convention center, can help reverse that perception.

At the same time, it would be naïve to assume that all such locations would be considered equal by all participants. A convention center conveniently situated in one part of town may feel dangerously "on the other side of the tracks" for some segments of the population. In the end, there may be no perfect location, but attention to this detail will have a definite impact on participants. Determining the location is an important task that should not be underestimated.

Create a Welcoming and Supportive Atmosphere

A welcoming atmosphere is a vital component of a safe deliberative space and can be achieved in a number of ways. America*Speaks*'s experience in creating these spaces suggests some key attributes, such as clear signage in multiple languages; having greeters to ensure that participants are not wandering around trying to figure out where they are supposed to go; incorporating public officials into the greeting process; having light snacks, coffee, or other beverages available for people to carry to their table; offering language interpretation as needed; and having someone responsible for taking the lead in breaking the ice and making introductions at the tables. For participants who may never before have experienced anything like a public deliberation and, further, who are being asked to sit at a table full of strangers, increasing their comfort in whatever ways possible is an important first step.

Another component of a welcoming and supportive atmosphere—and one that is critical to ensuring focused and productive work on the issue under discussion—is the presence, when appropriate, of representatives from constituency services agencies, such as social services, law enforcement, or licensing and permitting. Although citizens are attending the deliberation to make a contribution on the larger issues that have been identified, they may bring with them personal issues of concern that, although related to the larger topic, are tangential to the purpose of the process and to the eventual development of recommendations. In America*Speaks*'s experience, providing on-site capacity for personal issues to be heard and addressed enables affected individuals to participate fully in their table group and not be distracted from the larger discussion and goals.

PLAN TABLE SEATING TO ENSURE INTERACTION ACROSS GROUPS

The integrity of a deliberative process and the utility of the outcomes depend on planned table seating. It is human nature to seek out the comfort of friends or familiar-looking people in a public setting. If left to their own devices, deliberation participants will naturally cluster together at tables based on their previous relationships; their race, ethnicity, gender, and age; or other characteristics. Although natural, such self-segregating undermines the event's ability to surface shared priorities across differences. A room full of tables of like-minded people does little more than recreate the policy atmosphere in the outside world, in which many people attend principally to the media outlets that support their own worldview and hold steadfastly to their own positions on the issues.

To prevent this self-segregation, the planning team randomly assigns seating that creates a real demographic mix at each table and ensures that participants will have discussions with people with different points of view. Deborah Dalton, Senior Conflict Resolution Specialist at the U.S. Environmental Protection Agency (EPA), put it simply: "Our facilitators usually don't leave seating to chance" (Dalton 2012).

PROVIDE EXPERIENCED PROCESS FACILITATORS FOR EVERY TABLE

As described here, high-quality democratic dialogue depends on the ability of people of diverse opinions to air their differences with civility and respect and to develop shared understandings and mutually agreeable outcomes. This usually does not happen without help. Skilled, neutral facilitation is required—it is one of the most critical aspects of creating a safe public space for deliberation. Participants routinely say that the quality of the facilitation at their table was a major factor for success.

Facilitation of table discussions ensures that all participants feel comfortable expressing their points of view; that people actually listen in an effort to understand each other, and are not

FIGURE 8.1 HARD AT WORK IN A 21ST CENTURY TOWN MEETING

simply waiting for the opportunity to assert their own opinions. Facilitators help a group work through extensive or complicated informational material by attending to the time, tasks, and goals. They also make sure that summaries of the group's discussion fairly represent the diversity of views that have been expressed. Roger Bernier of the Centers for Disease Control and Prevention summarized it well when he said: "Neutral facilitation is key because people will not have to spend any energy wondering if what they are saying is being judged by somebody with a particular agenda" (Bernier 2012).

In short, the facilitator helps create a safe environment in which participants can be honest and really listen to one another, and in which there is discussion, not debate. By contrast, when people are allowed only to advocate for their beliefs and "be right," opportunities for real discussion are diminished. Table 8.1 summarizes the key distinctions.

Skilled process facilitators can be recruited locally from a number of professional fields, including organization development, human resources, education, and counseling. Faith-based groups are also a good source for skilled facilitators as long as they maintain neutrality on the topic. Regardless of the field, facilitators must have the capacity to effectively lead group dialogue, elicit discussion within a diverse group, and help participants discover their areas of shared agreement, all in a compressed time frame. They must be able to simultaneously facilitate the discussion and take notes. And they must have exceptional listening skills and the capacity to remain neutral and support the expression of many different points of view. There are numerous

TABLE 8.1 DEBATE VERSUS DISCUSSION

Debate	*Discussion*
There is a right answer, and someone has it.	Many people have pieces of the answer, and together they can craft a new solution.
Participants are combative and attempt to prove the other side wrong.	Participants work collaboratively together toward common understanding.
The debate is about winning.	The discussion is about exploring common ground.
Participants listen to find flaws and make counterarguments.	Participants listen to understand, finding meaning and agreement.
Participants defend assumptions as truth.	Participants reveal assumptions for reevaluation.
Participants critique the other side's position.	Participants reexamine all positions.
Participants defend their own views against those of others.	Participants admit that others' thinking can improve their own.
Participants search for flaws and weaknesses in other positions.	Participants search for strengths and value in others' positions.
Participants seek a conclusion or vote that ratifies their position.	Participants discover new options that satisfy all of their interests.

resources available on facilitation techniques from organizations such as the International Association for Public Participation, the International Association of Facilitators, the Organization Development Network, the American Society of Training and Development, and the National Coalition for Dialogue & Deliberation, among others.

A similar function is the moderation of online discussion. The downsides of open discussion online are well known: citizens sometimes attack each other personally; use inappropriate language; stray from the designated subject; or engage in a variety of other behaviors that can diminish the tone, quality, and outcomes of this work. Moderators play an important role in mitigating these problems. Recognizing that it is not possible to completely prevent uncivil behavior, it is essential that moderators monitor the discussion and intervene to keep it within the bounds to which the participants have agreed. To maintain online discussion that is engaging and trustworthy as well as open and transparent, it is important for moderators to quickly remove damaging content and respond to inappropriate or off-topic comments.

FIGURE 8.2 SKILLED PROCESS FACILITATION IS CRITICAL
TO CREATING A SAFE SPACE FOR DELIBERATION

Present Clear Expectations for the Work

Public managers understand well the importance of setting realistic expectations in any interaction with the public. There are two junctures at which this is particularly important: during the exploratory work that is done in communities, and during the deliberation itself.

In the preparation for a deliberation, transparent conversations that are part of a thorough educational process can help set and manage realistic expectations. Care should be taken in these consultations to ensure that community members do not get the impression that whatever they want is what will happen in the deliberation. Further, an overaccommodation of the needs of any one subgroup will detract from the credibility of the deliberation in the same way that disenfranchising any subgroup would.

Participants come to a deliberation with a wide range of expectations as well as personal objectives or desires. Some of these will be consistent with what has been planned for the deliberation, and some will not. In the end, people who have unrealistic expectations of what will transpire are likely to feel let down or conclude that the process was not safe or fair. It is therefore vital to begin the work by setting clear expectations about the process and the range of outcomes so that participants understand what will be possible to accomplish and what is outside the bounds of that particular deliberation.

Creating a Safe Public Space: Examples from Several Initiatives

Over nearly twenty years of practice, America*Speaks* has created many safe public spaces for deliberation. Although we consistently pursued the overarching objectives and tasks described earlier, each instance always had unique features. A few examples are highlighted here to demonstrate a range of possible scenarios in the creation of safe space. The initiatives will be familiar to the reader.

CREATING SAFE SPACE IN THE NEW ORLEANS COMMUNITY CONGRESSES

As described in Chapter Three, citizen engagement faced daunting challenges following Hurricane Katrina. In addition to the unprecedented destruction and loss across New Orleans, the long history of segregation and disenfranchisement of minority groups in the city had been greatly exacerbated by the disproportionate impact of the storm on these groups. To overcome citizens' distrust of governance processes, creation of a safe, deliberative space for the New Orleans Community Congresses was a top priority.

One of the unique aspects of New Orleans is the strong personal and cultural attachment residents have to their various neighborhoods. The French Quarter, the Garden District, Treme, the lower Ninth Ward, Gentilly, Algiers, and Lakeview, among others, all have a unique identity, history, style, and character with which residents proudly identify. In the lead-up to the Community Congresses, the core team spent time with citizens from all of these neighborhoods, making sure their individual cultures and perspectives were represented in the planning process and in the discussion agendas.

Another unique feature of New Orleans is that compared to many other American cities, it has an unusually high percentage of people whose families have lived there for generations (Ren 2011; City-data.com 2012a–e). To acknowledge this special fact, in addition to the standard questions about age, race, and income that are asked at the outset of every 21st Century Town Meeting so that participants, the media, and decision makers can see who is in the room, to lead off Community Congress II, participants were also asked: "How deep are your New Orleans roots?" Remarkably, nearly 30 percent of participants came from a family that had lived in the city for four generations or more.

During the deliberation, in keeping with the America*Speaks* model, skilled process facilitators were present at every table. In addition, as described earlier in Chapter Three, given the trauma that all participants had been through, local grief counselors were on-site to talk privately with those who needed a quiet space to do so. Every deliberation location hosted constituency services tables so that participants could get help managing their immediate needs and be better able to focus on the work of the deliberation.

In addition, planners meticulously attended to the physical environment so that people could do the difficult work in a space that had important symbols and energy expressive of their love of New Orleans. Participants in the Community Congresses were surrounded by the poetry, images, music, food, and culture of their city. A second-line parade played people into and out of the room to profound effect.

Finally, it is important to note that the Community Congresses took place in the New Orleans Convention Center. This was the site of heart-breaking tragedy in the aftermath of Hurricane Katrina and the flooding, and it quickly became symbolic of the complete disenfranchisement and abandonment of the citizenry by all levels of government. Housing citizen deliberation in this location was a dramatic way for New Orleanians to take back this important public space; to convert it into a place of healing and hope for their city.

CREATING SAFE SPACE IN THE WASHINGTON, DC, CITIZEN SUMMITS

In planning for the Washington, DC Citizen Summits, aimed at engaging the people of the District in budget and policy decision making, the choice of venue was a contentious issue from the start. In a city with a long history of stark racial and socioeconomic divisions, the physical geography was strongly associated with different population groups. Simply put, white people in the District who were more affluent lived west of the Anacostia River, whereas poorer, mostly African American people lived east of it. Daily lives and lines of commerce rarely crossed this natural boundary. An early recommendation for a location for the first Citizen Summit was auditorium space at the

University of the District of Columbia (UDC), which was well equipped and available at a reasonable cost. However, in vetting the idea, planners were quickly informed in no uncertain terms that many African Americans would not feel comfortable coming to UDC because of its location in the upper northwest section of the district.

After much consultation, the convention center in downtown Washington, DC was selected as the best venue for the Citizen Summit. Its location was central in the city, it was relatively accessible via public transit, and it was not "owned" by any subgroup of the population or political establishment. Further, the large, open space of the convention center enabled America*Speaks* to establish a specific environment that would build a feeling of familiarity and safety for participants. For every named neighborhood in the city, a banner with an iconic photograph was created and displayed in the hall so that when people entered they felt an immediate connection to their own neighborhood. They were also able to discover and appreciate the symbols that were important to their fellow citizens from other neighborhoods. It was quite a feeling to walk into the Citizen Summit and literally "see" the whole city surrounding the space in which people would be working together to make important budget and policy decisions that would have an impact on the city's future.

CREATING SAFE SPACE IN LISTENING TO THE CITY AND CALIFORNIA*SPEAKS*

Listening to the City and California*Speaks* were, in some respects, as distinct as any two deliberative exercises could be. The former was a response to a national tragedy, took place in one large urban area (New York City), and sought to produce recommendations on architectural and rebuilding plans for a major U.S. city. The latter was a deliberation about an ongoing public policy issue, took place simultaneously in eight different locations across California, and sought recommendations for statewide legislation. Despite the differences, these two initiatives shared a common feature: highly diverse participant demographics created the need to overcome significant language and cultural barriers in order to establish a level and safe deliberative space.

To encourage participation by undocumented immigrants in Listening to the City, the planning team modified the standard registration process so that providing identifying information would be optional. Further, the team took multiple steps to accommodate all participants' language needs and preferences. The event offered simultaneous spoken translation in Spanish and Chinese, with some of the table facilitators themselves being fluent in these languages. In addition, "whisper translation" (simultaneous translation by participants assisting their tablemates) was provided in these two languages, as well as in Russian for a group of immigrants from that community. The participant guide, outreach flyer, and memorial mission statement were translated into Spanish and Chinese. One of the promotional advertisements was also translated into Hebrew and Yiddish to be included in appropriate newspapers. The deliberation materials were made available in Braille and in large print, and there was sign language translation on-site during the event.

For California*Speaks,* across the eight deliberation locations, discussion guides and other printed materials were made available in Spanish and Chinese, as well as in large print. In addition, simultaneous interpretation via headset was provided in Spanish, Cantonese, and Mandarin. Thirty-three bilingual facilitators led table discussions in Spanish, and a number of tables across the eight sites had whisper translators simultaneously translating into Hmong, Thai, Laotian, and Vietnamese.

Taken together, all of these examples paint a picture of the considered and intentional steps needed to ensure, as much as possible, that citizens have a safe space in which to come together and deliberate. Although each deliberative context is likely to have unique features, the same overarching issues need to be considered while planning and designing any citizen engagement initiative.

FIGURE 8.3 LOCAL ARTIST DANIEL CAMACHO CAPTURED THE SPIRIT OF CITIZENS WORKING TOGETHER AT CALIFORNIA*SPEAKS*

THE PUBLIC MANAGER'S ROLE IN CREATING A SAFE PUBLIC SPACE

Although some of the concepts and strategies described in this chapter may seem logical and intuitive, the habit patterns of most public agencies do not reflect them. For example, the place, time, and process for a citizen deliberation undertaken by a public agency are often set to match the convenience of the agency rather than the needs of the participating communities. As noted earlier, this tends to leave participants with the sense that they are guests as opposed to true partners in the process. Deborah Dalton of EPA recognized the challenges that selecting a space can sometimes pose for public managers: "For most big EPA national discussions or meetings we are stuck with whatever room we can afford to rent that will fit the group, not cost a fortune, and be easy to reach and open to the public. We try not to choose EPA conference rooms as the biggest ones have horrible acoustics, and the other ones are not big enough to fit the group" (Dalton 2012).

Despite the challenges, there are some specific steps public managers can take to achieve a more level playing field for citizen engagement work. Foremost, they can embrace the importance and the nuances of providing a safe space for deliberation. They can then build their knowledge of the full range of constituent groups and stakeholders to identify factors that will increase or decrease safety. As discussed in this chapter, this information should be infused into every aspect of the planning process, such as the meeting location, the facilitation plan, and the nature of the agenda, to name a few.

To be sure, bringing a wider range of constituent groups into the process for consultation will mean more work in the planning phase. It will also mean moving the work to community venues and providing for more staffing during the deliberation (for example, greeters, content experts, constituency services representatives, and so on). If this additional work is done, there will be a greater possibility of success. If it is skipped, the resources put into the effort may not be used as efficiently and effectively as they could be.

Finally, managers must commit to having skilled process facilitators at all discussion tables. Circulating a handful of staff to support those tables that appear to be struggling is not sufficient. All tables, and all participants, must be able to move through the material with the same degree of comfort and success. Excellent facilitation is the way to ensure this.

Although there may be financial considerations attendant to these actions, substantially improved outcomes—as well as increased participant ownership of and commitment to those outcomes—will make the additional investment worthwhile. Patricia Milligan of the U.S. Nuclear Regulatory Commission put it this way: "It's true that there are a lot of travel expenses, staff time, lost time away from offices, and in some cases overtime when you do it this way. It is not cheap. But you cannot pay lip service to it [public involvement] and expect the results you want. The credibility that we create by investing in these processes builds real trust with the public and with our stakeholders. People don't believe information unless it comes from people and institutions they trust, so in the end, the trust we build really helps us do our work" (Milligan 2012).

Public Manager Perspectives

Building Capacity to Facilitate Public Dialogue

Deborah Dalton, Senior Conflict Resolution Specialist, Conflict Prevention and Resolution Center, U.S. Environmental Protection Agency

The Context

In the mid-1980s the Environmental Protection Agency (EPA) was concerned about high rates of litigation on environmental regulations. The agency's rule-making process sought input from the public and regulated industry only *after* a draft regulation had been developed. This input was frequently too late or too positional and adversarial to be useful. As a result, final regulations were often disputed, and, although the agency generally prevailed, the time and resources spent litigating delayed implementation and slowed progress on important environmental concerns.

In response to these challenges, EPA determined to pilot a new method for getting early and more complete public input on environmental regulations. The Administrative Conference of the United States (ACUS) suggested a new process, called Regulatory Negotiation (or Reg Neg), that would seek out all affected individuals, organizations, and groups and, through consensus-based deliberations, draft the rule. One of ACUS's central recommendations was to have neutral, third-

party facilitators convene and manage these deliberations. This would serve three purposes (1) enable all
parties to participate fully and equally, (2) increase the
likelihood that parties would work through impasses,
and (3) allow agency negotiators to focus on the substantive issues.

Unfortunately, at the time when Reg Neg was being
conceptualized there were no mechanisms for federal
agencies to identify and contract with facilitators for
nonlabor-related projects. Federal contracting was (and
remains today) a complicated, time-consuming process
with significant barriers to retaining a cadre of neutral
facilitators for public engagement. Program offices interested in involving stakeholders in decision making had
limited knowledge about contracting and even less
enthusiasm for taking on the challenges it presented.

Overcoming Barriers and Building Capacity

With these concerns in mind, over the next fifteen years
EPA pursued these specific steps to overcome contracting barriers and build the capacity necessary to bring
the public more robustly into agency rule-making:

- *Established in-house expertise.* As a critical first step, in
  1984 EPA established an in-house unit—the
  Regulatory Negotiation Project (RNP)—charged
  with assessing, managing, and evaluating public
  engagement projects. The RNP was the earliest
  federal unit dedicated to nonlabor and
  nonworkplace conflict prevention or dispute
  resolution. With a staff of two, and with informal
  consulting relationships with the MIT-Harvard
  Program on Negotiation and several experienced
  environmental mediators, the RNP began to
  determine which rules might best fit the process
  and assess the suitability of particular conflicts for
  new interventions. The rules found most suitable
  for Reg Neg were those with identifiable parties

interested in early resolution of issues; reasonable, identifiable deadlines; and adequate information available to all. When summarizing their findings, RNP mediators often suggested alternative ways to engage stakeholders.

- *Made it easy to access services.* In response to the challenges in retaining facilitators on a case-by-case basis, in 1988 the RNP took the unique step of designing and completing a multiproject "mission" contract specifically for facilitation and mediation—the first in the federal government. This initial contract (small by today's standards but extensive and unique at the time) provided a mechanism for EPA offices to easily identify and retain knowledgeable, skilled facilitators for projects that involved stakeholders in environmental decision making. Efforts to build internal rosters of experienced facilitators who could then be "lent" across agencies at no cost were ongoing.

  As in the movie *Field of Dreams,* RNP staff found that "if you build it, they will come." With the contracting barrier removed, EPA program officers were more willing to seek help in managing conversations, dialogue, and negotiations—they quickly began to use the new contract for a growing number of projects. Further, relieved of contracting and organizing burdens, program offices could direct their energies toward working directly with the public and stakeholders to design programs (such as cross-media permitting efforts), discuss specific EPA policies (such as solid waste definitions), and conduct on-site cleanup activities.

- *Built internal capacity.* In addition to establishing in-house expertise and removing barriers, building internal capacity for public engagement within EPA was also critical. The key pathways for this effort were laying out specific policies and guidance, establishing personnel competencies in this area, and providing training.

In the policy arena, EPA worked with ACUS to pass statutes (such as the Administrative Dispute Resolution Act of 1996, the Negotiated Rulemaking Act of 1996, and others) that officially authorized agencies to undertake these public engagement processes. The agency also supported legislation to establish the U.S. Institute for Environmental Conflict Resolution (US IECR), as well as Executive Orders on Environmental Conflict Resolution, Cooperative Conservation, and Open Government. All of these efforts contributed to the credibility of these processes within EPA. In later years, the RNP led EPA efforts to develop, update, and publish official agency policies on the use of alternative dispute resolution and public involvement.

In addition to policymaking efforts, the RNP (renamed the Conflict Prevention and Resolution Center, or the CPRC) continues to offer regular trainings to EPA staff and management on negotiation, public involvement, dispute resolution, and stakeholder engagement. In 2011 alone more than 1,500 employees were trained. The CPRC is also developing a multiyear training strategy to more comprehensively build these competencies. In its 2011–2016 strategy, the CPRC is looking to achieve even more public and stakeholder participation in environmental decision making.

Results

Building internal capacity is a long-term effort that requires strategic vision. When the RNP was reestablished as the Conflict Prevention and Resolution Center, it began to report directly to the Office of General Counsel of EPA. With a professional staff of more than six people, the CPRC has become the largest, most active nonworkplace dispute resolution unit in the federal government. The CPRC continues to offer in-house design, assessment, and facilitation services, and manages a contract of nearly 175 projects ranging from facilitation of public meetings and major public policy negotiations to mediation of enforcement cases. In partnership with the US IECR, the CPRC has also implemented a comprehensive evaluation program for agreement-centered mediated cases and is exploring an evaluation program for other stakeholder engagement processes.

The results of this work have been far-reaching. In the past five years EPA has used facilitators or mediators to resolve conflicts and settle cases in the cleanup of highly contaminated river sediments in the Hudson and Housatonic Rivers; in the negotiation of regulations for detecting E. coli bacteria in every public water system in the United States; in negotiating fish consumption and water quality standards in Oregon to protect subsistence fishermen; and in conducting public outreach on air regulations for coal-fired power plants, to name just a few.

Another notable product of more than twenty-five years of identifying and using facilitators and mediators has been the development of the field of environmental conflict resolution as a profession. In the 1980s there were fewer than a dozen mediators or facilitators with some experience in environmental issues. Today there are more than two hundred, and it is a full-time career for many. In 2000 the CPRC and the US IECR developed a public, searchable database of experienced environmental conflict resolution professionals.

Ongoing Challenges

Our work isn't done. There are many public outreach efforts and dispute resolution processes in EPA that have yet to take advantage of the new opportunities for enhanced public dialogue supported by the CPRC. In addition, economic downturns reduce resources for public outreach and facilitated discussion as well as for the travel this work often requires. This is an ongoing challenge. Finally, although the Internet and social media make it easier to transmit information to the public, challenges remain in ensuring that the information is both useful and fully accessible. Agencies are still working to discover how best to use new information-sharing tools to establish trust and credibility in resolving differences or disputes.

CHAPTER NINE

STRATEGY FIVE: INFORM PARTICIPANTS

I am a firm believer in the people. If given the truth, they can be depended upon to meet any national crisis. The great point is to bring them the real facts.

ABRAHAM LINCOLN*

Important conversations about public issues occur naturally among ordinary people. Yet to go beyond casual conversation and be able to contribute meaningfully to decision making on complicated policy concerns, or to make tough budget trade-offs, citizens require in-depth information that is accessible, neutral, and factual. This chapter explores the importance of providing such information within the context of a citizen engagement initiative as well as within the larger media environment. It presents case examples to illustrate the concepts and explores the challenges and opportunities for public managers.

WHY INFORMING PARTICIPANTS IS IMPORTANT

There can be little doubt that to participate in decision making on complex matters of public policy, citizens must be as informed

---

*Thomas, H. *Front Row at the White House: My Life and Times.* New York: Scribner, 2000, 74.

as possible about the issues under discussion. In the most basic sense, this means providing them with high-quality and easy-to-understand informational materials and guidance for their deliberations. Strategies for developing such materials are described in detail in this chapter. However, the task is more complicated than simply distilling and packaging the appropriate information. Any content that is provided for a deliberation will naturally intersect with the understandings, beliefs, and attitudes that citizens bring with them into the room. And it is these understandings, beliefs, and attitudes, based largely on the potentially biased information citizens have been able to access through various media channels, that can be problematic when it comes to achieving civil discourse. Several disturbing trends in the information sphere have combined to create an environment in which the American people have vastly different levels of understanding on public issues, and often hold views based on misinformation. These trends, described in this section, mean that attention to the detailed development of factual, neutral, and accessible materials for deliberation is more important than ever.

Advancements over the last two decades in society's capacity for information sharing and knowledge building are, to put it simply, quite astounding. With constant access to the World Wide Web at our fingertips, no question need ever go unanswered for more than a few minutes, or even seconds. Ordinary people now have access to the inner workings and daily efforts of nearly every organization and person that affects their lives, from the grocery store around the corner to the office of their member of Congress. The benefits of this information explosion are many: in addition to offering extraordinary data access, it has given voice to millions, significantly expanded participation opportunities, and created an army of citizen journalists, to name but a few.

And still, although the explosion in communication platforms and devices has made the creation and consumption of information a national passion and pastime, access to information has remained persistently inequitable across our society (this topic is discussed in Chapter Thirteen). Further, the information explosion has been accompanied by an increasingly ideologically driven media and the proliferation of disinformation campaigns. Both of these trends have a direct impact on citizens' capacity to understand the world around them and to participate effectively in governance.

An Ideologically Driven Media

In a well-functioning democracy, the media provides citizens with credible, unbiased information about their society and the actions of their government. This has been a long-held standard in our nation. Illustrating the point, in 1835 Alexis de Tocqueville observed: "As men become more equal and individualism more of a menace, newspapers are more necessary. The belief that they just guarantee freedom would diminish their importance; they sustain civilization" (de Tocqueville 2003, 601).

Today's media are a far cry from a sustaining force in our civilization. And, as the educational components of both traditional and new media have shrunk, commercial interests and ideologically oriented outlets (for example, Fox News and MSNBC) have created and encouraged the proliferation of content that is ever more slanted. The result is that instead of establishing a unified national narrative based on neutral, fact-based information, the "news" has simply become a set of reverberation chambers reflecting what different segments of the American population are predisposed to believe. And as more and more people gravitate to slanted news coverage of one variety or another, the provision of neutral, fact-based news by mainstream outlets becomes less economically viable and therefore even rarer. As Eli Pariser described it in *The Filter Bubble: What the Internet Is Hiding from You,* "Democracy requires citizens to see things from one another's point of view, but instead we're more and more enclosed in our own bubbles. Democracy requires a reliance on shared facts, instead we're being offered parallel but separate universes" (Pariser 2011, 5).

In addition to the problem of "separate universes," today's media are no longer a consistently credible source of factual information. One example of this can be seen in the increasingly corrupted use of the "doctrine of fairness"—the idea that all sides of a story should be presented equally. Once a central pillar of journalistic integrity, the doctrine, as it related specifically to the Federal Communications Commission's oversight of the media, was upheld as constitutional by the Supreme Court in 1969 but then overturned by the Reagan Administration in 1987. Subsequent efforts to reinstate it were vetoed by President George H. W. Bush. As a result, we have lost the legal protection of the original intent of the doctrine of fairness. Unfortunately, we are now seeing a profound distortion of that doctrine. Ideologically driven media take the idea that all sides of a story must be presented equally, and in the name of "fairness" provide equal coverage of all views regardless of their actual credibility.

Coverage of climate change over the last several years provides many examples of this phenomenon. According to Daniel J. Weiss, Senior Fellow and Director of Climate Strategy at the Center for American Progress, "Simply casting doubt on the science behind climate change is a strategy that has been very effective. The way the 'doctrine of fairness' is being used, every point of view gets equal airtime no matter how bogus" (Weiss 2012).

In the same vein as the misuse of the fairness doctrine is the media's overall willingness to allow narrative lines with no basis in fact to make their way into the mainstream. One of the better-known examples of this was the "Climategate" scandal of 2009 in which the media broadly reported that hacked emails from the Climactic Research Unit at the University of East Anglia demonstrated that climate research was being falsified. A number of outlets later retracted their stories, and the scientists—and their findings—were exonerated. Retractions like this are rare and, in the end, the imprimatur of authenticity from the original story tends to leave the public with a lasting, erroneous impression.

In a more recent example, in April 2012 a false rumor about South Carolina governor Nikki Haley was quickly converted into "fact" as it was tweeted, retweeted, and posted by reporters at the *Washington Post, The Hill* (a Washington, DC political newspaper), the Drudge Report (a popular news aggregation website), and other outlets. In this instance, Governor Haley was able to dispel the rumor the next day, with a letter from the IRS confirming that she was not, in fact, the subject of an investigation. However, the events demonstrated quite clearly what can happen when the media are so cavalier with facts: citizens lose their ability to reliably understand and evaluate the events of the day. One result, in the particular context of this book, is that people come to citizen engagement work with firmly held misconceptions about the issues under discussion. Writing about the false rumors surrounding Governor Haley, *Washington Post* columnist Kathleen Parker put it succinctly: "Most disappointing . . . was the failure of some legitimate news organizations to turn the rumor over and examine its underbelly before repeating it. . . . [I]ntegrity of information is the one thing newspapers can promise. . . . [U]ltimately it is a matter of helping protect freedoms that will become diminished as a less-informed citizenry surrenders responsibility to titillation" (Parker 2012, A19).

DISINFORMATION CAMPAIGNS

Hand in hand with an ideologically driven media is a trend among public figures to openly engage in disinformation campaigns. In late 2011, as the election season for the 2012 presidential race was getting under way, *Washington Post* columnist Michael Gerson called out this phenomenon. He reported that then-candidate Michele Bachmann had "criticized 'unnecessary foreign entanglements,' while also admitting, 'I do not know enough about it to comment on it.'" He then cited radio talk show host Rush Limbaugh for "accusing President Obama of sending American troops 'to wipe out Christians in Sudan, Uganda,' before promising 'to do some research on it.'" Gerson went on to say, "in both cases, it is remarkable that public figures feel no hesitancy—no internal check of propriety or shame—about offering opinions while admitting ignorance. Especially when a few minutes on the Internet would have sufficed" (Gerson 2011).

We are living in an era in which public figures, including elected officials, feel free to disregard facts and make up their own truths; in which a standard political strategy is to stake out a specific area of disinformation and repeat it so often over an extended period of time that it comes to be believed as fact. The rapidity and extended reach of information transmission over the Internet accelerate this process. Public opinion polling is often used to further such campaigns. Both political parties—or sides of an issue—routinely put polls in the field that are deliberately designed to elicit answers that support their respective positions, and they then portray the results as bona fide public opinion.

It is certainly ironic that as our access to information has increased exponentially, so too has the successful use of disinformation. In this equation, both citizens and democracy lose. Unable to come to stable views that are based in fact and reality, the American people are ripe targets for manipulation and disenfranchisement. They are likely to come into a deliberation with marked differences in their understanding of the "facts" at hand. Undertaking a series of strategies to account for these differences and to reintroduce fact-based information will help ensure that all participants have a sound basis on which to engage in a discussion.

STRATEGIES FOR INFORMING PARTICIPANTS

To deliberate effectively, citizens will need a discussion guide or background brief. They might also benefit from a mixed-media presentation, such as a video, that complements the written material and engages alternative learning styles. For virtual or networked community-based deliberations (described in Chapter Twelve), the information can be presented on a designated website that links to even more resources. Regardless of the format, the materials should provide a history of the issue, lay out the current facts surrounding it, and offer a starting list of potential options for action. The information presented should meet a short list of key criteria: it must be accurate, neutral, and accessible. It should also be flexible enough to incorporate in-the-moment additions from participants. If these criteria are not met, the integrity of the engagement work will be compromised, as will be any results or recommendations that come out of it.

Because producing materials that are accurate, neutral, accessible, and flexible can be more challenging than it might appear at the outset, a committee-based approach is strongly recommended. The membership of the content development committee must reflect all views on the issue; the "keepers" of official government data on the subject must also participate. Following is a review of specific strategies that content development committees can employ to meet these necessary thresholds.

FIGURE 9.1 ONE OF HUNDREDS OF "PARTICIPANT GUIDES"
AMERICA*SPEAKS* HAS PRODUCED

ACHIEVING ACCURACY

Although ensuring accuracy of materials may seem a straightforward and easily achievable task, this is not always the case. Complex policy and budget issues are often characterized by honest differences on the facts, which can complicate efforts to create a final product that people of diverse views will all accept as accurate. Different budgetary assumptions, for example, can produce distinctly different analyses about the impact of a proposed strategy, and varied stakeholder perspectives on an issue can shape the possible universe of options. Further, up-to-the-minute circumstances, such as a budget cut, or political realities, such as an election, can have an impact on the information landscape. Therese McMillan, Deputy Administrator at the Federal Transit Administration, commented on the complexity of the task: "Experience has taught us that although we might think we have a 'complete set of facts,' people can have very different interpretations and truths that about those facts. For example, if you're talking about potential reductions in services, the truth from a transit manager's perspective is that a 30% budget cut by the state leaves no choice but to cut service. However, from a rider's perspective, implementing a budget cut does represent a choice being made about his or her ability to get home from work after a midnight shift" (McMillan 2012). In the end, material developers must distinguish between differences of opinion, disinformation, and facts; respect all views; *and* adhere to standards of accuracy that are as strict as possible.

ACHIEVING NEUTRALITY

If an issue is sufficiently important and ripe that the public can have an impact on real-time decision making, chances are it is also contested in one way or another. Stakeholders, officials, and ordinary citizens may have lined up on different sides of the issue, and they may have begun to express, and in some cases become entrenched in, their strong opinions. Because the goal of authentic engagement work is to enable participants to reach across their differences and find common ground, it is extremely important that the information from which they are working not favor one position over another. Neutral information will in fact be the bridge across which citizens of diverse viewpoints can meet. To achieve this, a meticulously balanced content development committee is essential.

However, as noted earlier, achieving neutrality is often more difficult than might be anticipated. The task of creating informational materials for the Our Budget, Our Economy initiative illustrates the challenges. Larry Haas, a journalist and former White House communication strategist who was brought on to write the informational materials for Our Budget, Our Economy, described it this way:

> In Washington, budget policy is inherently contentious. Our Budget, Our Economy was designed to reassure our elected leaders that, in fact, they can come together around a plan to reduce deficits and debt because, all across America, average people from all walks of life could do so. To achieve that we had to create clear, concise, accessible written materials with which average Americans could understand the tough issues involved with cutting spending and raising taxes and, in turn, make their own choices.
>
> To develop the necessary material, we worked with a "Content Committee" of budget experts from across the political spectrum. Although we hoped to present basic budget information as objectively as possible, that proved no easy task. Liberal members of our committee worried that our materials would drive participants too much toward spending cuts, while conservatives worried that they would drive participants too much toward tax increases. We also struggled to explain the challenges of slowing health care costs in ways that average Americans would understand.
>
> In the end, our committee members compromised enough with one another to reach closure on the material. The experience, however, highlighted the very intense political nature of the budget debate and reminded everyone involved just how deadlocked that debate has become [Haas 2012].

The case study later in this chapter further illustrates the challenges in developing neutral, fact-based materials, as well as the value of a committee-based approach to this task.

ACHIEVING ACCESSIBILITY

America*Speaks*'s experience in developing more than one hundred participant discussion guides over nearly twenty years suggests that to make the content accessible to everyone in the community, an eighth-grade reading level is an appropriate target. Our experience also shows that although this goal is often easily agreed on, after the material is reviewed and edited by content experts, the reading level inevitably edges upward. Engaging someone without content expertise to read through the near-final material and edit it according to that standard is a useful strategy for ensuring it remains sufficiently accessible.

An additional consideration in regard to accessibility is whether and how to use multiple vehicles for disseminating information to accommodate a range of learning styles. Award-winning cinematographer and director Louie Schwartzberg noted that people use visual processing to take in the majority of the information they receive in a day (TEDxSF 2011). For many people, visual processing may be a preferred learning style. Therefore, a video presentation of the key information in the discussion guides can be an important tool for many deliberation participants. A video has the additional benefit of helping those with low literacy levels access the content. The contextual analysis undertaken for the initiative should lead to an understanding of the literacy levels among potential participants and guide organizers in their use of video.

Table facilitators must also know the content sufficiently well that if they observe a participant struggling to read and comprehend the material, they can provide assistance. Depending on the relevant demographics, translation may be a necessary component of ensuring accessibility. For the Washington, DC, Citizen Summits, the informational materials were published in five languages: English, Spanish, Mandarin, Korean, and Vietnamese. To meet very complex language demands, simultaneous translation devices may also be necessary. In 2005–2006 America*Speaks*'s international arm, Global Voices, collaborated on Meeting of Minds: European Citizens' Deliberation on Brain Science, which brought together 126 participants representing nine European countries and languages: Belgium, Denmark, France, Germany, Greece,

Hungary, Italy, the Netherlands, and the United Kingdom. Deliberation in nine languages was made possible through simultaneous translation at individual table discussions, multilingual documents, and roomwide translation during presentations.

Clearly, work like this requires significant effort and resources. Yet it is truly necessary for creating a level playing field that supports collective decision making. It is also true that many of the materials that are created can have a shelf life beyond a single deliberative event. For example, the discussion guides created for Our Budget, Our Economy are now being used as texts in both high school and college classrooms.

MAINTAINING FLEXIBILITY

To be sure, a discussion guide or brief that has been printed and distributed has limited capacity to be flexible. At the same time, authentic engagement of the public demands flexibility; it must acknowledge the views citizens bring to the table and incorporate the work they do once there. To do that, the engagement process and its materials must make room for the real-time inclusion of recommendations and options that come from citizens themselves—taking up ideas that the content development team had not included, or even those that had been considered but were rejected. Reflecting on a public engagement effort undertaken by the U.S. Forest Service, retired Deputy Regional Forester Richard Stem described the benefits of maintaining flexibility: "Throughout the public engagement process, trust between staff and stakeholders, and between stakeholder groups, had increased significantly... The public had so much empowerment once they had the information. We were able to devise some very effective options. By giving them power, they eventually gave it back to us" (Stem 2012). In addition to ensuring the integrity of the process, being open to the public's ideas for action often generates new alternatives or solutions that can then be explored.

For public managers who are steeped in expertise on a given subject—and who may be responsible for the outcomes of deliberative work—allowing for unanticipated content may be a difficult strategy to embrace. Yet it is essential. It may not be possible to give new material *equal* treatment, because there will be no time for data gathering and analysis. But table discussions and facilitation from the front of the room should nonetheless seek to incorporate and address emerging material wherever possible. Further, the informational materials themselves can explicitly state that the incorporation of new ideas is an expectation of the deliberation, and leave dedicated spaces and pages for this content. Additional work on new options suggested by the public can then be taken up after the deliberation has concluded.

Using Content Experts

No matter how much time and attention are put into the development of a discussion guide, background brief, or opening video, additional questions and issues for clarification will always arise during the course of the deliberation. This reality is best managed by having content experts available to participants during a deliberation. In the America*Speaks* model, content experts are *always* on-site. They circulate throughout the room and, when asked, provide clarification, additional information, and answers to specific questions. Across all of our projects, participating experts have noted afterward that they were extremely impressed by the public's understanding and the sophistication of their questions. Joe Minarik, Senior Vice President at the Committee for Economic Development, served as a content expert for the Our Budget, Our Economy initiative at the Philadelphia deliberation site. In reflecting on his experience, Minarik said:

> Even after absorbing the discussion material, participants often needed to dig deeper in order to resolve the range of opinions they were encountering at their tables. As I moved around the room, I found that their questions were far more sophisticated than I would have guessed they would be, and that once I gave them new or clarifying information, they were able to apply it immediately to the discussion. At the end of the day, though, I was most struck by the sincerity of their desire to find substantive areas of agreement with their tablemates—people they had only just met that morning [Minarik 2012].

Public managers have also learned through experience the importance of having content experts on hand. Patricia Milligan

FIGURE 9.2 PARTICIPANTS PRACTICE RAISING THEIR CARDS TO CALL FOR AN EXPERT

of the U.S. Nuclear Regulatory Commission (NRC) described it this way:

> When it comes to the cost and resource allocation for public engagement processes, you have to dedicate the amount that will be needed. In order to be credible, you need to be prepared with more than just canned or pre-prepared remarks and promises to "get back to you with the answer." Sometimes we have up to 20 staff at a meeting in order to have the right experts in the room. That way, when someone asks a specific question, about earthquakes for example, and we introduce our NRC expert to answer the question, it shows that the NRC takes its meeting

processes seriously—we supply the experts to answer the challenging technical questions on-the-spot. People respect that effort on our part, even if they disagree with us [Milligan 2012].

The following case study of a large-scale citizen deliberation on health care reform demonstrates the use of these various strategies for information development in a particularly high-stakes political environment.

INFORMING PARTICIPANTS: A CASE STUDY

In the middle of the last decade California was home to more than thirty-seven million people and was spending nearly $200 billion each year on a health care system that leaders readily acknowledged not only was inefficient but also allowed many people to fall through the cracks. In response, then-governor Arnold Schwarzenegger declared 2007 to be "the year of health care reform" (Harbage and Haycock 2008, 1), and major legislative proposals began to emerge from across the political spectrum. Many feared the issue would fall victim to politics as usual and began to seek strategies for pushing the issue to some satisfactory resolution. In February of that year the large-scale citizen engagement work of America*Speaks* caught the attention of business and philanthropy leaders, and the California*Speaks* initiative was launched.

Because rising health care costs were having an increasingly negative impact on the California economy, and because statewide health care reform had already been unsuccessfully attempted two times, elected officials, stakeholders, and the public were particularly anxious that California*Speaks* move the process forward. On the positive side, this sense of urgency led the governor and the legislative leadership of both parties to put core issues on the table, to be willing to openly identify the various pros and cons, and to bring the issues to the public for an honest debate. At the same time, the policy environment was extremely contentious, and as a result the preparatory work, in particular the development of the informational materials that would be the basis for the discussion, was very challenging.

Navigating Difficult Terrain

Health care reform is a uniquely complex public policy issue, combining matters of social policy, medical science, health economics, and health delivery systems. In California, as was true around the country, the terrain was also quite crowded with a wide range of well-connected policy experts, think tanks, and academics pushing for a sophisticated debate on the potential options. Further, many of the known content experts were also strong advocates for one option or another. And just about every existing data point on the issue was already in public use somewhere, to either support or refute various ideological positions. In this environment, finding a way to produce a neutral and broadly acceptable discussion guide was especially challenging.

To begin, it was necessary to create a well-balanced content committee made up of individuals with strong credibility across the ideological spectrum. People from each critical area of expertise also had to be represented on the committee: health policy, health economics, and health delivery systems. Extensive knowledge of the California budget was also key. Fortunately, the state of California has a nonpartisan state budget office (akin to the Congressional Budget Office at the federal level) that is widely understood to be a source of neutral and reliable information—in a number of states this function is filled by two legislative budget offices, one working for each political party. Finally, because state health policies inevitably intersect with national policies, the committee required both state- and national-level experts in all of the substantive areas. In the end, the team that came together to oversee the development of the discussion guide and materials included representatives from the Massachusetts Institute of Technology, Harbage Consulting, the Urban Institute, the Heritage Foundation, the California Health-Care Foundation, and the Insure the Uninsured Project at the UCLA Center for Health Policy Research.

Seeking to cover the breadth of policy issues in the area of health care reform and to directly reflect the legislative actions being considered in the state assembly and senate, the content committee focused on five key policy topics:

- Should employers be required to either offer insurance to employees or pay into a group insurance fund? If so, how much should they pay?

- Should the state government increase access to affordable health insurance for low- and moderate-income Californians?
- Should insurance companies be required to guarantee coverage to all applicants regardless of preexisting conditions? Should there be a limit on insurance companies' administrative fees and profits?
- Should individuals be required to have health insurance? Should employees be required to accept health insurance if their employer offers it?
- What can each part of the system do to help control costs while improving health outcomes?

For each topic, the group worked to agree on the range of possible options citizens could consider. The financial impacts for each option were then analyzed by the state budget office, and the material was closely reviewed by foundations that conduct technical research on issues pertaining to health care, by health policy staff in the governor's office, by key program managers in the state Department of Health Services, and by the minority and majority legislative leaders and staff in the state assembly and senate.

Once the content was laid out, the committee began to work on a framework for the discussion that would keep all of the options open for as long as possible. Again, given the contentiousness of the terrain and the fact that many participants were likely to come to the deliberation with strongly held views shaped by the media and ongoing advocacy efforts, it was important to ensure that all topics had an equal amount of discussion time. To achieve this aim, the committee devised a process whereby participants would identify what they liked, what concerned them, and what they felt was missing in each health care reform option and also lay out the range of conditions, if any, under which they would support each of the options.

HITTING A SNAG

As discussion materials were under development, it became apparent that one of the options for which some were advocating, a single-payer government-based system, was going to present problems. In the months before California*Speaks,* Governor

Schwarzenegger had vetoed single-payer health care reform legislation, and made it clear that if the legislature brought him another such bill as the result of the deliberation he would use his veto power again. Yet contextual analysis for California*Speaks* determined that there was public support for this option. Recent polling had shown that a significant portion of the public (just under 50 percent) was supportive of a single-payer system (DiCamillo and Field 2007), and strong and well-organized advocacy groups, such as the California Nurses Association, were behind it as well. Battle lines were drawn.

Given the importance of linking the deliberation agenda to real decision-making opportunities, after much work the content committee was able to reach a compromise. The discussion guide included information on the single-payer option but, acknowledging Governor Schwarzenegger's veto threat, was organized to focus the discussion first on the policy options in the two non-single-payer bills before the state legislature. The single-payer option would come up for discussion later in the agenda.

After two months and countless hours of work, the discussion materials and agenda for Califoria*Speaks* were set. In addition to a twenty-page discussion guide, translated into Spanish and Chinese, key information would be given to the assembly by video and a PowerPoint presentation.

RESULTS OF THE WORK

On August 11, 2007, 3,500 Californians gathered in eight different sites to participate in a daylong, in-depth deliberation about a range of health care reform options available to the state, and two pending legislative proposals in particular. The majority of California*Speaks* participants were drawn randomly. However, by oversampling and adding outreach for harder-to-reach groups, a close approximation of the state's demographics, health insurance statuses, and income levels was achieved.

Although legislative staff had been quite skeptical about whether ordinary citizens could carefully analyze such complex health care subjects, their concerns proved unfounded. This diverse group of citizens gave leaders an array of specific guidance on policy options related to employer, government, insurer, and individual responsibility. In just one example, approximately half of the participants across all eight locations indicated that they would support an employer requirement if it provided choice; addressed the issue of part-time, seasonal, and other nontraditional employees; ensured that employers would not be encouraged to reduce existing coverage or benefits; and incorporated a cap to prevent skyrocketing costs as well as protection for small businesses.

The single-payer compromise that had been crafted by the content committee worked well overall. However, in both Oakland and Humboldt County, a significant segment of the participants was frustrated that the single-payer option was not treated exactly the same as the other possibilities. This necessitated some in-the-moment adjustments to the program. Jeff Voorhees, who was the moderator in Humboldt County that day, described the experience this way:

> In Humboldt County, we had a large and vocal group who were advocating a single-payer plan, and who objected to the fact that it was not being included more directly in the discussion. We also had an elected State Senator present, Sheila Kuehl, who was a strong supporter of single-payer. Her presence at the event had a rallying effect on those who wanted a single-payer option to be considered as part of the discussion. I could see that the longer she stayed the bigger the problem was going to get in terms of being able to "stick with the script."

> We tried to handle things in the room for a while. Eventually, I went to her and talked about what was happening, what was at stake, and why the decision had been made to not include single-payer as a formal discussion option. She was very responsive, and we devised a plan through which the issue would be addressed from the stage in the main site in Los Angeles so that everybody in all eight sites would hear it. The Senator agreed to the plan, and soon after the presentation from Los Angeles she left the meeting, ensuring that participants could focus on their own authentic table work. Following that, we were able to proceed with the event, and people were engaged, respectful, and productive throughout the rest of the day [Voorhees 2012].

At the end of the day, a government-based health care system was, in fact, among the six final recommendations to emerge from California*Speaks*.

This sequence of events highlights the importance of maintaining sufficient flexibility for the real-time inclusion of recommendations and options that come from citizens themselves. It is particularly important to embrace unanticipated, or in this case anticipated but off-plan content when the issues for discussion are highly controversial. Responding creatively and satisfactorily to public dissent that emerged during the deliberation reinforced and preserved the credibility of the work.

Soon after the 21st Century Town Meeting, Governor Schwarzenegger and Assembly Speaker Fabian Núñez together filed health care reform legislation that aligned with most of the consensus views developed during California*Speaks*. Further, a subsequent independent analysis found that broader health care reform efforts in California shifted to better reflect the views expressed by California*Speaks* participants: "Of all 33 Reform Values and Options, the reform debate moved to more closely reflect 21, or 64% of the California*Speaks* priorities" (Harbage 2007, 1). The legislation developed by Schwarzenegger and Núñez passed the California State Assembly quickly and by a wide margin.

At this juncture, however, political gamesmanship reemerged as a factor. Senate Majority Leader Don Perata, who had been an active supporter of California*Speaks,* was simultaneously engaged in trying to move a complex water rights issue through the state legislature. Shortly after California*Speaks,* Perata tried to extract a vote on water rights from the governor and, when he was unsuccessful, stopped pushing health care reform at the same time. Part of his calculation was that a new $14 billion budget deficit projection—in large part caused by the subprime mortgage debacle in Southern California—had raised concerns about the $14.4 billion cost of the health care proposal and its underlying funding assumptions. Without Perata's open support, health care reform lost by one vote in the state senate. The insider politics along with the timing of the collapse of the housing market undermined the substantial public will that had been created to move forward on a vital public policy issue.

In the moment, and in retrospect given the limited success of subsequent national health care reform efforts, this result can be seen as a missed opportunity of extraordinary proportion. Larry

Levitt, then a health policy analyst for the Kaiser Family Foundation, summed it up well when he said: "Any progress in California would make a substantial dent in the problem of the uninsured nationally. Action in California would create real momentum, both in the presidential debate and in other states" (America-*Speaks* 2007).

And yet, although health care reform legislation failed again, California*Speaks* accomplished several important things. It enabled the state's top decision makers to hear citizens discover agreements on a complex and seemingly intractable issue. Elected officials then showed that they could work across party lines to create legislation that was consistent with the views of the people. In reflecting on the work, leaders noted the importance of citizens' involvement as well as the attention to neutrality and process. Kim Belshé, state secretary of health and services at the time, said: "This model is important in helping people move from raw,

FIGURE 9.3 PARTICIPANTS IN CALIFORNIA*SPEAKS*
TAKE ON HEALTH CARE REFORM

uniformed opinions to more informed judgments . . . and that is what makes a strong basis for helping to inform policymakers about these difficult issues" (America*Speaks* 2007). Speaker Núñez said: "When you facilitate that type of citizen participation, you end up with a better government" (America*Speaks* 2007).

The health care reform approach that Californians debated in 2007 turned out to be quite similar to the approach of the federal health care reform law enacted in March 2010. Recognizing that the federal law built on the work they had previously done, Governor Schwarzenegger and the legislature moved quickly to pass implementing legislation. Janet Coffman, a professor at the Philip R. Lee Institute for Health Policy Studies at the University of California, San Francisco, observed that "state health-care reform ultimately was not successful here in 2007 . . . but leaders had spent a lot of time defining what they wanted to see. While other states still are wrestling with some of the concepts behind federal health-care reform . . . we've been able to move swiftly from contemplation to implementation" (Mulholland 2010). As Governor Schwarzenegger was coming to the end of his term in late 2010, he appointed two of those who had led the 2007 effort—Chief of Staff Susan Kennedy and Health Secretary Kim Belshé—to the Health Benefit Exchange Board that was established to implement national health care reform legislation.

THE PUBLIC MANAGER'S ROLE IN INFORMING PARTICIPANTS

Public managers who are interested in significantly enhancing citizen engagement in their agency have an important role to play when it comes to ensuring that participants—and citizens in general—are well informed. Tony Faast of the U.S. Fish and Wildlife Service holds this view: "The quality of the input, and our ability to use it in decision-making, is proportional to the level of information we provide to educate meeting participants. . . . I have always believed that the rule should be: you have access to what we have access to, period" (Faast 2012). Richard Stem of the U.S. Forest Service expanded on the point: "With the right information, they can do better than our own professionals. The caveat is that you must manage the process properly and make sure that things are clear" (Stem 2012).

This section explores three strategies public managers can use to enhance the ways in which they inform the public: adopting a new approach to developing informational materials for participants; undertaking creative media work; and building on an agency's open government work.

ADOPTING A NEW APPROACH TO DEVELOPING INFORMATIONAL MATERIALS FOR PARTICIPANTS

Accurate, neutral, accessible, and flexible informational materials can be developed by pursuing the strategies described in this chapter. However, there are three unique challenges for public managers in stewarding the development of such materials. First, they may have to adjust their standard approach to preparing materials, which is likely to have focused on materials preparation for high-level policy discussions. For citizen engagement work, materials have to be easily understood by the general public. This is not an insignificant shift to make. Since the 1960s there have been a number of efforts to push government to simplify its written communication. The Obama Administration's Plain Writing Act of 2010 followed efforts by Richard Nixon, Jimmy Carter, and Bill Clinton to address this concern. Nonetheless, the *Washington Post* recently reported that "such executive actions haven't been enough to stem the tide of bureaucratic jargon. . . . [L]eft to their own devices, agencies have a tendency to develop inscrutably dense vocabularies" (Khimm 2011).

Second, in addition to simplifying language, public managers will need to challenge their assumptions about what the public needs to understand in regard to the technical aspects of a presenting issue. For example, sometimes understanding scientific details or the parameters of authorizing legislation is a prerequisite for making a contribution that can directly influence decision making. Participants may feel that they have been set up to fail if such details surface during the discussion without sufficient explanation, or if they do not surface during the discussion but are taken into account after the deliberation is over and citizens have departed.

Finally, public managers will have to open themselves up to the reality that for many citizens and public constituencies, government is a stakeholder just like other stakeholders on an issue. As a result, credibility and neutrality are not automatically conferred on informational materials simply because they are produced by the government. Such credibility must be earned by deliberate attention to a fair and equal presentation of all sides of an issue, and in some instances it may be important that the final product, though in large part created by a government agency, actually be written and published by an outside entity.

UNDERTAKING CREATIVE MEDIA WORK

Public managers can engage the media in the citizen engagement process in any number of creative and constructive ways. For example, in the Voices & Choices initiative (described in detail in Chapter Five), which brought together tens of thousands of citizens in regional planning in Northeast Ohio, a unique media partnership was instrumental in getting citizens the information they needed to participate productively on extraordinarily complex issues.

In the lead-up to the final event of this widespread, multimodal citizen engagement process, local philanthropies in Northeast Ohio and ten local television outlets collaborated to produce a series of educational programs on the key issues to be presented to the public. Five of the stations each developed one five-minute segment, either on education, equity, government, the economy, or quality of life. They then distributed their work so that all ten stations ended up with twenty-five minutes of programmed airtime. In the week before the final town hall meeting, the ten stations broadcast one segment each night during the nightly news (for example, education on Monday, equity on Tuesday, and so on).[1] As a result of these broadcasts, hundreds of thousands of Northeast Ohioans were exposed to, and educated about, the policy issues central to the initiative. Those people who saw the broadcasts and also attended the deliberations were better prepared to participate fully. This kind of collaboration is a great example of what is possible in pursuing creative partnerships with the media.

BUILDING ON AN AGENCY'S OPEN GOVERNMENT WORK

As will be discussed more fully in Chapter Twelve, public managers have a golden opportunity through the Open Government Initiative to deepen the impact of their citizen engagement work. Because the Open Government Initiative has predominantly focused on information-sharing and transparency improvements, it is particularly relevant to the work described in this chapter.

In a briefing paper for federal agencies, Joe Goldman, former Vice President of Citizen Engagement at America*Speaks,* and Joe Peters, founding partner of Ascentum, a Canadian public engagement firm, note several specific pathways through which public managers can build on their agency's open government work to keep the public better informed about critical issues. In particular, they emphasize making reports and videos from engagement work available online and using online platforms to further inform citizens and provide them with tools for taking action as well as for sharing information with their own networks. "Social media and social networking tools," they offer, "should help citizens who get involved feel like they are connected to the agency as a valued partner and member of a community. There should be a space for regular contests to collaboratively solve problems facing the agency or even present innovations that complement the agency's mission" (Goldman and Peters 2009, 2). Public managers can take advantage of the federal government's unprecedented hiring of young social media experts who are using these tools to connect government with the public. It is a specific skill set that most long-standing career civil servants do not possess because they came of age at a time when the tools did not exist.

The next wave of open government work is still in its infancy in most agencies, presenting public managers with a highly opportune moment to demonstrate their leadership in creating new practices that authentically engage the public.

Public Manager Perspectives

Be Fair, Be Open, Be Honest: Principles for Informing the Public and Regaining Their Trust

Tony Faast, retired biologist, U.S. Fish and Wildlife Service

The Context

In the late 1980s, faced with declining sturgeon numbers in the Lower Columbia River, fishery managers in the Oregon Department of Fish and Wildlife proposed a change in the legal catch size for these much-sought-after fish. The change would reduce the allowable catch by 20 percent or more for all sport, commercial, and tribal fishermen. This substantial cut was needed to meet the agency's biological sturgeon management objectives.

Anticipating that the planned change would not be a popular one, the director of our state department of fish and wildlife instructed me (the Agency's "go-to guy" for public involvement) to "hold a public meeting on the sturgeon regulations." As I understood my assignment, the goal was to get public input on the proposed change. I proceeded to set up a public meeting for forty to fifty participants in the Lower Columbia River town of The Dalles, Oregon.

As I was putting the final touches on the meeting details (room setup, mics, testimony table, seats for staff, participant seating, and so on), our chief of fisheries came in, ready to sit down and hear from the public on this issue. As he headed for his chair I asked him what we would tell participants about how the information gathered at the meeting would be used—a special report? Publishing the results in the local paper? Something else? He stopped, thought for a minute, and said: "Oh, we cut a deal with the tribes at 3:00 p.m. yesterday. It's already over." And so began a three-hour public meeting with a bunch of concerned citizens on an issue that had been decided the day before.

Unfortunately, this kind of scenario was not an anomaly. In fact, it was all-too-common practice in the early days of public engagement. The public, of course, suspected that such backroom dealings were going on. They often accused the agency of already having made up its mind, and of withholding information they needed to participate fully. Although they were quite often right, we continued to dutifully assure them that their input really counted. As you might expect, our trust level with the public in those days was minimal.

It was during those times, and specifically after the sturgeon regulations meeting, when a number of us handling public input on natural resource issues began to question our agency's practice (from the director on down) of simply going through the motions when gathering public comment. We concluded that there was no collective agency ethic against this practice, nor was there specific guidance about what to do instead. Just as noted conservationist Aldo Leopold had called for a land ethic to guide management actions concerning natural resources, we realized we needed an ethic to guide our agency's efforts in collaborative public interactions as well.

Developing a New Approach

In the mid-1990s agency staff determined to address this issue. We used the Cispus Workshop—an annual

interagency communication training session on collaboration and public involvement techniques—as a
vehicle for getting the work done. Through a series of
in-depth discussions over a few years, we closely examined our practices, focusing on two key questions: What
fundamental components of public involvement are
always in play when the work is successful? What components are always missing when the work fails? In the
end, we settled on three principles that constituted a
surprisingly simple yet comprehensive ethical framework
for public participation in our respective agencies: Be
Fair, Be Open, Be Honest.

Putting Principles into Practice

It is relatively easy to assess the principles of fairness,
openness, and honesty when looking retrospectively at
public involvement efforts. Process errors become glar-
ingly apparent through reports and news articles that
include such citizen testimony as: "It's not fair that they
got the information before we did . . . we told them
and nobody listened . . . they lied to us!" The difficult
part of applying any ethical framework is to do it continually in the present and to project it onto future
actions. In seeking to do this harder work, the agency
has learned some important lessons.

Be Fair. As practitioners and agencies, we need to
constantly ask ourselves questions like these:

- Is it fair to give one group more information than
  another?
- Is it fair to give the public only a few weeks to review
  a document that an agency spent two years writing?
- Is it fair to hold a single public meeting two
  hundred miles from the affected citizens and call
  that an adequate opportunity for participation?

I am often asked how any agency knows what is fair
with respect to an issue. My answer is simple: pick up

the phone, call a known opponent, and talk to him or her about it.

Be Open. In today's terminology, openness is often referred to as "transparency." The sturgeon regulations meeting described earlier is an excellent example of an absence of transparency. To adhere to the principle of being open, an agency should say so if it really does not want—or does not need—information from the public. Application of this principle in practice has produced some key guidance:

- Ideas and suggestions are often best sought early in a process when responses and actions are still malleable. Many issues can progress to a point where input is inappropriate, unhelpful, or even illegal in some cases. It is important to select a moment for public participation when input can actually be used, and to fully inform the public about the various stages of the decision-making process.
- The design of a public process must clearly and openly reflect the kinds of input an agency wants and needs for its decision-making effort. Do we need more factual information? Do we need new, creative ideas? Do we need specific proposals? Allowing people to stand up and talk at a microphone without informing them about what you are looking for does not make for a truly open process.

Be Honest. Agency professionals are not dishonest. But we are often loathe to divulge all relevant information about an issue. It's almost as if agency professionals don't really want the public to know as much (or as little) about an issue as they do! Concerning public engagement efforts, agency staff often say: "They don't need to know that" or "That will just confuse them." Assumptions like these lead to distrust. And they certainly don't stand up in court: "Your Honor, they knew this three months ago, and they didn't tell us."

If information relevant to decision making on an issue exists, it needs to be part of the discussion. It may be complicated or incomplete, but if it is what you have, it is what must be made public.

Regaining Public Trust

Over time, the straightforward ethic we devised proved to work in practice as well as in theory. With regular application of this ethic, we found that the public's trust in us increased. At our public meetings I began to routinely say things like: "Folks, I wish we had more time and more money to throw at this issue. I really wish we had more data as well, but we don't. Here's the legal box we are in, and the timeline for action is fixed. Help us figure out the next steps to resolve this." People would still rant about what the agency should have and could have done about an issue. But when we were truly fair, open, and honest about it, they respected us for being straight with them.

Respect is one of those elusive and often forgotten pieces of the "trust" puzzle. If respect is absent, there is no way we can expect people to trust us. Harvard University professor Sara Lawrence-Lightfoot says that respect is the single most powerful ingredient in nourishing relationships and creating a just society. We agree. If there is mutual respect in a collaborative effort, a solution can usually be reached. If respect is absent, no amount of agency meetings, processes, and events will work.

Agencies and consultants all have public involvement methods they believe are tried and true. My experiences have taught me not only that there is no magic bullet that can resolve thorny public issues but also that "involving" people simply by giving them a seat at the decision-making table is not enough. The public's involvement must be substantive, it must be based on a full set of information, and it must reflect the realities of an agency's decision-making processes. If we are ethical in our interactions with the public, we will gain (and retain) their respect and their trust.

When training staff on public engagement strategies, we explain it like this: "It's pretty hard to keep a three-ring binder full of policies and procedures in your head as you navigate a public engagement process." But you *can* look in the mirror every day and ask yourself a very simple question: "Is what we are doing fair, open, and honest?" If the answer is not a resounding "Yes," you need to go back to the drawing board.

CHAPTER TEN

STRATEGY SIX: DISCOVER SHARED PRIORITIES

The ignoring of differences is the most fatal mistake in politics or industry or international life: Every difference that is swept up into a bigger conception enriches society; every difference which is ignored feeds on society and eventually corrupts it . . . The true state must gather up every interest within itself. It must take our many loyalties and find how it can make them one.

MARY PARKER FOLLETT, 1920*

There are many purposes for engaging the public in deliberation. Civil discourse is vital, for example, for learning, for creating compromise, and for building relationships in diverse communities. This book focuses on an additional specific purpose: to give citizens a direct voice in the government decision making that affects their lives. This is a key to realizing our founders' aspirations for self-governance and to rebuilding Americans' trust in our institutions.

To achieve this purpose, citizens must go through deliberative processes that elevate commonly held perspectives and values and produce clear recommendations. Once they find shared priorities, citizens can not only provide specific guidance for a decision maker's actions but they can also form a solid constituency that

---

*Follett, M. P. *The New State: Group Organization: The Solution of Popular Government*. London: Longmans, Green, 1920, 40, 312.

will provide support and engagement as the decision is being implemented. This chapter discusses the importance of discovering shared priorities and offers concrete strategies and case examples to illustrate how it can be accomplished.

WHY DISCOVERING SHARED PRIORITIES IS IMPORTANT

Compromise is the sine qua non of a functioning democracy. The fiscal crisis that has engulfed our nation for the last several years provides a sobering example of what happens when Congress cannot, or will not, compromise. In summer 2011, unable to resolve significant differences about the federal debt ceiling, our divided and uncompromising national leadership punted: they passed legislation that did little more than forward the tough decision making into the future. Three months later, a dedicated congressional "supercommittee" similarly failed to reach agreements that would resolve the issue and put the nation on a path to a sound fiscal future. The polarized and rancorous political posturing that characterized both of these efforts made it clear that decision makers were unwilling to find compromise solutions when the moment demanded that they do so. In a 2012 op-ed piece in the *Washington Post,* Senator Bob Corker of Tennessee said that although elected officials on both sides of the political aisle claimed to be serious about reducing the deficit, "so far, this exercise has resulted in lots of talk but no real action. In fact," he said, "despite a national debt of $15 trillion and multiple failures to enact any significant legislation to address it, the Senate continues to pass the same fiscally irresponsible legislation that created our massive deficit problem" (Corker 2012).

In addition to perpetuating the nation's fiscal crisis, leaders' failure to act also put a simple fact into stark relief: without compromise, the governance of our country grinds to a halt. This is but one example of what has become a predictable trend in the nation's capital. As discussed earlier, America faces a host of other urgent challenges, from addressing our long-term energy needs, to rectifying our immigration policies, to taking action to ensure the strength of our economy in an era of global competitiveness. Yet as each issue takes its turn in the national spotlight, we see little more than our elected leaders' continued inability to make progress. Writing about the supercommittee debacle, Demos[1] senior fellow Richard Brodsky summed it up well:

> From the inception of our Constitutional system, we have depended on the willingness of the political class to compromise, to accept some things that it didn't like in order to achieve things it wanted. We remember the great compromises of years past as essential to our successes, including the big state/small state compromise in the Constitution, the strengthening of the Federal Government in response to the Depression, and the Civil Rights Era laws that ended legal segregation. Our major failures came when we couldn't find ways to bridge substantial gaps in conflicting ideologies, be it the Civil War, foreign military adventures, or our current debacle.

> Without compromise, the legislative process and democracy itself falter. In a nation so diverse, there will rarely be an issue that doesn't divide our people and our political class . . . and it is through that prism that the failure of the super committee and the failure of the Congress become intolerable, tragic and truly dangerous [Brodsky 2011].

Just as compromise is central to the legislative process, it is also vital when the public is deliberating. For citizens to have an impact on governance, decision makers must hear their agreed-on recommendations. Unfortunately, they often hear mostly divided and contradictory messages about the public's views, which they then use to justify their unwillingness to compromise and further entrench their respective positions. This happens because the way we design the majority of public engagement opportunities exacerbates differences and highlights opposition, thus leading to seemingly irreconcilable differences of opinion. Rather than acknowledge that we are creating such scenarios, we buy into the current national narrative that says compromise is fundamentally not possible. We are led to believe by politicians and elected officials of all stripes, as well as by the media, that the public's views are irretrievably entrenched and contradictory; that Americans would rather hold on to their ideology than reach across the table to discover common ground; and that as a people we are incapable of sustaining civil discourse.

To be sure, there is some truth in this narrative. We are a nation of determined individualists endowed with a strong belief in the righteousness of our views, as well as in our government-granted right to proclaim them. But the fact that we resort to yelling at each other under certain circumstances does not define us; it is not the sum of who we are and what we can do. In fact, the opposite is true.

The vast majority of us are delighted to have the opportunity to sit at a table with people who hold different views; share our thoughts with attentive listeners; and, in turn, listen to their ideas. We know that although we will not always come to agreement on everything, we will often be able to find common ground. Deliberating citizens quickly grasp that they do not have to adopt each other's philosophies. But because they want to solve the problems at hand, they are willing to compromise to find mutually agreeable alternatives. In bringing citizens together in this way, even under the most contentious of circumstances, America*Speaks* has seen that people are surprised to discover what they can accomplish together. Why are they surprised? Because television and other media constantly tell them that they cannot and will not be able to work together.

The public is quite capable of taking advantage of opportunities to discover shared priorities, and it is vital for our democracy that they are routinely given the chance to do so. Their collective work establishes a constituency that can support elected officials and other decision makers as they face the challenges that come with implementing policies. For example, after the citizen engagement work in New Orleans, hundreds of people came to previously legislated public hearing to ensure that the rebuilding and recovery plan they had crafted would not fall victim to politics as usual. The public's commitment to the shared priorities they developed powerfully linked public will with political will. The plan held.

STRATEGIES FOR DISCOVERING SHARED PRIORITIES

Each of the preceding six chapters has explored a strategy for bringing citizen voice into governance. Much ground has been covered, from approaches for conducting contextual analyses to specific roles and activities for decision makers. These chapters have discussed outreach strategies and tactics, recommendations for room configuration, and creative ways to work with the media. While each component is critical in its own right, all of these parts must be brought together in order to create an effective deliberative environment. In addition to all this groundwork, there are a number of specific strategies, discussed in the following subsections, that enable citizens to discover shared priorities.

ATTEND TO THE CONTENT AND SEQUENCE OF THE AGENDA

Bringing diverse citizens into a room and presenting a policy issue for discussion will not, in and of itself, surface shared views. To reliably achieve that result, the deliberative agenda must include a series of elements purposefully ordered.

Before any other work takes place, participants must know with whom they are deliberating. Coming to agreement requires some degree of mutual respect and understanding, which is difficult to achieve with complete strangers. Therefore, the first order of business is getting to know the other people sitting at your table. It must also be transparent to participants that the whole community is present in the room; that everyone's voice will be heard in developing collective recommendations for action. As discussed earlier, hand-held polling devices provide an effective way to demonstrate participant demographics. To create a climate of openness, participants must also have access to each other's views and values. America*Speaks*'s work therefore adheres to the following principle: the opening substantive discussion in a deliberation must be about values, vision, or both, not about positions and partisan ideology.

Values and vision work allows people to speak from their own experiences, connect with their deepest sense of priorities, and establish a shared vocabulary that will ultimately enable them to discover shared views. For example, in the Americans Discuss Social Security initiative, participants started the day by identifying the overarching values they wanted Congress to uphold while considering options for reforming the Social Security program. The majority of participants found that they shared a fundamental value that older people in our country should not be left in or forced into poverty at the end of their lives. Later in the day, when specific reform options were on the table and strong differences of opinion began to emerge, participants could go back to their commonly held view about preventing poverty among older Americans and use that shared value to work through their differences.

The Centers for Disease Control and Prevention's Roger Bernier offered a creative take on this: "In the final analysis," he said, "citizen engagement is not really about facts and figures because the recommendations are based on choices that have to do with values. When the bank robber Willie Sutton was asked why he robbed banks, he famously responded: 'because that's where the money is.' When a federal manager asks the question 'why should we involve citizens in our decision-making?' I say 'because that's where the values are'" (Bernier 2012).

Once commonly held values are established, an effective strategy for discovering shared views is to present the trade-offs that must be made to solve the issue under discussion. Reality-based scenarios that demonstrate what would happen if each choice were implemented can help participants test their understanding as well as their depth of commitment to different options. These comparisons and the discussions they engender are critical to the development of collectively shared views.

Finally, as the engagement process moves through the agenda's various issue discussions, it is important for participants to be kept up-to-date on the thinking of everyone who is participating, not just the work of their own small discussion group. In AmericaSpeaks's large-scale meetings this is done by moving back and forth between table discussions and plenary sessions in which the themes representing the work of everyone in the room are projected on large screens.

USE KEY PROCESS COMPONENTS

A number of process components go hand in hand with the agenda sequencing just described and are important to helping participants discover shared views. These process components were described in detail in Chapter Two and are briefly restated here. Small-group dialogue creates a safe space for participants to hear from each other and share their perspectives. Diverse table seating encourages participants to broaden their views beyond the ideas and understandings they bring with them. Neutral informational materials allow participants to come to decisions based on facts. Facilitation helps participants find bridges across their differences and reach decisions. Networked computers create an instant record of the ideas generated at tables and ensure that all voices are heard and no ideas are lost. Theming of these ideas enables participants to see how their views do and do not align with those of others. Electronic keypads enable the voting necessary to identify shared priorities.

Figure 10.1 Theme Team Working Intently

Hold the Line on Advocacy

Advocacy and stakeholder groups play an important role in our society and in our democracy. Few of us have the discretionary time to fully devote ourselves to all of the issues we care about.

FIGURE 10.2 A PARTICIPANT VOTING HER PREFERENCE

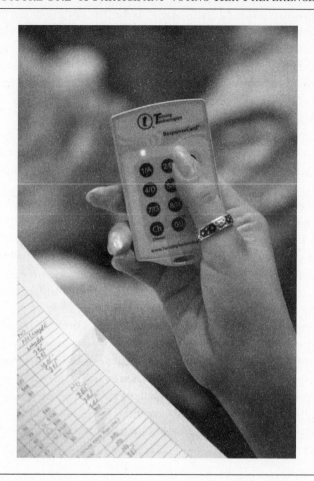

To participate in issue advocacy, we rely on existing organizations we can join. In the United States, we are fortunate that a well-endowed philanthropic sector has supported a rich advocacy infrastructure for many important issues.

Advocacy groups play a very specific role: they seek to secure or advance a particular outcome on a particular issue. Thus the kind of citizen engagement work described in this book, in which the outcomes are not known or determined in advance, presents a challenge when it comes to advocacy groups' participation. As discussed earlier, when operating as an advocate, intent on persuading as many people as possible to adopt a particular point of view, participating in an open dialogue aimed at a collective decision that is likely to reflect compromise is problematic. By contrast, unaffiliated citizens can participate in the development of shared priorities because they can check their preconceived notions and positions at the door and open themselves up to the views of others. Advocates and stakeholders are not likely to do this, nor should they be asked to. It is not their role.

Nevertheless, when advocates and stakeholders become aware that a citizen deliberation is planned for an issue on their agenda, they will naturally want to get involved and have an impact on the outcome. Advocates and stakeholders must be informed about the process, and because many will have knowledge about the issue, their ideas should be solicited. But they should not be allowed to influence the agenda and outcomes. If they do, the integrity of the citizens' deliberations as well as the results will be compromised. As an alternative, advocates can and should participate as individual citizens, distributed randomly around the room like all of the other participants.

To maintain the integrity of an open and safe deliberative space, there can be no compromising on these points. Further, when these guidelines are followed, there is often an interesting result: people who start out as advocates give up their individual positions because they see the value of participating as a member of the whole community. They are energized to be part of developing an authentic, collective set of recommendations that will influence decision makers.

DISCOVERING SHARED PRIORITIES: A CASE STUDY

As described earlier in this chapter, when our nation's mounting fiscal crisis came to a head in 2011, leadership once again failed to address the problem. However, the budgetary challenges we faced were known long before that time, and the consistently inadequate response had led democracy practitioners to wonder: Can we demonstrate what we know to be true, that the American people are better than our politics, even when it comes to complex, highly polarized issues? Can we support citizens in coming to specific, substantive recommendations where policymakers have been unable to do so?

The answer, as it turned out, was an emphatic yes. In summer 2010, in fifty-seven cities across the country, 3,500 Americans from every walk of life, including Tea Party and MoveOn.org members as well as average, middle-of-the-road citizens, came together and developed mutually agreeable strategies for reducing the nation's deficit by $1.2 trillion by 2025. In nineteen cities, large groups of citizens deliberated in a central location; in thirty-eight cities, smaller, volunteer-led conversations took place in people's homes and other community locations, such as libraries, businesses, and churches, and all were connected by webcast. In addition, a robust Internet presence and online engagement strategy directly linked another 12,000 people to the work.

Researchers who evaluated the initiative called it the "largest national experiment in structured public deliberation to date in the United States" (Esterling, Fung, and Lee 2010, 2). The story of the Our Budget, Our Economy national discussion provides important insights into the challenges a highly contentious stakeholder landscape can pose when citizens are seeking to find common ground.

DEVELOPING THE INFORMATIONAL MATERIALS

Participants in America*Speaks*'s Our Budget, Our Economy faced a difficult task. Simply understanding the complex issues underlying the nation's fiscal crisis was a tall order. But these citizens had to absorb this information quickly so that in a seven-hour period they could also discover mutually agreeable compromises and make collective decisions with fellow Americans they had only just met that day.

To help citizens achieve these goals, Our Budget, Our Economy organizers provided two informational resources that were created specifically for the initiative and designed to both establish a common, baseline understanding of the facts and support the discovery of shared priorities. The first document, a *Federal Budget 101* primer, offered basic definitions and an outline of spending and revenue categories in the federal budget. The

FIGURE 10.3 "FEDERAL BUDGET 101"

Federal Budget 101

An Introduction to the Federal Budget and Our Fiscal Challenges

June 26, 2010: Albuquerque, NM; Augusta, ME; Casper, WY; Chicago, IL; Columbia, SC; Dallas, TX; Des Moines, IA; Detroit, MI; Grand Forks, ND; Jackson, MS; Overland Park, KS; Louisville, KY; Missoula, MT; Philadelphia, PA; Portland, OR; Portsmouth, NH; Redlands, CA; Richmond, VA; San Jose, CA and elsewhere across the country...

 Peter G. Peterson Foundation
Our America. Our Future.

 W.K. KELLOGG FOUNDATION

 MACARTHUR
The John D. and Catherine T. MacArthur Foundation

primer reviewed the long-term debt and deficit projections our nation faces, as well as the risks of inaction given the implications of rising health care costs and an aging population. Finally, the primer debunked "magic bullet" theories that suggested, for example, that cutting waste, fraud, and abuse or ending the war in Afghanistan would be sufficient solutions to our fiscal crisis.

The second document was an options workbook that laid out forty-two possible actions for cutting spending and raising revenues. In the area of spending, action steps included making cuts to health care, Social Security, defense, and nondefense programs. In the area of revenue generation, they included raising existing taxes, reducing deductions and credits, reforming the tax code, and establishing new taxes. Revenue and savings estimates were provided for each option. With this information in hand, participants could take on the challenging target of reducing the deficit by $1.25 trillion by 2025.

The process of developing these materials was not simple. There were a number of core issues in dispute, such as whether Congressional Budget Office numbers were a legitimate baseline for citizens to use when considering possible cuts to the Medicaid and Medicare programs. The ideologically diverse content committee vigorously debated these issues. In the end, their conviction that the public had to be brought into the debate helped them rise above their differences and come to compromise positions.

To ensure accuracy and neutrality, the materials were reviewed by an equally ideologically diverse advisory committee of thirty prominent fiscal policy experts, including representatives from such organizations as the AARP, the American Enterprise Institute, The Brookings Institution, the Business Roundtable, the Center for American Progress, the Center on Budget and Policy Priorities, The Heritage Foundation, and the U.S. Chamber of Commerce, among others.

America*Speaks*'s standard procedure is to have informational materials written or edited by a professional writer to ensure they are accessible to average readers. In this instance, a freelance journalist, Larry Haas, was engaged to help write the materials. His perspective on the task was captured in the previous chapter.

Managing an Active Stakeholder Community

Despite bringing an array of experts who were equitably distributed across the ideological spectrum into the planning and development of Our Budget, Our Economy, the initiative's interaction with organized advocacy and stakeholder groups and coalitions was a significant challenge.

Not long before the launch of Our Budget, Our Economy, a national philanthropy invested $25 million in Social Security Works, a coalition made up of thirty-five organizations. The coalition was tasked with conducting constituent-based advocacy during upcoming federal fiscal negotiations, with the goal of preserving the Social Security program and ensuring no reduction in benefits. When Our Budget, Our Economy was announced, a prominent member of this coalition quickly posted a blog entry suggesting that whatever came out of the initiative would be biased because of the political leanings of one of the contributing foundations, which he considered "right wing." Soon we heard similar attacks from the other end of the ideological spectrum. Advocates and stakeholders, frightened that people would come up with answers that did not fit their own agendas, sought to impugn the results before citizens had a chance to sit down together. They falsely claimed that funders were influencing the development of the content for the deliberations. In actuality, the three principal funders, the Peterson Foundation, seen by many to be on the center right; the W. K. Kellogg Foundation, seen by many to be on the center left; and the MacArthur Foundation, seen by many to be in the middle, had been invited to listen in on the content committee's work but had no official role or ability to influence its decisions. Meetings with members of the Social Security Works coalition to explain the process by which the materials and agenda would be developed helped diffuse some of the disinformation campaigning, but did not stop it.

On the day of deliberation, small but vocal crowds of left-leaning protesters met participants in a few sites as they entered the building. The picketers sought to press their views on participants and convince them that the discussion was rigged. America*Speaks* staff worked with the people on the picket lines to ensure they were not harassing participants and also to offer them the opportunity to come in, as individual citizens, and join the conversation. Many of them did. Sue Lacy, one of the national outreach directors for the initiative, worked with the protesters outside the Philadelphia site and described the experience this way:

> There were probably about 40 people outside the First District Plaza in Philadelphia. Leading up to the event we had seen a good bit of email traffic from a range of organizations encouraging picketers, and a fairly diverse group showed up with signs about protecting Social Security, cutting the defense budget and other issues. The picketers lined the sidewalk and actively tried to convince people not to go in, telling them that they would be participating in something that was already pre-determined; that they were being used. The picketers were generally respectful but they were persistent, making some efforts to block the walkway into the entrance.

> About 30 minutes before the deliberation was set to begin, I went inside to get help from a man named Ed Schwartz, a long-standing liberal activist in Philadelphia who had, after bridging his own concerns about the initiative and its potential outcomes, joined the effort. He was a known and trusted presence in the community. Together, we delivered a very specific message to the picketers: you can stay out here and you will have absolutely no impact on the outcome of this deliberation, or you can come inside and participate and your voices will be part of what the President's Commission hears—it's your choice.

> From 30 years of community organizing experience I was able to say to them that I had been where they were on countless occasions—outside of rooms where decisions were being made and hoping my protests would have an impact. Today, I said, presented a very different kind of opportunity: Alice Rivlin and other influential people were in the room, and whoever was in there with them would be heard by them. Yes, I said, there would be a lot of conservative people in the meeting as well—so you can either sit at the table and work with your conservative colleagues from across the country to find some kind of compromise and unified messages to send to Washington or you can just yell at them as they walk past you.

In the end, the vast majority of the picketers chose to come in and participate. As I circulated among the discussion tables during the day I checked in with them—"How's it going?" "What do you think?" They said it was good—and nobody walked out [Lacy 2012].

FINDING SHARED VIEWS

Over the course of six hours, ordinary citizens working at table groups around the country produced plans that dramatically reduced the national deficit: nearly 60 percent of the groups achieved reducing the deficit by $1.1 trillion or reached the target of $1.2 trillion by 2025; more than 75 percent were able to reduce the deficit by $800 billion or more. Further, participants' shared views directly addressed all of the traditional "third rail" issues that officials and the media had claimed to be untouchable and intractable. For example, they very quickly understood and accepted that the nation would have to cut entitlements *and* raise revenues.

The collective views that emerged from Our Budget, Our Economy had a great deal of specificity:

- Eighty-five percent of citizens agreed to reduce defense spending by at least 5 percent.
- Sixty-eight percent agreed to at least a 5 percent reduction in spending on all nondefense programs.
- Sixty-two percent of participants expressed support for at least a 5 percent reduction in health care spending.
- Sixty percent (across every age group) agreed to raising the cap on payroll taxes to 90 percent of earnings, among other recommendations.

A week after the discussion, citizens' priorities were presented to the president's National Commission on Fiscal Responsibility and Reform, and then to the Senate and House Budget Committees as well as fifty-eight congressional offices. When the commission released its recommendations in November 2010, many of them closely tracked, or were influenced by, what citizens had said.

The fact that 3,500 citizens achieved this level of agreement speaks volumes about the untapped ability of our citi-

FIGURE 10.4 CITIZENS IN PHILADELPHIA TACKLE OUR NATIONAL DEBT AND DEFICIT

zenry to understand and discuss complex policy issues—as our founders envisioned, Americans clearly have the capacity for self-governance. It also demonstrates that the supposedly intractable polarization of the public on critical policy issues is largely a creation of the hyperpartisanship of today's politics and the media's choice to always highlight public meetings designed to generate conflict. One participant articulated this quite clearly when he said: "The conversation works. Americans [can] sit down and talk to each other regardless of the differences of opinion that they have—when they're not expected to be responding in the way that the media expects them to, or the parties expect them to" (America*Speaks* 2010).

LESSONS LEARNED

Our Budget, Our Economy sought to do something rare in this country—to give the public an opportunity to come to their own decisions on one of our most pressing issues: the national debt and deficit. The advocacy and stakeholder groups' efforts to obstruct citizens' deliberations in this project reflect a new and regrettable trend. Fearing that the collective judgment of the public would differ from the outcomes they wanted, they determined it was better to disrupt the process than to let democracy work. Our efforts to educate these groups and secure their support for the deliberative process for the most part fell on deaf ears. Despite that, many of their members did end up joining the discussion. Ironically, a liberal economist who put researchers outside the doors at Our Budget, Our Economy sites to try to show that participants were not demographically representative continued to attack the process while at the same time using some of the results to advance his own agenda.

It is unfortunate that throughout the development and planning process, on the day of the deliberation, and in the follow-up, the efforts of these groups consumed undue amounts of time from project leaders and forced a reallocation of precious communication resources to fight a disinformation campaign. Further, the disinformation has persisted over time. More than eighteen months after the deliberation, a Google search on "America*Speaks*" produces, among the top five entries, the false information that was put forward about a single funder driving the content of Our Budget, Our Economy. In this way, our Internet-dominated media environment gives an advantage to disinformation campaigns. It keeps them alive long after the actual events have concluded and even after their assertions have been shown to be false.

Despite these challenges, Our Budget, Our Economy proved that although partisan attacks are difficult to manage, well-organized citizen deliberation can withstand them. In the end, stakeholder efforts did not negatively influence the work of the 3,500 citizens who stepped up to participate. Independent evaluation research on the effort found that "liberals and conservatives seem to have given ground on their specific priorities in order to help achieve their goal of reducing the deficit. For example, conservatives became more supportive of raising taxes on the very wealthy. To a similar degree, liberals became more supportive of a 5% across the board cut to discretionary programs after one day of deliberation" (Esterling, Fung, and Lee 2010, 45).

The reason for these compromises is that deliberative work has a moderating impact on policy preferences. Deliberation participants *want* to solve problems and are willing to make the compromises necessary to arrive at collective decisions. When people deliberate across their differences, they move to the center rather than digging into existing positions on either extreme. Further, once they have reached a decision collectively, they own it and are committed to it.

In a healthy democracy, strong advocacy and the ability of general interest citizens to deliberate across their differences must coexist, even as the policy stakes get higher and the media environment becomes more partisan. One memorable incident from Our Budget, Our Economy illustrates this lesson. A participant in Missoula, Montana, had deliberately falsified his personal information when he registered. His intention was to "blow the cover" off of an initiative he assumed to be illegitimate. However, at the end of the deliberation, with some degree of embarrassment, he publicly acknowledged what he had done and asked that his information be corrected because he had seen the integrity of the process, was on board with the recommendations that had emerged, and wanted to remain involved going forward.

THE PUBLIC MANAGER'S ROLE IN DISCOVERING CITIZENS' SHARED PRIORITIES

Our founding fathers held a vision of a government "of the people, by the people, for the people." Helping citizens develop shared priorities that directly inform the decision making that affects them is fundamental to achieving this vision. Public managers are in a position to create opportunities for citizens to play this role in governance. To do so, however, they will in some cases have to change their views about the public. They will have to trust that the public is capable of absorbing factual information, understanding the issues at stake, listening to unique perspectives, and then setting aside their differences to focus on solutions that work for everybody. The Federal Transit Administration's Therese McMillan put it this way: "As a federal manager, you have to approach interaction with citizens from a humble perspective. If you go in believing that you have the 'correct answer' and the purpose of your public engagement effort is simply to have people confirm this, then don't bother. I came to this wisdom over time and now realize that not having all the right answers is not a bad thing. In fact, you can get better results through engagement if you start the process early enough so that public input can actually shape options. If you wait too long, you miss the opportunity" (McMillan 2012).

The next step for public managers is to lay out the zone of influence for the decision at hand: On what can the public realistically have an impact? Once the answer to this question has been established, public managers must ensure that the design of the agenda and the deliberation questions will lead to shared priorities as the end result. The work must ground people in their commonly held values and commit them to operating from their highest sense of purpose. From this foundation, the discussion areas and questions must build slowly and sequentially to achieve collective decisions. Again using the example of the Americans Discuss Social Security deliberation, if we had begun the day with the "hot" question in the media and Congress at the time, "Are you for or against private accounts?" participants would have immediately been polarized and stuck debating their positions. Instead we asked people to identify the values they wanted Congress to protect in reforming Social Security, which led participants to discover first what they had in common rather than highlighting their policy differences.

Next, the process components that have been proven effective in surfacing shared views must be put in place: small-group discussion, diverse table seating, neutral materials, theming of content, voting, and, most important, facilitation.

Finally, to ensure a safe deliberative space that will support the development of shared priorities, it is critical that advocates and stakeholders do not dominate the process. This principle should be reflected in every detail of the engagement work, no matter how small. Deborah Dalton of the U.S. Environmental Protection Agency (EPA) described her agency's approach this way:

We generally do not have the meetings hosted by one of the parties—even when they have better conference or hotel space than EPA—as folks seem to get leery about this. I can think of only one exception (the All Appropriate Inquiries Regulatory Negotiation) for which, after nine meetings in a barely suitable EPA conference room, we held the last meeting in the conference facilities of one of the parties to the negotiation. But this was only because EPA's larger room was not available and after we checked with each party *individually* to make sure they were comfortable. It worked at the end of the process, but I'm not sure it could have worked at the beginning even with groups that were generally friendly with each other [Dalton 2012].

Going beyond the design of an engagement process, another way public managers can help ensure that citizen input results in shared priorities is to encourage agencies to stop conflating polling-style information gathering with participation. Most of the new interactive platforms emerging from the Open Government Directive, such as new strategies for getting more comments on a pending rule, are little more than adaptations of polling techniques. As discussed in Chapter One, these methods do nothing to help individuals wrestle with an issue's complexity. They do not provide an accurate lens through which to consider someone else's views or reveal the trade-offs people would be willing to make in an effort to reach common ground. When agencies rely on such mechanisms to satisfy their participation requirements, they miss the opportunity to help citizens develop the shared views that can have a real impact on policymaking.

Further, information that is gathered this way may not accurately reflect citizens' views. In the Americans Discuss Social Security initiative, early polling had concluded that private retirement investment accounts had relatively strong support among the public. However, when citizens came together in live forums and teleconferences to discuss this issue, their responses to this option were mild to negative. The experience of authentic deliberation with fellow citizens produced a different set of views about the same policy question.

As public managers pursue robust citizen engagement work, they will be exerting an important counterforce against the impulse to treat polling as if it is real engagement. For that matter, they will be taking a stand against any form of engagement that produces discord as opposed to compromise.

Public Manager Perspectives

The Mountain Pine Beetle Coalition

Richard Stem, retired Deputy Regional Forester, U.S. Forest Service

The Context

Mountain pine beetles (or bark beetles) are frequent inhabitants of the forests in western North America, particularly in ponderosa and lodgepole pine trees. These small insects—no larger than a grain of rice—typically play a critical role in the ecosystem and life cycle of a forest. By attacking older, weakened trees they help thin out forests and therefore act as a catalyst for the growth and development of a younger, healthier forest. Their impact can become extreme, however, when climate conditions fluctuate. When there is a stretch of unusually hot, dry summer weather coupled with mild winter weather, forests filled with mature lodgepole pine trees can be overrun by beetles.

After several years of this weather pattern in the early 2000s in the mountains of Colorado, an unprecedented pine beetle epidemic was in full swing. Millions of beetles would fly in every summer and bore into the vulnerable trees. They laid their eggs, and in the process they introduced a blue stain fungus that blocked the flow of water in the tree, killing it within a year. By 2004 almost five hundred thousand acres had been infected in northwest Colorado, and the fungus was spreading.

The number of potentially affected industries was significant, including tourism, recreation, water quality and quantity, utility transmission, physical property and projected property values, roads and transportation infrastructure, and current and future construction. The U.S. Forest Service was the largest land manager in the region, but the problem affected multiple counties and cities, the state, the Bureau of Land Management, and more. The scourge of beetles was outrunning the Forest Service's capability to mitigate it, and everyone was upset at the prospect of forest and property loss.

Gary Severson, executive director of the Northwest Colorado Council of Governments, declared: "The very essence of Colorado's quality of life [was] placed in jeopardy by the little black beetles and their resulting impacts, not the least of which [was] catastrophic fire" (Wang and Severson 2007, 1).

Not surprisingly, many constituencies took different sides and began to develop their own positions about what to do. Taking into consideration the scope of the problem and the complexity of issues and jurisdictions involved, the Forest Service made the rare choice to build a coalition of the affected stakeholders. The goal was to deal with the problem as a team, rather than trying to work out recommendations and solutions along administrative lines and according to old power structures. The topic of dead and dying trees in northwest Colorado was an energizing topic, but it was not clear whether a large group of previously independent government entities, stakeholder groups, and citizens could collaborate at a level that would match the challenge at hand.

Public Engagement Strategies

In October 2005 a core group—a municipal, county, state, and federal intergovernmental cooperative spanning five counties and three national forests—was brought together to begin formulating a response. Structural and organizational changes were made at federal and state levels to give the newly formed coalition the freedom it needed to operate. The Colorado Bark Beetle Cooperative (CBBC) was launched.

The CBBC began with a process of clarifying core objectives to protect life and property, water supplies, and critical infrastructures. The collaborative model and the public engagement strategies focused everyone on working together in a sequence of small and large meetings to share information, to learn the technical implications and trade-offs within the various scenarios, and to prioritize the recommendations moving forward.

In the first few years of the CBBC, thousands of citizens attended many town hall meetings, conferences, and public meetings, and issues were debated, discussed, and advanced through dialogue. Newsletters, governor briefings, articles from national press outlets, and other forms of communication were generated by the different entities associated with the collaborative as means of sharing information and providing context to affected stakeholder groups and community members.

At the same time, congressional attention was sharpened with the direct personal involvement of Colorado's two senators and the congressman of the affected area. In addition, administration officials in Washington, DC came to know the collaborative by the visits that were championed by its members.

In 2006 the CBBC published the "Mountain Pine Beetle Strategy and Assessment," its first shot at addressing the full spectrum of problems and charting a realistic, successful plan for mitigation.

As the process moved on in 2007, the CBBC began to reach out and invite members of Colorado's active conservation community and other nongovernmental organizations (NGOs) to join the cooperative. These groups varied in their mobilization and influence on the issue, but were critical to getting broad-based support and input. The public engagement process eventually resulted in extended stakeholder involvement by NGOs, private landowners, interest groups, and water utilities. Four additional counties further expanded participation by municipalities and local government agencies.

Even after the initial date that was determined for the CBBC to expire, the group continued to expand its activities through collaborative efforts and increased community participation. The core team eventually included water utilities, emergency management, and the Western Area Power Administration, all representing the infrastructure needed to start a second phase of the collaborative with a newly formed steering committee. In summer 2008 the Colorado Forest Restoration Institute stepped in to help facilitate the growth and expansion of the CBBC and to help develop a viable consensus-building and decision-making process.

Powerful Outcomes

The CBBC's work led to important recommendations about the best ways to simultaneously protect human life, protect public infrastructure, and protect critical water supplies under extremely challenging circumstances. In the end, successful mitigation took place in fifty-five to seventy thousand acres across the nine CBBC counties. From a process perspective, some of the most powerful outcomes of this broad-based collaboration included the following:

- *Unified recommendations.* Cooperation among all relevant stakeholders and community members created unified recommendations and implementable plans to stem the tide of the epidemic.

- *Reduced competition increased available funding.*
  Reduced competition for existing funding, and
  collaboration to secure additional funding for the
  State of Colorado, resulted in securing over $10
  million from different sources.
- *Broader geographic impact.* The coalition eventually
  quadrupled the combined state, private, and
  federal acres treated.
- *No litigation.* There were very few disagreements,
  and as mitigation plans were implemented, there
  were no serious appeals or litigation that held up
  progress. That is not to say that there was not fierce
  debate during the process. There was. It was
  healthy debate that brought about better ideas.
  What was important was that the broad engagement
  from stakeholders in the collaborative ensured that
  it always worked toward a common end.
- *Common messages.* The creation of unified messages
  for all groups to use in their independent outreach
  accelerated public awareness efforts and united the
  coalition.

The Colorado Bark Beetle Cooperative remains in
existence today. Although its role has changed somewhat, working groups continue toward accomplishing
goals established in 2006, including developing a
communication plan and a vision statement as well
as monitoring the direction of project implementation that was agreed on by the government and the
cooperative.

CHAPTER ELEVEN

STRATEGY SEVEN: SUSTAIN CITIZEN ENGAGEMENT

Politics should be like this more often. This was a life changing event. I would do it again tomorrow.

OUR BUDGET, OUR ECONOMY TOWN MEETING
PARTICIPANT*

From planning to implementation, a high-quality citizen deliberation effort is a months-long, multifaceted process of citizen, policymaker, and stakeholder involvement. Although designing and convening the primary engagement forum may be the high point of the process, the work is not complete if robust public participation does not continue over time. Such sustained engagement means regular and ongoing opportunities are available for citizens to remain engaged and have an impact on the issues as they develop. It is also defined by observable increases in citizens' sense of civic agency and by a systemic embrace of participation by decision makers who embed the processes within the institutions they lead. Today this is the exception rather than the rule, but it is the long-term goal of this work. This chapter explores the importance of sustaining citizens' involvement and presents case examples to illustrate how it has been accomplished.

---

*America*Speaks*. Our Budget, Our Economy. *Archives.* 2011.

Why Sustaining Citizen Engagement Is Important

The body of independent evaluation research conducted on America*Speaks*'s work has shown that taking part in policy, resource, and planning discussions across differences is an empowering and transformative experience for the majority of participants. This finding makes it clear that the effort involved in assessing the landscape, getting the right people in the room, linking to decision makers, creating a safe space, and providing neutral information each and every time pays off in the form of inspiring democratic experiences, as well as real impacts on policy. It is also true that as soon as the outreach and communication efforts are over and team members leave the community, for the majority of participants there is no place, structure, or network through which they can continue what they found to be so empowering. There are few, if any, vehicles for sustaining their participation, and for holding decision makers accountable for ongoing action and results. When participants ask the question: "So what happens next?" there is seldom a satisfying answer.

Without mechanisms for real, sustained participation, people will soon lose their sense of agency. "A key challenge," says Richard Stem of the U.S. Forest Service, "is often the lack of follow-through. Failure comes when there is a 'meeting mindset' and it is just one and done. You need to help forge connections between the process milestones of initial conversation, collaborative planning, prioritizing and decision-making, and implementing. You cannot accomplish this if you are unwilling to follow through and be patient with the process each step along the way" (Stem 2012). As Stem makes clear, robust citizen engagement must include opportunities for future and ongoing involvement. It is not enough to engage citizens to solve a specific problem or weigh in on a policy choice. Roles for citizens in governance must be embedded and sustained.

The New Orleans Community Congresses provide an excellent example of sustaining involvement. This work was specifically aimed at responding to the Bush Administration's demand that the city and state present a unified voice to receive federal disaster recovery funds. The Community Congresses achieved that goal.

However, without additional effort, the potential for building on the momentum to fundamentally change governance processes and expectations in New Orleans would have been lost. Knowing this, a number of organizations that partnered with America*Speaks* on the Community Congresses and that were intricately involved in neighborhood recovery efforts came back together to explore ideas and opportunities for sustaining the work.

In summer 2008 approximately two hundred people representing the geographic and demographic diversity of the city joined together and formed nine action teams around specific components in a codified Citizen Participation Program. The teams pursued this work through the end of February 2009 and finalized a draft model. While this work was under way, in November 2008 lead organizations worked to secure an amendment to the city charter that would mandate citizen participation. An October 2010 resolution of the City Council further mandated that the amendment move forward. As this book went to press, enabling legislation that will further define and establish the necessary implementation structures was being developed, and pilot implementation projects were in the works. In addition, several city agencies, including the New Orleans Recreation Commission, the police department, and Capital Projects, were developing their own citizen input structures, aligning them fairly closely with the proposed citywide model. Keith Twitchell, President of the Committee for a Better New Orleans, which is helping lead these efforts, described it this way:

> Community Congress II was one of the most important events in the history of post-Katrina New Orleans. For those citizens who had previously been active in recovery efforts but were burned-out, it validated their efforts. We all saw real, tangible results, which was incredibly energizing; and the number of people involved—representing the diversity that is truly New Orleans—was so much greater than anything that had come before that it created strong momentum for an on-going, formal Citizen Participation Program (CPP). Several years later, the CPP is finally on the verge of being institutionalized, after successfully overcoming some persistent opposition [Twitchell 2012].

Strategies for Sustaining Citizen Engagement

There are many possible ways to sustain citizen engagement. In America*Speaks*'s experience they fall into four general categories:

- Connecting participants to existing networks, creating new networks, or both
- Increasing the availability of authentic deliberative opportunities
- Creating institutional mechanisms that sustain engagement
- Expanding current online interactions so that they are more meaningful and effective

Strategies in each of these categories are explored below.

Connecting Participants to Existing Networks or Creating New Ones

Participants feel empowered at the end of effective citizen engagement work. They want to stay connected, continue to make a difference, and contribute to their respective communities. On some topics or issues, they can readily connect to existing community organizations. More challenging circumstances emerge when there is no appropriate existing network. In these situations, conveners of the citizen engagement initiative will have to help citizens create one. At a very minimum, they can invite participants to share their contact information and disseminate contact lists. Following Listening to the City, one table group continued to regularly meet on its own for six months. Jane Berkow, a member of that group, described it this way: "Despite the fact that we were so different, and had rather lively disagreements during the meeting, we enjoyed it so much that we decided to stay in touch and collectively watch to see what would come of our input" (Berkow 2012).

Depending on the nature of the issue under discussion and the time frames in which action is important, laying out specific individual and group action steps can build on the relationships and momentum that are generated during a participation process. For example, at the end of the daylong California*Speaks* deliberation on health care reform, participants were invited to stay involved and were given specific actions to take, such as sending messages to their legislators about the outcomes of the deliberation, talking to friends and family, and using the initiative's website to receive updated information and additional actions. Follow-up polling with participants five weeks after the deliberation found that 95 percent had discussed the issue of health care reform with others, compared with 77 percent in a control group; 40 percent had contacted a government representative, compared with 12 percent in a control group; and 8 percent had contacted the media, compared with 3 percent in a control group (Fung, Lee, and Harbage 2008).

An excellent example of creating new networks to sustain participation can be found in the work initiated by the Public Life Foundation in Owensboro, Kentucky. In 2007 the We the People: America*Speaks* 21st Century Town Meeting initiative brought 650 people representative of the Owensboro and greater Daviess County communities together to deliberate about regional challenges, such as slow economic growth, underperforming schools, and environmental degradation. At the end of this deliberation, more than 300 participants signed up to be members of action groups in the five areas prioritized by citizens: education and learning; regional opportunity; "green and clean"; a healthy and caring community; and government for the twenty-first century. Several weeks later, 150 citizens reconvened to develop ninety-day work plans for these action groups, and three months later 150 citizens came together to assess progress. Since then, a We the People Leadership Council has met monthly to provide oversight, resources, and cross-initiative communication. Although the structure and leadership of the five groups have evolved over time, it is remarkable that to this day, over 1,300 citizens remain involved in We the People.

In one example of this ongoing work, since 2007 the Citizens for Good Government group has pursued an openness and transparency pledge with elected officials across county and city government. It has held public forums approximately four times per year on such subjects as basic civics, tax equity issues, and how

FIGURE 11.1 EVALUATION REPORT ON THE IMPACT OF THE
CALIFORNIA*SPEAKS* INITIATIVE

Public Impacts:

Evaluating the outcomes of the
CaliforniaSpeaks statewide
conversation on health care reform

Based on three independent
evaluations of California*Speaks* by:

Archon Fung, Harvard University & Taeku Lee,
University of California, Berkeley

Harder + Company Community Research

Peter Harbage, Harbage Consulting

californiaspeaks
Working Together for Better Health Care

to run for public office. And it has sponsored two nonpartisan candidate forums. After four years, the group continues to meet every month. Belinda Abell, who has volunteered to lead the Citizens for Good Government group since its inception, described her experience this way:

> Community involvement has always been a high priority for me. Whether it's our local Chamber or non-profits, I've always been involved. The most important efforts I've been involved with were our two *We the People* town meetings. After the first meeting there was an energy in the community that hadn't been there before. I think at that first meeting people realized they weren't alone in their thinking and, at the same time, that ideas different from theirs had merit. Many of us have stayed involved from the beginning either through hosting or participating in forums and have expanded our methods of seeking input by using focus groups.
>
> Communication has also improved from our local government entities to the community. Citizens now feel more comfortable in asking questions, they're seeing that their voices are heard and slowly but surely the focus is on a more participatory form of communication and decision-making. Of course you still have people who disagree but now the view is that we all are heard.
>
> All in all for me, the strength of the meetings has made a tremendous impact on how we as citizens view our role in the community [Abell 2012].

The 2007 We the People town meeting was so successful, and the work sufficiently embedded in the community, that three years later a second large-scale deliberation was launched. The goal was to build on the work of the first and further advance citizens' experience of agency. Owensboro and Daviess County citizens' ongoing commitment to participation has born real fruit. In 2011 the *New York Times* reported that more than $1 billion had been invested in revitalization projects in Owensboro, including a new hospital, an 8,500-square-foot expansion of the regional airport terminal, various road and drainage projects, and a new shopping center along the city's highway bypass (Schneider

2011). Rodney Berry, president of the Owensboro Public Life Foundation, described how the earlier citizen engagement work had laid the foundation for these improvements:

> The seeds for these initiatives were planted during an event four years earlier. On a chilly November day in 2007, more than 600 Owensboro–Daviess County, Kentucky residents devoted an entire Saturday—the first day of deer season—to participate in We the People: America*Speaks* 21st Century Town Meeting. During that effort, the need to "transform downtown" emerged as a top recommendation. Within a few months from now, construction will begin on a new riverfront convention center and hotel. A public plaza and the expansion of a riverfront park are under construction. Pedestrian-friendly streets and sidewalks are in the works. Several mixed use residential-office-retail projects are coming together. Most every leader agrees: Owensboro's downtown and riverfront initiatives would not have occurred had it not been for the public outcry to make this development a priority, and for the continuing dedication of citizens to keep pursuing it [Berry 2011].

INCREASING ENGAGEMENT OPPORTUNITIES

In summer 2008 America*Speaks* and the nonprofit organizations Everyday Democracy and Demos convened forty-nine advocates, scholars, and practitioners in a forum called Strengthening Our Nation's Democracy. The work aimed to develop an agenda and specific recommendations for addressing the increasing loss of people's trust in, and sense of connection to, our politics and governance. One of the conclusions reached by this group was that sufficient mechanisms must be available for citizens to deliberate about policy issues *on a regular basis,* as they do in the United Kingdom, for example, with citizen panels and citizen juries. More specifically, the group recommended that our federal government hold regular national discussions, of one million Americans or more, on the issues of highest public concern, such as jobs, energy, taxes, health care, and foreign policy. Citizens themselves are highly supportive of this concept. As noted in the Introduction, a National Conference on Citizenship survey found that more than 80 percent of respondents were supportive of the idea, and that the support crossed political lines. The survey found that 60 percent of Republicans and 70 percent of Democrats described themselves as "strongly" in favor of regular, organized national discussions on critical issues (National Conference on Citizenship 2008, 12).

To ensure as many appropriate and relevant opportunities for citizen engagement as possible, any national-level commitment, as recommended earlier, will have to be linked to work already under way at the regional, state, city, and community levels. In addition, the work at all these levels will have to be much more extensive and robust. Public managers, elected officials, and other leaders across all jurisdictions will continually have to increase the number of well-designed listening sessions, public hearings, stakeholder forums, and other more cutting-edge citizen engagement processes.

The U.S. Department of Health and Human Services (HHS) is an example of a federal agency that has done this. Over the last few years HHS has deliberately expanded its routine opportunities for participation, creating over 230 federal advisory committees. Notably, rather than limiting participation to expert stakeholders, HHS invites the public to participate on these committees. And HHS continues to explore how to expand its participation base even further (Lukensmeyer, Goldman, and Stern 2011).

Although increasing the volume of opportunities is a worthwhile objective in its own right, any new or expanded work would ideally incorporate citizen engagement implementation strategies along the lines of those recommended in this book. Further, any agency working to increase the volume of participatory opportunities it provides should ensure that individual instances are strategically linked to each other. A series of stand-alone events has limited capacity to build sustained involvement by citizens. Public managers and others should therefore ask themselves if their citizen engagement activities build on each other, and closely track the progress of the issues and choices under discussion. Each iteration of the work should not only attract new participants but also encourage and support repeat participation. By attending to these facets of the work, public managers can create a cohesive body of opportunity that sustains citizens' ability to have an impact on key issues. David Kuehn, Cochair of the Environmental Justice in Transportation Committee of the Transportation Research Board, thinks about it this way: "Engagement can be cyclical. Often the goal of sustaining engagement is to bring new people in, not only working with the same people over time. In the end, though, it is about continuously building capacity" (Kuehn 2012).

Creating Institutional Mechanisms That Sustain Engagement

Taking measures to increase the volume of citizen engagement work requires an institutional commitment as well as the specific mechanisms for making good on that commitment. As discussed earlier, most of our governing institutions neither are committed to increasing citizen engagement nor have the capacity to do this. For the most part, they have no budgets, authorizing mandate, administrative mechanisms, or systemic expectations for citizen engagement work. In short, agencies, and the individuals in them, have few incentives for undertaking enhanced citizen engagement practice, and there certainly are no consequences if they do not.

The lack of policies and resources to support citizen engagement does not mean we do not know what is needed. America*Speaks* has convened multiple gatherings of more than two hundred democracy practitioners and scholars, senior agency leaders, managers, and staff to discuss these issues, and they were readily able to identify critical avenues. In particular, they noted the importance of codifying policies and mechanisms that both require public officials to do engagement work and assess their performance doing it. They also focused on the need for sufficient technical assistance, capacity-building tools, and human and financial resources. More action steps for public agencies include the following (America*Speaks* 2009):

- Providing training on, and professional development opportunities for, civic engagement
- Establishing incentives via performance reviews, promotion and reward systems, or other vehicles
- Promulgating standards for the work so that consistency and quality can be maintained

- Establishing plans to evaluate the agency's work on an ongoing basis
- Creating positions and departments in which support and expertise can be developed and housed

Olivia Ferriter of the U.S. Department of the Interior was not part of these discussions, but independently drew some of the same conclusions. "A key sign that we were prioritizing public engagement was when it went into our performance plans," she said. "In addition, we invested in training people and in ongoing messaging internally. But above all else, leaders walked the talk from the highest level" (Ferriter 2012).

The U.S. Department of Health and Human Services' work, in particular as it relates to internal capacity building, offers concrete examples of how institutional mechanisms that support engagement can be created.[1] HHS has built a community of practice around citizen engagement that allows innovators within the agency to network, compare results, exchange and document best practices, collaborate to address shared challenges, and develop participation and collaboration tools for others in the agency to use. This support network serves as an internal consulting team that can be called on by those who want to involve the public in policy formulation or implementation but who lack the expertise and experience with citizen engagement to do so. Several different areas of specialty have emerged within this community, including an "ideas" subgroup and a "competition-focused" subgroup.

Further, the HHS open government teams have "open gov days," on which meetings are held with different centers throughout the agency. At these meetings, the teams present ideas and brainstorm with program staff about how to engage the public in their particular issue areas and offer better services. The meetings also enable employees to provide input and feedback on the offerings made available by the central open government team. Because demand for the practice network's services and expertise far exceeds its capacity, the group publishes white papers, conducts trainings on best practices and available tools, and relies heavily on www.howto.gov to help share knowledge without significantly increasing costs.

A Closer Look at Another Federal Agency's Efforts

When considering public engagement efforts in the federal government, The U.S. Environmental Protection Agency (EPA) has long been a leader.[2] Patricia Bonner, lead EPA staff member for public involvement after 1984, recalled: "Back in 1981, the EPA pioneered citizen engagement with its Public Participation Policy. Community-based water, air, Superfund, and risk communications work followed, as well as efforts to explore conflict prevention and resolution through dialogue. The agency used web-based dialogue with the public as early as 2000. EPA's 2003 Public Involvement Policy is recognized and used as a model worldwide" (Bonner 2012).

To extend these efforts, under the Open Government Directive EPA has focused intently on five distinct success factors:

- *Effectively integrating activities across the agency.* EPA has incorporated open government concepts and objectives into its core mission and strategic plan. EPA has also gone to significant lengths to involve employees from across the agency in shaping its participatory and collaborative projects. An open government management work group, which meets weekly to develop actions, provide input, and track progress, comprises senior managers from across the agency and includes representatives from regional offices.
- *Distinguishing types of participation.* Clear differentiation between varying levels and types of participation enables better evaluation of existing engagement initiatives as well as potential projects under consideration. EPA distinguishes public participation projects by level of engagement, ranging in intensity from pure information dissemination to empowered stakeholder action. This schema, along with expectations for its use, have been fully disseminated internally.

- *Attending to diversity of participation.* EPA makes specific efforts to ensure broad representation in its engagement work and to diminish the influence of stakeholders: participants offering input must reflect the composition of the communities that are influenced by a policy. Further, EPA seeks to connect with communities historically underrepresented in its decision making. The agency established a national work group to evaluate this concern, focusing on issues of electronic access and the digital divide and seeking ways to provide technical information so that it is clear, accessible, and timely for use by affected communities.

- *Effectively responding to citizen input.* EPA seeks to embed outreach efforts within a framework of genuine dialogue by consistently responding to public input. For example, it has committed to responding in full to each of the five most popular proposals on the "Open Government" page of the agency's website.

- *Maintaining a high level of comfort with experimentation.* EPA has been a leading agency in experimentation, particularly in regard to online rule-making. The agency has tried involving the public earlier in the process of revising a rule, for example by creating opportunities for discussion forums, sharing public meeting information, and distributing rule-making progress updates in advance of the legal requirement for public comment. Even before the Open Government Initiative's institutionalization, EPA had developed an automated public comment tool and process to bring the rule-making process online. The platform later became Regulations.gov, an online rule-making platform now employed across the federal government to alert the public about rules in development, publish documents related to each proposed rule, and solicit public comment.

EPA's focus on these five success factors demonstrates its commitment to adapting existing mechanisms and creating new ones in an effort to sustain citizens' involvement in its work. Other agencies would do well to follow EPA's lead. In *Investing in Democracy: Engaging Citizens in Collaborative Governance*, Carmen Sirianni (2009) of Brandeis University provides a more detailed look at how EPA has worked to sustain engagement and build not only internal capacity but also community capacity.

EXPAND CURRENT ONLINE OPPORTUNITIES

The information technology revolution is creating platforms and tools that enable government agencies at all levels to experiment with new methods of participation. The Open Government Initiative has placed a demand on all federal agencies to move in this direction as quickly as possible. Government data have been made more readily accessible and user friendly, via such sites as Data .gov, and federal agencies have created a new internal infrastructure to support the delivery of information. In addition, wikis, crowdsourcing platforms, e-petitions, and a broad range of online tools are now being used to solicit public feedback; generate innovative ideas from citizens, stakeholders, and employees; and increase participation in specific agency rule-making processes.

Although greater government use of online tools and platforms is a positive trend, simply increasing the *number* of public-to-government interactions is not enough. The information offered by citizens must be usable by agencies and then, in fact, be used. To achieve this goal, agencies must take a close look at their own practices: Is the information we are getting from citizens useable? If not, why not, and what can be done to increase its utility? What happens to this information when it arrives? What are the internal and external response mechanisms? What is the feedback loop?

The work of the National Aeronautics and Space Administration (NASA) in this area is an example of strong and effective practice. In describing its structure for responding to ideas gathered via the agency's IdeaScale platform, NASA said: "After the period for idea collection had ended, we began an extensive overview of the submitted ideas, classifying them into one of five categories: things we can do; things we do or have done; things we cannot do; unclear; and off-topic. The 'things we can do' ideas are then tagged to specific topic areas (e.g., education, public affairs, NASA spinoff) and relevant ideas are delivered to the corresponding NASA office along with an explanation of the engagement process" (Lukensmeyer, Goldman, and Stern 2011, 36). NASA's open government plan also expresses an intention to build on this process by devising a framework and procedures for handling ideas that are popular but not feasible by, for example, working with the contributor to make the idea more realistic or implementable (Lukensmeyer, Goldman, and Stern 2011). NASA's approach demonstrates commitment to taking public input seriously. The next generation of the work should add an important component: a transparent feedback loop that ensures participants understand their level of impact.

This section has reviewed four overarching strategies for sustaining citizen involvement: connecting existing participation networks or creating new ones; increasing the availability of powerful deliberative opportunities; establishing systemic or structural supports within institutional practice; and building out current online interactions so that they are more meaningful and effective. The following case study from the Washington, DC, Citizen Summits demonstrates how all four strategies can be integrated and institutionalized.

SUSTAINING CITIZEN ENGAGEMENT: A CASE STUDY

When it comes to the practice of democracy, Washington, DC is a study in contrasts. Bill Potapchuk, President of the Community Building Institute and longtime Washington, DC advocate, noted that the city is "simultaneously the capital of the free world and the only place in the United States that does not have a voting representative in Congress. . . . [L]imited home rule has existed only since 1974 . . . and federal intervention in the affairs of the District of Columbia is a prominent part of the political landscape. Members of Congress oversee the budget, review locally enacted laws, and, on occasion, insert unwanted restrictions on policy and budget" (Potapchuk 2002, 1–2).

In addition to bearing these anomalies of governance, Washington, DC is also a city with a long history of racial and socioeconomic divisions that are strongly in evidence during every election cycle, budget negotiation, or City Council hearing. On the positive side, one of the joys and important assets of working in the District is its rich tradition of citizen activism. Having achieved home rule in 1974, citizens of Washington, DC know that acting together they can make a difference. It is in this highly complex municipal landscape that a comprehensive, citizen-driven management cycle was implemented.

The Washington, DC Citizen Summits represent the longest-running series of large-scale town meetings in the United States. Between 1999 and 2005, input from thirteen thousand people significantly influenced the District's priorities on growth and development, annual spending, and a wide range of legislative initiatives. But beyond the specific policy and budget outcomes of the five large-scale Citizen Summits held during this period, significant progress was also made in sustaining engagement by embedding citizen voice in the daily operations of government. This was achieved through the mayor's Neighborhood Action Initiative.

NEIGHBORHOOD ACTION

Neighborhood Action was an integrated process designed and implemented by the administration of Mayor Anthony A. Williams. Citywide, as well as within and across neighborhoods, the work revolved around a cycle of strategic planning, budgeting, performance contracting, and public accountability, all linked together. At the start of each planning cycle, several thousand residents would come together at a Citizen Summit to review budget and policy options that the mayor and his cabinet had developed. Their task was to establish shared priorities. The priorities from the Citizen Summit were then used to develop the mayor's final budget and policy framework. Performance contracts and scorecards for each of the city's agency directors held them accountable for implementing the priorities that came out

FIGURE 11.2 STRATEGIC MANAGEMENT CYCLE

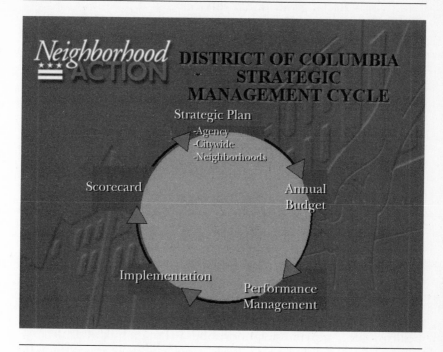

Source: America*Speaks 1999–2005*

of the Citizen Summit. City employees led follow-up planning and implementation work in every ward of the city. Figure 11.2 illustrates the strategic management cycle.

To achieve the desired goals, and to further embed citizen voice and participation in daily governance, the Neighborhood Action initiative put three new structures in place:

- *The Office of Neighborhood Action* took the lead on the citywide Citizen Summits and other ward- and neighborhood-based citizen deliberations. This office worked to link local neighborhood plans with city agencies' strategic plans as well as with the citywide strategic plan.
- *The Office of Neighborhood Services* coordinated service delivery in each of the city's eight wards through a cross-agency team approach to persistent problems. The work created a

transformative culture change from the District's long history of dysfunctional government services.

- *The Office of Neighborhood Planning* oversaw an expansion of the city's previous ward-based planning efforts. It increased the regularity of planning work, also coordinating it within and between neighborhoods and with the city-level strategic management cycle of planning and budgeting. This office also spearheaded the ongoing development of more public participation opportunities.

The city administrator's office coordinated the connections between these three offices, the mayor's office, and all cabinet agencies. These connections were the cornerstone of securing sustained involvement for citizens. As Potapchuk described it: "The linkage with Neighborhood Action provide[d] a vehicle for carrying neighborhood issues and priorities forward to the citywide strategic plan and budget. The linkage with Neighborhood Services relate[d] service interventions to longer term planning goals. With these linkages . . . Neighborhood Planning . . . [became] a powerful tool for building and maintaining healthy, safe, and vital neighborhoods" (Potapchuk 2002, 9).

Adding to these structural achievements, the city was an early leader in integrating the latest technology into its work. Although public dashboards of many varieties are now commonplace they were quite innovative in 2000, and were established in the District to enable citizens to more closely monitor the work of city agencies. Further, the Office of Planning worked with the offices of the chief financial officer and the chief technology officer to develop an online budget spreadsheet whereby the public could track agency actions on the recommendations that came out of the Citizen Summits. So, for example, if citizens at a Summit prioritized increasing funds for youth programming in the city's recreation centers, following that Summit citizens would have the same access as program managers to information indicating whether, when, and how those funds were being spent.

RESULTS

On the streets of the District of Columbia, Neighborhood Action yielded notable results. A groundbreaking neighborhood database took thousands of requests from a citywide call center and specific recommendations from the Citizen Summits, broke them down by ward and agency responsibility, and tracked their resolution. This high-accountability system resulted in a real change in the city's long-broken service delivery system and culture. As citizens repeatedly attended not only the biannual citywide Citizen Summit but also smaller-scale versions that were held in their neighborhoods and wards and designed on the same principles, they could see the cumulative impact of their ongoing participation. Street lamps were repaired. New resources came into their schools. Crime decreased. The "community learning" element of the initiative was also notable, with citizens building a solid understanding of government functioning and the roles they could play in it as well as the real policy and budgetary trade-offs involved in such complex issues as public safety, education, and employment.

Finally, the sustained involvement of the citizenry provided important political capital for Mayor Williams as he made and implemented policy during his terms in office. In the face of opposition from lobbyists or members of the City Council, the mayor would return again and again to data on citizens' priorities from the most recent Summit and use this information to successfully defend his choices. For example, in the 2001 Citizen Summit, one of the public's highest priorities was affordable housing. Following the Summit, having a strong public constituency enabled Mayor Williams to create an Affordable Housing Trust Fund that was "off-budget," meaning it could not be raided to fill budget gaps in other areas.

Neil Richardson, who was Executive Director of the Office of Neighborhood Action, noted that sustaining citizen involvement through a carefully crafted governance infrastructure was "a real win-win. The people of DC adopted a new role for themselves and, in real partnership with city leadership, were able to create a higher-functioning, more livable city" (Richardson 2012).

Unfortunately, even when a significant sustaining infrastructure for citizen engagement is built, the transition from one administration to the next creates political vulnerability. Although as a candidate for mayor Adrian Fenty promised to sustain citizen engagement, once elected he dismantled Neighborhood Action. Looking back on the loss of the initiative, Richardson commented:

"I don't think many people realize today how far away they are from the level of democratic input that they had. Neighborhood Action and the Summits created a tangible, accountable and transparent system of governance. I think a lot of people took that for granted" (Richardson 2012).

On a more positive note, in 2011 mayoral candidate Vincent Gray committed to reinstating robust citizen engagement in Washington, DC and, once elected, determined to make good on that promise. In March 2012 America*Speaks* worked with the Gray Administration to design and facilitate the One City Summit, which brought together 1,700 citizens representative of the diversity of the District of Columbia to take on the city's toughest issues. An additional 500 people viewed the deliberation online, with 150 of those participating actively in an online dialogue and voting process. The One City Summit enabled citizens of the District to develop a unified action agenda. Participants also came to agreement on four high-priority indicators through which the public can hold the District government accountable for progress toward achieving "one city." The key indicators are affordable housing; lower unemployment rates, particularly in Wards 7 and 8; reduced income disparity across the city; and increased high school graduation rates. Mayor Gray's commitment to annual citywide Summits as well as ward-based and issue-focused Summits lays the groundwork for citizen engagement in Washington, DC to flourish once again.

THE PUBLIC MANAGER'S ROLE IN SUSTAINING CITIZEN ENGAGEMENT

This chapter has laid out multiple pathways, as well as specific entry points, through which government agencies can sustain citizens' ability to make meaningful contributions to policymaking. Within the context of their own programs, public managers can work to increase the number and types of participatory efforts, and can ensure that successive initiatives are substantively connected and continuously build public and stakeholder commitment. Across their agencies, they can seek to instill a series of key success factors, some of which were described earlier in this chapter, that were derived from early analysis of agency open government plans. These success factors include the following (Lukensmeyer, Goldman, and Stern 2011):

- Effective integration of activities across departments within the agency
- An ability to distinguish participation levels across different engagement methodologies
- Attention to the diversity of participation
- Having a high comfort level with experimentation
- Incorporating extensive face-to-face engagement
- Investment in competitions
- Dedicated staffing
- Effectively responding to citizen input
- Having the capacity to make public commitments
- Building the internal support infrastructure

Public managers also have an important role to play in building public demand for sustained involvement. As described earlier, following a deliberation, public managers need to ensure timely communication of results and next steps to every participant, and they must also continue to provide regular updates about progress on the issues that were discussed. Public managers in every public agency should develop and maintain a database of participating citizens and stakeholders to facilitate the regular communication that builds public demand for involvement. Further, they can work to ensure that the range of information-sharing and information-gathering technologies and techniques their agency uses are aimed at the cocreation of innovative ideas, not just one-way exchanges. Joe Goldman, former vice president of citizen engagement at America*Speaks,* and Joe Peters, founding partner of Ascentum, summarized it well:

> Following participation opportunities, citizens and stakeholders should be able to go online to easily find reports and videos from the activities, and have an opportunity to comment on those reports and videos. Evaluations should be made available of the quality of the participation opportunities as rated by those who participate in them. Opportunities to take action in one's community in order to contribute to the agency's mission should

also be available on the web site . . . Citizens should be provided with tools to take action, educate others, collaborate with like-minded people to solve problems, and recruit their networks to get involved [Goldman and Peters 2009, 2].

Finally, public managers can strategically partner with local, regional, or even national groups that are in a position to help organize, implement, and follow up on engagement work. Agencies can provide funds for capacity building to strengthen existing organizations, or they can help create new ones to fill identified gaps. Chapter Thirteen highlights several types of organizations that can be strong partners.

To have an impact and effect a real change in agency culture, all of this work must be pursued with consistency. Long-term federal manager Rich Kuhlman, who led and managed a substantial body of public engagement work over several decades, noted: "It is not uncommon to see some people forget what they have learned and revert back to old practices. They use a collaborative process, get a great result, but then turn around and approach the next challenge with the old approach. This inconsistency will be evened out once engagement practices become part of the culture. But it requires buy-in and support at all levels of the Agency" (Kuhlman 2012). Richardson of Washington, DC concurred: "You have to be adaptive and nimble to be continually responsive to an ever-changing policy and budget environment," he said. "This work must be built into the reflex of government across the country" (Richardson 2012).

The agency-based examples offered in this chapter demonstrate that work to sustain citizen involvement can be and is being done. But the work will not be without its challenges. In many cases, in particular in the federal government, one or more of the essential elements—such as real support from top-level administrators and political appointees, the required resources, the availability of people in the agency with the requisite skills, or the inclusion of citizen engagement in program managers' performance goals—may not be in place. Or they may be in place but only tenuously because they are connected to a political appointee whose leadership is short-term. Further, except in some forward-looking agencies, there are not likely to be immediate rewards for these efforts. Too often, despite its labor-intensiveness, this work is seen as an add-on, with no simultaneous reduction in other responsibilities. In resource-strapped environments, building in the needed incentives, rewards, training, and support will take time, commitment, and diligence. Public managers will have to push through these challenges. Long-term manager Kuhlman described it this way: "Consistency is important. Because there is now a cultural expectation of continued public engagement, we are able to influence other agencies and increase their commitment to these kinds of processes as well. Over time this establishes momentum, which can reduce the impact of changes brought about through the election cycles" (Kuhlman 2012).

These last seven chapters have provided detailed strategies for designing and executing public engagement work that links citizen voices to government decision making. All of this information is fundamental to doing the work well. However, it would be a disservice to anyone wanting to learn to do this work not to also emphasize the importance of intuition and insight—and the need, at certain moments, to take a leap of faith. It would be possible to follow all of the guidance in this book to the letter and *still* miss the target if the nontechnical, non-data-driven, human elements are not respected and creatively utilized. Integrating the principles of practice with the intuition and insight that comes from experience leads to the most effective and empowering citizen engagement.

Equally important are the passion and motivation of the people doing this work. Thankfully, civil servants in our country *do* care passionately about the issues on which they work and *do* believe they can make a real difference in the life of our nation. They believe that government is an institution whose mission is to protect the public and the common good. In the end, the work described here is a critical vehicle for achieving these goals. And it is about much more than planning and executing a meeting. It is about supporting and sustaining the involvement of citizens in the governance of our nation. Public managers have an essential role to play in bringing citizens to the table in our democracy.

Public Manager Perspectives

Embedding Citizen Engagement in Government Policy Development Processes Through Advisory Councils

Bruce Gilbert is the Assistant Deputy Minister of the Rural Secretariat (Executive Council) in the Government of Newfoundland and Labrador, Canada. In light of his leadership, I recently had a number of conversations with Gilbert about the Rural Secretariat and the advisory councils it supports. The following is a summary of our conversations.

The Context

On the eastern edge of North America, Newfoundland and Labrador (NL) is a vast and rugged, largely rural territory about the size of California. The population in 2011 was 510,578, with about 40 percent residing in or near the only city of St. John's. NL has one of the fastest-growing economies in Canada due to booming oil and gas, mineral exploration, marine, and information technology industries. Despite impressive urban and suburban growth and prosperity in recent years, NL, like all other provinces in Canada, faces a number of complex challenges related to rural sustainability. These include an aging and shrinking rural population; youth out-migration linked to rural unemployment; and an aging infrastructure in seven hundred small communities spread across large distances. The Rural Secretariat (RS), a small entity within the Government of Newfoundland and Labrador (GNL), was created to engage citizens in deliberative dialogue about these rural sustainability issues and challenges. The goal was for rural citizens to inform the policy- and decision-making processes of government. In the early days of the citizen engagement process, however, the effort faced a number of challenges.

The Early Days

When the RS was launched in 2005, its citizen engagement work centered on supporting the efforts of ten government-convened, voluntary advisory councils (nine citizen-based regional councils and one stakeholder-based provincial council). Each council was made up of ten to fourteen volunteers who had been selected, after an open nomination process, by elected decision-makers within the Government of Newfoundland-Labrador. The formation of the ten councils was GNL's way of institutionalizing or embedding citizen engagement in governance. Although the term was not used at that time, these councils today would probably be considered a type of "open government" experiment.

The ten councils faced a considerable challenge. They had to build trust, respect, and mutual understanding among members. They had to inform themselves on issues in their region, on policy development processes, and on best practices from other jurisdictions. They had to wrestle with tremendously complex rural challenges that had eluded previous efforts at resolution. In addition, there were public questions about their legitimacy and usefulness. Some stakeholder groups working in related rural development areas believed the councils to be duplicating their efforts. Some others did not appear to understand or agree with the need for citizen engagement in policy processes. There were differing views both at the council tables and within the RS as to what amounted to useful advice, to whom it should be sent, and what constituted an appropriate and timely response.

The result of such challenges, not surprisingly, was that the councils got off to a relatively slow start in terms of actually developing and submitting advice. Some opposition party members publicly criticized councils for being inactive and ineffective. Few observers understood that a considerable amount of necessary learning and preparation work was under way behind the scenes. Some council members became frustrated, others reported feeling underappreciated, and several resigned. Most, however, refused to give up. They were committed to the idea that citizens can and should inform the policy- and decision-making processes of government. They wanted the councils to work, and they were going to do their best to realize their civic engagement potential.

Evolving and Strengthening the Councils

In 2008 senior officials at the RS were asked to assess the situation and to identify practical and timely ways to help councils reach their goals. After much consultation and dialogue with all involved, a number of important changes, adjustments, and realignments were made.

- *Increasing capacity to develop and provide advice.* In their first few years, councils were relatively slow to submit written advice to the GNL. This was not because they had nothing to say. Rather it was largely because many members were not content to submit advice based solely on the views of a small number of council members, and also because they knew that officials were more likely to seriously consider documents underpinned by evidence. To address this perceived need for evidence, the RS identified resources to support small-scale, council-driven, collaborative, and participatory research activities that would serve to generate data that could inform advice documents.

Also, the RS proactively supported councils interested in better engaging their fellow regional citizens on the topic under consideration. Moreover, RS officials worked closely with councils to build awareness of the relative merits of various types and degrees of evidence. They wanted members to understand that for some topics it may be appropriate to do regional-level research or additional citizen engagement work (that is, submit a report backed by research or informed by engagement activities), but for other topics it may be enough for the council members themselves— after considerable deliberation of course—to submit their own views concerning the matter at hand.

These efforts have had a very positive impact on the ability of councils to offer varied, timely, and sound advice. Over the past three years, sixty-one documents (for example, letters, reports, summaries of public engagement events) have been developed and submitted to the GNL. Government departments have responded to all submissions. Further, many departments are increasingly opting to meet with councils to discuss the documents, sometimes convening several times.

- *Clarifying advice and response processes.* In the early years, it was not clear how council documents would move through the bureaucracy. Some at the RS thought they should be reviewed, commented on, or even edited by officials before submission, whereas others thought officials should not interfere with them. Some thought they should enter at a relatively low level in the bureaucracy and work up to senior officials, whereas others thought the reverse. Expectations in regard to the degree, depth, and timeliness of department responses were also unclear. The RS worked to both specify and simplify the "inbound" and "outbound" processes and expectations, and confusion and questions have largely disappeared.

- *Strengthening the citizen engagement capacity of officials and members.* To increase the utility of council advice, it was clear that incorporating citizen engagement into their advice development process would be key. To better support councils in doing this, the RS sought out advanced training for officials in designing, conducting, and evaluating stakeholder and citizen engagement processes that aim to capture diverse views on policy questions. RS officials shared their new expertise with council members and worked with them to develop useful and appropriate activities. Since 2008 all councils have hosted citizen engagement activities, with the support of the RS, on topics ranging from land-use planning to health services; from aquaculture to waste management. Some engagement sessions have been small (10 to 20 people), whereas many others have been large by the standards of rural NL (50 to 60 people). There have been several multisite events involving 150 to 200 people. In two instances, nine rural communities engaged together through technology. In addition to producing more grounded advice for the GNL, these efforts have greatly improved the reputations of the councils and of the RS itself across rural NL. Indeed, early public questioning of the RS and councils has largely been replaced by accolades for their innovative and creative work.

Ongoing Challenges and Plans

The efforts of the councils and the RS have evolved and improved dramatically since 2008. Councils regularly develop and submit thoughtful and informed advice to senior officials across the GNL. Councils often engage the wider citizenry in their region to ensure that many voices are featured in advice documents. Department officials regularly meet with councils, and they work together on community-based research projects.

Notwithstanding these successes, challenges remain. Institutional barriers persist in some departments, with skepticism of the value of citizen-generated policy advice in some quarters. Also, responses from some departments have been described as "less than ideal" by some council members. In such cases RS officials will often contact the relevant department to request additional information on behalf of the council. On a number of occasions councils themselves have recontacted departments to ask for clarity on outstanding issues. The good news is that in all instances, communication between officials and members has been respectful and positive. In most instances, council members have been satisfied with additional explanations given to them.

More fundamentally, after numerous years of submitting advice to the GNL, some council members are asking: "How do we know our work is truly making a difference?" Such questions draw attention to the ongoing need to enhance the receptor capacity of advice-receiving departments, as well as their ability to provide quality and timely responses to councils. Of course, most council members are not seeking "proof" that their advice has been accepted, or that their recommendations can be directly linked to policy change. They understand that decision makers have multiple sources of data, input, and advice, and that tough choices often have to be made. What they want is more certainty that their advice is valued and thoughtfully considered.

Seven years ago, an experiment in citizen engagement was launched in NL. Despite a slow start, most of those involved—officials and citizen volunteers alike—remained committed to a constantly evolving and improving process. Learning occurred. Changes were made. Supports were found. The result: the advice floodgates opened up; public participation in advice development in regions dramatically increased; advice became much more informed by evidence; the vast majority of members now successfully ask to be reappointed to their council when their first or second term has expired; the GNL has recently demonstrated its overall commitment to the process by appointing thirty-two new members to councils; and responses from departments are constantly improving. In addition, officials from many departments are now proactively seeking the advice of councils on matters of interest. And there are even deeper results. Council members and citizens better understand government and the challenges and choices officials face. Officials are more aware of regional perspectives and needs, and understand that citizens deliberating together can produce useful and important ideas and recommendations. Trust, respect, and mutual understanding have also improved.

There is still much that can be done to improve this engagement process overall. Efforts are currently under way to implement a participatory evaluation of the advice and response processes. In the end, however, what is most important is that the GNL, the RS, council members, and many rural NL citizens are more committed than ever to the idea that through sustained dialogue and engagement, public policy, government decisions, and indeed modern democracy itself can be improved for all.

CHAPTER TWELVE

USING ONLINE TOOLS TO SUPPORT CITIZEN ENGAGEMENT

The urgent priority is to change the nature of the democratic conversation and to use this magnificent set of digital tools, on the World Wide Web, in social media, in apps, and elevate the role of reason and truth.

FORMER VICE PRESIDENT AL GORE, 2012*

Each of the seven previous chapters has referenced how technology, new media, or both can be used to achieve a particular citizen engagement strategy. This chapter takes a broader perspective. It reviews some of the early indications of how the ongoing information technology revolution is changing and enhancing the interaction between government and the public. It explores promising strategies for applying online tools to citizen engagement practice, and details some of the lessons that have been learned. The chapter concludes with a discussion of the importance of striking a judicious balance between online and face-to-face methodologies to ensure that citizens' voices have an impact on the policies that affect their lives.

---

*Gore A. "Al Gore and Sean Parker on Apathy SXSW 2012." *YouTube.* [http://www.youtube.com/watch?v=3eWacOwPsWw]. Accessed 2012.

A NEW WORLD FOR GOVERNMENT-PUBLIC INTERACTION

Continuously advancing information and communication technology is changing the way we interact with each other and with our world. Online platforms are giving the government many more options for meeting people where they are. They are helping agencies both reach a broader range of citizens, partners, and constituencies and establish more collaborative relationships. Finally, new platforms are creating opportunities for achieving a level of scale in citizen engagement work that had not been possible before.

Government efforts in this arena tend to fall into two general categories: increasing the variety and volume of data that are shared with the public and gathering public input and ideas. Both categories encompass activities that are valuable in and of themselves. At the same time, if these efforts are strategically expanded, they can make important contributions to the practice of robust citizen engagement.

DATA SHARING

As described in earlier chapters, the open government work that the Obama Administration has undertaken has greatly increased the flow of information from federal agencies to the public. Patricia Milligan of the U.S. Nuclear Regulatory Commission identified a broad portfolio of technology-based information-sharing methodologies in use in her agency:

> We are now starting to take advantage of greater technology. We are using Twitter, YouTube for videos, and blogs with updates. We "spotlight" emerging issues and put them on our front page to direct people to a special site with hot topics, etc. People who want information can find it quickly. We do not just communicate with the public at meetings. We have a great website that releases as much information as possible on a continuous basis—you can search by docket number and see all public documents available regarding a particular issue. We send out emails proactively with annual reports, as well as other interesting information about health effects [Milligan 2012].

There are now countless ways for citizens and groups to access and work directly with enormous quantities of federal data. They are using this information to build powerful applications for the web and for mobile devices, such as "accountability mashups" of congressional campaigns and voting records, or tracking mechanisms through which citizens around the world can work together to monitor the prevalence of common illnesses. The U.S. Department of Health and Human Services has developed an online Apps Expo that catalogues hundreds of citizen-created applications that use federal data to advance a wide range of health outcomes.

By using social media to disseminate and respond to information, government becomes a "platform" for interaction, creativity, and problem solving. It is no longer just a consumer of citizen resources, such as taxes, data, and complaints; a producer of public goods, such as space flight, national parks, and clean air; or a distributor of products and services to citizens, such as highways, social security, and passports. In this new world, government is like a marketplace, leveraging value-creating activity. And the newfound ability of citizens and government to cocreate public goods out of raw data has galvanized an entire generation of activists hungry for opportunities to improve democratic governance and outcomes for citizens.

Gathering Public Input and Ideas

A second major way in which government is using new platforms and technologies is by creating open innovation or crowdsourcing opportunities that seek to surface new ideas and solutions. As part of the Obama Administration's early open government work, the U.S. General Services Administration (GSA) set up crowdsourcing forums for all federal agencies through a platform called IdeaScale, so that each agency could gather input on its open government plans. A number of agencies have continued to use this and other platforms to gather the public's views on broader questions of policy and programming. Building on this work, in 2010 the GSA developed Challenge.gov, an interagency platform through which the public can help solve discrete problems that are either outside an agency's area of expertise or beyond its available resources to solve. In some instances, making these challenges public also fulfills other agency needs, such as increasing credibility or expanding its networks.

When this book went to press, over forty federal agencies had posted more than 175 challenges on Challenge.gov. The topics of these challenges are diverse, ranging from requests for educational videos from health awareness initiatives, to calls for detection algorithms that can find craters on the surface of Mars. The challenges often incentivize public participation through prizes, including cash awards.

FIGURE 12.1 A RECENT CROWDSOURCING EFFORT
BY THE FEDERAL GOVERNMENT

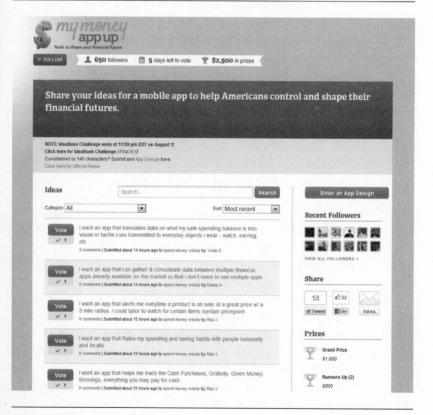

Source: Challenge.gov 2012

In one example, the U.S. Department of Defense's Defense Advanced Research Projects Agency (DARPA) regularly holds challenges related to the design of military support vehicles. In 2011 the winner—whose work stood out from among 159 entries involving more than twenty thousand designers—was Victor Garcia, an immigrant who came to the United States from Mexico at age five (Tuutti 2011). Challenges like these have become a popular way to link the public to the work of federal agencies. It is not uncommon for a well-run challenge that addresses an important topic of public policy to engage hundreds of thousands, if not millions, of citizens.

LINKING PARTICIPATION TO DECISION MAKING

Expanding citizens' access to government data and proactively seeking their input and ideas on challenging questions are valid and useful methods of fostering public participation. To the extent that these activities are part of a positive feedback loop through which citizens can see whether and how their ideas are being used, they can help drive increased interest and participation. However, in the context of the citizen engagement outcomes contemplated in this book, efforts like these are not enough.

As noted in Chapter Four, public participation strategies exist along a spectrum that begins with *informing* the public by providing data or information, or *consulting* with them by seeking their input in a one-way exchange. Public involvement intensifies along the spectrum when efforts *engage* the public to build on their input; when decision makers *collaborate* or partner with citizens on ideas and recommendations; and, finally, when government *empowers* citizens with actual decision-making authority (see Table 4.1, "Public Involvement Spectrum"). As involvement strategies move toward the empowerment end of the spectrum, the depth of the public's participation, and the potential for influencing decision making, increase.

Online tools and platforms offer real promise for moving practice toward the empowerment end of the spectrum to the extent that they are used to support meaningful participation at scale. The following three categories constitute a framework for sorting through the range of available online tools and strategies to find those that can best support citizen engagement that is explicitly linked to decision making:

- Online tools that extend the scope and reach of face-to-face deliberation
- Online tools that increase the value of ideation processes
- Online tools that seek to sustain participation over time

The three sections that follow provide a description of each category, explore some of the tools that are available, and offer brief case examples to illustrate their use.

ONLINE TOOLS THAT EXTEND THE SCOPE AND REACH OF FACE-TO-FACE DELIBERATION

Until recently, participation at public hearings, on expert panels, and in other "listening" sessions was generally limited to those who could be physically present—those not obligated to be at work, with family, or in school. With the processing and connective power of handheld devices, however, an entirely new landscape of participation has been revealed. Nearly half of American adults own a smartphone (Smith 2012), meaning a great many of us can run advanced applications from the palm of our hand, quickly finding data, for example, on how federal dollars are being spent in our neighborhood, or responding to instant polls on an issue of interest.

Although there is a long way to go before the use of these tools and techniques becomes an accepted governance practice, it is extraordinary to see high-level expert panels responding, in live broadcast discussions, to questions from television and web audiences via the 140-character bandwidth of Twitter. Social platforms like Facebook have enabled members of Congress and the Obama Administration to convene public meetings that feature interactive video and text chat.

These platforms can be applied to the complex deliberative events described in this book. As long as "virtual" participants are fully engaged in the deliberative process, as opposed to simply monitoring it and tossing in an occasional comment, then they too can have a direct impact on decision making. America*Speaks* has developed two adaptations to its 21st Century Town Meeting model—virtual summits and networked house parties—that enable citizens to participate in a substantive, interactive way without having to be physically present at an in-person forum. We have also begun to use a range of interactive media to extend the reach of our face-to-face deliberative efforts.

VIRTUAL SUMMITS

Virtual summits were designed by America*Speaks* to closely simulate the in-person experience of the 21st Century Town Meeting citizen engagement process. Through a webcast or television program, virtual participants learn about the issues under discussion. Additional informational materials can also be made immediately accessible to them on a website dedicated to the engagement initiative. After reviewing the information, these participants dial in to a conference line to join a small group in a facilitated, fifteen- to thirty-minute discussion at a "virtual table." The role of the online discussion moderator is crucial to ensuring that the discussion is productive and that all participants are as engaged as productively as possible. The ideas that emerge through these conversations are submitted online to a theme team, which identifies community-, city-, state-, or even nationwide themes from across all of the virtual tables. At the end of the discussion period, participants watch a report from the theme team via webcast or television and then use online voting tools to express their preferences. The process is repeated several times to ensure comprehensive coverage of the topics at hand.

This model is highly scalable, as it reduces the costs associated with creating physical environments and in person forums for discussion. Further, it is an inclusive methodology through which people who are unable to travel due to disability or any other circumstance can fully participate. Although it requires more organization and infrastructure than some of the other online methodologies described later in this chapter, a virtual summit provides the most engaging, scalable, deliberative experience to a distributed group of online participants that is possible with existing technology. This use of technology enables a substantially larger and more geographically diverse discussion than can be achieved through deliberation at central forums alone.

Using This Tool: Virtual Tables Expand a National Discussion on Autism Policy

The prevalence of autism has significantly increased over the past ten years. The national advocacy organization Autism Speaks reports that "around 1 in 88 American children [are] . . . on the autism spectrum . . . [and] more children are diagnosed with autism each year than with juvenile diabetes, AIDS or cancer, combined" (Autism Speaks 2012). When people with autism transition from childhood to adulthood, they face significant challenges in a society that does not have adequate resources to meet their needs. In November 2009 America*Speaks* facilitated a national town meeting aimed at developing the country's first-ever agenda for improving services and supports for adults with autism.

More than one thousand people across thirty-three cities participated in this discussion, establishing priorities for addressing policy concerns about housing, employment, community life, and other pressing issues for individuals with autism. The Advancing the Future of Adults with Autism (AFAA) initiative piloted the first application of virtual table technology. More than fifty people, across seventeen cities, watched a live webcast presentation from the national in-person discussions and then joined volunteer facilitators on a conference call. As these virtual participants came to agreement, their ideas were submitted online to a team of analysts who integrated them with those of citizens participating in the connected face-to-face deliberations taking place in sixteen other cities. Online polling keypads enabled virtual table participants to vote on their priorities over the course of the day. Sammi F. of Marysville, Washington, said this about her experience:

> The online autism forum was outstanding; the first of its kind that I am aware of where the forum is not professionals speaking about the current state of affairs, but predominantly focused on mothers like me who are facing the decision to turn their children over to independent living. The broadcasts came through clearly and were inspiring. We were able to instant message one another while also having group conversation through text and speaking on the phone. The real-time participation gave those of us at the virtual table a chance to be heard.
>
> I feel considerably more empowered since the forum, knowing that other parents are undergoing the same concerns I am with their autistic children coming of adult age. Other parents at my virtual table have invited me to an email group, a regional meeting group, social functions, as well as state lobby days. All this makes me feel connected to an effort that is serious about affecting legislation with and on behalf of our autistic children [America*Speaks* 2009].

Based on this work, AFAA created a national consortium and a policy agenda to advance the futures of adults with autism. In July 2010 the consortium hosted a congressional briefing in Washington, DC to discuss priorities for action in the public and private sectors. Having an activated coalition of organizations that could carry the work forward was an enormous gain in a field that had not had that kind of collective infrastructure prior to the initiative. Lisa Goring, a Vice President at Autism Speaks, noted that "AAFA founding members have continued to meet and collaborate—a direct result of the work of the AFAA consortium and the focus that was developed as a result of the engagement process. The needs of adults with autism are greater than any one organization, and the consortium provides a venue for many organizations to come together to work on common goals" (Goring 2012).

Networked House Parties

Like virtual summits, networked house parties seek to simulate the deliberative process that can take place in a central forum while enabling participants to gather remotely from their homes, neighborhoods, or communities. At these parties, groups of participants watch a live presentation via webcast or television, engage in face-to-face dialogue, and vote on priorities via text message or online. The small local gatherings are hosted by volunteers who are trained in facilitation methods. As participants come to agreement, they submit their ideas online to a theme team that identifies commonalities across all of the networked house parties. At the end of the discussion period, participants watch a webcast or televised report on the emerging themes and priorities and use voting tools to express their preferences.

By blending online and face-to-face methodologies, networked house parties bring an exciting new angle to web-based dialogue options. Each house party is connected to the larger deliberation virtually and creates a small community of face-to-face engagement.

Other Interactive Media

Participation in any face-to-face deliberative event, or in a virtual summit or networked house party, can be expanded and enhanced with additional media. For example, during Our Budget, Our Economy a group of participants engaged virtually by joining the discussion in "Second Life," a three-dimensional Internet-based world in which people can interact through avatars they create. The Second Life participants watched presentations from the national program via the webcast and used Second Life's chat function to deliberate about the issues. Their views were incorporated into the process and outcomes of the work.

Online chat is another example of an effective and relatively simple mechanism for discussion that can substantially broaden the participant base in an engagement initiative. Adding a voting component to online chat, especially one that is linked to voting in the face-to-face deliberation sites, can substantially increase the number of citizens who contribute to the development of recommendations.

FIGURE 12.2 SECOND LIFE AVATARS WORK THROUGH CHALLENGING
FISCAL ISSUES DURING OUR BUDGET, OUR ECONOMY

The second We the People 21st Century Town Meeting in Owensboro, Kentucky, described in the previous chapter, supported simultaneous online chat during its large-scale, in-person deliberation. As a great example of the connections that can be created, one of the chat participants was a young man, a native of Owensboro, who was serving in the Peace Corps in Costa Rica. Kevin Brown followed the event from afar through the entire day, offering comments on such issues as the community's perception of immigrants and greater use of school buses to improve the city's "green" plans.

Text messaging and tweeting are two more examples of interactive media that can be applied to enhance the reach of face-to-face citizen engagement work. The immediacy, familiarity, and high open rates with these media—which far exceed those of email—make them potentially powerful mechanisms. At the simplest level, advertising upcoming deliberative opportunities; recording votes on yes-no surveys; or managing short-answer quizzes; text messages and tweets can help generate participation from communities that can be hard to engage, such as young people or low-income and other demographic groups that lack regular Internet access.

There is also a strong likelihood that text messaging and tweeting may be able to go deeper in the future. For example, although text messages and tweets are limited to a certain number of characters, through theming or semantic analyses that identify recurring messages, they can reveal important aggregate data on users' views that could be incorporated into the themes emerging in the on-site deliberation. Experimentation with such analytic capacity is ongoing. As their use evolves, these media tools may have increasing utility in extending the reach of face-to-face engagement methods.

Online Tools That Increase the Value of Ideation Processes

There are numerous new tools and applications that can be used to gather input and ideas from the public. Under the general heading of "ideation processes," meaning they focus on idea or solution development, such tools are most often used in a one-way flow of information from the public to the government. If strategically adapted, however, they can also be used to foster more robust participation that is linked to decision making.

Crowdsourcing

As described earlier, federal agencies are increasingly using crowdsourcing tools. In July 2011 President Obama himself entered the fray, tweeting a direct question about which government costs should be cut and which investments kept to reduce the deficit. ThinkUp, a social networking resource, described it as "the first time that a President has ever posted directly to a social network from the White House . . . [and] the first time the President directly asked for feedback from users of a social network" (Baio 2011). President Obama got over 1,850 responses to his tweet, six times more than any White House tweet had received in the previous year.

This was an exciting use of new media. However, as noted, information gathering and other forms of "light touch" interaction are not equivalent to real participation. Further, many of the bells and whistles that make these vehicles appealing, such as a graph of Twitter traffic overlaid on the president's State of the Union address, are more like party tricks than a path to genuine public impact on policy decisions. To convert crowdsourcing into an engagement process that links to decision making, it must support users not only in forwarding their own ideas but also in modifying them based on the ideas others are submitting, voting on their priorities, and considering and potentially endorsing the consensus views that result.

Using This Tool: Crowdsourcing Offers Important Guidance on Health Policy

Shortly before the 2008 presidential election, America*Speaks;* the National Academy of Public Administration (NAPA); and Delib, a United Kingdom–based e-democracy organization, hosted a ten-day online conversation with U.S. citizens and stakeholders about realizing the benefits of information technology (IT) in the health care arena while also safeguarding privacy. At that time, crowdsourcing was a relatively new process that had only been used by a few agencies. Over the ten-day period, more than five hundred ideas and comments were posted on the initiative's site, and unique visitors hailed from every state and territory. In total, more than three thousand people discussed challenges in health IT, generated ideas, recommended principles, and came to a consensus in real time.

The dialogue on health IT targeted individuals and groups with an active interest in this area of concern and was open and accessible to the public at large. Participating stakeholders included consumer, disability, and patient rights advocates; federal and state government staff; health care providers; insurers and industry representatives; large and small businesses; open government advocates; researchers and students; and nonprofit organizations. Experts were on hand throughout the week to answer questions, make clarifications, and contribute a diverse range of viewpoints. The findings from the dialogue were delivered to a wide audience, which included the Office of Management and Budget, the federal Chief Information Officers Council, the Obama Transition Team, as well as dialogue participants.

Following the process a panel of experts (NAPA Fellows) conducted an in-depth analysis of the effort and reported three important outcomes. First, they were able to draw new and valuable insights into how ordinary citizens engage with issues of health IT and privacy, particularly how they view these concerns relative to the ways in which stakeholders, such as researchers and practitioners, view them. Second, they identified several specific issues that clearly needed more exploration, such as people's views on particular trade-offs and their understanding of best practices. Third, drawing from the full dialogue they were able to establish a set of principles to be a starting point for crafting policy in the future (Reeder et al. 2009).

COLLABORATIVE WRITING

Collaborative writing tools (for example, GoogleDocs or wikis) offer another way for citizens to play a direct role in decision making. These applications can provide the public with opportunities to help draft policies, laws, rules, directives, and the like. These are promising platforms for participation, but should be used advisedly. Accurate, effective writing is difficult under most circumstances but particularly when it comes to developing legal and policy documents. Writing "by committee" is even harder, especially on controversial subjects or when the contributing group is large. For these reasons, collaborative writing is often best combined with other methods of gathering input. Blending it with a crowdsourcing platform, for example, separates the conceptual work from the writing process itself, so that ideas are well developed and prioritized before any drafting takes place.

Another option is to incorporate a voting mechanism into the editing process to allow for maximum input and participation without users getting bogged down in multiple, competing versions of the same piece of writing.

Using These Tools: Crowdsourcing and Collaborative Writing Shape Open Government Plans

In summer 2009, while working to develop the particulars of the Open Government Directive, the Obama Administration put in place a three-phase process for gathering public input. In phase one, the crowdsourcing platform IdeaScale was used to generate ideas. Users posted more than forty-two thousand ideas, generating twenty-six thousand comments and nearly 350,000 votes. Following this effort, the White House Office of Science and Technology Policy launched a blog to gather input on issues that emerged in the first phase. Finally, the Administration used MixedInk, a free collaborative writing tool, which allowed citizens to help craft a set of final recommendations in the areas of innovative dispute resolution, incentivizing partnerships between public and private entities, and strengthening civic participation, among others.

The combined use of these participatory technologies by a sitting president on an active element of his governing agenda was groundbreaking. At the same time, the work was not without a number of challenges. Special interests dominated the crowdsourcing effort. Limited communication and insufficient moderation of the platforms made it difficult to effectively build and then manage participation. And the Administration's reluctance to frame the writing as actual draft material, as opposed to simply a collection of citizen input, undermined the credibility of that part of the effort. Each of these challenges, however, yields a valuable lesson for pursuing such work in the future. For example, increasing outreach to bring more people into the conversation will diminish the extent to which special interest groups can dominate. Limiting the number of steps involved in gathering input will diminish confusion and also facilitate broader public participation. Finally, the work confirmed one of the tenets of this book: public input processes are most effective when they focus on real questions and trade-offs that are on the table, as opposed to simply enabling a wide-ranging conversation that is not directly linked to decision making.

BLOGS

Another effective ideation tool is the blog. Blogs can allow policies and governance practices to be reviewed and discussed publicly. Decision makers can use this kind of forum to gather citizens' reactions and feedback, while simultaneously enabling large numbers of people to learn from the discussion. A blog's interface and reverse-chronological display encourage the exchange of information at regular intervals, and over time a community of regular readers and commenters can evolve. Adding voting functions to a blog can enable the conversation to progress and scale more efficiently because users can glance at the most popular suggestions instead of having to read through hundreds of posts to glean the same information.

Well-managed blogs can create an opportunity for educational and insightful engagement on an issue, which is beneficial to decision makers and members of the public alike. Blogs can create an immediate community that grows over time without the need for extensive outreach. At the same time, they tend to attract "repeat customers" and, to be successful, require a significant commitment to remain current and relevant, with new postings and responses required multiple times per week. The tracking metrics available on blogs provide real-time data concerning the number of unique viewers, commenters, and voters so that blog managers can tailor content to be continually relevant and engaging to target audiences. The downsides of blogs, from personal attacks to simply unproductive dialogue, can best be addressed through moderation and facilitation.

Using This Tool: Blogging at the U.S. Environmental Protection Agency Brings Citizens into Strategic Planning

In 2008 the U.S. Environmental Protection Agency (EPA) launched an official blog, called *Greenversations*. The blog is "written by EPA employees (and occasional guests) about the things they bring to their jobs every day" (U.S. EPA 2012). Although the posts do not represent official EPA policy, content, or language, hundreds of EPA staffers regularly contribute across more than sixty topic categories ranging from pesticides, to information management, to women in the sciences. *Greenversations* has an active public following; among the various mechanisms for accessing the blog, more than twenty-seven thousand people follow it on Twitter.

In summer 2010 EPA used *Greenversations* as a vehicle for gathering public input on the agency's 2011–2015 strategic plan. Kathy O'Brien, director of EPA's Office of Planning, Analysis, and Accountability, posted this at the time:

> Last month, I penned my first Greenversations post. I encouraged readers to share their ideas and feedback on a new component of the Draft FY 2011–2015 EPA Strategic Plan, the Cross-Cutting Fundamental Strategies. Since then, close to 2,000 individuals have checked-out our Discussion Forum and dozens have shared powerful and thoughtful ideas that will help us shape the way we do our work to protect the environment and human health. The Discussion Forum is a new tool for many of us at the Agency and it has provided EPA with a unique opportunity to engage with you. We have appreciated the feedback you have provided to date—about transparency, partnerships, environmental justice, children's health, science, and work force. And we welcome your additional ideas and advice as we turn the strategies into actions and take steps to tangibly change the way we do our work [O'Brien 2010].

One of the unique features of *Greenversations*, very unusual in the federal context, is that it is EPA program staff, not communications staff, who are the primary bloggers. Further, the consistency of staff postings has attracted and sustained a community of active followers.

Electronic Polls, Surveys, and Petitions

Electronic polls, surveys, and petitions are simple and increasingly familiar tools that can be quite powerful when used creatively. Unfortunately, despite an enormous range of technology-supported options, these tools are often used in only the most traditional manner: users respond on a form by selecting an option (often simply "yes" or "no," or scaled ratings like "very supportive," "moderately supportive," or "not supportive"); or users can, with a signature, support a petition that includes only a brief description of the issue and position. As discussed in Chapter One, with such limited tools, people tend to express largely superficial preferences that do not provide a solid basis on which decision makers can act.

A poll or survey is more likely to lead to input that can influence decision making if it requires respondents to think through the issues at hand, including tough trade-offs, as well as to consider the views of others. Because such extra effort can reduce completion rates, it helps if the mechanism is appealing and entertaining. A range of online applications can make run-of-the-mill surveys and questionnaires more engaging and educational, and produce responses that offer a more meaningful contribution to decision making. Some "educational surveys" take a more comprehensive approach. Using videos, links, and text to present facts, scenarios, and perspectives in a balanced and entertaining manner, they help users consider the complexities of policy or budget issues carefully before arriving at an opinion.

Mirroring the detailed discussion guides used for the face-to-face deliberations described throughout this book, these surveys can simulate real-world trade-offs and conditions and ask users to make the same difficult decisions government officials face. By standing in the shoes of policymakers, citizens come to better understand the challenges in balancing competing priorities. They gain important insights into the decision-making processes of government while actively participating in those very processes. The Voices & Choices regional planning initiative in Northeast Ohio, described in Chapter Five, used such a survey. Seventeen hundred citizens completed a Choicebook, designed by Ascentum, to express their priorities for regional development. A remarkable 94 percent of those who started a Choicebook completed it.

E-petitions can be another important tool because they seek a commitment from participants, in the form of a signature. We the People: Your Voice in Our Government is a White House platform that enables citizens to create a petition articulating a specific policy priority, mobilize their community to sign the petition, and find support from others on the site. The action threshold for these petitions is twenty-five thousand signatures received in thirty days. Within several months of its launch in September 2011, the website had already logged several million signatures on dozens of petitions. In January 2012, when two petitions opposing an Internet piracy bill logged more than fifty thousand signatures each, the Obama Administration formally responded and indicated that it would not support the legislation (Ciccone 2012). In the United Kingdom, e-petitions with more than one hundred thousand signatures are referred to the House of Commons and considered by the Backbench Business Committee, which is authorized to select issues for official debate (HM Government 2012). Beyond those discussed here there are a number of websites that now facilitate the development and dissemination of petitions in the United States and around the world.

E-petitions, a variant of the standard survey or poll, can also be reshaped to support more meaningful participation. They can be refashioned to provide, above the signature line, a wealth of engaging information on a specific issue through links to videos and web-based documents. They can also include links to decision-making exercises that will help citizens come to an informed position before deciding whether or not to sign.

ONLINE POLICY GAMES AND SIMULATIONS

There are increasing numbers of online games aimed at engaging citizens on civic issues and involving them in decision-making processes. Some of these games seek to influence people's thinking on a particular issue, whereas others seek to influence their behavior. Some offer points, badges, or leader boards to heighten competition and increase their appeal to potential users.

A sample of the kind of online game most closely linked to the work described in this book is a policy or budget simulation through which citizens work to resolve an issue using real-world information. By enabling users to make the same difficult choices facing decision makers, these policy and budget simulations help citizens better understand the challenges of balancing competing priorities. Local authorities and others can also use such simulations to build understanding and cohesion around important issues.

In a recent example, as the national debate about our debt and deficit was escalating in fall 2010, *New York Times* reporter David Leonhardt created a "Deficit Puzzle" on the newspaper's website through which readers could make their own attempts at closing budget gaps by selecting different program and policy choices and seeing their fiscal impact. In one week, the puzzle earned more than one million page views and over eleven thousand Twitter posts. The *New York Times* analyzed the responses and found the most popular choice to be reducing the military to less than what it was before the war in Iraq. The least popular choice was to let the Bush tax cuts expire for people with an income below $250,000 a year (Leonhardt 2010). Although Leonhardt readily acknowledged that the results were not scientific, the information that emerged was, nonetheless, a useful addition to the policy debate, and it is likely that the puzzle encouraged people who might otherwise have remained on the sidelines to learn about the issue and engage.

David Kuehn, Cochair of the Environmental Justice in Transportation Committee of the Transportation Research Board, offered these thoughts on the use of online games: "It is not always feasible to get people to see the effects of new transportation facilities and services, so creative uses of technology and virtualization—such as gaming activities and other table-top exercises that test scenarios and possible strategies—allow transportation professionals to accurately identify possibilities while keeping participants excited and engaged in the process" (Kuehn 2012).

ONLINE TOOLS THAT SEEK TO SUSTAIN PARTICIPATION OVER TIME

Because hundreds of millions of people around the world are spending time on Facebook, Twitter, and other social media platforms, it is important to explore the potential opportunities these vehicles offer for sustaining citizen engagement in decision-making processes. To be sure, they are convenient channels through which to educate the public about important issues, ask for their ideas, and inform them of upcoming deliberative opportunities. At the same time, new platforms as well as analytic and semantic tools are beginning to allow effective monitoring and theming of comments within and across multiple social networking sites and social network accounts. As a result, the most popular social networking sites have the potential to build communities that engage in real policy dialogue over time.

Achieving this goal may be accomplished faster by building new, stand-alone social networking sites (outside of Facebook or Twitter) and listservs around a particular geographic or policy niche. As examples of such online networks, GovLoop focuses on issues facing government employees, and Harringay Online focuses on a particular neighborhood in London. These kinds of tools are especially effective when used following significant face-to-face engagement initiatives. Although growing a self-sustaining network requires significant investment in the initial planning, design, and outreach, once established it can provide an ongoing infrastructure for discussion in a particular area or on specific issues that decision makers can tap into as needed.

Using This Tool: The American Square Seeks to Sustain Involvement

To sustain the citizen engagement work that was undertaken in the Our Budget, Our Economy initiative—and in response to a direct request from participants in that effort—in April 2011 America*Speaks* launched The American Square (www.theamericansquare.org). This stand-alone social networking site sought to enable and extend the respectful, nonpartisan conversations about the federal budget that took place during the face-to-face deliberation. Although the site initially focused on fiscal issues, it was hoped that over time it would serve as a discussion forum on a wide range of public issues that could be linked to decision-making processes. Content on the site included regular blog posts by high-profile, Washington, DC–based budget and deficit experts Alice Rivlin, Bob Bixby, and David Walker, among others. America*Speaks* regularly posted news, information, and polls to keep the site as current as possible, and moderated the discussions.

In The American Square's first six months, it attracted approximately one thousand members, thirteen thousand unique visitors, sixty-five thousand page views, and thousands of comments. Unfortunately, this level of traffic fell short of the hoped-for targets, and given the labor-intensiveness of the effort, sustaining the site was a challenge. At the same time, the experts who had been contributing to The American Square had come to value the way it directly connected them with the public in a dialogue on these issues, and they expressed a strong interest in keeping it going. In early 2012 America*Speaks* transferred the site to The Concord Coalition, a nonpartisan, grassroots organization whose mission is advocating responsible fiscal policy, and which had the necessary capacity to manage the site.

America*Speaks*'s experiences with The American Square offer a number of important lessons for using social networks to help sustain citizen engagement. The first is a confir-

FIGURE 12.3 THE AMERICAN SQUARE: DELIBERATING
TOUGH CHOICES ONLINE

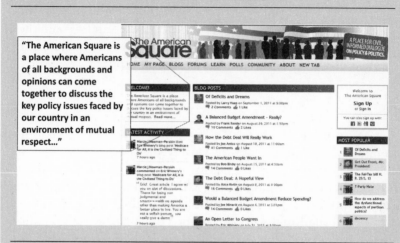

mation that healthy cross-partisan dialogue can happen online—we saw innumerable interesting and insightful policy discussions on The American Square. At the same time, ensuring consistently healthy, civil dialogue takes a significant investment in moderation. We had hoped to deputize some community members to help with moderation, but until a greater scale was reached we found it difficult to find trusted, motivated community leaders who could and would play this role. In addition, our work on The American Square clearly demonstrated that the community needed a significant volume of new content to consume and discuss if members were to return regularly. Because America-*Speaks* is not primarily a policy shop, we struggled to publish new content at the clip required to foster an exponential growth rate on the site. Finally, our work led us to the conclusion that dialogue does not automatically sell itself online, especially when it involves being exposed to ideas and information that challenge people's worldview. Whereas cute kitten videos may easily go viral on YouTube, "discussion" is unlikely to do so. Public agencies seeking to use social media platforms for online deliberation will face some of these same challenges. They will need skilled moderators to keep the site civil, the capacity to continually update content, and the resources to drive a large enough audience to the site to make it meaningful for both the agency and the public.

The online tools that have been described here constitute a brief sampling among a wide variety of options for extending citizen engagement work. Leading networks in the participation and deliberation communities (the Deliberative Democracy Consortium, the National Coalition for Dialogue & Deliberation, and the International Association for Public Participation, among others) are cataloguing the array of tools that are available. One of the most comprehensive of these lists can be found at http://participatedb.com/tools.

INSIGHTS AND LESSONS LEARNED

Although the application of online technologies and new media to citizen engagement is completely natural to younger generations of public managers, for the great majority, these tools and platforms are still relatively new. Exciting as they are, there is a long way to go before they can be universally adopted and well used. Backlogs of records, bottlenecks in administrative processes, and political division thwart efforts to get more valued data online quickly. Many challenges go unanswered and prizes go unclaimed, and many great ideas are never implemented or adopted broadly by the public. Today much of the input that goes into online forums is not productive and wastes everyone's time, attention, and goodwill. It would not be a stretch to say that, to date, there may be more promise than delivery when it comes to the use of online tools by government. However, the opportunities these tools offer for expanding the scale and substance of citizen engagement are real, and as a result the emerging lessons from their use are highly relevant.

Be Strategic

The allure of technology and the vast reach of the Internet too often cause people to focus on tools and methods before strategies, and to jump on board with the latest and most exciting platform. Such media experiments often do not end up fully supporting the strategic plans and priorities that have been established by a given agency, and they may produce little in the way of useful results. In addition to the loss of valuable time and effort, a lack of results erodes confidence among those who participated and reduces the likelihood of future participation.

Before selecting a tool, public managers must be clear on the purpose of the engagement, the target audience, and the desired outcomes. A series of questions can help point to the type of public engagement that is appropriate. These include the following (Goldman and Peters 2011):

- What do we want from participating communities? Are they to explore an issue? Validate options already determined? Reconcile or prioritize trade-offs? Identify competing interests?
- What is the initiative's commitment regarding immediate follow-up, and ongoing participation opportunities?
- To best inform decision makers and support their action steps, what volume of participation is needed, and who needs to be at the table?
- How contentious is the issue, and what is the timeline for engagement?
- What resources are available to support the process?

Finally, it should be noted that online tools differ significantly from one another in how they are administered and moderated, and in the degree to which they integrate social media and voting systems, among other features. Each platform has advantages and disadvantages, making a well-researched and considered selection important.[1] In short, before selecting a tool, be strategic. Know the purpose of the engagement, the target audience, the desired outcomes, and the nature of the tool.

Build In the Necessary Capacity

Using new media in a meaningful way requires significant organizational capacity. The field is evolving at a remarkable pace. As President Clinton quipped in 2011: "When I took office in January of 1993, there were a total of fifty sites on the Internet . . . more than that have been added since I was introduced [for this speech]" (Ford Foundation 2011). Keeping pace with this rapid growth requires staffing and commitment. Further, to maintain utility and credibility, agency blogs and special interest communities require multiple posts per week over months, and even years, as well as regular monitoring and moderation of content.

Jim Mayer, Executive Director of California Forward, a nonpartisan, statewide effort to enhance democracy and improve government performance, commented that by creating five different regional Facebook pages, California Forward has dramatically increased public and stakeholder responses to and participation in its work. However, California Forward has found this new media environment to be a brutal taskmaster. To sustain what the organization has built, new content must be added every day. "My staff understand the importance of it," he said, "but it takes a tremendous amount of work to feed the beast" (Mayer 2012).

Level the Playing Field

As is true with face-to-face deliberation, it is critical to make sure that citizens and stakeholder groups can participate on equal footing in online engagement efforts. Stakeholder organizations often have the resources and are positioned to offer formal or detailed online comments on anticipated government actions or plans. Average citizens may not be aware of these submissions, or of their opportunity to influence them. One way for agencies to level the playing field between participating stakeholder organizations and citizens, is to make stakeholder submissions on an issue available to the public in a user-friendly, accessible library. When such information is transparent to all, the general public can engage from a position of knowledge.

Be Aware of the Trade-Offs

The principal value of incorporating online interactive channels into citizen engagement work is the potential they offer for broad reach. These processes are highly scalable, cost little, and make it easy and appealing to regularly invite public input. However, although the channels are open to the entire public—arguably even more so than standard participatory mechanisms like voting, which is limited by citizenship status, age, and criminal history— they are only available to those with access to technology and the capacity to use it. Online platforms tend to self-select for people who are already interested in these media, and familiar with how they operate. It is therefore important to consider the trade-off between simply achieving high numbers of users via online plat- forms and the exclusion of populations that do not have access to, or the capacity to use, these technologies.

In fact, any discussion of the exciting potential of online tools to build citizen engagement must acknowledge the digital divide in our country and its impact on citizens' ability to participate in the decision making that affects their lives. The next chapter describes the digital divide and some of its implications. It is a significant and persistent challenge that must be addressed.

Commit to Outreach

To offset the self-selection phenomenon just described, ongoing measurement of online participation numbers and demographics followed by targeted outreach to underrepresented populations is critical. Such an analysis can be supplemented by increasingly available research on rates of technology use among different population groups. This information can help engagement initiative planners ensure balanced participation. However, who participates online and how they do it is constantly changing and must be continually reassessed.

These lessons briefly encapsulate some of the knowledge that is building in this emerging field. It is essential that agencies share their experiences and learning in this arena. The next step is to develop a set of standards and write case studies that highlight best practices so that these can be widely disseminated and used by public managers who are just beginning to engage citizens online.

STRIKING A BALANCE BETWEEN ONLINE AND FACE-TO-FACE ENGAGEMENT METHODS

This chapter has explored a wide range of online tools that can increase citizens' interaction with government. Taken as a whole, they offer exciting opportunities for practitioners in the field of deliberative democracy. Given the Internet's extensive reach, it might be easy to conclude that application of these various tools is *all* that is necessary to engage large numbers of citizens in governance. That is not the case.

Even with the modifications discussed in this chapter, when used alone, today's online methodologies still struggle to support meaningful discussions that build shared views. This is particularly noticeable when online discussions are compared to those that take place during a well-crafted face-to-face deliberation. The efforts of The American Square, described earlier, illustrate this point. During the Our Budget, Our Economy deliberation that prompted the development of that social networking site, the 3,500 citizens who came together found a great deal of common ground on complex issues of grave importance, despite their widely divergent political views. Participants in this work noted with surprise and appreciation the civility and productivity of their conversations. Although The American Square explicitly intended to continue that work, this goal proved quite difficult to achieve. The posts and dialogues on The American Square were often characterized by strong partisan accusations and nonproductive arguing. The experience offered evidence that at the moment it remains extremely difficult to simulate online the moderating impact of face-to-face interaction that creates civility and compromise in citizen engagement work.

This is not surprising. Well-crafted face-to-face deliberation produces civil discourse because in-person experiences are fundamental to the creation of trust and respect, both of which are necessary precursors of civility. More simply put, it is through the act of conversation, complete with all of its visual and aural cues, that trust between people can fully develop.

Although there is a level of intuitiveness to this assertion, it has also been confirmed in research. In June 2010 *TimeScience* reported on a recent study by Kevin Rockmann of George Mason University and Gregory Northcraft at the University of Illinois in which two hundred students were asked to problem-solve on a project either by email, through a videoconference, or in person. Among other findings, *TimeScience* reported that "those who met in person showed the most trust and most effective cooperation" (Luscombe 2010). Frank Bryan's seminal study of more than 1,500 town meetings in Vermont over three decades reaffirms the point. His work has demonstrated that when trying to build community and a movement of committed people, one of the primary elements that promotes that work is the experience of being face-to-face and creating something together (Bryan 2003). Emerging platforms, such as Cisco's new TelePresence system, are seeking to create interactive environments of face-to-face quality. It will be interesting to watch these technologies evolve, and to see whether they can produce the same levels of mutual trust and willingness to compromise that can come from face-to-face engagement.

There can be no doubt that the unique capabilities of the Internet are quickly advancing our capacity to connect citizens and government. When this connection is specifically aimed at influencing decision making, thereby requiring citizens to present a slate of collective views and recommendations, we must maintain a judicious balance between online and face-to-face methodologies. Online tools provide the opportunity for an unprecedented level of reach and scale, whereas face-to-face processes can enable meaningful civic dialogue and shared decision making among people who hold strongly divergent views. In other words, each has a distinct and important role to play, and one should not replace the other. Citizen engagement efforts that can seamlessly and effectively blend the two approaches are the new frontier in the field of deliberative democracy. The efforts described in this chapter illustrate progress toward that goal, but we are only just beginning.

CHAPTER THIRTEEN

INFRASTRUCTURE NEEDS IN A DEMOCRACY

The first reform needed in our political practice is to find some method by which the government shall continuously represent the people . . . When we have a state truly representative of our collective citizenship, then fear of the state will disappear because the antithesis between the individual and the state will have disappeared.

MARY PARKER FOLLETT, 1920*

In a healthy, fully functioning democracy, institutional systems, such as Congress, the media, public education, and others, support and reinforce democratic behaviors and outcomes. But today the United States is not a healthy, fully functioning democracy. There are significant systemic failures across our electoral and governance processes and structures, and, as a result, the fundamental trust between citizens and their government has been broken. On the electoral side, a number of key issues have to be addressed: redistricting policies that secure political advantage for incumbents; ever greater infusions of money unduly influencing politics; policies and practices that suppress voter participation—to name just a few. On the governance side, efforts are under way to make important systemic reforms such as limiting the power of the filibuster, reducing delays in presidential appoint-

---

*Follett, M. P. *The New State: Group Organization The Solution of Popular Government.* London: Longmans, Green, 1920, 11, 141.

ments, and establishing an annual fiscal report that all leaders must accept as the basis for decision making.

But efforts like these are not enough.

This book has a very specific objective: to see our nation's practice of democracy reflect the aspirations for self-governance that were embedded in our founding documents; to actually be a governing system "of the people, by the people, for the people." We must have systems and mechanisms in place to achieve that goal. So, as we call on citizens, decision makers, and our federal government to adopt new citizen engagement practices, we must simultaneously commit to building the infrastructure that will support those efforts. Together, new practices *and* the appropriate robust infrastructure can generate a strong, reinforcing pattern of authentic democratic behavior.

This chapter seeks to articulate a vision for the infrastructure our country will need to support a highly functioning democracy. It describes seven specific components of this infrastructure, assesses where we stand on each one, and outlines where there are promising pathways. The challenges in making this vision a reality are significant and complex. They are well beyond what any individual, organization, or sector could possibly achieve alone. But, as in all major change or transformation processes, the greater the number of people who share a common vision of the goal, the more possible it is to align objectives and strategies to reach that goal. We all have a stake in the outcome, and we all have an important role to play in bringing it about.

SEVEN INFRASTRUCTURE COMPONENTS THAT SUPPORT DEMOCRACY

To realize the vision of millions of Americans routinely discussing and informing critical government decision making, our nation needs an embedded, supporting infrastructure of seven fundamental components. Each is described briefly below and then explored at greater length in the chapter.

1. *A legislative mandate for participation.* To be widespread and consistent, citizen engagement and the structures necessary

to implement it must be mandated by legislation, with government playing designated roles. Our largely nonlegislated, nongovernmental structure for citizen engagement has proven to be scattershot and inadequate.

2. *Safe, accessible physical spaces.* Democratic and productive deliberation enables diverse citizens to confidently and civilly air their differences; it ensures that every voice is heard. A safe, accessible deliberative space in which everyone feels welcome and able to participate is required to achieve these goals.

3. *Broader access to technology.* To fully participate in their democracy, citizens need reliable access to accurate and neutral information. In today's world, this means having high-speed Internet access and the capability to use it. Our national approach to technology access has produced a significant digital divide that obstructs our ability to keep all of our citizens well informed and networked.

4. *A facilitation infrastructure.* Informed, high-quality democratic deliberation requires strong facilitation. To support a marked increase in the use of citizen engagement around the country, an ever-expanding "bank" of skilled process facilitators will be required.

5. *An organizational infrastructure.* In our large and diverse nation, securing widespread citizen engagement will require the help of mediating organizations and structures that have the trust and confidence of the public. Today we have a rich range of organizations advocating for particular agendas, but we do not have a strong network of organizations whose mission is to support bringing citizen voice into governance. We need to build it.

6. *A trustworthy, fact-based media.* The public needs trustworthy information to make good decisions and act democratically. The media has an important role to play in providing this information, but has become ideologically driven and seemingly unconcerned with the facts. To play its core role in our democracy, the media must once again be fact-based and nonideological.

7. *Robust civic education.* Americans' knowledge of basic civics is disappointingly sparse (Lane 2008), and trends in democracy-specific volunteering are not positive. As a result, practitioners

of civic engagement spend much time and energy "pushing" people to get involved and persuading them to become good citizens. When citizens know about participatory opportunities and, more important, demand to be part of them, we will have a thriving national civic life.

This vision and framework for an infrastructure that supports democracy are derived from America*Speaks*'s experience of conducting citizen engagement work in all fifty states in the United States and in fifteen countries around the world. Throughout nearly twenty years of practice, America*Speaks* has encountered infrastructure gaps often enough to be able to identify seven that are the most chronic, the most pervasive, and the most likely to thwart democratic objectives. For example, in community after community we have faced the lack of adequate deliberation spaces; we have worked many times to overcome a biased media's presentation of the "facts" surrounding a deliberation topic; and we have struggled to generate enthusiasm about participation among citizens whose previous experiences of public meetings had left them uninspired and disengaged.

Further, and perhaps most critical, in the course of our work we have seen which gaps have had the strongest negative impact on larger issues of democracy and social justice. For example, the nation's structural inability to support bringing the full diversity of the public into decision making means that already-engaged subgroups will continue to have their voices heard while underrepresented voices will continue to be left out.

In addition to knowing how the seven components were derived, it is important to understand the motivation behind the development of this framework. Over the years, as America*Speaks* became increasingly successful in creating initiatives to bring citizen voices into policymaking, budget allocation, and planning, we began to recognize that there was rarely, if ever, adequate infrastructure in the communities in which we were working to sustain the work after we left, or for the communities themselves to initiate and embrace citizen engagement as a routine practice. This realization shifted our understanding of our leadership role in this work. Instead of simply proving the efficacy of citizen engagement over and over again, we had to pay attention to building supporting infrastructure in these communities. The strategies for sustaining engagement discussed in Chapter 11 are an important part of this work, but the challenge is much larger than that. In each of the seven components explored in the following sections there is significant work to be done to create the infrastructure necessary to ensure an ongoing, routine, authentic connection between public will and political will. Only then will we realize our founders' aspirations for a democracy in which citizens are the central actors.

LEGISLATIVE MANDATE FOR PARTICIPATION

This book has offered a number of powerful case studies in which elected officials have embraced citizen engagement to achieve important policy and budget goals. It has been noted in each instance that such work is regrettably sporadic. It is principally found where individual leaders understand the value added by citizen engagement and are also willing and able to absorb the political risks inherent in opening up a decision-making process to the public. As has also been noted, one reason for the scarcity of these initiatives is that there are almost no budgets, authorizing mandates, or legislated expectations for citizen engagement within our government at any level. Finally, the legislated participatory mechanisms we do have at the federal level, such as the 1964 Administrative Procedure Act (discussed in Chapter One), are quite weak when it comes to offering broad opportunities for participation. The fact that they are mostly used by lobbyists and stakeholder groups speaks volumes about how effective they are as vehicles for public participation.

All of these factors combine to produce an environment in which decision makers have few incentives for getting involved in this work. In short, we lack a legislative mandate for citizen participation that will actually embed it as a core part of our governance.

At the federal level, the Obama Administration's Open Government Directive (OGD) sought to address this problem by institutionalizing for the first time a mandate for transparency, participation, and collaboration in the work of federal agencies.

However, the implementation of the OGD has focused almost exclusively on transparency and data access efforts, leaving the participation goals and objectives insufficiently developed and monitored. America*Speaks*'s close analysis of the twenty-nine open government plans found, among other concerns, that little had been included in most plans to ensure that agencies engaged the public on critical policy issues.

There is no mystery about what the desired elements of a legislative mandate for participation would be. They have been explored and documented. In just one example, in summer 2006 America*Speaks* convened a gathering of practitioners and scholars in a series of conversations aimed at conceptualizing and designing a more comprehensive participatory governance structure that could be put in place through legislation at the national level. Although the goal of the group was to create a blueprint for an overarching concept, by the end of three days together, five concrete participatory mechanisms that could be legislated had emerged (America*Speaks* 2006):

1. Establishing a biennial, citizen-initiated legislation process through which a citizens' assembly would identify one issue for the congressional agenda for which Congress would be held accountable to voters
2. Authorizing an independent, quasi-governmental Policy Review and Analysis Center that would provide technical assistance and process tools on public engagement
3. Developing a set of benchmarks for federal agency and staff performance on citizen engagement practices
4. Creating an independent panel to assess the performance of elected public officials on fostering active and effective citizen engagement in governance
5. Launching a Key National Indicators System to engage citizens in the identification of, and monitoring of progress toward, national priorities such as better health outcomes or higher-quality public education

It is exciting to imagine how robust citizen participation in our country would be if all these elements were in place. It should be noted that the last recommendation was formally made to

Congress by the Government Accounting Office in 2006 and has, in fact, been implemented. In 2010 the U.S. government authorized the creation of the first ever Key National Indicator System (KNIS), overseen by an eight-member, bipartisan commission appointed by Congress.

The National Academy of Sciences, in partnership with the nonprofit organization State of the USA, is preparing for the implementation of this system. The overarching purpose of the KNIS is to make quantitative information about the country as a whole more accessible and useful for civic dialogue. The KNIS will present a limited number of high-quality measures in a state-of-the-art, web-based "scorecard," covering such areas as education, the economy, families and children, civic and cultural life, innovation, health, safety and security, energy, housing, the environment, and infrastructure. Chris Hoenig, President and CEO of The State of the USA, described the work this way: "As a nation we face many challenges and opportunities. But we can only manage what we can agree to measure. Striving for credible simplicity to inform Americans about complex issues is a problem worthy of serious investment by our society. We all have the right and the responsibility to assess progress by seeing the data for ourselves" (Hoenig 2012).

In addition to mandating the other parts of a participatory governance structure, the vehicles needed to carry out such mandates also have to be defined and funded through legislation. Fortunately, there is precedent for this. As noted in Chapter Seven, the Federal Mediation and Conciliation Service (FMCS) was established in 1947 to help federal, state, and local government agencies resolve disputes and build capacity for constructive conflict management. Today, there are FMCS field offices in more than fifty cities. A similarly structured "Federal Office of Public Participation" could build capacity for public engagement in the field operations of every federal agency and stimulate cross-jurisdictional participation work among federal, state, and local agencies.

Further, there could be a quasi-governmental agency or independent, congressionally linked organization tasked with securing public participation. The Congressional Budget Office (CBO), established in 1974 to provide Congress with objective and timely analyses of federal programs, is an example of this kind of organization. The CBO has thrived for over three and a half decades despite some seemingly problematic aspects of its design. In his April 2010 remarks to the Economic Club of Washington, DC, former CBO Director Peter Orszag said that if you looked closely at the CBO—at the fact that it doesn't report to anyone, has no independent board, and is subject to the whims of Congress—you might safely assume it was not a very powerful organization and would be unlikely to succeed. And yet, he went on to say, the standard of professionalism, nonpartisanship, and quality established by its first director, Alice Rivlin, has been upheld by every succeeding director, such that more than thirty-five years later the CBO has proved that this kind of structure is indeed viable (Economic Club of Washington 2010). A similarly structured organization could be tasked with ensuring high-quality public participation on the toughest issues facing the country.

The National Academy of Public Administration (NAPA) is yet another example of a quasi-governmental organization whose structure could serve as a model for a national public participation organization. Chartered by Congress in 1967, NAPA is a coalition of top public management and organizational leaders that, through fostering peer-to-peer leadership, seeks to improve the quality, performance, and accountability of government by helping it respond effectively to the nation's most pressing challenges. As described in the previous chapter, in 2008 the Office of Management and Budget invited NAPA "to pilot an interactive, web-based discussion platform—labeled a 'National Dialogue'— as a means to engage members of the public on relevant issues" (National Academy of Public Administration 2009, 1). NAPA reached out to America*Speaks* to partner in designing and implementing this work.

The U.S. Institute for Environmental Conflict Resolution (US IECR) offers yet another model. Established by Congress in 1998, the US IECR is an independent federal program that supports finding workable solutions to tough environmental conflicts and improving environmental decision making. In addition to taking on and managing its own dispute resolution cases, the US IECR works to increase the capacity of agencies and other affected stakeholders and practitioners to manage and resolve conflicts themselves. It also provides leadership on conflict resolution practice and policy development within the federal government.

The Federal Mediation and Conciliation Service, Congressional Budget Office, National Academy of Public Administration, and U.S. Institute for Environmental Conflict Resolution are all viable models for organizations tasked with carrying out a public participation mandate nationally. Public demand and inspired political leadership could easily create the legislative mandate necessary to bring citizen voices to the table in governance.

SAFE, ACCESSIBLE PHYSICAL SPACES

In 1998 America*Speaks* launched its inaugural project, Americans Discuss Social Security, which brought together almost fifty thousand people across nearly all fifty states to develop collective recommendations on this critical issue of national policy. One of the early surprises in this work was finding that most communities around the country did not have a public space for deliberation that was physically adequate, inexpensive or free, and located in a place that was both neutral and convenient for all subgroups of the population. It was eye-opening to experience this gap in the nation's infrastructure.

What we found, and what has remained a consistent concern in our work over the ensuing two decades, is that in most communities in the United States, if adequate space (such as a convention center) exists, the business model governing its use identifies it solely as a profit center, not as a public asset. In this business model, multiple contracts with independent vendors are necessary to use such a space for public participation. The physical requirements must be built into the space for every event, and all necessary services—the electricity, food, technology, and so on—carry a charge. Because very few communities have more than one such space, the entire enterprise is likely to be largely noncompetitive and therefore quite expensive. As discussed in Chapter One, this is a change from previous practice, when such spaces were often made available for public use at little or no cost.

As a result, it is a sad truth in our nation today that decision makers in the public sector must spend significant amounts of money, and undertake substantial logistical work, to listen to their citizens. As noted in Chapter One, to hold the first Washington, DC Citizen Summit in the downtown convention center, the city had to pay the same fee that Microsoft had paid the week before for its annual exposition. Similarly, nearly $350,000 in philanthropic money was spent to hold Listening to the City in New York City's Jacob Javits Center. We must do better than this. One possibility is to return to a business model for convention centers in which some level of free public use is presumed or required. Another is to offer incentives, as new spaces are built in communities, to ensure they have the capacity to accommodate multiple civic uses.

The University of Wisconsin–Madison has recently followed this course. Jay Ekleberry, Mini-Courses Director for the Wisconsin Union, was keenly interested in regenerating and expanding the student union debating society tradition through which students regularly deliberated and spoke up about vital issues of the day. He hoped the university would be able to routinely engage not only large numbers of students but also community members. His vision was to make real the idea that "the borders of the campus are the borders of the state," and demonstrate how a public university exists for the good of all citizens (Ekleberry 2011).

When the opportunity arose, in 2008, to rebuild one of the Wisconsin Union's two campus buildings, Ekleberry spearheaded an effort to make sure that the large ballroom in the new building would also be a fully equipped public meeting space, one that could serve civic purposes beyond the walls of the university. He researched options and gathered specific suggestions from visioning work America*Speaks* had done on the design and architecture of deliberative spaces. The full support of the Wisconsin Union leadership as well as the financial backing of a local corporate benefactor ensured the success of the project.

The new Varsity Hall opened in April 2011 with the capacity to seat hundreds of people at round tables, each with computer and Internet capacity. The room has three large, high-definition video display screens visible to all in the room as well as a portable stage. In its first six months of operation, Varsity Hall supported such university-based activities as a nine-hundred-person "campus town hall meeting" on the issue of diversity in university admissions and a one-thousand-person shared reading assembly. Varsity

Hall has also already hosted a facilitated dinner and dialog event with the larger community on the future of higher education. There are plans for a similar event entitled "The Promise of American Democracy." The University of Wisconsin–Madison's success in creating a multipurpose venue demonstrates how an increase in the availability of deliberative spaces across the country can be achieved.

Imagine the significant impact on democratic participation if communities all across the country had a public space designed for and dedicated to convening citizens and decision makers on critical issues.

BROADER ACCESS TO TECHNOLOGY

Technology is a critical part of the infrastructure needed to support democracy. Our deliberative spaces, like the one created at the University of Wisconsin–Madison, have to be technologically equipped to support authentic discussion among large numbers of people. Equally important, greater access to technology, broadband in particular, is required if citizens across the country are to have the information they need to participate actively in their democracy.

In today's world, having access to accurate and neutral information requires high-speed Internet access, not just reading newspapers and watching television. Recognizing this, a number of countries are declaring access to broadband a right and are working to substantially expand the availability of this resource. In Estonia, Internet access has been considered a basic human right since 2000; in 2009 France followed suit, as did Costa Rica in 2010. In 2009 Finland legislated speeds of at least one megabit per second for all Internet connections. In June 2011 the Human Rights Council of the United Nations General Assembly declared disconnecting people from the Internet to be a violation of their civil and political rights (United Nations General Assembly Human Rights Council 2011).

Leaders around the globe have determined the power of the Internet, and therefore access to it, to be as essential to the future of humanity as the air we breathe and the food we eat. Once we accept this as the "new reality," we quickly see how behind the curve we are in the United States, where there are enormous disparities in citizens' direct access to high-speed Internet. Large swaths of the American public, as many as one hundred million homes, have no access at all (Federal Communications Commission [FCC] 2010). In 2011 the Federal Communications Commission reported that the United States ranked ninth in per capita mobile broadband adoption among thirty member nations of the Organisation for Economic Co-operation and Development (OECD), and twelfth for per household fixed (that is, DSL or cable) broadband. This put us behind South Korea, the United Kingdom, Canada, and Germany, among others (FCC 2011). Also in 2011 we ranked seventeenth in net increases in broadband penetration, or the amount of the Internet market that has high speed or broadband access (OECD 2012b). If we persist in our current approach, it could take the United States sixty years to reach *current* Internet speeds in South Korea (Communications Workers of America 2009)—and who knows how fast the South Koreans' Internet will be by then?

Our poor international status in broadband penetration reflects a number of systemic problems. First and perhaps foremost, it reveals the extreme economic stratification we allow to persist in America. Most poor people and communities simply do not have the resources with which to purchase high-speed Internet access at current market rates. Our reliance on a technology infrastructure that is largely governed by private sector financial incentives ensures the persistence of these disparities. Powerful corporate interests rarely make equal access to their products a priority. About 78 percent of U.S. homes have access to only two wireline broadband service providers (meaning those delivering the service by cable, fiber optic, or older landline systems) (Kang 2010).

To be sure, tight budget times make it that much more challenging for the nation to shoulder the high costs associated with significantly expanding Internet access across the country. The FCC has estimated that as much as $350 billion may be needed for an infrastructure that will bring rapid broadband access (with speeds as high as one hundred megabits per second) to all Americans; a lesser commitment, meaning fewer people and speeds of only up to three megabits per second, is estimated to cost about $20 billion (Reardon 2009). After much negotiating, President Obama was able to secure only $7.2 billion in 2009 stimulus dollars for expanding broadband access in rural and underserved areas.

Another stark reminder of the persistent inequities in information access comes from the fact that we allow the publicly supported information access points we do have, such as libraries and schools, to be among the first resources cut back in economic downturns. In the wake of the extremely difficult fiscal times of 2009–2010, for example, nineteen states reported cuts in funding for public libraries; in more than half of these, the cuts were greater than 10 percent (American Library Association [ALA] 2011). In some parts of the country, library cuts were even more substantial. To cite just a few examples: 74 percent was cut statewide in New Jersey (Linehan 2010), and 23 percent was cut in Los Angeles (Linthicum 2010). In Troy, Michigan, the public library was slated for closure altogether (ALA 2011). Cuts like these result in reduced hours, weekend closures, and other service losses that greatly diminish one of the few public access points for Internet use.

Responding to these various concerns, in fall 2010 the FCC issued America's first national broadband plan. The plan's goals include substantially expanding affordable access for all Americans and in public institutions in every American community; ensuring that the United States has the fastest and most extensive wireless networks of any nation; establishing a nationwide, wireless public safety network; and enabling every American to use broadband to track and manage real-time energy consumption. The plan details a complex array of strategies to educate the public, increase competition, upgrade networks, use government-controlled assets more efficiently, and reform laws that stand in the way (FCC 2010).

Bringing all of this to fruition will require a significant reconfiguration of the industry, not just literally, in terms of who holds how much of the various resources, but in terms of values as well. As noted, for many years U.S. broadband access has operated almost exclusively in a market context. More widespread and equitable use of this resource will require that a combination of market and government forces be in play. If we can make this shift, significant portions of the American public will finally gain access to the information they need to actively participate in our society.

Although the democratization of information remains incomplete, it should not go without saying that the astounding advances in technology we have seen over the last two decades, and with them the unparalleled adoption of new platforms and devices, create an exciting and promising foundation on which to build.

FACILITATION INFRASTRUCTURE

Informed, high-quality democratic deliberation requires strong process facilitation. To come to shared views that can have a real impact on decision making, diverse citizens must be able to confidently and civilly air their differences and express their individual perspectives, no matter how divergent. They must feel free to change their viewpoints as they learn. Facilitation is critical to supporting this kind of deliberation. It stands to reason, then, that the more deliberation we have, the more facilitators we will need.

When it comes to the availability of process facilitators for citizen engagement, there is a wealth of existing resources in the United States. To begin, a number of democracy organizations have developed networks of people trained in democratic process facilitation who can and should be put to regular use in supporting deliberations among citizens. To cite just a few examples: the International Association for Public Participation has more than one thousand trained facilitators in its network; America*Speaks* has more than six thousand; and the National Issues Forums has more than ten thousand. To add to this, a number of organizations, such as Everyday Democracy and the National Issues Forums, as well as America*Speaks,* provide training and technical assistance to communities across the country in need of facilitators for citizen engagement.

Directly related fields, such as conflict resolution, mediation, counseling, and coaching, also have large numbers of practitioners with the core skills and attributes of excellent process facilitators. In addition, entities in such fields as organization development and education, as well as religious institutions, can provide facilitation resources. Organizations in all of these areas have long recognized the importance of process facilitation skills, and used them extensively to accomplish their respective missions.

In America*Speaks*'s experience, professional people from all of these fields are ready and willing to give back to their community, to expand their skills and professional networks, or to help advance citizen engagement. For the Voices & Choices initiative, more than 550 individuals volunteered to help facilitate the work of over 20,000 people from sixteen counties in Northeast Ohio as they sought to develop a public mandate and specific strategies for improving life in that region. The Listening to the City initiative provides perhaps the most powerful example from America-*Speaks*'s work. Following the tragic events of 9/11 there was an outpouring of public desire to help New Yorkers, but often there was little that one could do other than send money. Believing that people with great process facilitation skills would be honored to assist with the healing and rebuilding, America*Speaks* sent out a notice about the need for table facilitators to only three professional listservs. The invitation went out on a Thursday evening. By the following Tuesday morning we had more than 500 volunteers representing all fifty states who were willing to pay for their own transportation and housing expenses to support New Yorkers. This desire to help crossed international boundaries as well. Facilitators from Canada, England, Australia, South Africa, Columbia, and Denmark joined the effort. One woman from Australia was so eager to help facilitate that she convinced Qantas Airlines to give her a free round-trip ticket so she could make the trip.

When it comes to building a nationwide infrastructure of facilitators, we should also be thinking outside the usual boxes. Youth, for example, should become a regular part of the equation. There are a number of youth networks in the country, such as City Year, AmeriCorps, 4-H, Youth Service America, Girl Scouts, and YMCA Youth and Government, that routinely train young people in process facilitation, knowing that such skills are enormously useful in a democratic society.

In Washington, DC, Mayor Anthony Williams put this often underused resource to the test. In 2000 he held The City Is Mine: Youth Summit in which 1,400 young people ages fourteen to twenty-one were brought into program and policy decisions related to safety and violence, education, and job training. More than 100 youth received training to facilitate the roundtable discussions at the Youth Summit. Each youth was paired with an adult who had been trained to play a support role. The facilitation skills these young people gained have had long-term benefits. A number have gone on to pursue work and activism in urban planning, public affairs, city government, and social services.

Melvin Moore, who was a Youth Commissioner for Washington, DC at the time and a member of the planning team for The City Is Mine, said:

> The Youth Summit pursued the spirit of engagement work, where making an immediate connection with the people at your table is so important. For participating youth, having the table facilitator be one of their own gave them a real sense of comfort in expressing their voices, raising concerns and making recommendations. For the youth facilitators themselves, it was a significant leadership exercise. To qualify, they had to be able to demonstrate certain skills, like listening, communication, writing, and mediation. But to be able to then apply these skills outside of a school setting, in the real-world and with real consequences, was enormously powerful [Moore 2012].

In addition to expanding facilitation resources, it will be important to pool together the ones we already have. Individual organizations that do participatory work currently are limited by the size of their own network of facilitators. Like the emerging resource network for environmental conflict resolution described in the public manager case study in Chapter Eight, by establishing a national, shared database of citizen engagement facilitators, all these organizations and others would have increased capacity. Imagine an online map showing the location of the country's skilled process facilitators who want to support citizen engagement. In the geographic areas that have fewer resources, democracy practitioners could step up and partner with a local university or community college to develop a curriculum aimed at building facilitation capacity in that geographic area. Many of these kinds of efforts are scattered across the country. At the University of Wisconsin–Madison, for example, the human resources department has launched a certification program on public participation and engagement. This program, Fully Prepared to Engage, trains faculty in collaborative engagement processes and skills, seeking to "significantly increase the capacity of the University to bring people together around important issues and engage those participants' energies in a constructive, synergistic manner." A parallel track for students who want to develop large-group facilitation skills is under consideration (Ekleberry 2011).

Substantially increasing citizen engagement in our democracy will require a corollary increase in the skilled human resources available to support the work. Fortunately, the United States is already resource-rich in this regard. As a result, achieving the necessary facilitation infrastructure nationwide is easily within our grasp.

ORGANIZATIONAL INFRASTRUCTURE

The case studies in Chapters Three and Seven illustrate how extensive, strategic outreach efforts were required to meet the participation goals in New Orleans following Hurricane Katrina and in New York City after 9/11. These efforts reflect a larger truth: many communities lack a reliable, robust network of mediating organizations that can quickly and effectively support non-issue-specific democracy work. The fact that both of these efforts took place in large cities, which arguably have a more substantial organizational infrastructure than do rural areas of the country, makes the point vividly. Although mediating organizations abound in this country, the challenge as it relates to supporting a high-functioning democracy is to make sure the collective infrastructure they provide remains up-to-date, is nimble, and includes a sufficient number of issue-neutral organizations.

One concern is that long-standing organizations must continually adapt to an ever-changing world. They must frequently adjust their mission, reorient their operating strategies, and refresh themselves. Change like this can be difficult, and mediating organizations sometimes become more focused over time on ensuring their own survival than on serving the people and issues in whose interest they were established. For example, during the pre-event interviews for the first Washington, DC Citizen Summit, America-*Speaks* found that in six of the city's eight wards, residents felt that their local community development corporation was serving the needs of the organization more than the needs of the people. This anecdote is not offered to disparage Washington, DC, or community development corporations. Rather, it demonstrates a common and perhaps even natural phenomenon among long-standing community organizations, and serves as a reminder that the connections between the people and these organizations must be kept vital and authentic.

We must also pay attention to which population groups have no mediating organizations representing them. These groups are usually the most marginalized in the community. Existing organizations may have to shift to meet the needs of these groups, or, if there is none that can do so, traditional community organizing may be necessary to fill the gaps. When this is the case it is an indicator that new mediating organizations will eventually have to be created to serve these population groups.

As noted, another critical aspect of the organizational infrastructure is having a sufficient number of groups that are simply prodemocratic—that is, not affiliated with a particular issue or ideology. When a community needs to resolve a vexing or nuanced concern, such as prioritizing strategies for regional growth in an unsteady budget environment, there must be a neutral convener trusted by all parties to move the conversation forward. Organizations affiliated with a particular agenda are not well suited to host a discussion in which *any* outcome representing the will of diverse citizens will be respected and become the basis for action. Rather, successful deliberative democracy practice requires mediating organizations in which the whole community has confidence. These are organizations whose job is to bring representative groups of citizens to the table; provide neutral, reliable information about a critical issue; and help foster discussion that uncovers shared views.

There are effective models of such organizations around the country, a number of which are listed in Appendix B. For example, the North Dakota Consensus Council, a nonpartisan, nonprofit organization established in 1990, connects leaders, stakeholders and citizens in order to build public agreements that improve government policies, services, and structures. The West Virginia Center for Civic Life creates opportunities in communities around the state for citizens to become involved in deliberative dialogues on common problems, such as prescription drug abuse and childhood obesity. The challenge is in making sure there are enough of these kinds of organizations in communities across the country.

An additional challenge is that many of the better-known, non-issue-specific organizations, such as the League of Women Voters, the National Civic League, or the Boy Scouts and Girl Scouts, have in some respects come to be seen as "old school" by younger generations or are perceived as being aligned with certain political views or power structures in the community. This phenomenon has been well documented by Theda Skocpol (2004) and Robert Putnam (2000) at Harvard University, Carmen Sirianni (2009) at Brandeis University, Peter Levine (in press) at Tufts University, and others. Such organizations are vital to our democratic health and are working hard to shift these perceptions. However, the vacuum left in their absence has been filled, not by a surge of new, nonaligned organizations, but rather by ever greater numbers of advocacy groups and ideologically identified organizations. As a result, opportunities to participate civically have become much more circumscribed. In some places it's hard to find a way to get active *other* than by lobbying or advocating on a specific issue.

Peter Levine, Director of the Center for Information and Research on Civic Learning and Engagement (CIRCLE) at Tufts, assessed it this way: "While traditional membership organizations (e.g., the Knights of Columbus, the NAACP, and the Rotary) cannot be held directly responsible for deliberative democracy, they did have somewhat diverse memberships, especially with respect to class, and they inducted people into civic roles and responsibilities that went beyond their own membership. They had incentives and resources to recruit people into civic life and to develop their skills and interests. If these old organizations are defunct, we need a new, functional equivalent" (Levine Nov. 2010).

Two national public institutions that have historically played an important role in the democratic life of our communities have also suffered reduced resources in recent years. First is our system of land grant universities, which were originally called "democracy colleges" because they sought to increase access to higher education for a broader array of Americans, thereby encouraging them to take a more proactive role in civic life. Like most public educational institutions, in our current economy land grant universities are experiencing shrinking resources and are having to limit many programs, including some that promote an active civic life.

Second is our public library system. Although in communities all across the country libraries are reawakening to larger civic goals, most are also being forced by economic necessity to reduce their staff and services. In a 2010 *Los Angeles Times* opinion piece, author and library advocate Marilyn Johnson framed it very starkly when she said: "The U.S. is beginning an interesting experiment in democracy: We're cutting public library funds, shrinking our public and school libraries, and in some places, shutting them altogether . . . Those [people] in cities that haven't preserved their libraries, those less fortunate and baffled by technology, and our children will be the first to suffer. But sooner or later, we'll all feel the loss as one of the most effective levelers of privilege and avenues of reinvention—one of the great engines of democracy—begins to disappear" (M. Johnson 2010).

In the end, the infrastructure that institutions like these once provided now exists only in pockets, in many places simply because committed people happen to live there or because the right combination of private resources was available at the right time.

To demonstrate the fragility of the organizational infrastructure overall, in 2010 Levine developed a map of the civic renewal field. The map is an illustration and analysis of the links and networking capacity of 117 organizations working in the arena of participatory democracy. He drew a series of conclusions from this exercise that are instructive:

> While certain groups play active bridging roles, we badly need an active and robust organization—with a staff and a budget— to fill a national-level, lead role in unifying and building the democracy reform field. We also need more organizations with grassroots constituencies; with a few exceptions, the organizations that have the most citizen members are peripheral to civic renewal, and the pure civic renewal groups are grant-supported professional organizations or foundations. While there is a reasonably broad ideological spectrum, we need more diverse leadership—at least 90% of the top leaders of these 117 organizations are white and have college degrees [Levine Oct. 2010].

Levine's assessment provides guideposts around which we must build a more robust organizational infrastructure that will support widespread and diverse citizen participation in this country.

Notably, 2012 marked the 150th anniversary of the Morill Act, through which Abraham Lincoln established our land grant universities. This is an excellent reminder of the importance of revitalizing organizational infrastructures that help instill a sense of civic duty and engage citizens in the important issues of the day.

TRUSTWORTHY, FACT-BASED MEDIA

In a highly functioning democracy, the media is a primary source for providing citizens with credible information about their society and the actions of their government. Sadly, for as long as our nation has held this belief, the media has struggled to fulfill its obligations. In 1814 Thomas Jefferson made this point quite clearly: "I deplore, with you, the putrid state into which our newspapers have passed, and the malignity, the vulgarity, and mendacious spirit of those who write them . . . These ordures are rapidly depraving the public taste, and lessening its relish for sound food. As vehicles of information, and a curb on our functionaries, they have rendered themselves useless, by forfeiting all title to belief" (Jefferson 2010, 373).

Over the years, particularly in the last century, there have been consistent efforts to address these issues; to push the media to maintain a more neutral and educationally oriented role. The Communications Act of 1934 (which established the Federal Communications Commission) was intended, according to New America Foundation President Steve Coll, "to ensure that the commercial broadcasting industry helped strengthen the country's democracy by educating the public and promoting civil, inclusive debate" (Coll 2010), To achieve this, the act required networks it licensed to dedicate "not less than 4% nor more than 7%" of their programming to public interest—that is, educational—programming (Committee on Energy and Commerce 2003, 193). Since then, securing industry compliance with this rather miniscule requirement has been a great challenge. Coll summed it up this way:

The Federal Communications Commission oversees the formal "public interest obligations" undertaken by broadcasters in exchange for their spectrum licenses. There has always been an eye-of-the-beholder aspect to these obligations, but during the 1960s and 1970s, broadcast networks and local stations understood that serious news reporting, public service announcements and education programming were required of them. In recent years, influenced by industry lobbyists, the rules have been so watered down that commercial broadcasters do little more than self-report on their service to the public; they do not have to file their reports with anyone but themselves, as long as those filings are available during office hours. The neutered system is symbolic of deeper failures of private media to serve the public interest [Coll 2010].

A steady stream of commissions have studied such concerns about the media and offered remedies. For example, in 1948 the Commission on Freedom of the Press, widely known as "the Hutchins Commission" sought to promote an overarching code of social responsibility for the media. In 1967 the Carnegie Commission on Educational Television raised concerns about media quality. In the same year, President Lyndon Johnson signed the Public Broadcasting Act in the hope of stimulating risk-taking, creativity, and innovation in public programming and to fill the quality gap that was consistently left by the networks. The next year, the National Advisory Commission on Civil Disorders, known as the Kerner Commission, issued a report that was particularly critical of the media's failure to provide a balanced—especially racially balanced—perspective on current events. Most recently, in 2009, following two years of study, the Knight Commission on the Information Needs of Communities in a Democracy issued a detailed strategy document aimed, in part, at improving the quality of information that is made available to the public.

Despite these efforts, the educational components of our media, both traditional and new, have continued to shrink, while ever more slanted and biased media have proliferated. The fragmentation and lack of trustworthiness in today's media have had a direct impact on the behavior of our public officials. It has become quite commonplace, for example, for politicians who have reneged on a pledge or committed some misdeed to deflect attention from their behavior by pointing to bias in media coverage. Because much coverage is, in fact, ideologically biased these days, the complaint feels legitimate and the underlying concern is lost. When media outlets operate as advocates instead of as neutral observers and reporters, their ability to hold decision makers accountable for their commitments and behaviors is undermined.

All of this must be understood within the context of the significant sea change in the media industry as a whole. In *Informing Communities: Sustaining Democracy in the Digital Age,* the Knight Commission found that "journalistic institutions that have traditionally served democracy . . . are themselves in crisis from financial, technological, and behavioral changes taking place in our society" (Knight Commission on the Information Needs of Communities in a Democracy 2009, xii). The Commission reported a decrease of more than 30 percent, over the last six years, in newspaper staff reporters covering their respective statehouses on a full-time basis. It further reported that nearly three-quarters of Associated Press managing editors felt that shrinking staffs hurt their capacity to keep readers informed (Knight Commission 2009). By all accounts, the news industry as we once knew it is disappearing.

Peter Shane, Executive Director of the Knight Commission from 2008 to 2009, assessed the changing media landscape, and the opportunities it presents, in this way:

Local news and information constitute what economists call a "public good," and there are plenty of reasons to worry whether the U.S. is contributing sufficient social resources to their production. But, when you think about the tools that are available to us, the scope of literacy in the nation, people's access to information and the possibilities for participating in an authentic way, it's hard to imagine a better time for promoting local communication flow than right now.

The task ahead of us is not, "How do we save the local paper and return to 1975?" Even the so-called Golden Age of Journalism was far from optimal. But we can create a renaissance going forward by ensuring that the new resources we have actually give communities the information they need to thrive civically.

Unfortunately, we have very little vocabulary to describe a healthy community information environment, much less a reliable metric on whether people are getting the information they need. But there are some exciting early steps being taken to gather such data, and communities are finding innovative ways to meet their information needs—through local online forums, community radio and citizen journalism, among other strategies. None of these provides a full cure for our national shortfall in full-time professional reporting, but they are all key directions for the future [Shane 2010].

To be a positive force in our democracy, our ideologically biased media must begin again to adhere to long-held journalistic standards of fact-based reporting, balance, fairness, and a commitment to real public education. And media outlets must re-own their neutral public function. In addition to enabling citizens to take up their respective roles in democracy, the media should once again be a core avenue through which citizens can hold government accountable for pursuing the will of the people.

ROBUST CIVIC EDUCATION

A robust civic education grounds Americans in the expectation of participation and enhances their ability to undertake it. In 1910, in his well-known "Man in the Arena" speech, President Theodore Roosevelt offered a strong statement about the importance of civic responsibility:

> A democratic republic such as ours—an effort to realize [in] its full sense government by, of, and for the people—represents the most gigantic of all possible social experiments, the one fraught with great responsibilities alike for good and evil . . . Under other forms of government, under the rule of one man or very few men, the quality of the leaders is all-important. But with you and us the case is different . . . success or failure will be conditioned upon the way in which the average man, the average woman, does his or her duty. The average citizen must be a good citizen if our republics are to succeed [Roosevelt 1910, 3].

One hundred years later, noting an ongoing decline in civic activism in this country, Lee Hamilton, a thirty-five-year veteran of the U.S. House of Representatives, reiterated President Roosevelt's point: "If Americans increasingly disengage—if more and more Americans are less and less interested in civic responsibility," he said, "then the entire American democratic enterprise is at risk, and the country simply will not work" (Hamilton 2011).

Our nation is falling quite short when it comes to nurturing democratically focused civic activism: today's volunteers tend to focus on service-related work, and "politically oriented" activities are most often linked to specific issues or causes. Americans are less and less engaged in basic democratic efforts, such as civic leadership development activities, voter education and registration, working to ensure high-quality and diverse election slates, or running or attending community meetings.

In considering the causes of these trends, a 2010 study by the Intercollegiate Studies Institute found a strong link between lower levels of civic activism and a lack of civic knowledge. The Institute reported that "no other variable, including age, income, race, gender, religion, or partisanship, was found to exceed both the breadth and depth of civic literacy's positive impact on active political engagement" (Intercollegiate Studies Institute 2012).

And yet, as a nation, we demonstrate a very weak commitment to civic education. In 2012 Arne Duncan, U.S. Secretary of Education, summarized the problem this way: "Unfortunately, we know that civic learning and democratic engagement are not staples of every American's education today. In too many schools and on too many college campuses, civic learning and democratic engagement are add-ons, rather than an essential part of the core academic mission" (Duncan 2012).

Even more disturbing, the availability of academic offerings that build civic knowledge and stimulate participation is correlated with race and income. A 2008, California-based study reported these findings: "In our study of high school civic opportunities, we found that a student's race and academic track, and a school's average socioeconomic status (SES), determine the availability of the school-based civic learning opportunities that promote voting and broader forms of civic engagement. High school students attending higher SES schools, those who are college-bound, and white students get more of these opportunities than low-income students, those not heading to college, and students of color" (Kahne and Middaugh 2008, 3).

The results of these trends are plain to see. In addition to decreased civic activism, far too many Americans lack basic knowledge about how our democracy works. In one brief illustration, in 2011 *Newsweek* magazine gave one thousand U.S. citizens the national citizenship test. The results were dismal: "29 percent couldn't name the vice president. Seventy-three percent couldn't correctly say why we fought the Cold War. Forty-four percent were unable to define the Bill of Rights. And six percent couldn't even circle Independence Day on a calendar" (Romano 2011). Such limited knowledge of basic civics has been a problem in our country for a long time. In their well-regarded 1997 study of this issue, Michael Delli Carpini and Scott Keeter concluded that "despite the numerous political, economic and social changes that have occurred since World War II, overall political knowledge levels in the United States are about the same today as they were forty to fifty years ago" (Delli Carpini and Keeter 1997, 270).

In short, our current approach to civic education is, and has long been, insufficient. It does not ensure that all of our nation's young people develop a strong, positive, and knowledgeable identity as citizens and, more important, have the requisite skills to act on it. In January 2012 the Obama Administration, in partnership with a wide range of organizations, announced efforts to address this challenge. One major thrust of the work is being conducted through the American Commonwealth Partnership, an effort aimed at bringing civic learning back into higher education through a series of initiatives. These initiatives include: an awareness-building, deliberative dialogue effort in partnership with the National Issues Forums Institute, the Pedagogies of Empowerment and Engagement Initiative to build civic instruction the Campus-Community Civic Health Initiative, and an initiative focused on state and federal policies related to civic learning, among others (DemocracyU 2012).

In conjunction with these efforts, based on the work of the National Task Force on Civic Learning and Democratic Engagement, the U.S. Department of Education has also committed to taking a series of action steps to enhance civic education in America. These include efforts to "reinvest in the fundamental civic and democratic mission of schools . . . enlarge the current national narrative that erases civic aims and civic literacy . . .

advance a contemporary, comprehensive framework for civic learning . . . foster progressively higher levels of civic knowledge, skills, examined values, and action as expectations for every student . . . [and] expand the number of robust, generative civic partnerships" (National Task Force on Civic Learning and Democratic Engagement 2012, vi).

Ideally, efforts like these (additional examples are listed in Appendix B) will help move the nation toward the more robust civic life we so clearly need. America*Speaks*'s work has repeatedly shown that once people experience a deliberative process linked to live policy outcomes they are "hooked" and will seek out the experience again and again. But in a country as vast and complex as ours, providing opportunities for real democratic participation to a relatively small number of people will never be enough. The impetus for civic participation must be much more broadly felt. Robust civic education that nurtures widespread demand by citizens for opportunities to participate is a tall but necessary order.

THE PUBLIC MANAGER'S ROLE IN BUILDING AN INFRASTRUCTURE THAT SUPPORTS DEMOCRACY

As described in this chapter, every component of an infrastructure that supports democracy already exists in some form in places across the country. However, these are only isolated instances. Public managers have a unique opportunity to help build the necessary infrastructure in the communities in which they work. For example, when planning engagement work, public managers might ask themselves questions like these: "As I return to this community to hold public hearings, what can be done differently this time to help institutionalize the capacity to have this conversation in a more robust and routine way? Which local organizations can be supported to take on this role? Can more people be trained to facilitate these processes? How can the public be systematically educated about these issues so that their participation is even more valuable to decision making?" Answering questions like these will go a long way toward building local infrastructure and capacity for high-quality citizen engagement. And, as more and more public managers do this, their combined efforts will make an important contribution to the development of a community-based national infrastructure for deliberative democracy.

The infrastructure we need to support and sustain vigorous citizen engagement in this country is multifaceted and far-reaching. We must ensure not only that every component of this infrastructure is present in communities across the country but also that all of these elements fit together in an interconnected system to support national deliberation on the most important issues facing our country. This is a steep mountain to climb, but not an insurmountable one. The good news is that millions of Americans are ready to join the ascent.

WHO IS RESPONSIBLE FOR OUR NATION'S DEMOCRACY? WE ALL ARE!

I know of no safe depository of the ultimate power of the society but the people themselves, and if we think them not enlightened enough to exercise their control with a wholesome direction, the remedy is not to take it from them, but to inform their discretion.

THOMAS JEFFERSON*

We are at risk of losing our democracy. Partisan redistricting, winner-take-all election rules, voter suppression strategies, an ideologically driven media, and outrageously increasing amounts of money in politics are unduly influencing who we elect and how our country is governed. This has dangerously eroded public trust in our democratic institutions. The end result is that citizens are thoroughly disaffected and critical public concerns hang in the balance. Whose job is it to fix all these things? And where do we begin?

It is natural to want to shy away from such big and overwhelming questions. Yet I believe that readers who have come this far actually want to take on these challenges. You recognize the gravity of the situation and know that you have an important role to

---

*Thomas Jefferson to William Charles Jarvis, September 28, 1820. *The Thomas Jefferson Papers Series 1: General Correspondence. 1651–1827.* [http://hdl.loc.gov/loc.mss/mtj.mtjbib023901]. Accessed August 2012.

play in transforming our democracy to ensure that citizen voices are heard.

This book has argued that reengaging citizens in the governance of our nation is one of the critical pathways to taking on the major, structural challenges facing American democracy. Three core constituencies will have to climb this mountain together. Elected officials will have to declare this is the way the public's business will be done. Public managers will have to embrace these practices and embed them in their everyday work. The public will have to demand their place at the table and actively participate.

To accomplish this transformation, all three of these groups will have to work on both day-to-day strategies and the long-term structural issues facing us. Accordingly, this book has deliberately moved back and forth between these two challenges. Undertaking the day-to-day strategies will not, alone, accomplish the broader sea change necessary in our democracy. For that we will have to build the infrastructure needed to support it. At the same time, tackling the larger issues without making adjustments to daily practice will only undermine the stability of any structural changes that are achieved. It is vital that we attack both of these challenges at the same time.

This book has focused on public managers among the three core constituencies because they are uniquely positioned to work directly with both citizens and elected officials—and to connect the two. Not only do they run or have management responsibility for a wide range of specific programs that can be strengthened by citizen engagement but from their vantage point in policymaking, they can influence the larger issues as well. As I said at the outset, I am a passionate advocate for strengthening democracy in our country *and* for the importance of public service. This book has sought to make explicit the necessary and vital connection between the two.

KEY TRUTHS ABOUT US

After nearly twenty years of working to bring citizens into authentic connection with their elected officials and other decision makers, I am willing to posit a number of truths. Together they are a strong foundation on which we can build a movement to transform American democracy. At a time when our system is broken, they can inspire us to bring citizens' voices to the table and realize our founders' aspirations for self-governance. These truths are as follows:

- Our people are better than our politics. The vast majority of Americans care more about solving problems than rigidly holding on to ideological positions.
- Given the opportunity, Americans thrive in environments in which they are able to talk with and listen to people who think differently than they do about the key challenges facing our country.
- Given the opportunity, elected officials embrace citizen engagement and take action on recommendations that reflect the collective voice of the public.
- When people own the outcomes of a policy decision, budget allocation, or planning process, they are willing to stay engaged to ensure that their recommendations are implemented.
- Today, we have a willing public, the outreach capacity to bring them together, the policy expertise to educate them about the facts and options, the design capability to engage them in meaningful discussion with people who think differently than they do, the technology platforms necessary to take the discussion to scale and make collective decisions, and elected officials who are willing to listen.

These truths have been demonstrated over and over again in citizen engagement work practiced across the United States, and elsewhere in the world. The work has demonstrated these truths over and over again. So why is this not the way we routinely do the public's business in a nation founded on the philosophy of self-governance?

WHAT'S MISSING

What we are missing is the will—both public and political—to remake our democratic institutions with the voices of the people at their center. "Of the people, by the people, for the people" can only come to life in our democracy today if we the people demand it.

This book began with an observation by Alexis de Tocqueville, one of the most insightful and prescient observers of American life. "The great privilege of the Americans does not consist in being more enlightened than other nations," he said, "but in being able to repair the faults they may commit." Citizen engagement is a compelling and viable path for repairing the public's trust in governance. We know the underlying principles, have demonstrated successful strategies, and have the technical tools to do it. Now we must find the will to get it done.

REFERENCES

Abell, Belinda. Private email message to Wendy Jacobson, Feb. 1, 2012.

America*Speaks*. "Americans Discuss Social Security." *Archives*. 1998.

America*Speaks*. "Citizen Summits." *Archives*. 1999–2005.

America*Speaks*. *Designing 21st Century Governance Mechanisms: Report from an America*Speaks *Democracy Lab Conference*. Washington, DC: America *Speaks*, 2006.

America*Speaks*. "California*Speaks:* Working Together for Better Health Care." [http://americaspeaks.org/resources/videos/], 2007.

America*Speaks*. "Advancing Futures for Adults with Autism National Town Meeting." *Archives*. 2009.

America*Speaks*. *Champions of Participation Executive Summary*. Washington, DC: America*Speaks*, Mar. 2009.

America*Speaks*. "America*Speaks:* Our Budget, Our Economy." [http://americaspeaks.org/resources/videos/]. Aug. 2011.

America*Speaks*. Our Budget, Our Economy. *Archives*. 2011.

American Library Association (ALA). *The State of America's Libraries*. Chicago: American Library Association, 2011.

Apfel, Ken. Private email message to Carolyn J. Lukensmeyer, Feb. 3, 2012.

Appreciative Inquiry Commons. "Definitions of Appreciative Inquiry." [http://appreciativeinquiry.case.edu/intro/definition.cfm]. Mar. 2012.

Atkins, P., Blumenthal, P., Edisis, A., Friedhoff, A., Curran, L., Lowry, L., St. Clair, T., Wial, H., and Wolman, H. *Responding to Manufacturing Job Loss: What Can Economic Development Policy Do?* Washington, DC: Brookings Institution Press, 2011.

Autism Speaks. "What Is Autism?" [www.autismspeaks.org/what-autism]. Accessed 2012.

Baio, A. "Lessons Learned from the President's Tweet." [http://expertlabs.org/2011/07/lessons-learned-from-the-white-houses-twitter-town-hall.html]. Jul. 2011.

Beer, S. "Thesis." *Platform for Change*. West Sussex, UK: Wiley, 1975.

Beinart, P. "Why Washington Is Tied Up in Knots." *Time*. [www.time.com/time/magazine/article/0,9171,1966451,00.html]. Feb. 2010.

Berkow, Jane. Private email message to Wendy Jacobson, Apr. 20, 2012.

Bernier, Roger. Private email message to Jesse Sostrin, Jan. 20, 2012.

Berry, J. "The Holy City of New Orleans." In D. Rutledge (ed.), *Do You Know What It Means to Miss New Orleans? A Collection of Stories and Essays Set in the Big Easy.* Seattle: Chin Music Press, 2006.

Berry, R. "Owensboro Town Meeting Bears Good Fruit." [http://americaspeaks.org/blog/owensboro-town-meeting-bears-good-fruit/]. Nov. 2011.

Bonner, Patricia. Private email message to Wendy Jacobson, Jan. 23, 2012.

Brodsky, R. "The Super Committee, Austerity, Stimulus, and Compromise: The Collapse of American Politics." *Huff Post Politics: The Blog.* [www.huffingtonpost.com/richard-brodsky/super-committee-fail_b_1108473.html]. Nov. 2011.

Bryan, F. M. *The New England Town Meeting and How It Works.* Chicago: University of Chicago Press, 2003.

Campbell, T., Sostrin, J., and Masters, B. *How to Educate the Public about the ACA: Recommendations from California*Speaks. Washington, DC: America*Speaks.* Apr. 13, 2011.

Center for Deliberative Democracy. *By the People: Hard Times, Hard Choices: Michigan Residents Deliberate.* Battle Creek, MI: W. K. Kellogg Foundation, Jan. 2010.

Center for Responsive Politics. "527s: Advocacy Group Spending." [www.opensecrets.org/527s/index.php]. Mar. 2012.

Challenge.gov. "My Money App Up." *Challenge.gov.* [http://ideabank.mymoneyappup.challenge.gov/]. Accessed 2012.

Chupp, M. Voices of Citizens: Analysis of Citizen Interviews, a Preliminary Report. Cleveland, OH: Cleveland State University, Dec. 2005.

Ciccone, A. "The White House Officially Responds to SOPA Petition." [www.thetechupload.com/2012/01/the-white-house-officially-responds-to-sopa-petition/]. Jan. 2012.

Citizens United v. *Federal Election Commission*, 558 U.S. 50, 2010.

City-data.com. "Races in Atlanta, Georgia (GA) Detailed Stats: Ancestries, Foreign Born Residents, Place of Birth." [www.city-data.com/races/races-Atlanta-Georgia.html]. Accessed 2012a.

City-data.com. "Races in Memphis, Tennessee (TN) Detailed Stats: Ancestries, Foreign Born Residents, Place of Birth." [www.city-data.com/races/races-Memphis-Tennessee.html]. Accessed 2012b.

City-data.com. "Races in New Orleans, Louisiana (LA) Detailed Stats: Ancestries, Foreign Born Residents, Place of Birth." [www.city-data.com/races/races-New-Orleans-Louisiana.html]. Accessed 2012c.

City-data.com. "Races in St. Louis, Missouri (MO) Detailed Stats: Ancestries, Foreign Born Residents, Place of Birth." [www.city-data.com/races/races-St.-Louis-Missouri.html]. Accessed 2012d.

City-data.com. "Races in Washington, District of Columbia (DC) Detailed Stats: Ancestries, Foreign Born Residents, Place of Birth." [www.city-data.com/races/races-Washington-District-of-Columbia.html]. Accessed 2012e.

Coll, S. "Why Fox News Should Help Fund NPR." *New America Foundation.* [http://newamerica.net/node/39228]. Oct. 2010.

Committee on Energy and Commerce, U.S. House of Representatives. *Compilation of Selected Acts Within the Jurisdiction of the Committee on Energy and Commerce Communications Law as Amended Through December 31, 2002.* Washington, DC: U.S. Government Printing Office, 2003.

Communications Workers of America. *SpeedMatters: A Report on Internet Speeds in All 50 States.* Washington, DC: Communications Workers of America, Aug. 2009.

Conrad, Kent. Private email message to Carolyn J. Lukensmeyer, Feb. 3, 2012.

Corker, B. "Sen. Corker: Senate Must Face Fiscal Reality in Pending Highway Bill." *Washington Post.* [www.washingtonpost.com/opinions/sen-corker-senate-must-face-fiscal-reality-in-pending-highway-bill/2012/02/28/gIQAtf6VuR_story.html]. Mar. 2012.

Cottman, M. "A View From the Summit: D.C. Residents Turn Out to Hash Out Their City's Future." *Washington Post,* C01. Nov. 21, 1999.

Dalton, Deborah. Private email message to Carolyn J. Lukensmeyer, Apr. 18, 2012.

Daly, C. B. "Rick Perry Says Social Security Is a 'Ponzi Scheme' and a 'Monstrous Lie.'" [http://www.cbsnews.com/8301-503544_162-20098635-503544.html]. Aug. 2011.

Danish Board of Technology. "111 Responses Concerning Bill on Abolition of the Danish Board of Technology." [www.tekno.dk/subpage.php3?article=1848&toppic=kategori11&language=uk]. Feb. 2012.

Deliberative Democracy Consortium. *Where Is Democracy Headed? Research and Practice on Public Deliberation.* Washington, DC: DDC, 2008.

Delli Carpini, M. X., and Keeter, S. *What Americans Know about Politics and Why It Matters.* New Haven, CT: Yale University Press, 1997.

DemocracyU. "About DemocracyU and American Commonwealth Partnership." [http://democracyu.wordpress.com/about/]. Accessed 2012.

de Tocqueville, A. *Democracy in America: And Two Essays on America* (G. Bevan, trans.). London: Penguin Books, 2003.

de Tocqueville, A., and Spencer, J. C. *Democracy in America*. (H. Reeve, trans.). Vol. 1. New York: J. & H. G. Langley, 1841.

DiCamillo, M., and Field, M. *California Voter Views of the Health Care System*. San Francisco: Field Research Corporation, 2007.

Dietz, T., and Stern, P. C. (eds.). "Panel on Public Participation in Environmental Assessment and Decision Making." *Public Participation in Environmental Assessment and Decision Making*. Washington, DC: National Academies Press, 2008.

Duncan, A. "Secretary Arne Duncan's Remarks at 'For Democracy's Future' Forum at the White House." U.S. Department of Education. [http://www.ed.gov/news/speeches/secretary-arne-duncans-remarks-democracys-future-forum-white-house]. Jan. 2012.

Economic Club of Washington. "2009–2010 Season." [http://www.economicclub.org/page.cfm/go/videos/id/11]. Apr. 2010.

Eggler, B. "Planning Process OK, Speakers Say Continued Public Participation Urged as Document Is Revised." *Times-Picayune*, Mar. 8, 2007.

Ekleberry, Jay. Private email message to Wendy Jacobson, Oct. 28, 2011.

Esterling, K., Fung, A., and Lee, T. *The Difference That Deliberation Makes: Evaluating the "Our Budget, Our Economy" Public Deliberation*. Chicago: John D. and Catherine T. MacArthur Foundation, 2010.

Faast, Tony. Private email message to Jesse Sostrin, Jan. 12, 2012.

Fahrenthold, D. A. "American Town Halls More Contentious Than Ever, in Part by Design." *Washington Post*. [www.washingtonpost.com/politics/american-town-halls-more-contentious-than-ever-in-part-by-design/2011/08/25/gIQAhKWHjJ_story.html]. Aug. 2011.

Federal Communications Commission (FCC). *Connecting America: The National Broadband Plan*. Washington, DC: Federal Communications Commission, Mar. 2010.

Federal Communications Commission (FCC). *In the Matter of International Comparison Requirements Pursuant to the Broadband Data Improvement Act International Broadband Data Report*. Washington, DC: Federal Communications Commission, May 2011, DA 11-732, IB Docket No. 10-171.

Ferriter, Olivia. Private email message to Jesse Sostrin, Jan. 19, 2012.

Fishkin, J. S. *Democracy and Deliberation: New Directions for Democratic Reform*. New Haven, CT: Yale University Press, 1993.

Flaherty, J. "On the Fifth Anniversary of Katrina, Displacement Continues." *San Francisco BayView: National Black Newspaper*. [http://sfbayview.com/2010/on-the-fifth-anniversary-of-katrina-displacement-continues/]. Sept. 6, 2010.

Follett, M. P. *The New State: Group Organization the Solution of Popular Government*. London: Longmans, Green, 1920.

Ford Foundation. "Wired for Change: A Special Address from President Clinton." [http://vimeo.com/20611694]. Mar. 2011.

"FORTUNE 500: Our Annual Ranking of America's Largest Corporations." *CNNMoney* [http://money.cnn.com/magazines /fortune/fortune500/2011/cities/]. Mar. 2012.

Fung, Archon. Private email message to Carolyn J. Lukensmeyer, Jan. 26, 2012.

Fung, A., Lee, T., and Harbage, P. *Public Impacts: Evaluating the Outcomes of the California*Speaks *Statewide Conversation on Health Care Reform.* Washington, DC: America*Speaks*, 2008.

Gastil, J., and Keith, W. M. "A Nation That (Sometimes) Likes to Talk: A Brief History of Public Deliberation in the United States." In J. Gastil and P. Levine (eds.), *The Deliberative Democracy Handbook: Strategies for Effective Civic Engagement in the Twenty-First Century.* San Francisco: Jossey-Bass, 2005.

"Georgia Joins Health-Care Reform Lawsuit." *Atlanta Business Chronicle.* [www.bizjournals.com/atlanta/stories/2010/05/10/daily56.html? page=all]. May 2010.

Gerson, M. "The Worthy Mission to Get Joseph Kony." *Washington Post.* [www.washingtonpost.com/opinions/the-worthy-mission-to-get -joseph-kony/2011/10/17/gIQAny5YsL_story.html]. Oct. 2011.

Goldberger, P. "Groundwork: How the Future of Ground Zero Is Being Resolved." *New Yorker,* May 2002. Reprinted by permission of the author.

Goldberger, P. "Shaping the Void: How Successful Is the New World Trade Center?" *New Yorker.* [www.newyorker.com/arts/critics /skyline/2011/09/12/110912crsk_skyline_goldberger]. Sept. 2011.

Goldman, J., and Peters, J. *Participation and Open Government Websites.* Washington, DC: America*Speaks* and Ottawa, Ontario: Ascentum, 2009.

Goldman, J., and Peters, J. *10 Questions: Is Your Organization an Eagle or an Ostrich?* Washington, DC: America*Speaks* and Ottawa, Ontario: Ascentum, 2011.

Gore A. "Al Gore and Sean Parker on Apathy SXSW 2012." *YouTube.* [http://www.youtube.com/watch?v=3eWacOwPsWw]. Accessed 2012.

Goring, Lisa. Private email message to Wendy Jacobson, Jan. 12, 2012.

Haas, Larry. Private email message to Carolyn J. Lukensmeyer, Jan. 27, 2012.

Hamill, P. "Thrilling Show of People Power." *New York Daily News: Sports Edition Final.* Jul. 22, 2002.

Hamilton, L. H. "Educating for Democracy: What Is Civic Literacy?" *The Center on Congress at Indiana University*. [http://congress .indiana.edu/educating-democracy-what-civic-literacy]. Mar. 2011.

Harbage, P. California*Speaks* and the Evolution of the California Health Reform Debate. Sacramento, CA: Harbage Consulting, 2007.

Harbage, P., and Haycock, H. "Health Care Reform '07: Fixing Compromised Care with a Compromise Solution." *Harvard Law and Policy Review*, 2-2, 1–4, 2008.

Heintz, Stephen. Private email message to Carolyn J. Lukensmeyer, Mar. 23, 2012.

HM Government. "How E-Petitions Work." [http://epetitions .direct.gov.uk/how-it-works#commons]. Accessed 2012.

Hoenig, Chris. Private email message to Carolyn J. Lukensmeyer, Apr. 25, 2012.

Honomichl, J. "The 2011 Honomichl Top 50 Report." [www .marketingpower.com/ResourceLibrary/Publications /MarketingNews/2011/6–30–11/Hono.pdf]. Jun. 2011.

Intercollegiate Studies Institute. "2011 Summary." [http://www .americancivicliteracy.org/2011/summary_summary.html]. Accessed 2012.

International Association for Public Participation. "IAP2 Spectrum of Public Participation." [http://www.iap2.org/associations/4748 /files/spectrum.pdf]. Accessed 2012.

Jefferson, T. "To Dr. Walter Jones, Monticello, January 2, 1814." In P. L. Ford (ed.), *The Works of Thomas Jefferson, Vol. XI: Correspondence and Papers 1808–1816*. New York: Cosimo, 2010.

Johnson, Laurie. Private email message to Wendy Jacobson, Sept. 10, 2010.

Johnson, M. "U.S. Public Libraries: We Lose Them at Our Peril." *Los Angeles Times*. [http://articles.latimes.com/2010/jul/06/opinion /la-oe-johnson-libraries-20100706]. Jul. 2010.

Jones, J. "A Sustainable Discussion." *Daily News-Record*, Jun. 1, 2009.

Kahne, J., and Middaugh, E. *Democracy for Some: The Civic Opportunity Gap in High School, Circle Working Paper 59*. College Park, MD: Center for Information and Research on Civic Learning and Engagement (CIRCLE), 2008.

Kamensky, John. Private email message to Wendy Jacobson, Jan. 23, 2012.

Kang, C. "How the FCC's New National Broadband Plan Is Expected to Affect Consumers." *Washington Post*. [http://voices .washingtonpost.com/posttech/2010/03/how_the_fccs_new _national_broa.html]. Mar. 2010.

Kassarjian, Sevanne. Personal communication with Carolyn J. Lukensmeyer, May 10, 2012.

Katz, B. "Editor's Overview." In B. Katz (ed.), *Reflections on Regionalism.* Washington, DC: The Brookings Institution Press, 2000.

Kettering Foundation. "Public Deliberation in Democracy." [http:// www.kettering.org/ketterings_research/public_deliberation_in _democracy]. Accessed 2012.

Khimm, S. "Pushing the Government to Speak Plainly." *Washington Post.* [www.washingtonpost.com/opinions/pushing-the -government-to-speak-plainly/2011/11/18/gIQA7TmpLO _story.html]. Dec. 2011.

Kia-Hway, Liou (trans.). *Œuvres complètes.* Paris: Editions Gallimard, 1969.

Knight Commission on the Information Needs of Communities in a Democracy. *Informing Communities, Sustaining Democracy in the Digital Age.* Washington, DC: The Aspen Institute, 2009.

Knighton, Betty. Private email message to Wendy Jacobson, Oct. 19, 2010.

Koppelin, Andy. Personal communication with Carolyn Lukensmeyer. Jan. 20, 2012.

Krupa, M. "Survey Backs Plan for Smaller Footprint but Demographics of Voters Questioned." *Times-Picayune,* Oct. 29, 2006.

Kuehn, David. Private email message to Jesse Sostrin, Jan. 17, 2012.

Kuhlman, Rich. Private email message to Jesse Sostrin, Jan. 11, 2012.

Lacy, Sue. Private email message to Wendy Jacobson, Jan. 27, 2012.

Lane, E. "America 101: How We Let Civic Education Slide—And Why We Need a Crash Course in the Constitution Today." *Democracy: A Journal of Ideas.* [http://www.democracyjournal.org/10/6643.php? page=all]. Fall 2008.

Larsson, S., and Nordvall, H. *Study Circles in Sweden: An Overview with a Bibliography of International Literature.* Linköping, Sweden: Linköping University Electronic Press, 2010.

Leighninger, M. *The Next Form of Democracy: How Expert Rule Is Giving Way to Shared Governance—and Why Politics Will Never Be the Same.* Memphis, TN: Vanderbilt University Press, 2006.

Leisner, I. *Technology with a Human Face: Teknologirådet, the Danish Board of Technology.* Copenhagen, Denmark: Danish Board of Technology, May 2005.

Leonhardt, D. "How Readers Chose to Fix the Deficit." *New York Times.* [www.nytimes.com/2010/11/21/weekinreview/21leonhardt .html]. Nov. 2010.

Levine, P. "A Map of the Civic Renewal Field." *Peter Levine: A blog for civic renewal.* [http://www.peterlevine.ws/mt/archives/2010/10/a -map-of-the-ci.html]. Oct. 2010.

Levine, P. *We Are the Ones We Have Been Waiting For: The Philosophy and Practice of Civic Renewal.* Oxford: Oxford University Press, in press.

Levine, Peter. Private email message to Carolyn J. Lukensmeyer, Nov. 8, 2010.

Lincoln, A. "On Government." In J. G. Nicolay and J. Hay (eds.), *Abraham Lincoln: Complete Works, Comprising His Speeches, Letters, State Papers, and Miscellaneous Writings.* Vol. 1. New York: Century, 1907.

Linehan, M. "State Cuts to Hit Libraries Hard." *The Middle Township Gazette.* [http://www.shorenewstoday.com/snt/news/index.php/2010-04-07-20-18-16/middle-township-news/908-]. May 2010.

Linthicum, K. "L.A. Book Lovers to Protest City Library Budget Cuts." *Los Angeles Times.* [LATimesblogs.com http://latimesblogs.latimes.com/lanow/2010/05/la-book-lovers-to-protest-city-library-budget-cuts.html]. May 2010.

Long, R., and Beierle, T. C. *The Federal Advisory Committee Act and Public Participation in Environmental Policy.* Washington, DC: Resources for the Future, Jan. 1999.

Lukensmeyer, C. J. "Large-Scale Citizen Engagement and the Rebuilding of New Orleans: A Case Study." *National Civic Review,* Fall 2007. DOI: 10.1002/ncr.182, 3–13.

Lukensmeyer, C. J., and Brigham, S. "Taking Democracy to Scale: Creating a Town Hall Meeting for the Twenty-First Century." *National Civic Review,* 2002, *91*(4), 351–366.

Lukensmeyer, C. J., Goldman, J., and Stern, D. *Assessing Public Participation in an Open Government Era: A Review of Federal Agency Plans.* IBM Center for the Business of Government Fostering Transparency and Democracy Series. Washington, DC: IBM Center for the Business of Government, 2011.

Lukensmeyer, C. J., and Torres, L. *Public Deliberation: A Manager's Guide to Citizen Engagement.* IBM Center for the Business of Government Collaboration Series. Washington, DC: IBM Center for the Business of Government, 2006.

Luscombe, B. "Why E-Mail May Be Hurting Off-Line Relationships." *TimeScience.* [www.time.com/time/health/article/0,8599,1998396,00.html#ixzz1kON7Ys1B]. Jun. 2010.

Madison, J. "The Federalist No. 49: Method of Guarding Against the Encroachments of Any One Department of Government by Appealing to the People Through a Convention." *Independent Journal,* Feb. 1788. [http://constitution.org/fed/federa49.htm]. Accessed 2012.

Mansbridge, J. J. *Beyond Adversary Democracy.* Chicago: University of Chicago Press, 1983.

Mayer, Jim. Private email message to Carolyn J. Lukensmeyer, Apr. 10, 2012.

McMillan, Therese. Personal communication with Jesse Sostrin. Apr. 6, 2012.

Melville, K., and Kingston, R. J. "The Experience of the National Issues Forums." In D. Yankelovich and W. Friedman (eds.), *Toward Wiser Public Judgment*. Memphis, TN: Vanderbilt University Press, 2011.

Miller, Ron. Private email message to Carolyn J. Lukensmeyer, Jan. 6, 2012.

Milligan, Patricia. Private email message to Jesse Sostrin, Jan. 31, 2012.

Minarik, Joe. Private email message to Carolyn Lukensmeyer, Jan. 9, 2012.

Moore, Melvin. Private email message to Wendy Jacobson, Jan. 17, 2012.

Mulholland, J. "California: A National Model for Health Benefit Exchanges?" [www.governing.com/topics/health-human-services/California-national-model-health-benefit-exchanges.html]. Nov. 2010.

Nabatchi, T., Gastil, J., Leighninger, M., and Weiksner, M. (eds.). *Democracy in Motion: Evaluating the Practice and Impact of Deliberative Public Engagement*. New York: Oxford University Press, 2012.

National Academy of Public Administration. "A National Dialogue on Health Information Technology and Privacy." Washington, DC: National Academy of Public Administration, 2009.

National Coalition for Dialogue & Deliberation. *NCDD Engagement Streams Framework*. Boiling Springs, PA: National Coalition for Dialogue and Deliberation, 2010.

National Conference on Citizenship (NCOC). *2008 Civic Health Index: Beyond the Vote*. Washington, DC: National Conference on Citizenship, 2008.

National Task Force on Civic Learning and Democratic Engagement. "A Crucible Moment: College Learning and Democracy's Future." Washington, DC: Association of American Colleges and Universities, 2012.

NE Indiana Regional Partnership. "Vision 2020 Process Reveals Support for Regional Collaboration: Preliminary County Data Reports Focus on Regionalism, Local Assets." [www.chooseneindiana.com/news.aspx/2010/5/17/vision-2020-process-reveals-support-for-regional-collaboration]. May 17, 2010.

New Orleans Community Support Foundation. *The Unified New Orleans Plan: The Road to Recovery*. New Orleans: New Orleans Community Support Foundation, 2006.

Obama, B. "Transparency and Open Government." [http://www.whitehouse.gov/the_press_office/TransparencyandOpenGovernment]. Accessed 2012.

O'Brien, K. "Cross-Cutting Fundamental Strategies: Share Your Ideas by Friday!" *Greenversations* [http://blog.epa.gov/blog/2010/07 /share-your-ideas-by-friday/]. Jul. 2010.

Olshanky, R. B., and Johnson, L. A. *Clear as Mud: Planning for the Rebuilding of New Orleans.* Chicago: American Planning Association (Planners Press), 2010.

Organisation for Economic Co-operation and Development (OECD). *Promise and Problems of E-Democracy: Challenges of On-Line Citizen Engagement.* Paris: Organisation for Economic Co-operation and Development, 2003.

Organisation for Economic Co-operation and Development (OECD). "OECD Guiding Principles." [www.goodpracticeparticipate .govt.nz/benefits-of-community-participation/oecd-principles .html]. Accessed 2012a.

Organisation for Economic Co-operation and Development (OECD). "1d. OECD Fixed (Wired) Broadband Penetration (per 100 Inhabitants) Net Increase June 2010–2011, by Country." [www.oecd.org/document/54/0,3343,en_2649_34225_38690102 _1_1_1_1,00.html]. Accessed 2012b.

Orr, David. Private email message to Carolyn J. Lukensmeyer, Feb. 2, 2012.

Orszag, P. "Memorandum for the Heads of Executive Departments and Agencies, SUBJECT: Open Government Directive, M-10-06." [http://www.whitehouse.gov/sites/default/files/omb/assets /memoranda_2010/m10-06.pdf]. Dec. 8, 2009.

Panopoulou, E., Tambouris, E., and Tarabanis, K. "eParticipation Initiatives: How Is Europe Progressing?" *European Journal of ePractice*, 7, 15–26, Mar. 2009.

Pariser, E. *The Filter Bubble: What the Internet Is Hiding from You.* New York: Penguin Press, 2011.

Parker, A. "For Federal Employees, a Feeling of Being Targets in the Budget Wars." *New York Times.* [www.nytimes.com/2010/12/06 /us/06federal.html?_r=1&partner=rss&emc=rss]. Dec. 2011.

Parker, K. "Whispering Campaigns Can Take Flight in New Media." *Washington Post.* [http://www.washingtonpost.com/opinions/whispering-campaigns-can-take-flight-in-new-media/2012/04/10/gIQA7tr78S _story.html]. Apr. 2012.

Participatory Budgeting Project. "History of Participatory Budgeting." [www.participatorybudgeting.org/]. Accessed 2012.

Partnership for Public Service. "2011 Finalist—Citizen Services Medal." [http://servicetoamericamedals.org/SAM/finalists11/csm /braunstein.shtml]. Accessed 2012.

Pew Research Center for the People & the Press. *Distrust, Discontent, Anger and Partisan Rancor: The People and Their Government.* Washington, DC: Pew Research Center for the People & the Press, 2010.

Potapchuk, W. R. "Neighborhood Action Initiative: Engaging Citizens in Real Change." In David D. Chrislip (ed.), *The Collaborative Leadership Fieldbook.* San Francisco: Jossey-Bass, 2002.

Putnam, R. *Bowling Alone: The Collapse and Revival of American Community.* New York: Simon and Schuster, 2000.

Reardon, M. "The Price of Universal Broadband." *CNET.* [http://news.cnet.com/8301-30686_3-10364590-266.html?tag=mncol;txt]. Sept. 2009.

Reeder, F. S., Balutis, A. P., Christopherson, G. A., Lyles, C. A., and Payton, S. *A National Dialogue on Health Information Technology and Privacy.* Washington, DC: National Academy of Public Administration, 2009.

Ren, P. "Table 1, Place of Birth for the United States and Puerto Rico by Region and State: 2010." *Lifetime Mobility in the United States: 2010.* ACSBR/10-07. [www.census.gov/prod/2011pubs/acsbr 10–07.pdf]. Nov. 2011.

Richardson, Neil. Private email message to Wendy Jacobson, Jan. 11, 2012.

Rigamer, G. *New Orleans: One Year After Katrina.* New Orleans, LA: GCR & Associates, 2006.

Rivlin, S., and Rivlin, A. "Public Opinion on Health Care Reform 1993 and 2009. Is This a New Day or Just Groundhog Day?" *Pollster.com: Articles and Analysis.* [www.pollster.com/blogs/rivlin_rivlin_public _opinion_o.php]. Mar. 2009.

Robertson, Le'Kedra. Private email message to Wendy Jacobson, Oct. 15, 2010.

Rodriguez, Yolanda. Personal communication with Carolyn J. Lukensmeyer. Apr. 2, 2012.

Romano, A. "How Dumb Are We?" *The Daily Beast.* [http://www .thedailybeast.com/newsweek/2011/03/20/how-dumb-are -we.html]. Mar. 2011.

Roosevelt, T. "The Man in the Arena: Citizenship in a Republic." *Almanac of Theodore Roosevelt.* [http://www.theodore -roosevelt.com/images/research/speeches/maninthearena.pdf]. Apr. 1910.

Rutledge, D. (ed.), *Do You Know What It Means to Miss New Orleans? A Collection of Stories and Essays Set in the Big Easy.* Seattle: Chin Music Press, 2006.

Saad, L. "Americans Express Historic Negativity Toward U.S. Government: Several Long-Term Gallup Trends at or Near Historical Lows." [www.gallup.com/poll/149678/americans -express-historic-negativity-toward-government.aspx]. Sept. 2011.

Salant, J. D., and O'Leary, L. "Six Lobbyists per Lawmaker Work on Health Overhaul." *Bloomberg.* [www.bloomberg.com/apps/news ?pid=newsarchive&sid=aqMce51JoZWw]. Aug. 2009.

Sangha, S. "Putting In Their 2 Cents." *New York Times.* [www.nytimes .com/2012/04/01/nyregion/for-some-new-yorkers-a-grand -experiment-in-participatory-budgeting.html?ref=nyregion]. Mar. 2012.

Sangha, S. "The Voters Speak: Yes to Bathrooms." *New York Times* [www.nytimes.com/2012/04/08/nyregion/voters-speak-in-budget -experiment-saying-yes-to-bathrooms.html?_r=1&scp=1&sq= participatory%20budgeting&st=cse]. Apr. 2012.

Schneider, K. "A Kentucky City Reinvents a Faded Downtown." *New York Times.* [www.nytimes.com/2011/11/16/realestate /commercial/in-owensboro-ky-a-tax-increase-helps-revitalize -downtown.html?_r=2&scp=1&sq=A%20Kentucky%20City%20 Reinvents%20a%20Faded%20Downtown&st=cse]. Nov. 2011.

Schwartz, T. F. "Lincoln Never Said That." *Illinois Historic Preservation Agency.* [http://www.illinoishistory.gov/facsimiles.htm]. Accessed 2012.

Shane, Peter. Private email message to Wendy Jacobson, Nov. 11, 2010.

Simpson, Alan. Private email message to Carolyn J. Lukensmeyer, Apr. 25, 2012.

Singer, N. "Harry and Louise Return, with a New Message." *New York Times.* [www.nytimes.com/2009/07/17/business/media /17adco.html?_r=1]. Jul. 2009.

Sirianni, C. *Investing in Democracy: Engaging Citizens in Collaborative Governance.* Washington, DC: Brookings Institution Press, 2009.

Skocpol, T. *Diminished Democracy: From Membership to Management in American Civic Life.* Norman: University of Oklahoma Press, 2004.

Smith, A. "Nearly Half of American Adults Are Smartphone Owners." [www.pewinternet.org/Reports/2012/Smartphone-Update-2012 .aspx]. Mar. 2012.

Snowe, O. J. "Olympia Snowe: Why I'm Leaving the Senate." *Washington Post.* [http://www.washingtonpost.com/opinions /olympia-snowe-why-im-leaving-the-senate/2012/03/01 /gIQApGYZlR_story.html]. Mar. 1, 2012.

Stem, Richard. Private email message to Jesse Sostrin, Mar. 12, 2012.

TEDxSF. "Louie Schwartzberg—Gratitude." [www.youtube.com /watch?v=gXDMoiEkyuQ], Jun. 2011.

Teixeira, R. "Public Opinion Snapshot: Health Care Reform Still Popular." [www.americanprogress.org/issues/2009/08/opinion 080309.html]. Aug. 2009.

Tempest Williams, T. "Commencement." *The Open Space of Democracy.* Great Barrington, MA: The Orion Society, 2004.

Thomas, H. *Front Row at the White House: My Life and Times.* New York: Scribner, 2000.

Thomas Jefferson to William Charles Jarvis, September 28, 1820. *The Thomas Jefferson Papers Series 1: General Correspondence. 1651–1827.* [http://hdl.loc.gov/loc.mss/mtj.mtjbib023901]. Accessed August 2012.

Treasury Board of Canada Secretariat. "What Are the 10 Elements of MAF?" [www.tbs-sct.gc.ca/maf-crg/overview-apercu/elements-eng .asp]. Jun. 2011.

Triplett, Vera. Private email message to Carolyn J. Lukensmeyer, Jan. 20, 2012.

Tuutti, C. "Government Stars Rock the House at FedTalks 2011." *Federal Daily, Management Watch.* [http://federaldaily.com/blogs /management-matters/2011/10/government-rock-stars-at-fedtalks.aspx]. Oct. 2011.

Twitchell, Keith. Private email message to Wendy Jacobson, Jan. 18, 2012.

Ullner, J. "Proud to Serve: It's Time to Stop Bashing Federal Employees." *Washington Post.* [http://www.washingtonpost.com /opinions/i-work-for-uncle-sam-and-im-proud-of-it/2012/02/14 /gIQAVDcdcR_story.html]. Feb. 29, 2012.

United Nations General Assembly Human Rights Council. *Report of the Special Rapporteur on the promotion and protection of the right to freedom of opinion and expression, Frank La Rue.* Seventeenth session, Agenda item 3, A/HRC/17/27, May 2011.

U.S. Census Bureau. "Selected Population Profile in the United States: 2005 American Community Survey." [http://factfinder2.census .gov/faces/tableservices/jsf/pages/productview.xhtml?pid=ACS _05_EST_S0201&prodType=table]. Accessed 2012.

U.S. Department of Health and Human Services (HHS). *HHS Pandemic Influenza Plan.* Washington, DC: U.S. Department of Health and Human Services, 2005.

U.S. Department of Health and Human Services (HHS). "HHS and DHS Announce Guidance on Pandemic Vaccination Allocation." [www.hhs.gov/news/press/2008pres/07/20080723a.html]. Jul. 2008.

U.S. Environmental Protection Agency (EPA). "It's Our Environment: About." *Greenversations.* [http://blog.epa.gov/blog/about/]. Accessed 2012.

U.S. General Services Administration. "Federal Advisory Committee Act (FACA) Management Overview." [www.gsa.gov/portal /content/104514]. Accessed 2012.

Voorhees, Jeff. Private email message to Carolyn J. Lukensmeyer, Jan. 21, 2012.

Wang, T., and Severson, G. "Beetles and Collaboration." Northwest Colorado Council of Governments. [http://www.nwccog.org /docs/cbbc/beetles_and_collaboration.pdf]. Nov. 1, 2007.

Warburton, D. *An Evaluation of Your Health, Your Care, Your Say.* London: U.K. Department of Health, Jul. 2006.

Weick, K. E., and Sutcliffe, K. M. *Managing the Unexpected: Resilient Performance in an Age of Uncertainty.* San Francisco: Jossey-Bass, 2007.

Weiss, Daniel J. Private email message to Wendy Jacobson, Feb. 17, 2012.

Williams, Anthony. Personal communication with Carolyn Lukensmeyer. Apr. 2, 2012.

Williamson, A. "Citizen Participation in the Unified New Orleans Plan." Unpublished doctoral dissertation. Cambridge, MA: Kennedy School of Government, Harvard University, 2007.

Wilson, P. A., Padgett, J. D., and Wallace, J. *New Orleans Community Congress II: Towards the Next Era of Participatory Democracy.* Washington, DC: AmericaSpeaks, 2007.

Wortham, J. "With Twitter, Blackouts and Demonstrations, Web Flexes Its Muscle." *New York Times.* [www.nytimes.com/2012 /01/19/technology/protests-of-antipiracy-bills-unite-web.html? _r=3]. Jan. 2012.

Yankelovich, D. *Coming to Public Judgment: Making Democracy Work in a Complex World.* Syracuse, NY: Syracuse University Press, 1991.

Yankelovich, D. *The Magic of Dialogue: Transforming Conflict into Cooperation.* New York: Touchstone, 2001.

Zernike, K. "George Gallup Jr., of Polling Family, Dies at 81." *New York Times* [www.nytimes.com/2011/11/23/us/george-gallup-jr-of -polling-family-dies-at-81.html?_r=1]. Nov. 2011.

BIBLIOGRAPHY

Life experience and reading have been among the cornerstones of my personal and professional development. It is in this spirit that I share with readers the most complete bibliography I can reconstruct, relevant to the work presented in this book. I am sure there are many titles missing. Ideally, something included here will inspire you to challenge your thinking as well.

CONTEMPORARY CRITIQUES OF DEMOCRACY AND POLITICS

Broder, D. S. *Democracy Derailed: Initiative Campaigns and the Power of Money.* San Diego, CA: Harcourt, 2000.

Edwards, M. *The Parties Versus the People: How to Turn Republicans and Democrats into Americans.* New Haven, CT: Yale University Press, 2012.

Edwards, M. *Reclaiming Conservatism: How a Great American Political Movement Got Lost—and How It Can Find Its Way Back.* New York: Oxford University Press, 2008.

Gerzon, M. *A House Divided: Six Belief Systems Struggling for America's Soul.* New York: Jeremy P. Tarcher/Putnam, 1996.

Greider, W. *Who Will Tell the People? The Betrayal of American Democracy.* New York: Simon & Schuster, 1992.

Johnson, H., and Broder, D. S. *The System: The American Way of Politics at the Breaking Point.* Boston: Little, Brown, 1996.

Mann, T. E., and Ornstein, N. J. *It's Even Worse Than It Looks: How the American Constitutional System Collided with the New Politics of Extremism.* New York: Basic Books, 2012.

Mann, T. E., and Ornstein, N. J. *The Broken Branch: How Congress Is Failing America and How to Get It Back on Track.* New York: Oxford University Press, 2008.

McWilliams, W. C. *Redeeming Democracy in America.* Lawrence: University Press of Kansas, 2011.

Rauch, J. *Demosclerosis: The Silent Killer of American Government.* New York: Times Books, 1994.

Wolfe, A. *Does American Democracy Still Work?* New Haven, CT: Yale University Press, 2006.

DELIBERATIVE DEMOCRACY: RESEARCH, THEORY, AND PRACTICE

Barber, B. R. *Strong Democracy: Participatory Politics for a New Age.* Berkeley: University of California Press, 1984.

Barber, B. R. *A Place for Us: How to Make Society Civil and Democracy Strong.* New York: Hill and Wang, 1998.

Becker, T., and Slaton, C. D. *The Future of Teledemocracy.* Westport, CT: Praeger, 2000.

Bryan, F. M. *Real Democracy: The New England Town Meeting and How It Works.* Chicago: University of Chicago Press, 2004.

Buss, T. F., Redburn, F. S., and Guo, K., eds. *Modernizing Democracy: Innovations in Citizen Participation.* Armonk, NY: M. E. Sharpe, 2006.

Crosby, N. *Healthy Democracy: Empowering a Clear and Informed Voice of the People.* Edina, MN: Beaver's Pond Press, 2003.

Dowlen, O. *Sorted: Civic Lotteries and the Future of Public Participation.* Toronto: MASS LBP, 2008.

Dryzek, J. S. *Deliberative Democracy and Beyond: Liberals, Critics, Contestations.* New York: Oxford University Press, 2000.

Duval, J. *Next Generation Democracy: What the Open-Source Revolution Means for Power, Politics, and Change.* New York: Bloomsbury, 2010.

Elster, J., ed. *Deliberative Democracy.* Cambridge, UK: Cambridge University Press, 1998.

Engaging with Impact: Targets and Indicators for Successful Community Engagement by Ontario's Local Health Integration Networks—a Citizens' Report from Kingston, Richmond Hill and Thunder Bay. Toronto: MASS LBP, 2009.

Fishkin, J. S. *Democracy and Deliberation: New Directions for Democratic Reform.* New Haven, CT: Yale University Press, 1991.

Fishkin, J. S. *The Voice of the People: Public Opinion and Democracy.* New Haven, CT: Yale University Press, 1995.

Fung, A., and Wright, E. O. *Deepening Democracy: Institutional Innovations in Empowered Participatory Governance.* London: Verso, 2003.

Gastil, J. *By Popular Demand: Revitalizing Representative Democracy Through Deliberative Elections.* Berkeley: University of California Press, 2000.

Gastil, J. *Political Communication and Deliberation.* Thousand Oaks, CA: Sage, 2008.

Gastil, J., Deess, E. P., Weiser, P. J., and Simmons, C. *The Jury and Democracy: How Jury Deliberation Promotes Civic Engagement and Political Participation.* New York: Oxford University Press, 2010.

Gastil, J., and Levine, P., eds. *The Deliberative Democracy Handbook: Strategies for Effective Civic Engagement in the Twenty-First Century.* San Francisco: Jossey-Bass, 2005.

Jacobs, L. R., Cook, F. L., and Delli Carpini, M. X. *Talking Together: Public Deliberation and Political Participation in America.* Chicago: University of Chicago Press, 2009.

Kay, A. F. *Locating Consensus for Democracy: A Ten-Year U.S. Experiment.* Augustine, FL: Americans Talk Issues Foundation, 1998.

Leib, E. J. *Deliberative Democracy in America: A Proposal for a Popular Branch of Government.* University Park: Pennsylvania State University Press, 2004.

Leighninger, M. *The Next Form of Democracy: How Expert Rule Is Giving Way to Shared Governance—and Why Politics Will Never Be the Same.* Nashville, TN: Vanderbilt University Press, 2006.

Mansbridge, J. J. *Beyond Adversary Democracy.* Chicago: University of Chicago Press, 1983.

Phillips, C. *Constitution Café: Jefferson's Brew for a True Revolution.* New York: W. W. Norton, 2011.

Polletta, F. *Freedom Is an Endless Meeting: Democracy in American Social Movements.* Chicago: University of Chicago Press, 2002.

Rough, J. *Society's Breakthrough! Releasing Essential Wisdom and Virtue in All the People.* Bloomington, IN: 1stBooks Library, 2002.

Sirianni, C. *Investing in Democracy: Engaging Citizens in Collaborative Governance.* Washington, DC: Brookings Institution Press, 2009.

Skocpol, T., and Fiorina, M. P., eds. *Civic Engagement in American Democracy.* Washington, DC: Brookings Institution Press, 1999.

Yankelovich, D. *Coming to Public Judgment: Making Democracy Work in a Complex World.* Syracuse, NY: Syracuse University Press, 1991.

DEMOCRATIC THEORY AND PRACTICE

Chickering, A. L. *Beyond Left and Right: Breaking the Political Stalemate.* San Francisco: Institute for Contemporary Studies Press, 1993.

Dahl, R. A. *On Democracy.* New Haven, CT: Yale University Press, 2000.

Dunn, J., ed. *Democracy: The Unfinished Journey, 508 BC to AD 1993.* New York: Oxford University Press, 1993.

Elshtain, J. B. *Democracy on Trial.* New York: Basic Books, 1995.

Follett, M. P. *Creative Experience.* 1924. New York: Peter Smith, 1951.

Follett, M. P. *The New State: Group Organization the Solution of Popular Government.* London: Longmans, Green, 1920.

Fullinwider, R. K., ed. *Civil Society, Democracy, and Civic Renewal.* Lanham, MD: Rowman & Littlefield, 1999.

Gutmann, A., and Thompson, D. *Democracy and Disagreement: Why Moral Conflict Cannot Be Avoided in Politics, and What Should Be Done About It.* Cambridge, MA: Belknap Press, 1996.

Heclo, H. *On Thinking Institutionally.* Boulder, CO: Paradigm, 2008.

Herbst, S. *Politics at the Margin: Historical Studies of Public Expression Outside the Mainstream.* New York: Cambridge University Press, 1994.

Ostrom, E. *Governing the Commons: The Evolution of Institutions for Collective Action.* Cambridge, UK: Cambridge University Press, 1990.

Posner, R. A. *Law, Pragmatism, and Democracy.* Cambridge, MA: Harvard University Press, 2003.

Putnam, R. D. *Making Democracy Work: Civic Traditions in Modern Italy.* Princeton, NJ: Princeton University Press, 1993.

Putnam, R. D. *Bowling Alone: The Collapse and Revival of American Community.* New York: Simon & Schuster, 2000.

Rosenthal, A., Loomis, B. A., Hibbing, J. R., and Kurtz, K. T. *Republic on Trial: The Case for Representative Democracy.* Washington, DC: CQ Press, 2003.

Sennett, R. *Together: The Rituals, Pleasures and Politics of Cooperation.* New Haven, CT: Yale University Press, 2012.

Sloterdijk, P. *Critique of Cynical Reason.* Minneapolis: University of Minnesota Press, 1987.

DIGITAL DEMOCRACY

Barabási, A. L. *Linked: The New Science of Networks.* Cambridge, MA: Perseus, 2002.

Davis, S., Elin, L., and Reeher, G. *Click On Democracy: The Internet's Power to Change Political Apathy into Civic Action.* Boulder, CO: Westview Press, 2002.

Diamond, E., and Silverman, R. A. *White House to Your House: Media and Politics in Virtual America.* Cambridge, MA: MIT Press, 1995.

Fountain, J. E. *Building the Virtual State: Information Technology and Institutional Change.* Washington, DC: Brookings Institution Press, 2001.

Grossman, L. K. *The Electronic Republic: Reshaping Democracy in the Information Age.* New York: Viking Press, 1995.

Grossman, L. K., and Minow, N. N. *A Digital Gift to the Nation: Fulfilling the Promise of the Digital and Internet Age.* New York: Century Foundation Press, 2001.

Hindman, M. *The Myth of Digital Democracy.* Princeton, NJ: Princeton University Press, 2009.

Kamarck, E. C., and Nye, J. S., eds. *Democracy.com? Governance in a Networked World.* Hollis, NH: Hollis, 1999.

Noveck, B. S. *Wiki Government: How Technology Can Make Government Better, Democracy Stronger, and Citizens More Powerful.* Washington, DC: Brookings Institution Press, 2009.

Pariser, E. *The Filter Bubble: What the Internet Is Hiding from You.* New York: Penguin Press, 2011.

Powers, W. *Hamlet's Blackberry: Building a Good Life in the Digital Age.* New York: Harper Perennial, 2011.

Rash, W. *Politics on the Nets: Wiring the Political Process.* New York: W. H. Freeman, 1997.

Rheingold, H. *The Virtual Community: Homesteading on the Electronic Frontier.* Cambridge, MA: MIT Press, 2000.

Shane, P. M., ed. *Democracy Online: The Prospects for Political Renewal Through the Internet.* New York: Routledge, 2004.

Sunstein, C. *Republic.com.* Princeton, NJ: Princeton University Press, 2001.

Tapscott, D., and Williams, A. D. *Wikinomics: How Mass Collaboration Changes Everything.* New York: Portfolio, 2006.

Wilhelm, A. G. *Democracy in the Digital Age: Challenges to Political Life in Cyberspace.* New York: Routledge, 2000.

GENERATIONS, GEOGRAPHY, DEMOGRAPHICS, AND CULTURE

Bishop, B. *The Big Sort: Why the Clustering of Like-Minded America Is Tearing Us Apart.* Boston: Houghton Mifflin, 2008.

Chinni, D., and Gimpel, J. *Our Patchwork Nation: The Surprising Truth About the "Real" America.* New York: Gotham Books, 2010.

Garreau, J. *The Nine Nations of North America.* Boston: Houghton Mifflin, 1981.

Strauss, W., and Howe, N. *Generations: The History of America's Future, 1584–2069.* New York: William Morrow, 1991.

Winograd, M., and Hais, M. D. *Millennial Momentum: How a New Generation Is Remaking America.* New Brunswick, NJ: Rutgers University Press, 2011.

Woodard, C. *American Nations: A History of the Eleven Rival Regional Cultures of North America.* New York: Viking Press, 2011.

HISTORICAL PERSPECTIVES: FOUNDING FATHERS

Bailyn, B. *To Begin the World Anew: The Genius and Ambiguities of the American Founders.* New York: Alfred A. Knopf, 2003.

Ferling, J. *A Leap in the Dark: A Struggle to Create the American Republic.* New York: Oxford University Press, 2003.

Kiernan, D., and D'Agnese, J. *Signing Their Lives Away: The Fame and Misfortune of the Men Who Signed the Declaration of Independence.* Philadelphia: Quirk Books, 2009.

Needleman, J. *The American Soul: Rediscovering the Wisdom of the Founders.* New York: Jeremy P. Tarcher/Putnam, 2003.

Padover, S. K., ed. *Thomas Jefferson on Democracy.* New York: Mentor Books, 1939.

Wilentz, S. *The Rise of American Democracy: Jefferson to Lincoln.* New York: W. W. Norton, 2005.

HISTORICAL PERSPECTIVES: INFORMED CITIZENS AND SELF-GOVERNANCE

Brown, R. D. *The Strength of a People: The Idea of an Informed Citizenry in America, 1650–1870.* Chapel Hill, NC: University of Chapel Hill Press, 1996.

Morone, J. A. *The Democratic Wish: Popular Participation and the Limits of American Government.* New York: Basic Books, 1990.

Wiebe, R. H. *Self-Rule: A Cultural History of American Democracy.* Chicago: University of Chicago Press, 1995.

HISTORICAL PERSPECTIVES: NATIVE AMERICAN CONTRIBUTIONS TO OUR SYSTEM OF GOVERNMENT

Barreiro, J., ed. *Indian Roots of American Democracy.* Ithaca, NY: Akwe:kon Press, 1992.

Johansen, B. E. *Forgotten Founders: How the American Indian Helped Shape Democracy.* Boston: Harvard Common Press, 1982.

Wallace, P.A.W. *The White Roots of Peace.* 1946. Saranac Lake, NY: Chauncy Press, 1986.

HOW GOVERNMENT WORKS

Bok, D. *The Trouble with Government.* Cambridge, MA: Harvard University Press, 2001.

Eggers, W. D., and O'Leary, J. *If We Can Put a Man on the Moon . . . Getting Big Things Done in Government.* Boston: Harvard Business Press, 2009.

Hibbing, J. R., and Theiss-Morse, E. *Stealth Democracy: Americans' Beliefs About How Government Should Work.* Cambridge, UK: Cambridge University Press, 2002.

King, C. S., and Stivers, C. *Government Is Us: Public Administration in an Anti-Government Era.* Thousand Oaks, CA: Sage, 1998.

Morse, R. S., Buss, T. F., and Kinghorn, C. M., eds. *Transforming Public Leadership for the 21st Century.* Armonk, NY: M.E. Sharpe, 2007.

Salamon, L. M., ed. *The Tools of Government: A Guide to the New Governance.* New York: Oxford University Press, 2002.

Troxel, J. P., ed. *Government Works: Profiles of People Making a Difference.* Alexandria, VA: Miles River Press, 1995.

INSIGHTS FROM OTHER FIELDS OF INQUIRY

Rosenberg, T. *Join the Club: How Peer Pressure Can Transform the World.* New York: W. W. Norton, 2011.

Thaler, R. H., and Sunstein, C. R. Nudge: *Improving Decisions About Health, Wealth, and Happiness.* New York: Penguin Books, 2009.

Vedantam, S. *The Hidden Brain: How Our Unconscious Minds Elect Presidents, Control Markets, Wage Wars, and Save Our Lives.* New York: Spiegel and Grau, 2010.

INTERNATIONAL PERSPECTIVE AND PRACTICE

Beer, S. *Platform for Change.* West Sussex, UK: Wiley, 1975.

Boulding, E. *Building a Global Civic Culture: Education for an Interdependent World.* New York: Teachers College Press, 1988.

European Commission. *Democracy and the Information Society in Europe.* New York: St. Martin's Press, 2000.

Inoguchi, T., Newman, E., and Keane, J., eds. *The Changing Nature of Democracy.* Tokyo: United Nations University Press, 1998.

Knight, B., Chigudu, H., and Tandon, R. *Reviving Democracy: Citizens at the Heart of Governance.* London: Earthscan, 2002.

Manji, I. *Risking Utopia: On the Edge of a New Democracy.* Vancouver: Douglas & McIntyre, 1997.

Myers, S., ed. *The Democracy Reader.* New York: International Debate Education Association, 2002.

Selee, A., and Peruzzotti, E., eds. *Participatory Innovation and Representative Democracy in Latin America.* Washington, DC: Woodrow Wilson Center Press, 2009.

Shark, A. R., and Toporkoff, S., eds. *Beyond e-Government and e-Democracy: A Global Perspective.* Washington, DC: Public Technology Institute/ITEMS International, 2008.

Troxel, J. P., ed. *Participation Works: Business Cases from Around the World.* Alexandria, VA: Miles River Press, 1993.

Valadez, J. M. *Deliberative Democracy, Political Legitimacy, and Self-Determination in Multicultural Societies.* Boulder, CO: Westview Press, 2001.

THE MEDIA

Fallows, J. *Breaking the News: How the Media Undermine American Democracy.* New York: Pantheon Books, 1996.

Jones, A. S. *Losing the News: The Future of the News That Feeds Democracy.* New York: Oxford University Press, 2009.

Ladd, J. M. *Why Americans Hate the Media and How It Matters.* Princeton, NJ: Princeton University Press, 2012.

McChesney, R. W. *Rich Media, Poor Democracy: Communication Politics in Dubious Times.* New York: New Press, 1999.

Patterson, T. E. *Out of Order: An Incisive and Boldly Original Critique of the News Media's Domination of America's Political Process.* New York: Vintage Books, 1994.

Rosen, J. *What Are Journalists For?* New Haven, CT: Yale University Press, 1999.

NEW ORLEANS

Horner, J. *Breach of Faith: Hurricane Katrina and the Near Death of a Great American City.* New York: Random House, 2006.

Olshansky, R. B., and Johnson, L. A. *Clear as Mud: Planning for the Rebuilding of New Orleans.* Chicago: American Planning Association (Planners Press), 2010.

Piazza, T. *Why New Orleans Matters.* New York: HarperCollins, 2005.

Rutledge, D., ed. *Do You Know What It Means to Miss New Orleans? A Collection of Stories and Essays Set in the Big Easy.* Seattle: Chin Music Press, 2006.

NEW YORK CITY POST-9/11

Goldberger, P. *Up from Zero: Politics, Architecture, and the Rebuilding of New York*. New York: Random House, 2004.

Williams, R. *Writing in the Dust: After September 11*. Grand Rapids, MI: William B. Eerdmans, 2002.

REVITALIZING DEMOCRACY AND CIVIL SOCIETY: THEORY, PRACTICE, AND PROPOSALS

Bellah, R. N., Madsen, R., Sullivan, W. M., Swidler, A., and Tipton, S. M. *Habits of the Heart: Individualism and Commitment in American Life*. Berkeley: University of California Press, 1985.

Boren, D. *A Letter to America*. Norman: University of Oklahoma Press, 2008.

Breyer, S. *Active Liberty: Interpreting Our Democratic Constitution*. New York: Alfred A. Knopf, 2005.

Eberly, D. E, ed. *Building a Community of Citizens: Civil Society in the 21st Century*. Lanham, MD: University Press of America, 1994.

Eberly, D. E. *Restoring the Good Society: A New Vision for Politics and Culture*. Grand Rapids, MI: Baker Books, 1994.

Fineman, H. *The Thirteen American Arguments: Enduring Debates That Define and Inspire Our Country*. New York: Random House, 2008.

Hessel, S. *Time for Outrage*. (M. Duvert, trans.). New York: Twelve, 2011.

Hill, S. *10 Steps to Repair American Democracy*. Sausalito, CA: PoliPointPress, 2006.

Hirsch, E. D. *The Making of Americans: Democracy and Our Schools*. New Haven, CT: Yale University Press, 2009.

Kemmis, D. *Community and the Politics of Place*. Norman: University of Oklahoma Press, 1992.

Kemmis, D. *The Good City and the Good Life*. Boston: Houghton Mifflin, 1995.

Lappé, F. M. *Democracy's Edge: Choosing to Save Our Country by Bringing Democracy to Life*. San Francisco: Jossey-Bass, 2006.

Lappé, F. M. *Getting a Grip 2: Clarity, Creativity and Courage for the World We Really Want*. Cambridge, MA: Small Planet Media, 2007.

Levine, P. *The Future of Democracy: Developing the Next Generation of American Citizens*. Medford, MA: Tufts University Press, 2007.

Liu, E., and Hanauer, N. *The Gardens of Democracy: A New American Story of Citizenship, the Economy, and the Role of Government*. Seattle: Sasquatch Books, 2011.

Mathews, D. *For Communities to Work.* Dayton, OH: Kettering
    Foundation Press, 2002.
Mathews, D. *Reclaiming Public Education by Reclaiming Our Democracy.*
    Dayton, OH: Kettering Foundation Press, 2006.
Purdy, J. *For Common Things: Irony, Trust, and Commitment in America
    Today.* New York: Vintage Books, 2000.
Williams, T. T. *The Open Space of Democracy.* Great Barrington, MA:
    Orion Society, 2004.

VOTING AND POLITICS

Crenson, M. A., and Ginsberg, B. *Downsizing Democracy: How America
    Sidelined Its Citizens and Privatized Its Public.* Baltimore: Johns
    Hopkins University Press, 2002.
Hacker, J. S., and Pierson, P. *Winner-Take-All Politics: How Washington
    Made the Rich Richer—and Turned Its Back on the Middle Class.* New
    York: Simon & Schuster, 2010.
Patterson, T. E. *The Vanishing Voter: Public Involvement in the Age of
    Uncertainty.* New York: Alfred A. Knopf, 2002.
Piven, F., and Cloward, R. A. *Why Americans Still Don't Vote: And Why
    Politicians Want It That Way.* Boston: Beacon Press, 2000.

ACKNOWLEDGMENTS

As a prolific reader, I have often marveled at the acknowledgments sections of books. How could the author possibly be indebted to so many people and be clear about what each contributed?

Now I know.

This book could not have been written without the support and contributions of so many generous and gifted people. And the work described in the book would never have come to be without the passion and effort of so many dedicated and talented individuals.

Over the years many people, more than I could name here, have urged me to write about America*Speaks*'s work and share stories that might be an inspiration to others to get involved. But two stand out who must be named. The first is Jody Telfair, a dear friend and colleague of thirty years, who has never wavered in her belief that my voice should be read as well as heard. Her conviction kept me going when mine was wavering.

The second is Jesse Sostrin, a friend and colleague in the America*Speaks* network, who gave me the gift of "retreating" with me for three days to a cabin in the wilds of West Virginia in March 2009 to clarify my vision for the book and set up a structure in an already overcommitted life to make it happen. The journey from there to here has been very different from what we imagined that weekend. But I made the commitment, and Jesse has been there to do whatever needed to be done to help me cross the finish line.

As a first time book author, I am most indebted Dangling, and needs a subject, to the person without whom this book truly could not and would not have been written: Wendy Jacobson. Wendy has written many documents for America*Speaks* and knows our work well. I have been blessed across the course of my career to have experienced many profound collaborations—times when I have known that what has been produced is a whole that is larger than the sum of its parts. That has been the case with *Bringing Citizen Voices to the Table.* Wendy has worked tirelessly to take my ideas and drafts and craft them into a narrative that preserves my voice and improves the writing. I owe a huge debt of gratitude to Wendy.

A special thanks to Lars Hasselblad Torres and David Stern for editing and strengthening the chapter on online engagement. Any skepticism readers may detect concerning online engagement's ability to strengthen collective citizen voice in decision making is entirely my own.

Mark Abramson, Peter Levine, and Jeff Voorhees all made major editorial contributions that improved both the structure of the book and its syntax, and I am very grateful for their guidance.

I also received valuable edits from Lyman Orton, the Board Chair of the Orton Family Foundation; Dan Prock, an organization development consultant; and Don Zauderer, professor of public administration at American University.

A very special thanks to each of the current and former federal managers who provided interviews and case studies for this book, sharing best practices and lessons learned on effective citizen engagement that is linked to decision making: Jane Berkow, Roger Bernier, Deb Dalton, Tony Faast, Olivia Ferriter, Bruce Gilbert, David Kuehn, Patricia Milligan, Therese McMillan, Rich Kuhlman, and Richard Stem.

Key members of the America*Speaks* project teams as well as client partners were essential in providing important data and stories about the America*Speaks* cases represented in the book. Many thanks to Rodney Berry, Theo Brown, Tom Campbell, Daniel Clark, Janet Fiero, Sue Lacy, Shelly Nichols, Neil Richardson, and Le'Kedra Robertson.

Because the primary audience for the book is public managers, it was very important for me to have the benefit of the editorial eye of people with that experience. I am indebted in this regard to several career public servants whom I am fortunate enough to also count as close colleagues and friends. Jane Berkow, Mark Funkhauser, Ron Redmon, and Margaret Yao were kind enough to read the book from cover to cover and sharpen its insights and language.

Eric Diters, my executive assistant, ably served as the primary researcher for the book while gracefully carrying out all of his other duties. Setting out on this journey, I could not have imagined the volume of detailed work necessary to turn a complete draft manuscript into a "book" ready for the publisher's editorial team. The permissions, licenses, photos, and so on, were also a result of Eric's tireless, unerring work.

Elana Goldstein, the newest member of the America*Speaks* team, did the groundwork for Appendix B on organizations and networks, and she turned the piles of books in my office and library into the bibliography.

This book could not have been completed without the generous financial support of the following foundations and individuals: the Nathan Cummings Foundation, the Public Life Foundation, the Vermont Community Foundation, the Whitman Institute, Grant Abert, Michael Berman, Laura and Richard Chasen, Carl Haefling and Pam Johnson, Ed and Sonia Nevis, Cynthia and Leo O'Harris, Lyman Orton, Norm Rice, Ernie Urquhart, and George Vradenburg.

Finally, a very special thank you to the current America*Speaks* team, who had my back and made it possible for me to carve out the time to finish this book.

And now to the citizen engagement work itself . . .

The body of work presented in this book is the creation of many people over almost two decades. The original vision and blueprint for the implementation of America*Speaks*'s model for citizen engagement linked to government decision making were mine. Its evolution and current capabilities are the result of the creativity and dedication of the talented and committed people with whom I have been honored to collaborate at America*Speaks*. I am often asked how I can continue to bring the energy and enthusiasm that I do to this work. The answer is simple and clear: the people with whom I have been and am blessed to work.

There are a few members of the America*Speaks* staff and associates to be highlighted for their extraordinary contributions to the breakthroughs in, and evolution of, our work: Steve Brigham,

Ashley Boyd, Janet Fiero, Joe Goldman, Susanna Haas-Lyons, Lars Hasselblad-Torres, and Daniel Stone.

Current and former staff members at America*Speaks* are and have been passionately committed to citizen voices being at the center of governance and have contributed to the high standards to which we hold ourselves in doing our work. We have made the road by walking, and I am deeply appreciative of everyone's contributions over the years. Thank you to each and every one of you from the bottom of my heart for helping to make my vision a reality: Sujeet Ahluwalia, David Anstett, Marianne Bottiglieri, Alayna Buckner, Josh Chernila, Daniel Clark, Erzuile Coquillon, Mary Lauran Crary-Hall, Holly Davis, Dianna Dauber, Eric Diters, Cara Elkins, Brian Foyer, Elana Goldstein, Andress Green, Megan Hamilton, Hala Harik Hayes, Kecia Jackson, George Koch, Janice Kruger, Melvin Moore, Darrick Nicholas, Evan Paul, Audra Polk, Michael Ravvin, Jeff Rohrlick, Andrea Scallon, Julie Segal-Walters, Kim Sescoe, Anne Shoup, David Stern, Elizabeth Stoops-Johnson, Ron Thomas, Roberta Travis, Stefan Voinea, Irene Wairimu, and Elizabeth White.

America*Speaks* could not deliver its large-scale projects without the dedicated professionals in our Associates Network, each of whom was involved in one or more of the major cases shared in this book. Every one of these people is passionate about the transformation of American democracy: Diane Altman Dautoff, Frances Baldwin, Ann Begler, Deanna Berg, Jane Berkow, Juanita Boyd-Hardy, Theo Brown, Tom Campbell, David Campt, Mary Cogan, Katherine Curran, Shelley Durfee, Don Edwards, Bernardo Ferdman, Ka Flewellen, Katie Fry, Scott Gassman, Laura Gramling, Dedoceo Habi, Jonno Hanafin, Mattice Haynes, Damon Hemmerdinger, Peter Hyson, Stephen Jenks, Gregory Keidan, Bob Kolodny, Sue Lacy, Matt Larson, Becca Lewis, Harold Massey, Jacqueline McLemore, Hubert Morgan, Shelly Nichols, Steven Ober, Anita Perez-Ferguson, Linda Perkins, William Potapchuk, Ruthann Prange, George Reed, Le'Kedra Robertson, Tracy Russ, Diane Schwartz, Sally Sparhawk, Benjamin Stephens, Elizabeth Stoops-Johnson, Clare Stroud, Julia Sullivan, Elizabeth White, Vickey Wilcher, Jennifer Wilding, Gary Willoughby, Jennifer Wright, and William Zybach.

Equally important, and at the heart of our work with the public, are the six-thousand-plus professional process facilitators in the America*Speaks* Facilitators Network. Every time we do a 21st Century Town Meeting, each table is supported by a VOLUN- TEER table facilitator who ensures a safe, democratic space for everyone at the table. I am humbled whenever I think of the gift these people give to our democracy. America*Speaks* could not do its work without their generosity and commitment.

America*Speaks* would be unable to do its large-scale work in so many locations simultaneously without the technology and production members of our team. Special thanks to Lenny Lind, Todd Erickson, Josh Kaufman, Karl Danskin, Christian Saucedo, and Laura Gramling of Co-Vision; Mike Smith of One Counts; and Constance Chatfield-Taylor, Lynn Hanford, and Erin Murphy of Flying Colors.

Anyone who leads a nonprofit organization in our country knows that there are times when you have to have a strong advo- cate in your corner to get done what needs to be done. I would especially like to thank Bill Hauck, Stephen Heintz, Damon Hem- merdinger, Don Kellerman, Sterling Spiern, and David Walker for believing in me and in America*Speaks*'s ability to make sure citizen voices would be heard when it mattered most.

A special thank you to colleagues in the field of deliberative democracy, too numerous to list here, who have been cocon- spirators at so many points along the way—and who believe as passionately as I do that there is a nascent, broad-based democ- racy reform movement yet to be ignited across this country.

And, most important, gratitude and great thanks to the found- ing generations of Americans who envisioned, stood up, spoke out, and fought for our freedoms in the revolution that created the United States of America. And to all Americans who know that our democracy is a fragile gift, and who are ready to stand up for a government "of the people, by the people, for the people."

THE AUTHOR

Carolyn J. Lukensmeyer, PhD, is the first Executive Director of the National Institute for Civil Discourse (NICD) at the University of Arizona. NICD is a national advocacy, research, and policy center that seeks to strengthen America's democratic traditions and improve governance and public decision making.

Carolyn founded America*Speaks* in 1995 and served as its President for seventeen years. Under her leadership, the organization earned a national reputation as a leader in the fields of deliberative democracy and democratic renewal and won numerous awards, including two from the International Association for Public Participation, the Organization Development Network's Sharing the Wealth Award, a Housing and Urban Development award for best practices, a distinguished service award for outstanding leadership from the Federal Managers Association, and a best practice award from the National Training Laboratories Institute.

Prior to founding America*Speaks,* Carolyn served as consultant to the White House chief of staff, as the Deputy Director for Management of the National Performance Review, and as Chief of Staff to Governor Dick Celeste of Ohio. Carolyn also led her own successful organizational development and management consulting firm for fourteen years, working with public and private sector organizations on four continents.

Carolyn earned a PhD in organizational and systems behavior from Case Western Reserve University and completed postgraduate training at the Gestalt Institute of Cleveland.

An avid traveler and outdoors adventurer, Carolyn led the first all-women's rafting expedition down the Colorado River, tracked panda bears in the remote Sichuan Province of China, and has trekked in major mountain ranges all over the world. She currently lives in Washington, DC and Damariscotta, Maine.

Wendy Jacobson is a consultant specializing in research, analysis, writing, and editing on a wide range of social policy issues. She has written numerous publications, including many for America-*Speaks* over the last 14 years. Prior to launching a consulting practice, Wendy served as a Special Assistant in the U.S. Department of Health and Human Services, ran the Center on Budget and Policy Priorities' Earned Income Credit Campaign, and was the first Policy Director at Georgians for Children, a statewide child advocacy organization. Wendy has a BA in history from Yale University, an MSW from the University of Georgia, and was a 1997 fellow with the Annie E. Casey Foundation.

BIOGRAPHIES OF PUBLIC MANAGERS WITH CASE STUDIES IN THIS BOOK

Jane Berkow, MS, has had an accomplished career as an organizational development consultant and management development trainer in both the private and public sectors. Since 1994 she has worked as an internal organizational development consultant for the Animal and Plant Health Inspection Service (APHIS) of the U.S. Department of Agriculture. She currently is the lead strategic planner for plant protection and quarantine. In 1996 Jane designed and facilitated the first Future Search conference within the federal government. In 2004 she was involved in providing change management support with the transfer of 2,500 agriculture inspectors to the Department of Homeland Security, for which she received the Secretary of Agriculture's Honor Achievement Award.

Since 1999 Jane has been an associate with America*Speaks*. In 2002 she served as project manager for Listening to the City, which convened 4,500 people from the New York City area to provide input to policymakers on the future of lower Manhattan and Ground Zero. She has served in various other capacities on other America*Speaks* citizen engagement projects.

Jane earned her master's degree in organization development from American University in 1987. She is a member of the National Training Laboratories Institute of Applied Behavioral Science and has served as a practicum adviser and learning community facilitator for the American University master's program in organization development.

Roger Bernier has had a thirty-year career in public health at the local, national, and international levels. Roger obtained his MPH from Yale University in 1974 and his PhD in epidemiology from the Johns Hopkins University in 1978. He served in the Centers for Disease Control and Prevention (CDC) as an Epidemic Intelligence Service Officer, and was assigned to the Division of Immunization, where he has worked as the chief of the Epidemiologic Research Branch, as Associate Director for science, as coordinator of the Infant Immunization Initiative, and most recently as the Senior Adviser for Scientific Strategy and Innovation.

In 2001 Roger requested a special assignment to explore how the CDC could increase public participation in decision making about vaccines. Struck by the polarization between the CDC and some segments of the public, Roger worked to create a new model for engaging unaffiliated citizens as well as representatives of stakeholder organizations. The model's goal was to better inform CDC decision making over the short term and to build trust over the longer term. Since then the model or a modified version of it has been employed successfully multiple times, and the model was the cowinner of the Project of the Year award issued in 2007 by the International Association for Public Participation.

Roger retired from the CDC in July 2010 and is currently adjunct professor in the College of Public Health at the University of Georgia. In addition, he is consulting on public engagement and revamping the *Epidemiology Monitor,* an international newsletter for epidemiologists and public health professionals he has edited and published since 1980.

Deborah Dalton is a Senior Conflict Resolution Specialist with the Conflict Prevention and Resolution Center of the U.S. Environmental Protection Agency (EPA). She advises EPA program and regional offices on public involvement and dispute resolution processes for developing rules, policies, permits, and enforcement actions, with a specialty in negotiated rule-making. Deb brings more than thirty years of EPA experience in pesticides, toxic substances, and hazardous waste, in addition to three years of experience as a private sector mediator, primarily in Superfund. Deb is co-project officer for EPA's national dispute resolution contract, which provides facilitators and mediators for EPA public involvement and dispute resolution activities nationwide.

She has a BS in psychology from the College of William and Mary and an MS in environmental biology from the University of Virginia, and has taken PhD courses from the University of Maryland in environmental toxicology. She has more than four hundred hours of training in negotiation, mediation, and public involvement and has taught negotiation, mediation, and public involvement with the EPA, the U.S. Office of Personnel Management, and the U.S. Department of Justice

Tony Faast is a wildlife biologist with thirty years' experience conducting over one hundred public meetings and involvement activities with state and federal natural resource agencies. His successful facilitation of many task groups, commissions, public meetings, and strategy sessions—often under trying circumstances—has earned him the coveted title of "combat facilitator." Tony's twenty-year career with the Oregon Department of Fish and Wildlife included such positions as hatchery technician, hunter education coordinator, habitat staff biologist, education supervisor, and public involvement coordinator (that agency's first).

After joining the U.S. Fish and Wildlife Service in 1994, Tony was involved in the initial development of a pioneering outreach effort to bring a new approach to interacting with the many and varied publics of the Fish and Wildlife Service. He served fifteen years as a staff biologist for the Division of Wildlife and Sport Fish Restoration in the Pacific region of the service.

Bruce Gilbert is the Assistant Deputy Minister of the Rural Secretariat (Executive Council) in the Government of Newfoundland and Labrador, Canada. The Rural Secretariat is a unique government entity that strives to advance rural Newfoundland and Labrador (NL) sustainability by supporting citizens to develop policy advice for government on matters critical for rural survival; engaging citizens in dialogue about the future of their respective communities and regions; facilitating and conducting research that informs policy- and decision making; and supporting rural stakeholders, including government departments, to collaborate more effectively for change.

Bruce has spent much of his career working with and for nongovernmental organizations. His experience includes serving as Managing Coordinator for the Canadian Climate Impacts and Adaptation Research Network (Dalhousie University); Executive

Director for Conservation Corps Newfoundland and Labrador; founding partner of the Communication for Survival Initiative (NL); Community Mobilization Adviser for OXFAM-Canada in Namibia; Field Coordinator for Memorial University: Extension; Education Officer for the Newfoundland and Labrador Human Rights Association; Group Leader for Canada World Youth in Indonesia and Malawi; and Provincial Coordinator with Katimavik (Canada's former national "youth service" program).

Bruce has a master's degree in adult education from St. Francis Xavier University, with a concentration in popular education and community mobilization, and an interdisciplinary PhD from Dalhousie University in public engagement, collaboration, and sustainability. He recently conducted postdoctoral research at Memorial University on effectiveness in academic-community partnerships. He has received a doctoral fellowship from the Social Sciences and Humanities Research Council, several Canadian International Development Agency awards, and the St. Francis Xavier University award for excellence in international adult education practice.

Bruce lives in St. John's, NL, with Camille Fouillard and their children, Léo and Esmée.

Therese McMillan joined the Federal Transit Administration (FTA) as the newly appointed Deputy Administrator on July 2, 2009. Therese assists the administrator in leading a staff of more than five hundred in the Washington, DC, headquarters and in ten regional offices throughout the United States. Therese worked with FTA staff in allocating $8.78 billion for 1,072 Recovery Act grants, which created or retained over 12,500 jobs and strengthened and enhanced public transportation for working Americans and their communities. Therese also leads a special task force on civil rights to comply with the increased—and welcome—attention that the Obama Administration and Secretary Ray LaHood have placed on the entire body of civil rights responsibilities that the U.S. Department of Transportation (DOT) and all federal agencies are expected to carry out on behalf of the American public. Therese also serves on the Partnership for Sustainable Communities with fellow DOT colleagues, EPA and the U.S. Department of Housing and Urban Development.

Prior to her appointment, Therese was the Deputy Executive Director of Policy at the San Francisco Bay Area Region's Metropolitan Transportation Commission (MTC). Serving in that role for nine years, she was responsible for strategic financial planning and for MTC's management of federal, state, and regional funding for public transit, highways, roadways, and other modes of transportation; state and federal legislative advocacy; and public affairs and community outreach. Therese received her BS in environmental policy and planning analysis from the University of California, Davis, in 1981, and a joint MCP/MS in city planning and civil engineering science in 1984 from the University of California, Berkeley.

Richard Stem has twenty-eight years of resource management experience in government organizations and an incident command background, and he is recognized for his ability to develop and lead diverse external and government teams and organizations. His experience in program management and conflict resolution covers the industries of engineering, forestry, biology, geology, archeology, construction, finance, administration, and logistics.

His last assignment with the U.S. Forest Service was as Deputy Administrator for the twenty-two-million-acre, five-state Rocky Mountain region, consisting of eleven national forests; 2,400 employees; and a budget greater than $350 million.

As an independent contractor, he has worked directly for the governor of Wyoming, solving issues in resource management. He has also worked for various energy companies (on retainer and on individual projects), working through myriad avenues and process steps involved in securing permits for energy exploration and construction. At present Richard is working for a four-county coalition in Wyoming, and he also acts as an ongoing contractor sent out to assist the Federal Emergency Management Agency with issues related to project implementation. Wise multiple use of private and government lands is of the highest priority in Richard's current endeavors.

ORGANIZATIONS AND NETWORKS PRACTICING IN THE FIELD OF DELIBERATIVE DEMOCRACY IN THE UNITED STATES

The landscape of organizations and networks committed to deliberative democracy work is fluid. The following list is not intended to be exhaustive, but rather to provide an entry point for those wanting to explore the various practices in this field.

NATIONAL ORGANIZATIONS AND NETWORKS

AMERICAN DEMOCRACY PROJECT
www.aascu.org/programs/ADP

The American Democracy Project is a multicampus initiative aimed at preparing the next generation of engaged and informed citizens. The initiative is sponsored by the American Association of State Colleges and Universities, in partnership with the *New York Times*, and includes 240 participating higher education institutions that are committed to producing civically engaged graduates.

AMERICANS FOR INDIAN OPPORTUNITY
www.aio.org

Americans for Indian Opportunity (AIO) supports and encourages cultural, political, and economic opportunity for indigenous peoples. Based in traditional indigenous philosophies, AIO works with indigenous communities to develop leaders and create community-based solutions.

CAMPUS COMPACT
www.compact.org

Campus Compact is a national alliance of 1,200 college and university presidents who are committed to promoting civic engagement through higher education. Campus Compact promotes the development of students' citizenship skills through public service; it helps campuses create community partnerships; and it provides resources for faculty to incorporate civic learning in their curricula.

CENTER FOR DELIBERATIVE DEMOCRACY
www.cdd.stanford.edu

A deliberative poll considers the preferences and opinions of citizens both before and after they are presented with relevant information and exposed to the views of fellow citizens. The technique was first developed in 1988 by James Fishkin, a professor at Stanford University, and has been adopted by local and regional governments across the world. Currently, the Center for Deliberative Democracy at Stanford is committed to researching deliberative polling and its impacts.

CENTER FOR INFORMATION AND RESEARCH ON CIVIC LEARNING AND ENGAGEMENT
www.civicyouth.org

The Center for Information and Research on Civic Learning and Engagement, or CIRCLE, researches civic education in schools and communities, as well as young Americans' patterns of political participation and civic engagement. It is based at the Jonathan M. Tisch College of Citizenship and Public Service at Tufts University.

CITYCAMP
www.citycamp.govfresh.com

CityCamp supports "unconference," or participant-driven meetings, which bring together local government officials, experts, programmers, designers, citizens, and journalists. The meetings are focused on innovation for municipal governments and community organizations, specifically in regard to how the Internet can be used to develop more effective and open local government.

DAVENPORT INSTITUTE
http://publicpolicy.pepperdine.edu/davenport-institute

The Davenport Institute, formerly known as Common Sense California, strives to engage citizens in the policy decisions that have an impact on their lives. Housed within the Pepperdine University School of Public Policy, the institute works with governments, schools, and organizations to sponsor citizen engagement projects, connect institutions to citizens, and advocate for citizen involvement in finding policy solutions. The institute believes that a more involved, informed citizenry will produce better policy outcomes.

DELIBERATIVE DEMOCRACY CONSORTIUM
www.deliberative-democracy.net

The Deliberative Democracy Consortium (DDC) is a membership-based coalition of practitioners and researchers collaborating to enrich the field of deliberative democracy. The DDC supports research, develops publications, and convenes collaborative meetings throughout the world.

DEMOCRACY COMMITMENT
www.thedemocracycommitment.org

The Democracy Commitment is a national civic engagement project for community colleges that aims to engage community college students in civic learning and democratic practice. The project is modeled after the American Democracy Project, described above.

DEMOCRACY IMPERATIVE
www.unh.edu/democracy

The Democracy Imperative is a coalition of scholars, campus leaders, and civic leaders dedicated to enriching democracy in higher education. It produces open-source resources through its website, and offers workshops, conferences, and webinars. Membership is free, and there are currently over six hundred member organizations and individuals.

EVERYDAY DEMOCRACY
www.everyday-democracy.org

Everyday Democracy works with organizations and governments to help communities find ways for people to come together and solve problems. The organization addresses a wide range of issues, including poverty and economic development, education reform, racial equity, early childhood development, police-community relations, youth, and neighborhood concerns.

HANDSON NETWORK
www.handsonnetwork.org

The HandsOn Network is the volunteer-focused arm of Points of Light Institute with more than 250 HandsOn Action Centers in sixteen countries. The network has over seventy thousand organizations that contribute volunteers and together they give over 30 million hours of community service annually.

HARWOOD INSTITUTE
www.theharwoodinstitute.org

The Harwood Institute is a nonprofit, nonpartisan organization that supports the cultivation of public innovators. The institute works with communities and organizations across the country to encourage individuals to innovate and improve community life.

INTERNATIONAL ASSOCIATION FOR PUBLIC PARTICIPATION
www.iap2usa.org

The International Association for Public Participation (IAP2) is a nonprofit organization that provides members with resources to create high-quality public participation processes, and supplies outside groups, such as governments, resources to improve the participation opportunities they foster. IAP2 is an international organization, with active groups in the United States, Canada, and Australia.

JEFFERSON CENTER
www.jefferson-center.org

The Jefferson Center is the originator of the Citizens Jury process. In a Citizens Jury project, a random, demographically representative panel of citizens meets to examine an issue of public significance and offer recommendations. The Jefferson Center offers resources and strategies for those interested in creating a Citizens Jury.

JOINT CENTER FOR POLITICAL AND ECONOMIC STUDIES
www.jointcenter.org

The Civic Engagement and Governance Initiative of the Joint Center for Political and Economic Studies works to increase the political participation of minority citizens, as well as to provide tools for civic engagement. The Joint Center publishes a biennial analysis of African American voters, and founded the National Policy Alliance, whose membership includes over eleven thousand African American officials from all levels of government.

KETTERING FOUNDATION
www.kettering.org

The Kettering Foundation engages with community organizations, governments, and scholars to produce research related to making democracy work. The foundation's research focuses on citizens, communities, and institutions. In addition, the Kettering Foundation produces extensive materials, including issue books and videos for the National Issues Forums.

LOGOLINK
www.logolink.org

LogoLink is a global coalition of civil society organizations, research institutions, and governments committed to growing citizen engagement at the local level. Currently, LogoLink comprises nine partners from Africa, Asia, Latin America and the Caribbean, North America, and Europe.

MOBILIZE.ORG
www.mobilize.org

Mobilize.org encourages millennials, individuals born between the years 1976 and 1996, to identify and solve social problems. The site has invested in more than forty Millennial-led projects, including Democracy 2.0 summits.

NATIONAL ASSOCIATION OF LATINO ELECTED AND APPOINTED OFFICIALS (NALEO)
www.naleo.org/civicengagement.html

The National Association of Latino Elected and Appointed Officials (NALEO) has a program on civic engagement that aims to foster civic participation and engagement within the Latino community. NALEO's strategy focuses on three areas: naturalization assistance and promotion, voter engagement, and census-related work.

NATIONAL CENTER FOR MEDIA ENGAGEMENT
www.mediaengage.org

The National Center for Media Engagement provides resources for public media platforms to encourage citizen participation and develop community relationships. The center provides station-specific services such as an online community engagement portal of resources and links. In addition, the center supports content producers through partnerships for learning and customized fee-based services.

National Coalition for Dialogue & Deliberation
www.ncdd.org

The National Coalition for Dialogue & Deliberation (NCDD) serves as a resource database and community for groups and individuals in the dialogue and deliberation fields. With a network of over 1,300 members, NCDD produces educational resources and convenes dialogue and deliberation practitioners through conferences.

National Conference on Citizenship
www.ncoc.net

The National Conference on Citizenship (NCoC) is a nonprofit chartered by Congress to measure and strengthen citizenship. The NCoC convenes conferences, facilitates working groups, and shares its research to stimulate the national conversion surrounding civic engagement.

National Issues Forums
www.nifi.org

National Issues Forums (NIF) is a coalition of organizations committed to the promotion of public deliberation.[1] In addition to promoting locally sponsored public forums on a wide-ranging set of issues, the network produces nonpartisan issue books that help foster citizen deliberation.

National League of Cities
www.nlc.org

The National League of Cities (NLC) is a resource and advocate for thousands of cities, towns, and villages across the United States. NLC works at the federal level to ensure that communities have a strong voice in the policies that affect them, provides leaders with the tools to address their communities' challenges, and builds and strengthens networks between community leaders through conferences and educational opportunities. NLC also partners with forty-nine state municipal leagues and with major corporations to improve communication, increase competitiveness, and strengthen local governments.

PUBLIC AGENDA
www.publicagenda.org

Public Agenda is a public opinion research and public engagement organization that is committed to helping communities handle complex public policy issues. The organization engages with voters through issue guides and other civic participation tools. The academic arm of the organization's public engagement side, the Center for Advances in Public Engagement, studies the impact of engagement and produces research publications.

PUBLIC CONVERSATIONS PROJECT
www.publicconversations.org

The Public Conversations Project (PCP) facilitates dialogues on a wide range of contentious issues around the world. The PCP uses these dialogues to support the development of more effective public communication. In addition to hosting dialogues, the PCP provides workshops and trainings that teach people to use its dialogue methods.

UNITED WAY
www.unitedway.org

The United Way is a nonprofit organization that works with local United Way offices throughout the country to support community-based programming. The organization currently focuses its work on three major goals: improving education and cutting the number of high school dropouts in half; helping people reach financial stability and economic independence; and promoting family and individual health.

UNIVERSITY NETWORK FOR COLLABORATIVE GOVERNANCE

www.policyconsensus.org/uncg

The University Network for Collaborative Governance is composed of university programs that create opportunities for scholarship around issues of dialogue, discussion, and conflict resolution. The network helps support related university programs, convenes conferences, and acts as a hub for information exchange.

VIEWPOINT LEARNING

www.viewpointlearning.com

Founded in 1999, Viewpoint Learning designs and conducts dialogues on complex issues for governments, companies, and organizations throughout North America and Europe.

STATE AND LOCAL ORGANIZATIONS

CENTER FOR DEMOCRACY AND CITIZENSHIP—JANE ADDAMS SCHOOL FOR DEMOCRACY

www.augsburg.edu/democracy/jas.html

The Jane Addams School for Democracy brings together diverse participants, such as immigrant families, college students, and refugees, to do public work and learning. The unique, non-hierarchical structure of the school enables people from a wide range of cultural backgrounds to work together and address issues that affect their lives.

CENTER FOR MICHIGAN

www.thecenterformichigan.net

The Center for Michigan works to combat hyperpartisanship and develop a citizens' agenda for Michigan. The center's work concentrates on three main areas: engagement through dialogue and polling, informing the public through independent public affairs journalism, and providing leadership training and coalition-building for improved public policy. In addition, the center publishes papers related to the challenges facing Michigan.

Center for Public Deliberation at Colorado State University
www.cpd.colostate.edu

The Center for Public Deliberation (CPD) promotes deliberative democracy within the northern Colorado region through three main avenues: enhancing local civic culture, expanding collaborative decision making, and improving civic knowledge and teaching. In pursuit of these goals, CPD hosts student and community workshops and facilitates academic research on topics related to deliberative democracy.

Citizens League
www.citizensleague.org

Based in Minnesota, the Citizens League fosters civic capacity throughout the state through policy recommendations and civic leadership development. The Citizens League regularly publishes policy reports and provides opportunities for civic education and capacity building.

David Mathews Center for Civic Life
www.mathewscenter.org

The David Mathews Center for Civic Life works to build infrastructure and capacity for more effective civic engagement and decision making. Although the center originally focused locally on Alabama, it has now taken on a broader mission and works on national issues. The center offers a series of core programs, whose topics range from local concerns to capacity building.

Hampton Roads Center for Civic Engagement
www.hrcce.org

The Hampton Roads Center for Civic Engagement (HRCCE) develops and facilitates civic engagement processes that create productive collaboration between citizens and their governments. HRCCE supports fact-based dialogues and uses outside deliberative democracy programs to run its citizens' discussions. In addition, HRCCE focuses on civic capacity building in the southeastern Virginia region and intends to develop a civic engagement research program.

HEALTHY DEMOCRACY OREGON

www.healthydemocracyoregon.org

Healthy Democracy Oregon works to strengthen the ballot initiative process through its Citizens' Initiative Review, whereby a group of randomly selected and demographically balanced voters comes together to evaluate a ballot measure. This citizen panel hears from supporters and opponents of the bill as well as from policy experts before issuing a "citizen statement" about the measure, which is published in all voters' election pamphlets.

INSTITUTE FOR LOCAL GOVERNMENT

www.ca-ilg.org/public-engagement

The Institute for Local Government's public engagement program aims to help local officials and communities in California make decisions about how to implement public engagement initiatives in their communities. Resources include tip sheets, how-to guides, and best practices.

NEW HAMPSHIRE LISTENS

www.carseyinstitute.unh.edu/nhlistens/home.html

New Hampshire Listens fosters deliberation concerning complex, challenging issues at the local and state levels, often facilitating efforts to address these concerns. As part of the Carsey Institute at the University of New Hampshire, the organization provides resources and facilitator trainings, and serves as a network hub of engaged communities in New Hampshire. The organization also works with local and state leaders to develop opportunities for citizen-leader conversation and dialogue.

PENN PROJECT FOR CIVIC ENGAGEMENT
www.gse.upenn.edu/pcel/programs/ppce

Housed within the University of Pennsylvania, the Penn Project for Civic Engagement collaborates with community groups, government agencies, and businesses to conduct conversations on important topics. The project hopes to bring together citizens and experts to create civic action. Past projects have included the development of community forums on topics ranging from immigration to health care, as well as government-sponsored town hall meetings.

PUBLIC LIFE FOUNDATION
www.plfo.org

Based in Owensboro, Kentucky, the Public Life Foundation works to create broad-based, meaningful citizen participation and to support the development of public life. Focusing on three process areas, information, deliberation, and empowerment action, the foundation fosters citizen-based problem solving and citizen engagement.

WEST VIRGINIA CENTER FOR CIVIC LIFE
www.wvciviclife.org

The West Virginia Center for Civic Life is a nonprofit organization that engages citizens in discussions concerning pressing public issues. The center focuses on civic engagement through community dialogue and deliberation, as well as on moderator training and issue framing. The organization connects interested communities with resources and assistance to ensure that community dialogues are successful.

APPENDIX C

AMERICA*SPEAKS* PROJECTS BY SUBJECT AREA

Projects that are described in this book are identified by this symbol: ◆. Some projects appear in more than one category. Full project descriptions are available on the America*Speaks* website at www.americaspeaks.org.

BUDGETING

- ◆ Our Budget, Our Economy, National Discussion (2010). Albuquerque, NM; Augusta, ME; Casper, WY; Chicago, IL; Columbia, SC; Dallas, TX; Des Moines, IA; Detroit, MI; Grand Forks, ND; Jackson, MS; Los Angeles County, CA; Louisville, KY; Missoula, MT; Overland Park, KS; Philadelphia, PA; Portland, OR; Portsmouth, NH; Richmond, VA; and Silicon Valley, CA
- • San Francisco Listens (2005). San Francisco, CA
- ◆ Washington, DC, Citizen Summits I, II, III, and IV (1999–2005). Washington, DC
- • Colorado 100 Leadership Summit (2003). Denver, CO
- • Fixing New York's Fiscal Practices (2003). Palisades, NY

DISASTER RECOVERY

- • National Urban Areas Security Initiative & Homeland Security Conference (2011). San Francisco, CA
- • DC Emergency Preparedness Forums (2009). Washington, DC
- • Rebuilding Lives Summit (2009). Lake Charles, LA

- New Orleans Community Congresses (2007). New Orleans, LA; Atlanta, GA; Baton Rouge, LA; Dallas, TX; and Houston, TX
- One New Orleans City Wide Planning Day (2007). New Orleans, LA
- Gulf Coast Business Reinvestment Forum (2005). Washington, DC
- National EMS Preparedness Initiative Policy Summit (2005). Washington, DC
- Louisiana Recovery and Rebuilding Conference (2005). New Orleans, LA
- Listening to the City (2002). New York, NY
- Federal Emergency Management Agency Long-Term Disaster Recovery (2004). Charlotte, DeSoto, and Hardee Counties, FL

ENVIRONMENT

- Green Communities Summit (2012). Dallas, TX
- Mid Atlantic Regional Council on the Ocean (MARCO) (2009). New York, NY
- National Conversation on Climate Action (2009). Los Angeles, CA, and seventy other communities
- Seal the Deal Global Town Hall (2009). Daejeon, South Korea
- The 2010 Imperative: A Global Emergency Teach-In (2007). New York, NY, and forty-seven countries
- Economic Benefit of Local Climate Action (2007). Fayetteville, AR
- Washington Board of Trade Potomac Conference (2007). Washington, DC

HEALTH CARE

- California*Speaks* 2 (2011). San Diego, San Leandro, Riverside, San Luis Obispo, Fresno, Pasadena, and Sacramento, CA
- Advancing Futures for Adults with Autism National Town Meeting (2009). Chicago, IL; Atlanta, GA; Boston, MA; Chapel Hill, NC; Cleveland, OH; Dallas, TX; Kansas City, MO;

Long Beach, CA; Long Island, NY; Miami, FL; Newark, NJ;
Philadelphia, PA; Phoenix, AZ; Pittsburgh, PA; Sacramento,
CA; and Washington, DC

- Advancing Futures for Adults with Autism Think Tank (2009). New York, NY
- Calvert County Pandemic Planning Project (2008). Huntington, MD
- A National Dialogue on Health IT and Privacy (2008). Nationwide
- Shaping America's Youth (2007). Memphis, TN; Dallas, TX; Philadelphia, PA; Chicago, IL; and Des Moines, IA
- California*Speaks* (2007). San Diego, Los Angeles, Riverside–San Bernardino, San Luis Obispo, Fresno, Sacramento, Oakland–San Francisco, and Humboldt County, CA
- Urban Zen (2007). New York, NY
- Citizens' Health Care Working Group (2006). Nationwide
- Tough Choices in Health Care (2005). Biddeford and Orono, ME
- Your Health, Your Care, Your Say (2005). Birmingham, United Kingdom

INTERNATIONAL

- Positive Visions for Biodiversity Stakeholder Summit (2010). Brussels, Belgium
- Seal the Deal Global Town Hall (2009). Daejeon, South Korea
- Clinton Global Initiative University (2008). New Orleans, LA
- The 2010 Imperative: A Global Emergency Teach-In (2007). New York, NY, and forty-seven different countries
- City of Port Phillip (2007). Port Phillip, Australia
- Clinton Global Initiative International I, II, and III (2005–7).
- Meeting of Minds: European Citizens' Deliberation on Brain Science (2005–2006). Brussels, Belgium
- World Economic Forum: Global Town Hall (2005). Davos, Switzerland
- Your Health, Your Care, Your Say (2005). Birmingham, United Kingdom
- Dialogue with the City (2003). Perth, Australia

National Policy

- America*Speaks:* Capacity Building and Strategy Workshop (2010). Lansdowne, VA
- Our Budget, Our Economy, National Discussion (2010). Albuquerque, NM; Augusta, ME; Casper, WY; Chicago, IL; Columbia, SC; Dallas, TX; Des Moines, IA; Detroit, MI; Grand Forks, ND; Jackson, MS; Los Angeles County, CA; Louisville, KY; Missoula, MT; Overland Park, KS; Philadelphia, PA; Portland, OR; Portsmouth, NH; Richmond, VA; and Silicon Valley, CA
- Advancing Futures for Adults with Autism National Town Meeting (2009). Chicago, IL; Atlanta, GA; Boston, MA; Chapel Hill, NC; Cleveland, OH; Dallas, TX; Kansas City, MO; Long Beach, CA; Long Island, NY; Miami, FL; Newark, NJ; Philadelphia, PA; Phoenix, AZ; Pittsburgh, PA; Sacramento, CA; and Washington, DC
- Advancing Futures for Adults with Autism Think Tank (2009). New York, NY
- Equal Voice for America's Families Campaign (2008). Los Angeles, CA; Chicago, IL; and Birmingham, AL
- Power and Promise of Philanthropy (2008). National Harbor, MD
- Shaping America's Youth (2008). Memphis, TN; Dallas, TX; Philadelphia, PA; Chicago, IL; and Des Moines, IA
- National Rural Assembly (2007). Washington, DC
- Economic Benefit of Local Climate Action (2007). Fayetteville, AR
- Citizens' Health Care Working Group (2006). Nationwide
- Americans Discuss Social Security (1998–1999). Nationwide

Planning and Growth

- Green Communities Summit (2012). Dallas, TX
- Walter Reed Re-Use Plan Public Workshops and Town Hall (2012). Washington, DC
- Ward 8 Community Summit (2011). Washington, DC
- Near Southeast/Southwest Community Summit (2011). Washington, DC

- 2010 Build Nebraska Housing Summit (2010). Kearney, NE
- Envision Prince George's (2010). Prince George's County, MD
- Power of 32 (2010). Thirty-two counties in Maryland, Ohio, Pennsylvania, and West Virginia
- Our Region, Our Plan—Charleston Regional Workshops (2010). Berkeley, Charleston, and Dorcester Counties, SC
- We the People: America*Speaks* 21st Century Town Meeting (2010 and 2007). Owensboro, KY
- Build Nebraska Housing Policy Summit (2009). Lincoln, NE
- Boston Civic Summit—A Citywide Town Meeting (2008). Boston, MA
- Creating Tomorrow Today: A Forum on the Future of Northwest Indiana (2008). Merrillville, IN
- Calvert County Pandemic Planning Project (2008). Huntingtown, MD
- Lancaster 2020—Shaping Our Future (2008). Lancaster, PA
- Cleveland Jewish Community Downtown Dialogues (2008). Cleveland and Beachwood, OH
- City of Port Phillip (2007). Port Phillip, Australia
- Seaport Speaks (2006). New York, NY
- Voices & Choices (2005–2006). Northeast Ohio
- Louisiana Recovery and Rebuilding Conference (2005). New Orleans, LA
- Oakland Mills Village Meetings I & II (2004–2005). Columbia, MD
- Redevelopment of Skyland Mall Shopping Center (2004). Washington, DC
- The Region Speaks (2003). Charlotte, NC
- Dialogue with the City (2003). Perth, Australia
- Hamilton County Community COMPASS (2002). Hamilton County, OH
- Listening to the City (2002). New York, NY
- Common Ground (2001). Chicago, IL
- Marshalling Regional Cooperation Colloquium (2001). Cincinnati, OH

YOUTH AND EDUCATION

- Seal the Deal Global Town Hall (2009). Daejeon, South Korea

- Youth Truth Assembly (2009). Nationwide
- Clinton Global Initiative University (2008). New Orleans, LA
- Grantmakers for Children, Youth & Families Policy Summit (2008). Washington, DC
- New Mexico Children's Cabinet Career Cluster Initiative (2008). Albuquerque, NM
- Shaping America's Youth (2007). Memphis, TN; Dallas, TX; Philadelphia, PA; Chicago, IL; and Des Moines, IA
- United Agenda for Children (2004). Charlotte, NC
- The National Conversation on Youth Development in the 21st Century (2002). Washington, DC
- DC Youth Summit follow-up (2001). Washington, DC
- The City Is Mine: Youth Summit (2000). Washington, DC
- D.C. Youth Roundtable (2000). Washington, DC

STAKEHOLDER SUMMITS

- ConvergeUS (2011). San Francisco, CA
- NOAA Senior Executive Service Conference (2011). Annapolis, MD
- 2010 Build Nebraska Housing Summit (2010). Kearney, NE
- America*Speaks:* Capacity Building and Strategy Workshop (2010). Landsowne, VA
- Build Nebraska Housing Policy Summit (2009). Lincoln, NE
- Chicago Jazz Town Hall (2009). Chicago, IL
- Mid Atlantic Regional Council on the Ocean (MARCO) (2009). New York, NY
- RPRP CommunityForum Training (2009). Denver, CO
- The State of the USA Key Indicators Project (2008). Washington, DC
- Cleveland Jewish Community Downtown Dialogues (2008)
- Grantmakers for Children, Youth & Families Policy Summit (2008). Washington, DC
- Lancaster 2020—Shaping Our Future (2008). Lancaster, PA
- Power and Promise of Philanthropy (2008). National Harbor, MD
- Cleveland and Beachwood, OH National Performing Arts Convention—Taking Action Together (2008). Denver, CO
- Clinton Global Initiative (2005–2008). International

- National EMS Preparedness Initiative Policy Summit (2007). Washington, DC
- National Rural Assembly (2007). Washington, DC
- Washington Board of Trade Potomac Conference (2007). Washington, DC
- One New Orleans City Wide Planning Day (2007). New Orleans, LA
- Pittsburgh Nonprofit Summit (2006). Pittsburgh, PA
- National Conference on Citizenship Citizens' Forum (2005). Washington, DC
- World Economic Forum: Global Town Hall (2005). Davos, Switzerland
- American Camping Association Tri-State Conference (2004). New York, NY, and Washington, DC
- Academy of Natural Sciences (2003). Philadelphia, PA
- Colorado 100 Leadership Summit (2003). Denver, CO
- Colorado College (2003). Colorado Springs, CO

CONVENING LEADING PRACTITIONERS AND SCHOLARS

Since the mid 1990s, America*Speaks* has convened a series of gatherings aimed at developing recommendations for improving the practice of democracy in America.[1] Participants at these gatherings considered a wide range of strategies, including broader and enhanced practice of citizen engagement. More information and reports can be found on the America*Speaks* website, www .americaspeaks.org, under "Democracy Lab/Convenings."

TABLE D.1 PRACTITIONER AND SCHOLAR CONVENINGS

Convening	Date	Participants
Taking Democracy to Scale I	1995	A diverse group of sixty elected officials, community leaders, corporate officers, scholars, technology experts, journalists, and young people
Designing for Democracy	1997	Civic innovators from three regions (Snohomish County, Washington; the fourteen-county region around Charlotte, North Carolina; and across Kentucky) and a national resource team of leaders in public deliberation and the use of technology for civic engagement

(*Continued*)

TABLE D.1 *(Continued)*

Convening	Date	Participants
Taking Democracy to Scale II	2002	Thirty leading researchers and practitioners in the emerging field of deliberative democracy
Millions of Voices	2002	More than a dozen leading citizen engagement practitioners
Champions of Participation I	June 2006	Twenty-four federal managers and staff
Designing Governance Mechanisms for the 21st Century	July 2006	Twenty-five leading democracy scholars and practitioners
Strengthening Our Nation's Democracy	July 2008	Forty-nine democracy advocates, scholars, and practitioners
Champions of Participation II	March 2009	Thirty-four federal managers and staff from twenty-three agencies and offices
Champions of Participation III	May 2009	Nineteen senior leaders from thirteen federal agencies and departments
Strengthening Our Nation's Democracy II	August 2009	Eighty-nine leaders and thinkers across a broad range of sectors, including federal managers, community organizers, deliberative democracy practitioners, election reformers, transparency advocates, e-democracy practitioners, media reformers, educators, key leaders from the Obama Administration, and others

NOTES

Introduction

1. See Appendix A for brief biographies of the public managers with case studies in this book.

Chapter One

1. See Appendix B for descriptions of organizations practicing in the field of deliberative democracy in the United States.

Chapter Two

1. For an excellent synopsis of the history of public deliberation in the United States, see Gastil and Keith (2005).
2. The 21st Century Town Meeting is trademarked by America*Speaks*. For purposes of readability, the trademark symbol will not be used after this point.
3. A complete list of America*Speaks* projects can be found in Appendix C.
4. Parts of this section were originally published in Lukensmeyer, C. J., and Brigham, S. "Taking Democracy to Scale: Creating a Town Hall Meeting for the Twenty-First Century." *National Civic Review*, 2002, *91*(4), 351–366.
5. Parts of this section were originally published in Lukensmeyer, C. J., and Brigham, S. "Taking Democracy to Scale: Creating a Town Hall Meeting for the Twenty-First Century." *National Civic Review*, 2002, *91*(4), 351–366.

Chapter Three

1. Content in this chapter was originally published in Lukensmeyer, C. J. "Large-Scale Citizen Engagement and the Rebuilding of New Orleans: A Case Study." *National Civic Review*, Fall 2007, DOI: 10.1002/ncr.182, 3–13.
2. The term "diaspora" refers to a group being dispersed outside its traditional homeland, forced to relocate by circumstances and decisions beyond its control. New Orleanians—as well as the city's

press corps—used the term in the aftermath of Hurricane Katrina and the flooding. It is a powerful reminder of the fact that tens of thousands of people boarded airplanes out of New Orleans literally not knowing where they would land.

3. The importance of contextual analysis for citizen engagement work is explored in Chapter Five.

4. Chapter Seven explores strategies for achieving diverse participation in citizen engagement.

5. In February, 2010, having returned to New Orleans, Glenda Harris died of a heart attack at age 52.

6. In New Orleans tradition, the "main line" of a parade is the front section, made up of the organization or musicians who are sponsoring the parade or who hold the parade permit. The "second line" is the group of people who spontaneously join the parade as it moves through the streets, dancing or walking or sometimes playing instruments of their own. In New Orleans, almost every public parade includes a boisterous second line.

7. Chapter Six explores the importance of decision makers' participation in engagement processes and lays out a range of approaches for involving them.

8. Chapter Eight explores in detail strategies for creating safe public spaces.

9. Chapter Nine explores strategies for informing participants.

10. Chapter Ten explores strategies for helping citizens discover shared views.

11. Chapter Eleven explores a range of strategies for ensuring that deliberative efforts extend beyond a single event.

Chapter Four

1. Parts of this section were previously published in Lukensmeyer, C. J., and Torres, L. *Public Deliberation: A Manager's Guide to Citizen Engagement.* IBM Center for the Business of Government Collaboration Series. Washington, DC: IBM Center for the Business of Government, 2006.

2. See Appendix D for a description of these convenings.

3. Parts of this discussion of the public involvement spectrum were originally published in Lukensmeyer, C. J., and Torres, L. *Public Deliberation: A Manager's Guide to Citizen Engagement.* IBM Center for the Business of Government Collaboration Series. Washington, DC: IBM Center for the Business of Government, 2006.

4. Parts of this section were originally published in Lukensmeyer, C. J., Goldman, J., and Stern, D. *Assessing Public Participation in an Open Government Era: A Review of Federal Agency Plans.* IBM Center

for the Business of Government Fostering Transparency and Democracy Series. Washington, DC: IBM Center for the Business of Government, 2011. This report provides a more extensive and detailed analysis of early open government implementation efforts.

Chapter Five

1. The appreciative inquiry (AI) technique was developed in the early 1980s by doctoral students at Case Western Reserve University and has been refined and used over the years by a broad range of practitioners. David Cooperrider, one of the technique's originators, describes it as "the cooperative search for the best in people, their organizations, and the world around them. It involves systematic discovery of what gives a system 'life' when it is most effective and capable in economic, ecological, and human terms . . . AI involves the art and practice of asking questions that strengthen a system's capacity to heighten positive potential. It mobilizes inquiry through crafting an 'unconditional positive question' often involving hundreds or sometimes thousands of people" (Appreciative Inquiry Commons 2012).

Chapter Seven

1. Parts of this section were originally published in Lukensmeyer, C. J., and Brigham, S. "Taking Democracy to Scale: Creating a Town Hall Meeting for the Twenty-First Century." *National Civic Review,* 2002, *91*(4), 351–366.
2. The Title VI Circular provides guidance to recipients of FTA funds—state departments of transportation, metropolitan planning organizations, and transit operators—about how to implement Title VI.
3. When a federal agency drafts a new regulation, or makes amendments to an existing regulation, the material is called a "proposed rule." Under the Administrative Procedure Act of 1946, agencies must publish a proposed rule in the *Federal Register* (the daily newspaper of the federal government) at least thirty days before the rule is to take effect, and provide mechanisms by which the public can comment on it.

Chapter Nine

1. A compilation of the programs can be viewed on the America*Speaks* website at http://americaspeaks.org/projects/topics/planning-growth/voices-and-choices/

Chapter Ten

1. Demos is a national nonprofit organization that undertakes research, policy development, and advocacy on the economy, democracy, and the role of the public sector.

Chapter Eleven

1. Parts of this discussion of HHS's work were previously published in Lukensmeyer, C. J., Goldman, J., and Stern, D. *Assessing Public Participation in an Open Government Era: A Review of Federal Agency Plans.* IBM Center for the Business of Government Fostering Transparency and Democracy Series. Washington, DC: IBM Center for the Business of Government, 2011.

2. Parts of this discussion of EPA's work were previously published in Lukensmeyer, C. J., Goldman, J., and Stern, D. *Assessing Public Participation in an Open Government Era: A Review of Federal Agency Plans.* IBM Center for the Business of Government Fostering Transparency and Democracy Series. Washington, DC: IBM Center for the Business of Government, 2011.

Chapter Twelve

1. For a detailed exploration of this topic, see Leighninger, M. *Using Online Tools To Engage—And Be Engaged By—The Public.* Washington, D.C.: IBM Center for the Business of Government, 2011.

Appendix B

1. For a comprehensive list of organizations using the NIF model, please see Carcasson, M. *Democracy's Hubs: College and University Centers as Platforms for Deliberative Practice.* Dayton, OH: Kettering Foundation, 2008.

Appendix D

1. America*Speaks* was the sole convener of the listed meetings with the exception of the two Strengthening Our Nation's Democracy meetings. America*Speaks*'s partners in those two convenings included Everyday Democracy, Demos, the Ash Center for Democratic Governance and Innovation at Harvard University, the Deliberative Democracy Consortium, the Council for Excellence in Government, the Taubman Center for State and Local Government at Harvard University, and the National Civic League, among others.

INDEX

Page references followed by *fig* indicate an illustrated figure; followed by *t* indicate a table. Federal agency entries are listed under U.S.